THE
BRAVEST MAN

THE BRAVEST MAN

Richard O'Kane and the Amazing Submarine Adventures of the USS *Tang*

William Tuohy

PRESIDIO
PRESS

BALLANTINE BOOKS • NEW YORK

2006 Presidio Press Mass Market Edition

Copyright © 2001 by William Tuohy

Published in the United States by Presidio Press, an imprint of The Random House Publishing Group, a division of Random House, Inc., New York.

PRESIDIO PRESS and colophon are registered trademarks of Random House, Inc.

Originally published in hardcover by Sutton Publishing in 2001.

ISBN 0-89141-889-X

Cover photograph: © National Archives

Printed in the United States of America

www.presidiopress.com

OPM   9   8   7   6   5   4   3   2

To Rose Marie and Cyril

In each ship there is one man who, in the hour of emergency or peril at sea, can turn to no other man. There is one who alone is ultimately responsible for the sage navigation, engineering performance, accurate gunfire, and morale of his ship. He is the Commanding Officer. He is the ship!

—JOSEPH CONRAD

Contents

THE
BRAVEST MAN

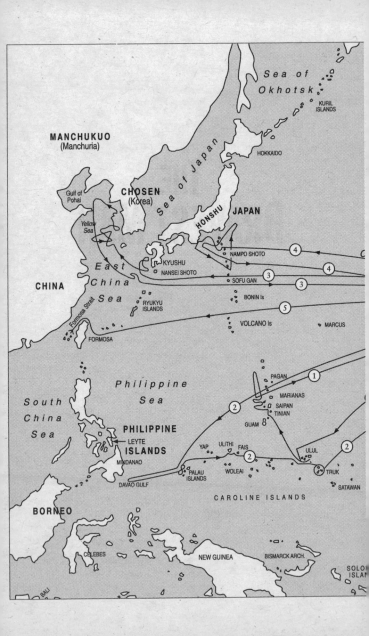

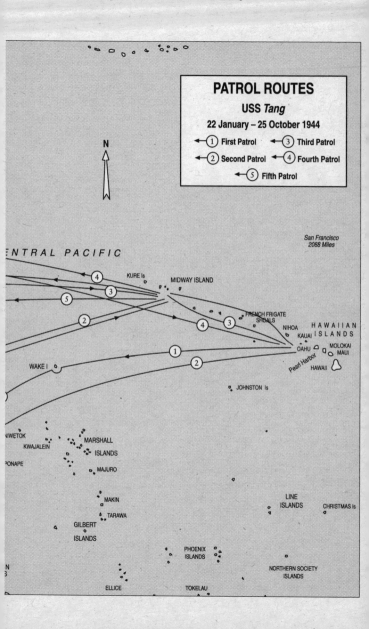

PATROL ROUTES

USS *Tang*

22 January – 25 October 1944

←①← First Patrol   ←③← Third Patrol
←②← Second Patrol   ←④← Fourth Patrol
←⑤← Fifth Patrol

N

San Francisco
2088 Miles

CENTRAL PACIFIC

KURE Is
MIDWAY ISLAND
④
③
⑤
②
FRENCH FRIGATE
SHOALS
NIHOA
HAWAIIAN
④ ③
KAUAI
ISLANDS
OAHU
MOLOKAI
MAUI
①
Pearl Harbor
WAKE I
②
HAWAII
JOHNSTON Is
NIWETOK
KWAJALEIN
MARSHALL
ISLANDS
PONAPE
MAJURO
MAKIN
LINE
ISLANDS
CHRISTMAS Is
TARAWA
GILBERT
ISLANDS
PHOENIX
ISLANDS
N
NORTHERN SOCIETY
ISLANDS
ELLICE
TOKELAU

Introduction

The United States Submarine Force in World War II was known as the Silent Service because the heroic deeds of submariners were kept secret. This slender force, with only 1.6 percent of the total personnel of the U.S. Navy, sunk fully 55 percent of the 10 million tons of Japanese warships and merchantment accounted for by Allied sea and air armadas.

The price of this remarkable success was shatteringly high. Fifty-two boats were lost; 22 percent of submarine crewmen died in action. Their ships became their steel coffins. This was the highest fatality rate of any branch of the U.S. Armed Forces.

Seven submariners won the Medal of Honor, the nation's highest decoration for valor. Thirty-seven submarines were awarded the elite Presidential Unit Citation; another thirty-six boats were recipients of the slightly lesser Navy Unit Commendation—by far the highest ratio of any class of warship.

To achieve this shining record, young submarine skippers overcame outdated peacetime tactics, weaknesses in command strategy, and defective weapons. The failure of U.S. torpedoes to function properly amounted to a secret wartime scandal, bordering on the criminal. Flawed torpedoes cost many submariners' lives—and needlessly prolonged the war against Japan. Despite all adversity, the skippers left a valiant legacy to the captains of today's huge, nuclear, ballistic boats: not since World War II has an American submarine fired a torpedo in combat. Only 465 officers commanded the

U.S. submarines that went on 1,682 war patrols in World War II. Some failed. More succeeded. Many died.

Of the gallant conduct of this Nelsonian band of brothers, Captain Edward L. Beach, who was one of them, noted: "World War Two saw the last of the old species of naval warfare in which the fate of nations hung on the ability of a few fearless men to rise above the shocking disruption of mind, and terror of painful annihilation by drowning, suffocation, burning or scalding to do their duty in spite of it all."

This is the story of Richard O'Kane, America's undersea ace of aces, and a few fearless men, submariners all.

CHAPTER ONE

"Wahoo Is Expendable"

At the first, pale light on a January morning in 1943, *Wahoo* carved through the calm waters of the South Pacific with her crew at full alert. In the breaking, shimmering dawn, the sleek, matte-black American submarine strained on the surface at full speed, 18 knots, her powerful diesel engines leaving a boiling wake astern. *Wahoo* was approaching the Vitiaz Strait, a narrow waterway separating the Solomon Sea from the Bismarck Sea off the northeast coast of the big island of New Guinea. The strait was a maritime chokepoint, patrolled by Japanese aircraft and anti-submarine vessels from nearby New Britain Island—dangerous water for U.S. submarines.

Wahoo's seventy-one crewmembers shared an edgy expectancy. They were embarked on a war patrol to seek out armed, enemy ships. They would be risking all. Thousands of miles from a friendly port, they would face the enemy alone. Defeat would mean death in their own iron coffin, in a nameless deep. They were heading into a no man's sea, and *Wahoo* was fair game for foe, or even friend—patrol planes from Australia had a nasty habit of dropping bombs on American submarines. Normal doctrine called for *Wahoo* to dive beneath the surface at first light and proceed submerged. But the situation was not normal. *Wahoo* was holding to a breakneck pace to reach a Japanese-occupied harbor, and running on the surface would save precious hours.

Now, seven days out of the U.S. Submarine Base at Brisbane, Australia, *Wahoo* was several hours ahead of schedule heading for her patrol area around the Japanese-held Palau Islands east of the Philippines. En route to her assigned area,

Wahoo had orders to make a slight detour, if possible, to re-connoiter the anchorage of Wewak on the north coast of New Guinea, captured by the Japanese in the conquest of the East Indies the year before. It was used by the Japanese as a staging area to support amphibious operations in the Solomon Islands chain. Thanks to her four powerful diesel engines *Wahoo* was able to maintain an 18-knot speed, almost 21 statute miles per hour. (A knot, a nautical mile per hour, is 1.15 statute miles an hour.) To fit in the requested reconnaissance, *Wahoo* was running at full speed on the surface despite the proximity of Japanese airfields. Submerged on batteries, her speed would have been reduced to 5 or 6 knots at best.

Though crewmembers were apprehensive, they were curiously confident. For *Wahoo* on her third war patrol was commanded by two officers whom they trusted, and whose leadership was soon to become famous throughout the U.S. Submarine Force. The sense of confidence was pointedly shared by the executive officer, Lieutenant Richard O'Kane, a handsome 31-year-old sailor with light-brown almost rusty hair, a strong jaw, firm set to his mouth, and an open face. Dick O'Kane was of medium height and in fine physical condition. A New England Yankee, O'Kane was energetic and outgoing, but sometimes sharp-tongued. His temperament was changeable, the crew thought. He could be voluble, or he could be quiet. The XO seemed by turns charming or curt, warm or irascible. But whatever his mood, he had a reputation as a hard-charger.

O'Kane put *Wahoo* into commission on June 15, 1942, as executive officer under then skipper, Commander Marvin Kennedy. O'Kane was delighted with the vessel's name. U.S. fleet boats were named after marine life and a wahoo is a large, swift, game fish. But "Wahoo" sounded to O'Kane and the crew like the name of an Indian tribe. So her battle flag pictured an American Indian headdress.

Despite *Wahoo*'s early promise and well-trained crew, O'Kane, the number two, was frustrated at Captain Kennedy's performance as skipper on the first two Pacific war patrols. He believed Kennedy was not aggressive enough, and failed to press attacks against choice enemy targets, including an aircraft carrier. Dick O'Kane decided he would not make a third war patrol under Marvin Kennedy. He would ask for a transfer off *Wahoo*.

O'Kane's unstated feelings were shared by the enlisted men and other officers, and that mood translated into ragged morale among the crewmen, who were all volunteers prepared to risk their lives on patrol. *Wahoo,* with only one confirmed enemy ship sunk, had not made much of a record. Captain Kennedy may have had his excuses, but the crew did not want excuses. They wanted a good record. They wanted to sink enemy ships.

What buoyed the morale of Dick O'Kane and *Wahoo*'s men was the presence of a dynamic new skipper, Lieutenant Commander Dudley W. Morton, thirty-five, a tall, dark-haired, broad-shouldered athlete, with ham-hands, a friendly smile, and an approachable manner. Morton exuded confidence and ability. He was familiar with the crew, having made the second war patrol aboard *Wahoo* as the Prospective Commanding Officer—the PCO, or "makee-learn" in sub slang.

Kentucky-born and Florida-raised, Morton acquired his nickname, Mush, short for "Mushmouth," at the Naval Academy because of his heavy Southern drawl. Mush Morton liked roaming the boat chatting with the sailors. *Wahoo*'s engineer, Lieutenant George Grider, thought Mush was built like a bear and playful as a cub.

Dick O'Kane was familiar with Mush Morton's record. Morton was a varsity football player and wrestler who had been in command of the ancient submarine *R-5* in the Atlantic. Mush had vainly fired two torpedoes at what he thought was a German U-boat. Transferred to the Pacific as a Prospective Commanding Officer (PCO), Morton was assigned to the venerable *Dolphin* as relief crew skipper. He looked the boat over, took her out on a training exercise off Pearl Harbor, and decided the sub was too creaky and should be retired—or assigned solely to training duties. "*Dolphin* is a death trap," Morton told the executive officer. "I'm going to try to get off her. I advise you to do the same."

This high-handed attitude, which branded Morton a maverick in the eyes of some squadron commanders, resulted in his removal from command of *Dolphin*. He was on the verge of being "surfaced" out of submarines to regular duty when he was rescued by a senior staffer, Captain John H. "Babe" Brown, also an Academy football player. Brown kept Morton in the PCO pool at Pearl Harbor. He was assigned as a PCO passenger aboard *Wahoo* for the second war patrol, which left Pearl Harbor traveling through the South Pacific to Brisbane. Mush Morton was determined to vindicate himself and Babe Brown's confidence in him.

During *Wahoo*'s second patrol, Morton shared O'Kane's view that Captain Kennedy was far too cautious. The higher authorities in Brisbane concurred, and on the last day of 1942, Mush Morton was given command of *Wahoo*.

Dick O'Kane was impressed by Mush Morton's first action on taking control. Calling the crew together, Mush said quietly, "I am glad to have everyone of you aboard *Wahoo* personally. What I have to say can be stated simply. *Wahoo* is expendable. We will take every reasonable precaution, but our mission is to sink enemy shipping. We are going out there on this war patrol to search for Japs. Every smoke trace on the horizon, every contact on watch will be investigated. If it turns out to be the enemy, we are going to hunt him down and kill him."

Morton paused. "Now if anyone doesn't want to go along under these conditions, just see the yeoman. I am giving him verbal authority to transfer anyone who is not a volunteer. Nothing will ever be said about your remaining in Brisbane."

A half-hour later, just before sailing time, Morton checked with Yeoman Second Class Forest J. Sterling, the ship's clerk.

"Any customers, Yeo?"

"Not a one, Captain."

Morton grinned. "That's the kind of stuff I like in a crew."

Now, sailing into combat, *Wahoo* had a captain and an executive officer who seemed to form a command team infused with fighting spirit, which radiated a mood of cockiness and assurance. Mush Morton clearly placed full trust in Dick O'Kane, and the exec repaid his skipper's faith with loyalty and expertise.

Dick O'Kane was eager to fight. At the U.S. Sub Base in Brisbane a few days earlier, he learned that his first submarine, the elderly USS *Argonaut,* had been reported overdue and presumed lost—after a depth charging by a Japanese destroyer in waters near New Britain, not far from the *Wahoo*'s present transit area. What better way to avenge this personal loss, O'Kane thought, than by using the training he gained from *Argonaut* to help *Wahoo* score against the enemy? After three war patrols, O'Kane knew that submariners liked being on a boat with a good combat record. They wanted skippers and execs who could conduct a war patrol that would make them proud.

As for the crew's view, Yeoman Sterling sensed *Wahoo* was different this time out, with a strong spirit growing in her. There was more of a feeling of freedom, of camaraderie, Sterling thought, of men being trusted to get their jobs done. The ship was no longer uptight but relaxed, though still taut and alert. The yeoman thought that *Wahoo* would make her own luck.

Heading for Wewak, Mush Morton posted additional lookouts at the bridge—rather than submerging at a much-reduced speed. Daylight surface running was a new innovation, since U.S. subs usually spent the day submerged when they were anywhere near enemy air searches. Morton's bold tactic did not sit well with everyone. Some *Wahoo* junior officers, going into battle under the aggressive new skipper, had qualms—and wondered whether their skipper wasn't taking too many chances. George Grider, a tall, thoughtful pipe-smoker from Memphis, Tennessee, believed some of Mush Morton's bolder comments during *Wahoo*'s second patrol reflected the absence of a reasonable degree of caution. Running on the surface in daylight near Japanese airfields seemed to Grider to be rash, if invigorating. With Captain Morton on the bridge, Grider was Officer of the Deck (OOD) when the lookouts spotted a plane in the far distance. Grider prepared to scramble down the bridge hatch for the expected crash dive.

"Let's wait till he gets in to six miles," Mush Morton said quietly.

"Great Lord," Grider thought, "we're under the command of a madman." The enemy plane closed to $6^{1}/2$ miles and then veered away. By not diving, Morton saved hours. The tactic had worked, Grider grudgingly admitted, but he wasn't sure he was in favor of it.

Entering Vitiaz Strait, from *Wahoo*'s flying bridge Captain Morton watched the skies for Japanese planes. A lookout reported a Mitsubishi bomber that had sneaked in four miles away.

"Clear the bridge," Morton ordered. "Dive! Dive!"

"AHOOGAH, AHOOGAH." Two raucous blasts sounded from the diving klaxon. Lookouts tumbled below through the bridge hatch to the conning tower, followed by Grider and Morton, who ordered, "Take her down." The bridge hatch clanged shut. The Quartermaster dogged it down.

"Green board," reported Chief of the Boat, Russell "Pappy" Rau at the "Christmas tree" control board. "Pressure in the boat."

Wahoo slipped quickly beneath the surface. The main air induction valve had slammed shut with a wheeze. Water gurgled into the ballast tanks as air hissed and sputtered out. Throbbing diesels abruptly stopped as the ship shifted to battery-powered, electric drive to run smoothly under water. *Wahoo* was closing Wewak and Morton decided to run submerged the rest of the day.

In the control room, the officers discussed tactics. George Grider suggested that the instruction "reconnoiter" meant to take a periscope look outside Wewak harbor, and simply note the shipping activity.

Captain Morton countered, "No, boy, the only way you can reconnoiter a harbor is to go right into it and see what's there." With that, George Grider glanced in consternation at fellow officers—Roger Paine Jr., lean, dark-haired with a ready smile who ran the torpedo data computer; and Richie Henderson, tall, thin, and serious. It was clear, Grider decided, that the captain had advanced from rashness to outright foolhardiness. It would be crazy for *Wahoo* to submerge and enter an enemy harbor whose very location on the map they couldn't pinpoint.

For *Wahoo*'s navigating team had discovered a serious problem: their out-of-date charts showed only a ragged coastline for New Guinea, the world's second largest island. The name "Wewak" did not appear on their maps. But Allied air reconnaissance had reported heavy Japanese shipping in a harbor at latitude 4 degrees south, and longitude 144 degrees east. Such rough coordinates covered a large area, however, leaving a considerable margin for error.

George Grider had learned that a senior enlisted man, Motor Machinist's Mate First Class Dalton C. Keeter, had purchased an Australian school atlas in Brisbane to bring home to his children. The atlas had a large fold-out map of Northern Australia and Eastern New Guinea and it provided a reasonable close-up of Wewak anchorage, identified as such, and the protecting islets called Kairiru, Karsau, and Mushi—which was quickly dubbed "Mush." The thought struck George Grider that only a couple of weeks before the idea of entering an enemy roadstead with the help of a school geography book would have been too ridiculous even to be funny. Now, he almost hugged the book and hurried to the wardroom with it as if it were the key to the destruction of the entire Japanese Navy.

An amateur photographer, Grider set up his Graflex camera as a projector. With the help of Dick O'Kane, he enlarged the map onto fine tracing paper, producing a workably accurate, large-scale chart of the harbor. *Wahoo* slowly approached the Wewak anchorage and just before dawn on Sunday, January 24, the submarine was off Mush Island. Morton called, "Battle stations submerged." The "BONG, BONG" chimes sounded the battle alarm.

Ever the iconoclast, Mush Morton devised a unique system for underwater attack. Instead of manning the periscope himself, which was customary in U.S. submarines, Mush assigned Dick to operate it and make the sightings—freeing the captain to conn the ship, supervise the attack team, and concentrate on the tactical situation. Few skippers showed such confidence in their execs, but during his previous PCO cruise, Morton had developed complete trust in Dick O'Kane.

"Dick," Mush Morton said, "you'll make all of the approach and attack periscope observations or with the torpedo data computer if we're on the surface. I'll conn *Wahoo* to the best attack position, and you'll fire the torpedoes."

Morton broke into a broad smile. "This way I'll never get scared."

The crew was tense. No American submarine had been so adventurous as to penetrate a Japanese-held port, let alone rely for guidance on a school geography book.

In the war, submarine captains tried to strike a reasonable balance between courage and caution. Finding the right mix was always a difficult problem. When did aggressiveness become recklessness? That was the gnawing question. An experienced submarine officer, George Grider thought about the matter while he was serving with the gung-ho Morton–O'Kane team. It was one thing to be aggressive, he believed, and another to be foolhardy. It would be a mistake to think that the average submariner was a fire-breathing buccaneer who never thought of his own hide. Grider believed most submariners, in calculating risks, factored in that they were worth more to the Navy alive than dead—and to their wives and children as well. The problem with Mush, George thought, was the only risk he recognized was the risk of not sinking enemy tonnage. Grider also worried about Dick O'Kane, whom he liked. Dick had absolutely no reservations about their new captain. The skipper and exec, it seemed, agreed about everything. Grider thought the exec was occasionally given to bravado talk. He displayed mood swings—one day lenient and carefree, the next abrupt and regulation. His style was far from reassuring. With Mush and Dick in the saddle, how would *Wahoo* fare? Grider wondered. The crew would soon find out.

Wewak was a dog-leg anchorage about 7 miles long with various indentations, sheltered by the three islets. Morton ordered *Wahoo* forward. The battle approach team was ready in the conning tower. Dick O'Kane glued his eye to the rubber buffer of the periscope's eyepiece. He did knee bends as the periscope was raised or lowered. He ordered the scope popped up for quick sighting to avoid leaving a feather wake that might be spotted. O'Kane tersely reported bearings of peaks and promontories to establish their position. He noted light patches of sea, which indicated shallower water. Signalman Deville Hunter monitored the opposite side of the periscope, reading bearings from it. Soundman James Buckley gave depth readings and bearings of distinctive beach noises. A strong current running through the anchorage complicated sightings. The current swept *Wahoo* so close to shore that O'Kane could see a Japanese soldier sitting under a coconut tree. His orders and responses were given quietly—submarine attack teams prided themselves on a cool demeanor, especially in emergencies.

Finding no targets, Morton ordered *Wahoo* to move up the harbor. Dick O'Kane spotted a ship. It looked like a freighter or tender at anchor at the end of the dog-leg.

"Well, Captain," someone in the conning tower joked, "we've reconnoitered Wewak. Let's get out of here and report there's a ship in there."

"No," Morton insisted, "we're going to go in and torpedo him." Dick asked Mush to look through the scope and help identify the target. They were both surprised. It was not a tender. It was a destroyer—a lethal hunter of submarines.

"We'll take him by surprise, Dick," Morton said. "He won't be expecting an enemy submarine in here."

True, George Grider thought, no one in his right mind would expect a U.S. submarine in such a confined space—a nearly landlocked harbor.

Inside *Wahoo,* all noise-making equipment was shut down, including the air conditioning. Compartment door handles were dogged down to make them watertight. The temperature soared above the 100-degree mark. Sweat covered the faces and bodies of the attack team in the conning tower and control room. Radioman James Carter, the control room talker, relayed the running action to the crew over the intercom.

"Open outer doors," Morton ordered, referring to the torpedo tubes.

O'Kane reported the range to target: "Three thousand yards." "Stand by," Morton said evenly.

At the periscope cylinder, O'Kane flipped his thumbs up to show he needed the scope raised for a final sighting. He

rode the handles up, pressing his face to the eyepiece. He
grabbed a quick look.

"Down scope," he ordered. "Captain, she's gotten underway heading out. Angle on the bow, 10 degrees port."

The tactical plan was suddenly awry: the sitting duck was
moving rapidly toward them.

Instantly Morton devised a new attack plan.

"Right full rudder," he ordered helmsman Alfred Simonetti.

Wahoo was turning her stern to the onrushing destroyer to
fire her rear torpedoes at right angles as the enemy warship
passed. An accelerating target whose speed was difficult to
judge through the tiny lens complicated the tactical solution.

"Up periscope," O'Kane ordered. "Mark! Target has zigged.
Angle on the bow forty starboard."

This meant the destroyer was crossing *Wahoo*'s bow.

"Any time, Dick," Morton said.

"Ready," O'Kane said. "Fire One . . . Fire Two . . . Fire
Three!'"

Morton's palm hit the firing plungers. The submarine
shuddered as three torpedoes burst from the forward tubes,
and a poppet valve vented compressed air from the tubes
back into the boat. The pressure hit everyone's eardrums.

"All hot, straight, and normal," soundman Buckley reported. Three torpedoes at 8-second intervals raced across
the water. They were 20 feet long and 21 inches in diameter.
Their engines were driven by steam, which left a distinct
wake, wide as a highway.

O'Kane raised the periscope again. "They're heading for
him," he said, as three tin fish churned through the water at
46 knots. Then the bad news.

"The first one missed astern," O'Kane said, eye to scope.
"The second one missed astern . . . The third one missed
astern."

The attack party had underestimated the destroyer's speed
in their torpedo firing set up.

"Get another set-up," Captain Morton ordered. "Use
twenty knots."

"Ready," O'Kane said. "Fire Four!"

O'Kane, pressing against the periscope, exclaimed, "Target turning away."

"Damn!" Mush said.

"The fourth missed," Dick O'Kane reported. "She's swinging around. She's headed right at us."

The situation quickly collapsed into every submariner's nightmare: a destroyer armed with depth charges attacking in shallow and constricted water, which severely limited the boat's ability to evade. The Japanese tin can had merely to follow the torpedo wakes to their source: USS *Wahoo*.

Only two torpedoes remained in the forward tubes. There was no time to bring the stern tubes to bear.

"That's all right," Captain Morton said. "Keep your scope up and we'll shoot the son-of-a-bitch down the throat."

A down-the-throat shot was a tactic that had been discussed in submarine wardrooms and officers' clubs but never before tried in Pacific combat. At best, a torpedo fired directly at an oncoming destroyer would strike its bow, or it would scare the enemy skipper into an emergency turn which presented a broadside target, increasing the chances of a hit. At worst, the torpedo would miss the narrow target—only 20 feet wide—and give the sub's position away, subjecting the boat to a devastating depth charge attack. In a shallow harbor with no deep water to protect it—nowhere to hide—the submarine stood little chance of survival.

Dick O'Kane coolly watched the destroyer approach showing a white "V" bow wave.

"Stand by," Morton ordered, his voice low.

O'Kane steadied the periscope's hairline wire, bisecting the destroyer's bow.

"Left a hair," O'Kane told helmsman Simonetti.

"Any time, Dick," Morton said.

"Fire Five!" O'Kane said, as the submarine lurched downward. "Periscope is under water. Bring me up." The scope moved up.

"Captain," O'Kane said. "He's still coming. Getting close." The range was now 850 yards.

"Stand by to fire Six," Morton ordered.

Listening to talker James Carter's laconic play-by-play

over the intercom, Yeoman Sterling experienced the stoic certainty that he was going to die. He wondered how this could be. It was unreal. He thought, "It can't be happening to me!"

"When shall I fire, Captain?" O'Kane asked.

"Any time, Dick."

"Fire Six!" O'Kane ordered.

"Take her down," Morton commanded. "Rig for depth charge."

Wahoo's diving officer, George Grider, flooded the negative buoyancy tanks and she started down. But since Grider had no idea of the depth of the anchorage he ordered the boat levelled at 90 feet keel depth. Grider realized that *Wahoo* was no longer the aggressor. All the crew could do was grab on to something and stand by for the final depth charging of *Wahoo*. "Our time has come," Grider thought, and they awaited the end almost calmly. Dick O'Kane braced himself between the scope and the torpedo data computer. The propellers of *Wahoo*'s last torpedo were blanked out by the sound of the destroyer's screws, roaring through the sub's conning tower. An explosion sounded loud and near, breaking light bulbs, and sending cork insulation flying.

The crew waited for the next blast that could crush the submarine's pressure hull. Silence. The second explosion never came.

Men looked at one another. Terror turned to hope. The underwater sound of steam belching from the tin can's boilers crackled through the boat.

"Jesus," came a voice from below. "We hit the son-of-a-bitch!"

In the conning tower, Captain Morton heard the remark and laughed. "By God, maybe we did," he said.

Morton ordered Grider, "Bring her back up to periscope depth." The scope was raised and O'Kane peered into it.

"There she is," he said, "Broken in two."

Grider, as the ship's photographer, raced up the ladder to the conning tower to take a picture of the sinking ship. The destroyer appeared bent in two: her skipper had tried to turn at the last minute and been hit broadside. O'Kane reported that some of the destroyer's crewmen were trying to fire a deck gun at *Wahoo*'s periscope. The gun tilted skyward. Morton, suddenly relaxed, offered anyone nearby a look through the periscope. The destroyer was identified as the *Harusame,* which had led the Japanese flotilla during the struggle for Guadalcanal.

All Forest Sterling could think of was an impromptu prayer: "Good Lord, let's get to hell out of here. Make him get out of here. I'll be a minister. I'll go to church every Sunday. I'll do anything you want. Only, let's get to hell out of here."

An aircraft bomb landed close aboard and Mush Morton ordered a fast underwater retreat from Wewak—relying on landmarks recorded inbound to guide *Wahoo* from the anchorage to the safety of deep water. The conning team relaxed as they passed the 40-fathom curve: deep water at 240 feet. They knew what the submarine expression meant: life begins at forty.

The crewmembers were elated. They had sunk an enemy warship even before reaching their patrol station—a feat rarely accomplished. That qualified them to wear the prestigious submarine combat insignia on their uniforms. Their captain and exec had measured up. In the mess room, after securing from battle stations, there was a babble of talk among the excited crew.

Signalman Fertig Krause, who manned the plotting board in the conning tower, exclaimed, "Mush really knows his business. Between Mush and O'Kane, they make a great team." Signalman Hunter, who helped O'Kane with the periscope, added, "You should have seen O'Kane. He's the coolest cucumber you'd want to see in an emergency."

Krause nodded his head in agreement. "Man," he said, "O'Kane stayed on that periscope and looked right down their throats with that destroyer coming in plenty fast and shooting right at us. I've never seen anything like it."

The officers, who had been uncertain of Dick O'Kane's style, also altered their view of their executive officer. George Grider marvelled at the change that had come over O'Kane once the attack began. He was calm, terse, and utterly cool.

It was as if during the talkative, even boastful months under Captain Kennedy, O'Kane had been seeking his true element. Now it was found. This was the most dramatic example Grider had seen of a man transformed under pressure from what seemed almost adolescent petulance into a prime-fighting machine. But Roger Paine, who manned the torpedo data computer, believed O'Kane, while performing superbly, might have urged more restraint on Morton, who was asking for trouble. He thought *Wahoo* was fortunate to get out of Wewak alive.

During *Wahoo*'s hasty exit, Mush Morton checked into the mess room and instructed Pharmacist's Mate Leslie J. Lindhe—inevitably known as "Doc"—to "pass out that depth-charge medicine," which consisted of miniature bottles of bourbon, scotch, or brandy. The use of alcohol was officially forbidden on U.S. Navy ships, but the pharmacist's mates—the medics—kept a liquid store for emergencies and celebrations. Depending on the individual skipper, these were duly rationed out to the crew when the occasion called for it. In *Wahoo*'s case, it was 3-star Hennessy brandy. Doc Lindhe brought around the bottles with the announcement, "Get your depth charge medicine here."

Two hours after dark, well away from Wewak, Mush Morton ordered *Wahoo* surfaced in the Bismarck Sea and set a base course for the Palau Islands—the assigned patrol zone in the Western Carolines. As the conning tower rose above the sea, O'Kane instructed, "Crack the hatch." The round hatch to the bridge was partly opened by the Quartermaster to expel—with a loud whoooosh—the build up of compressed air inside the boat.

"Open the hatch," O'Kane said, and clambered up the ladder to the bridge. He ordered two big, sixteen-cylinder Fairbanks Morse diesels on propulsion, with the other two engines charging the batteries, which had been depleted by the long day underwater in Wewak. Hatches were opened, exposing the boat to fresh air, which after 12 hours underwater, came as a startling, strange smell. The crew could take it easy. The cooks treated them to a sumptuous meal—

submarines were renowned for having the best food in the Navy.

Mush Morton and Dick O'Kane decided to celebrate *Wahoo*'s crossing of the Equator. The crew had already "crossed the line" to get to Brisbane, but because of former CO Kennedy's restrictions, no ceremonies were held. Only O'Kane and a few other crewmen had been formally initiated into the Ancient Order of the Deep. So Mush Morton turned over temporary command of *Wahoo* to Dick O'Kane so that he could preside over shellback ceremonies, acclaiming a crewmember's crossing of zero degrees latitude. O'Kane ordered *Wahoo* to dive under the Equator as he assumed the role of His Majesty Neptunus Rex. Yeoman Forest Sterling was designated Davy Jones. In outlandish, homemade costumes the shellbacks aboard subjected the pollywogs—led by Captain Morton and other officers—to paddling. They stuffed them with foul-tasting bread dough laced with Tabasco sauce, red chili powder, a touch of iodine, castor oil, and vinegar. *Wahoo*'s entire crew were transformed from polliwogs to shellbacks. The men loved it, and Sterling gave them all laminated cards signed by Neptunus Rex and Davy Jones on January 25, 1943, declaring them official shellbacks.

The mood was uplifted by the hijinks, but after a few hours of levity, a more serious tone set in. Every sailor aboard knew *Wahoo* was again headed into harm's way.

CHAPTER TWO

"Shoot the Sons of Bitches"

As executive officer, Dick O'Kane was *Wahoo*'s link between captain and crew. O'Kane believed it was essential in a well-run ship that the exec knew everything of importance on board before the captain, so he took a turn through the claustrophobic spaces of his 312-foot-long vessel, making his way into the compartments, checking the ship's condition, congratulating the crew, and getting the thumbs up sign in return. It was his way of taking the crew's collective pulse.

Like the standard, 1,500-ton fleet boats of her class, *Wahoo*, SS-238, was of double-hull construction. The inner, welded, cylindrical "pressure" hull was divided into eight watertight compartments. The outer hull encased water ballast and fuel tanks which held enough diesel oil to give *Wahoo* a 12,000-mile range. Ton for ton, a U.S. fleet submarine was the most complex, compact, and deadly war machine in the world. For historical reasons, submarines though warships were called "boats," not "ships"—from "pig-boats," because early subs traveled with a bobbing movement like a porpoise, or "sea-pig."

Wahoo's eight compartments were divided into upper and lower levels by a metal platform deck. The forward torpedo room had six tubes, with sixteen torpedoes stored in them or lashed to the reload racks. One hatch led to the deck and could be used as the emergency escape trunk. Another hatch was used for torpedo loading. Torpedomen treated their "tin fish" with great care. Each day they pulled them out of the tubes for inspection: checking gyroscopes, air pressure, igniters, engines, and the double tandem propellers. The torpedoes, launched from the tubes by a blast of compressed air, were really mini-subs with their own turbines run by steam which was created by compressed air burned with alcohol. The gyroscope, which held the torpedo on course to the target, the water pressure device that maintained a pre-set depth, and the 500-pound TNT warhead all needed frequent inspection. The room could berth a dozen crewmen, their bunks placed over and under the spare torpedoes.

To the rear of the torpedo room was the forward battery compartment whose lower half, under the decking, contained 126 huge battery cells. This was the "can"—each cell weighing 1,600 pounds—that provided power for underwater propulsion. The batteries were sensitive and easily damaged by depth charging. If they were penetrated by significant amounts of salt water, deadly chlorine gas would be generated. With new batteries, a boat could make some 8 to 9 knots submerged. But this high speed discharged the battery in an hour and was known as the "one hour rate." Running at 3 knots, a submarine could travel submerged for up to 48 hours—or 150 miles distance. But when the boat ran out of battery power, it had to surface, like it or not.

The upper part of the compartment contained the officers' staterooms, wardroom, pantry, the chief petty officer's quarters, and a tiny ship's office, with Yeoman Sterling's typewriter and stencils. The pantry was presided over by steward's mates who took the food from the galley to keep it warm for officers coming off watch. They were often Filipinos or Guamanians, whose English was imperfect. One steward wanted to transfer off a submarine because he didn't like the idea of undergoing "death" charges: he was reassured when an officer explained they were only "depth" charges. When under red interior lights or using red goggles to adjust their night vision, officers and men played with cards whose numbers and suits were outlined in black, since red could not be distinguished through the red glasses.

In *Wahoo*'s mid-section lay its nerve center—the control room. Here were the diving mechanisms, including the manifold levers for flooding ballast tanks with seawater to cause the ship to sink, or blowing the tanks with compressed air forcing out the seawater to make *Wahoo* rise. Seawater was pumped forward or aft to the trim tanks to give the boat an even keel underwater. Two large wheels controlled the bow and stern diving planes, which kept the ship on an even keel—or at the desired up or down angle ordered by the diving officer. A glass tube shaped in an arc with an air bubble in the center—or to either side—showed the diving planesman the steepness of the submarine's angle, acting like a carpenter's level. Hence the submariner's expression: "Keep a zero bubble!"

A prominent feature was the "Christmas tree," a board, which showed whether valves for pressure hull openings were open or closed—with red (open) or green (closed) lights. A "green board" meant the boat was sealed, watertight, and ready for diving. With a green board showing, a slug of compressed air was pumped into *Wahoo* as a test. The sharp increase of pressure felt in the eardrums meant the submarine was safely sealed—"pressure in the boat." As a *Wahoo* officer described it, "The art of diving, like flying by the seat of the pants, involved getting the feel of the boat, whether it was heavy or light overall, forward or aft. Some officers learned it instinctively. Some never got the magic touch."

The hydraulic diving manifold was the battle station of the chief of the boat (COB), Chief Torpedoman "Pappy" Rau, a short, muscular, father figure for the crew. He was the senior enlisted man aboard. The COB like the CO and the XO did not stand watches but rather kept an administrative eye on all—except during Battle Stations. The chief of the boat was not necessarily an older man. It was up to the captain and the exec to pick someone who was a natural leader, and who could serve as a conduit between the crew and the executive officer. Fulfilling the role took a special quality that not every chief petty officer possessed. Some preferred to duck the added responsibilities of chief of the boat.

Behind Pappy Rau during an attack stood the boat's engineer and diving officer, George Grider, an officer who was considered to have a fine diving "touch." He had the use of a new instrument—the bathythermograph, which showed the location of a temperature gradient in the ocean. Enemy sonar waves bounced off a gradient, which hid the submarine lying below the temperature differential.

Exec O'Kane checked the emergency alarms in the control room: diving, surface, collision, fire. Each had a different shaped knob in case they had to be used in the dark. Below the control room was the pump room, which contained machinery to transfer air or water from one tank to another, and into or out of the submarine; the air conditioning equipment; air compressors; the main hydraulic plant; a fresh water tank; a fresh water distiller; and a cold storage space for meat and perishable food.

Above the control room, reached by a ladder, was the battle center, the conning tower—an 8-foot by 14-foot cylindrical addition to the boat's pressure hull. This critical space held the twin periscope eyepieces, sound and radar equipment, the torpedo data computer (hooked up directly to the torpedo room and factoring gyro angles into the torpedoes), the steering helm, and the torpedo firing mechanism. This was Mush Morton's and Dick O'Kane's station for Battle Submerged—along with their attack team. During Battle Stations, the conning tower was filled with nine or ten men and a tense, electric atmosphere. The room was crammed with navigational instruments, fathometers, and charts, and at night was bathed in an eerie red light to protect the night vision of those who had to climb to the bridge for lookout duty. The crucial piece of gear was the torpedo data computer, or TDC. The TDC officer cranked in the target's track and the submarine's own course was automatically entered to give a correct gyro angle for the torpedoes to intercept. The assistant TDC operator set the spread of a torpedo salvo to insure hits.

A ladder and hatch in the conning tower led to the bridge, where the officer of the deck was in charge when the submarine was surfaced. The bridge hatch was only 26 inches across. The bridge held a gyro compass; a target bearing transmitter (TBT) (hooked up to the torpedo data computer) with binoculars, a microphone to the ship's intercom system, and the diving klaxon, sounded twice with the verbal order "Dive, Dive."

Captain Morton and Dick O'Kane took over the bridge for Battle Surface stations. The twin periscopes rose above the superstructure, called the fairweather, along with the radar mast. There were small metal perches for lookouts on the periscope shears. Aft of the flying bridge was the "cigarette deck," which held the 20-millimeter machine gun. Crewmen could grab some air or a smoke there. Some men on patrol declined the offer to go topside while the sub was surfaced: they preferred the warm feeling of the womb-like confines of the submarine. They were proud that they would not see daylight until the end of a war patrol, a couple of months later. Forward of the bridge was the 4-inch deck gun.

Aft of the control room was the radio room. Next was *Wahoo*'s largest compartment, which held the galley, the messroom, and the crews' quarters—up to forty berths with leatherette mattresses and personal lockers. Below the decking was the after battery space—another 126 huge cells. Very occasionally, there weren't enough sleeping racks to go around, which resulted in the practice of "hot-bunking" with a couple of crew sharing the same berth. When one sailor was on watch the other slept, and vice versa. The stainless-steel galley was a masterpiece of compression where the cooks turned out meals and bakery products three times a day—with fresh sandwiches around the clock.

A good ship's cook was a treasured crewmember. The same food was prepared for crew and officers. A huge 10-gallon urn was always full of hot coffee. The messroom with four tables seating twenty-four men doubled as the rec room for the crew. It was filled with off-watch sailors: reading, studying for rate advancement, gabbing, snacking, playing acey-ducey or pinochle. Here the crew exchanged gossip and traded rumors.

Dick O'Kane bantered briefly with the sailors. He knew there were few secrets among the crew. On *Wahoo,* officers' stewards would wander back to the mess room to give the crew a fill-in on what their seniors in the wardroom were saying. Stowed in the messroom were a phonograph and 78 rpm records, and the library; paperbacks, which soared in popularity during the war, were favorites because they could be stuffed in pockets and the pages turned easily. The messroom and the sleeping compartment behind, above the after battery room, held pin-up pictures by *Esquire*'s George Petty and Varga, along with photos of Hollywood stars like Betty Grable and Rita Hayworth.

There were two showers for the crew. Likewise there were a couple of tiny "heads," or toilets. For the uninitiated, these devices could lead to messy embarrassment. The underwater heads were not easy to operate. Directions for use were stamped on a bulkhead plate in the heads. Thus: "Before using, see that Bowl Flapper Valve A is closed, Gate Valve C in discharge line is open, Valve C in water supply line is open. Then open Valve E next to bowl to admit necessary water. Close valves D and E. After using, pull Lever A, release Lever A. Open Valve C in air supply line. Rock Air Valve Lever F outboard to charge measuring tank to 10 pounds above sea pressure. Open Plug Cock B and rock Air Valve F Lever inboard to blow overboard. Close Valves B and C. For pump expulsion, open Plug Cock B. Pump waste receiver empty. Close Plug Cock B. Close Valve C. If on first inspection, the expulsion chamber is found flooded, discharge the contents overboard before using the toilet." Many sailors did not master this intricate operation at first; air valves pressed incorrectly resulted in a spray from the bowl, often onto the user's face or shirt—known as "dingleberries."

Rearward in tandem were the forward and after engine rooms, each containing two huge diesels that drove the boat on the surface and recharged the batteries. The engine noise was ear shattering. With all diesels running, the sound was like the hammers of hell. Enginemen wearing earplugs communicated with each other by hand signals and the "general quarters" alarm was a blinking red light. The diesels were each attached to main generators. The air necessary to run the engines came from the main induction valve under the cigarette deck, the largest on *Wahoo*—40 inches in diameter. When the diving alarm sounded, the main induction was shut, the diesels stopped, and the batteries took over to provide power for the twin screws. The diesels were in the charge of motor machinist's mates, or "motor macs." (In the Navy, machinist's mates looked after steam propulsion on bigger warships.)

The diesel engines were hooked by electric generators to main motors in the next compartment aft, the motor room, which through reduction gears drove the boat's twin propeller shafts, the screws. On the upper level was the maneuvering room, the main propulsion control board, which received orders from the conn. Electrician's mates had 5 million watts of power at their disposal to control the output of the generators from the engines or batteries to the motors, which drove the screws. They could switch power to charge the batteries if necessary. The electrician mate's in the maneuvering room transmitted orders from the conning tower or bridge into actual speeds: standard speed 15 knots, full speed 18 knots, flank speed 20 knots, and emergency speed whatever they could squeeze out of the machinery, possibly 21 or even 22 knots. It was difficult to maintain the highest speeds for long before burning out the electrical gear.

The rear compartment was the after torpedo room, with four tubes, eight torpedoes, and a dozen more bunks for the torpedomen. To these torpedomen, Dick O'Kane gave an assurance that if possible, their war fish would be the next to be fired at the enemy—the forward and after torpedo room gangs competed to see which could ring up the best scores. O'Kane noted that the rowing machines provided by high-minded shore authorities to maintain the crew's physical fitness, and originally stored in the torpedo room, had been deep-sixed along the way. A submarine's storage space was so restricted that the exercise machines deprived torpedomen of sleeping space.

Making his way through *Wahoo,* Dick O'Kane marveled at the boat. The submarine was a maze of valves, gauges, meters, and operating levers, which controlled the flow of water, air, and fuel lines that served as *Wahoo*'s capillaries and veins. The ubiquitous electrical cables were its nervous system. Though O'Kane had become accustomed to it, the submarine's pungent smell was distinctive—compounded in equal parts by ripe human scent, cooking odours and diesel oil fumes. The crew called it "fug."

Like all submarine officers, O'Kane was constantly concerned with the state of the pressure hull, which was constructed of inch-thick, welded, high-tensile steel, designed to resist enemy depth charges and deep sea pressure. *Wahoo*'s test depth was 300 feet, which meant that the boat should have a 100 percent safety factor that far down. Anything lower was in the risky zone, but in theory a submarine could descend twice its test depth and survive. Farther down, the hull would begin imploding.

As far as Dick O'Kane was concerned, the most important protection for a submarine was a well-trained and disciplined crew. He had vetted them all when they were assigned aboard: torpedomen, electricians, motor machinists, gunners, signalmen, radiomen, quartermasters, cooks, stewards. Every officer and man was expected to learn most every other job aboard *Wahoo* before being designated "qualified for submarines" and permitted to wear the prized twin-dolphin insignia. A pharmacist's mate, for instance, might stand watch as a soundman or radar operator. O'Kane stressed to newcomers that each sailor aboard *Wahoo* depended on everyone else—and on each man doing his job correctly. Any major mistake could make *Wahoo* their coffin: on the conduct of each depended the fate of all. "There's no margin for mistakes in submarines," O'Kane drilled into the crew. "You're either alive or dead."

O'Kane considered that "the men back aft" did a masterful job keeping machinery running, often improvising, sometimes under hairy, life-and-death conditions. He was aware, too, as perhaps younger crewmen were not, that the rising toll among the submarine force personnel had reached more than 20 percent killed in action—the highest fatality rate of any branch of the U.S. Armed Forces. There was scarcely a skipper or exec in the Sub Force who hadn't learned that a boat he once served aboard was now "overdue and presumed lost." Every submariner by now had lost friends on sunken submarines.

The nervous strain of submarine war imposed the need for men of stable temperament. Advancement of personnel to positions of greater responsibility within the ship was rapid: there was no room for dead weight. Since *Wahoo* had no medical officer, the crew's good physical condition was a necessity. Living conditions on board involved close quarters

for officers and men for long periods of time: amiable dispo-
sitions and clean habits were a must. O'Kane knew that work
on a submarine was hard and life was dangerous. So for him,
constant vigilance was the price of safety. He agreed with
the Navy axiom that a taut ship was a happy ship. The crew
thought O'Kane was sometimes stern but always fair, and
being treated fairly was important to them. O'Kane also accepted the Navy truism that in a well-run ship, the skipper
was the good guy and the exec the bad guy. Mush Morton
was the quintessential good guy, increasingly beloved by the
crew. O'Kane knew that a good exec's role was not to seek
popularity. His job was to keep everyone fine-tuned. O'Kane
ran the ship administratively through Pappy Rau. This allowed Mush Morton to concentrate on tactics and strategy.

Heading back to the control room, O'Kane felt confident
about *Wahoo,* a feeling shared by the crew.

In a popular gesture, Mush Morton directed that photos of
Japanese vessels, which had been pasted around the ship by
the previous captain, be replaced by some of the prettiest
pin-up pictures in the Navy—which Morton had obtained
during a visit to a Hollywood studio. In addition, he ordered
Yeoman Sterling to put up a placard with an exhortation attributed to Army General Leslie McNair—which was criticized by some American clergymen—reading:

WE MUST FIGHT
WE MUST SHOOT TO KILL
FOR OUR ENEMIES
HAVE POINTED THE WAY
TO SWIFTER SURER
CRUELER KILLING

Forest Sterling, on Mush Morton's orders, distributed bright
red cards in each compartment with the admonition:

SHOOT THE
SONS OF
BITCHES

Under former skipper Kennedy, the crew had been ordered not to use the showers in order to save fresh water. Only sponge baths were permitted. But Mush Morton, with O'Kane's enthusiastic approval, urged the crew to shower and use fresh water to keep their clothes clean. COB Pappy Rau, the submarine equivalent of an Army top sergeant, passed along Morton's new rules that showers and clothes-washing water were in order. Cleanliness was a privilege—and *Wahoo* sailors turned up for dinner with clean dungarees and freshly washed tee-shirts. Sometimes Mush washed his own khakis in a bucket of soapy water in the engine room. It was a gesture of solidarity with the crew and they loved it.

Dick O'Kane was pleased that Mush Morton respected his position as executive officer—the key administrator aboard ship working closely with the chief of the boat—rather than short-circuiting him, as Captain Kennedy did by giving orders directly to junior officers and chief petty officers. O'Kane's days of being the last to know were over. Skipper Kennedy had also insisted that O'Kane stand regular watches along with the other officers—a practice Dick thought detracted seriously from his main duties as executive officer, which included being navigator, assistant attack officer, and the ship's administrator. O'Kane believed his regular watch-standing as Officer of the Deck (OOD) in two four-hour hitches in a 24-hour cycle undermined *Wahoo*'s potential fighting ability. The exec's time was better used running the ship, freeing the captain to concentrate on strategic and tactical planning.

O'Kane thought that the relationship between the commanding officer and the executive officer was critical on a submarine: uneasy bonds between the two key officers on several boats had led to conflicts that affected their vessels as fighting units. O'Kane and his fellow officers knew his relationship with Kennedy had not been easy. Happily, it was soon clear to *Wahoo*'s crew that Mush trusted Dick completely.

As exec, O'Kane worked closely with Yeoman Sterling, who ran the ship's office. O'Kane told Sterling to throw away the Captain's Mast book, the record of minor crew offenses: he would handle disciplinary matters on board without official action. O'Kane was an officer who came to a crewman's rescue if he got into trouble ashore; he looked out for the crew. Problems were settled quickly and quietly. No big deal. The crew respected him for this.

Dick usually kept his Irish temper under control but Sterling liked to be flip with O'Kane, sometimes just for the hell of it. O'Kane took the joshing with good grace—up to a point. But Sterling knew you could only go so far with the exec: O'Kane was still the guy who kept *Wahoo* shipshape so that Mush could relax with the crew.

Sterling would quip to the crewmen, when asked how he got along with O'Kane, "We get along fine. I always get the last word in."

"You do?" he'd be asked in surprise.

"Yeah, I always say, 'Yes, sir,' and he walks away."

Aboard ship, new crewmembers soon learned that any Navy officer from the rank of ensign, through lieutenant junior grade, full lieutenant, lieutenant commander, commander, and four-stripe captain can command a warship, depending on the vessel's size and type. But every commanding officer, or CO, is also known as "Captain" or "skipper" regardless of actual rank.

Relations with officers on *Wahoo* were highly informal: nobody stood on ceremony. "You leave your rank on the dock," went the saying. But everyone knew who was who in the chain of command. On a U.S. fleet submarine, the seven to ten officers were expected to be able to perform each other's duties. All but the skipper and exec stood four-hour watches as officer of the deck (OOD)—in charge of conning the boat until the captain took over. The junior officers served as engineer, torpedo officer, torpedo data computer man, communication officer, gunnery officer, and the lowliest ensign, known as "George"—for "let George do it"—was generally assigned to commissary duties until he moved up the seniority ladder. Officers called each other by their first names, though junior officers would wait until their seniors told them to do so. Everyone called the skipper "Captain."

On *Wahoo,* if an engineering officer like George Grider

showed flair for diving the ship or running the torpedo data computer, a good skipper would use him in that role during Battle Stations. Mush and Dick didn't stand on ceremony when assigning an officer to a specific battle station: he served where he was best suited.

The exec was normally the submarine's navigator, as was Dick O'Kane. On a submarine operating for long periods underwater in dangerous surroundings, accurate navigational fixes were paramount. O'Kane introduced assistant navigator Fertig Krause, a Signalman First Class, to the mysteries of celestial navigation, sun lines and star shots through the sextant, using familiar stars like Sirius, Arcturus, Betelgeuse, Rigel, Aldebaran, Vega, and the Southern Cross constellation, as well as the planets Venus, Jupiter, and Mars. A proper fix from the sun and stars was essential.

O'Kane found that a submarine's war patrol was often influenced by its first combat action, which set a pattern. So with the patrol's first sinking behind them, Dick O'Kane looked forward to the rest of the voyage, even though a Pacific War patrol usually ran from forty to sixty days—a standard patrol allowed for thirty days on station, with ten days transit time each way, but these could run longer if targets were scarce, or shorter if torpedoes were expended. Between patrols, submarines underwent a refit at a sub base with a relief crew coming aboard while the regular crew had two weeks of rest and recuperation.

As *Wahoo* headed into battle again, Dick O'Kane sprang a pleasant surprise on the crew. He had quietly brought aboard a load of Sunday newspaper comic sections his wife had saved from the *San Francisco Chronicle* and *San Francisco Examiner* over a period of months. He began parcelling them out to the crew, a single set at a time. They passed eagerly from hand to hand. It was a nice lift for morale.

Two days north of Wewak, *Wahoo* charged forward, diesels throbbing. OOD George Grider's voice bellowed from the loud speaker on the bridge, "Smoke on the horizon, broad on the port bow."

Wahoo went to Battle Stations.

CHAPTER THREE

"One-Sub Wolf Pack"

For *Wahoo* in wartime, smoke was a submariner's delight. It signified a target on or over the horizon. By spotting smoke many miles away, a submarine could plot the course of Japanese ships over the horizon, follow them, and prepare for an attack out of the quarry's visual range. After Wewak, morale was high: no one knew what was making the smoke, but no one had any doubt that Mush and Dick would track it down.

Morton ordered *Wahoo* to flank speed on the surface at 20 knots to reach a position well ahead of the enemy. Lookout Deville Hunter, hanging from his perch on the periscope shears, reported two sets of top-masts emerging on the horizon—giving Morton a better fix on the course and speed of what was shaping up as a two-ship Japanese convoy, zigzagging. Moving ahead with the range closing, Morton pulled the plug and took *Wahoo* under. The boat crept toward the convoy, which was now headed *Wahoo*'s way.

Dick O'Kane manned the search periscope, the scope with the larger lens for longer distance sightings. (The second periscope was the attack scope. It had a smaller lens, but was harder for escort ships to sight.) O'Kane commented tersely on his sightings and identified the leading freighter as a Dakar Maru class. Morton's tactical plan was to lay about 1,000 yards off the leading target, and fire three fish at the lead freighter. He would then swing the boat to the left and fire the other three bow torpedoes at the second Japanese cargo ship. The maneuver required precise timing. Unexpectedly, O'Kane reported the freighters were going faster than estimated, bringing them too close to *Wahoo*. If fired, the torpedoes would not have enough running room—450 yards—to arm before impacting.

Improvising quickly, Morton turned the boat to bring the stern tubes into position for firing, a complex maneuver that could provide only two torpedoes per target. O'Kane worked expertly at the periscope: in minutes, *Wahoo* was ready with the new attack set-up. As O'Kane rattled off target angles, bearings, ranges and estimated speeds, Roger Paine cranked the information into the torpedo data computer, and gyro angles were set for the torpedoes. Morton supervised, giving orders to the helmsman and diving officer.

At O'Kane's instruction "Mark!" the target bearing was fed into the computer from the compass notations around the periscope. "Set," Paine said, indicating the data was cranked in and the torpedo was ready for firing. O'Kane shot two torpedoes at the leading freighter, the *Fukuei Maru*. He shifted to the second target and unleashed two more. As the four fish cut through the sea, Morton swung the submarine into a half circle to bring the bow tubes to bear for a follow-up attack.

"All hot, straight, and normal," soundman Buckley reported. Torpedoes One and Two hit the first target in the bow and stern. Torpedo Three ran ahead of its target, but Torpedo Four struck home. Three hits out of four!

As *Wahoo* completed the turn, O'Kane raised the periscope. He reported, "There's the first one. She's listing to starboard and sinking by the stern. Mark! Here's the other one—she's headed for us, but coming slow. Mark! Here's another ship, angle on the bow ninety starboard, range eighteen hundred." O'Kane decided the third ship looked like a troop transport. The situation was becoming confused: one vessel sinking; a damaged ship heading at *Wahoo;* a big new ship appearing on the scene. But this was the kind of situation that showed the Morton–O'Kane team at its best.

"Let's get the big one next," Mush Morton said.

O'Kane fired three bow torpedoes at the large transport in the distance, the *Buyo Maru*. Two hits. One miss. He turned his attention to the oncoming damaged freighter that was heading *Wahoo*'s way despite the earlier hit.

"It's a zero angle," O'Kane reported, peering through the periscope.

"That's all right," Morton said. "We'll shoot the son-of-a-bitch down the throat."

O'Kane thought: "Oh, no. I hoped never to hear those words again, much less in just three days." But he knew that Mush Morton believed there was no point in mastering a new technique if you didn't keep in practice.

O'Kane ordered two torpedoes fired from the bow tubes. One hit. But the plucky skipper of the cargo ship kept plodding toward *Wahoo*. Morton ordered deeper submergence to avoid having the conning tower rammed. Explosions stunned *Wahoo*. At first, O'Kane thought they were depth charges, but then realized they must be boiler explosions from their last hit on the target.

Morton ordered the torpedo tubes reloaded. Then he called for *Wahoo* to rise to periscope depth. O'Kane peered through the lens and reported the first target sunk. The second ship, which had tried to ram, was losing speed, and steering erratically, but moving off. The larger vessel, the troop transport *Buyo Maru,* was afloat but motionless— with soldiers all over the decks, some shooting weapons at *Wahoo*'s periscope.

"Let's finish him off," Morton said exultantly. "Dick, any time."

O'Kane conned the boat to within 1,000 yards of the target, took careful aim, and fired. He reported the track of the single torpedo.

"It's heading straight at him. They're shooting at it. It's going under . . . Oh, hell." The torpedo failed to explode.

Morton was furious at the dud weapon. Faulty torpedoes were the bane of the submarine force, and generated much friction between complaining sub skippers and Washington's Bureau of Ordnance officials who insisted American torpedoes were flawless.

"Stand by to shoot another," Morton ordered angrily. "Same set-up."

"Fire!" O'Kane said. His eye pressed to the periscope, O'Kane reported the fish running directly toward the target.

The fire control party cheered it on. The whole *Wahoo* crew could hear the blast.

"There it goes," O'Kane exclaimed. "What a hit!"

The torpedo struck under the transport's stack, ripping apart her midsection, and causing a fatal roll from which the ship couldn't recover. George Grider rushed to get a photo through the periscope, which showed masses of soldiers slithering down the vessel's sides. Seconds later, the stern shot up, the bow went under and the transport sank.

Morton wasted no time in congratulations. He directed O'Kane to find the second freighter, which had tried to ram them. Though hit twice, the hardy Japanese captain kept his ship afloat and was now staggering off at a half-dozen knots. But *Wahoo*'s batteries were getting dangerously low. It was now past noon, and the crew had been at Battle Stations since early morning. Morton ordered O'Kane to keep an eye on their quarry.

In a fresh sighting, O'Kane reported a fourth Japanese ship on the horizon. A second look indicated the ship was a large tanker. The wounded freighter headed toward the tanker and the two ships began to disappear over the horizon. Morton brought *Wahoo* to the surface. Finding himself surrounded by two-dozen boats carrying the troops from the sunken transport, he ordered: "Battle Stations—man all guns."

O'Kane looked at Morton questioningly.

"Dick," Morton said, "the army bombards strategic areas, and the air corps uses area-bombing so the ground forces can advance. Both bring civilian casualties. Now without civilian casualties, I will prevent these soldiers from getting ashore. Every one who does can mean an American life. I have to do it, Dick."

O'Kane felt hesitant but agreed there was no option. Japanese soldiers could easily reach the New Guinea coast, where Allied troops were engaged in bloody conflict with Japanese forces. To allow them to do so, he thought, would be aiding and abetting the enemy. Sailors quickly manned the 4-inch deck gun as well as the machine guns on the cigarette deck. During the Pacific War, some sub skippers developed an intense, almost personal, hatred for the Japanese enemy. Mush Morton, despite his easy-going nature, was one. Dick O'Kane, while less viscerally hateful of the enemy, still intended to take any measures that would end the war at the earliest opportunity. Other officers, like George Grider, were less emotional and viewed their mission with more detachment—if no less dedication.

The next minutes were among the most controversial in U.S. wartime submarine operations.

His voice turning cold, Mush Morton told Dick O'Kane, "I'll order a single 4-inch round at the largest craft, and we'll continue in to see if we draw any return fire. Keep your crews in protected areas until I order commence firing. It'll be your job to chase the troops out of their boats."

Morton instructed the gunner, "Chief Carr, you smash up the boats. There's only time for a single pass so use the maximum rate of fire."

Wahoo opened fire on the boats, about twenty of them. One shot back. In reply, *Wahoo*'s machine guns drove most of the Japanese soldiers in life-jackets from the splintering and sinking boats. The 4-inch gun crew demolished the bigger Japanese boats. Some crewmen reported the water was so thick with enemy soldiers that it was impossible to cruise through them without brushing them aside like driftwood. O'Kane knew they were uniformed troops bound for New Guinea to fight and kill Americans, and the officers sensed Mush Morton's overwhelming hatred of the enemy.

During the firing, two men manning the 20-millimeter machine gun were injured. Engineman Henry Glinski suffered two mangled toes when a shell exploded, blowing fragments out the rear breech. Seaman Wesley Gerlacher had metal embedded in his shoulder. O'Kane called Pharmacist's Mate Leslie Lindhe to the bridge to attend the wounded. Lindhe got the two seamen below. Motor Machinist's Mate Fred Chisholm produced a pair of wire cutters from his toolbox. The cutters were boiled in water to sterilize them, and Lindhe removed the remnants of Glinski's two toes. Lindhe saved the third toe by suturing it and dousing the wounds with sulfa powder.

O'Kane was impressed with Lindhe's performance, and by

the job that pharmacist's mates, also called hospital corpsmen, did in the Sub Force. As the only medic aboard a boat, the pharmacist's mate had no doctor to turn to. He was beyond the reach of professional advice. Most also had a battle station and performed well as a radar or sound operator.

Dick O'Kane reported that some Japanese troops were undoubtedly hit during the action, but no individual was deliberately shot in the boats or in the sea. The boats were legitimate targets. By the time *Wahoo* had completed a broad half-circle and Morton ordered ceasefire, the boats were nothing but flotsam. O'Kane said the action happened quickly, taking about 15 minutes, and that *Wahoo* shot at the boats to sink them. Roger Paine agreed with O'Kane. Forest Sterling believed the fire from the Japanese boats had provoked Morton's response.

Some commentators later raised the question of whether shooting boats laden with enemy soldiers was legitimate, while firing at Japanese troops in the water was not. Aboard *Wahoo,* officers and crewmen believed Morton was defending the ship, and killing Japanese soldiers was the basic nature of their duty, however it was done. The incident, when later recounted around officers' clubs in various versions, left some skippers uneasy.

After clearing the debris, Morton resumed a surface chase of the fleeing vessels. In late afternoon, *Wahoo*'s lookouts sighted the enemy ships. Morton began a classic submarine maneuver known as an end-around. This consisted of tracking and overtaking a target at a wide distance with the advantage of the submarine's 20-knot speed on the surface, finding a position forward of the convoy and off its bow, then submerging and waiting for the enemy ships to pass within torpedo range. It was a long, painstaking operation because the difference in the relative speeds of hunter and hunted was usually fairly small.

The two-ship convoy was now zigzagging frantically, but that maneuver aided *Wahoo* because it slowed the Japanese ships' overall advance along their base course. By dusk, Morton was in a favorable attack position. *Wahoo* submerged. Morton selected what looked like a tanker as the first target.

At the periscope, Dick O'Kane fixed the hairline on the ship and ordered three bow torpedoes fired at a range of a mile. They were the last fish left in the forward tubes.

One hit, but the vessel kept going. Morton ordered *Wahoo* swung around to line up the stern tubes with the four remaining torpedoes. The enemy ships kept zigzagging, which made them difficult targets. Finally, after grueling minutes, Morton worked out the zigzag plan, maneuvered his stern into position, and O'Kane fired two torpedoes at the target at a range of 1,850 yards. The second torpedo hit amidships. The vessel appeared to sink quickly.

Three ships down, but another only damaged: the crippled *Pacific Maru* had gallantly staved off *Wahoo* since early morning, though it had absorbed two hits.

Whatever his regard for his Japanese counterpart, Mush Morton determined to put him under. He ordered Battle Surface to track the fleeing vessel by another end-around. Then the freighter opened fire with deck guns, the shells falling close to *Wahoo*'s bridge.

"He's a nervy devil," Morton said admiringly, and ordered a dive. Mush was chagrined to be driven under by a mere freighter. A young lookout, Seaman Jesse Appel, piled down the hatch from the bridge, quite shaken up.

"They was shooting right at me," he told his shipmates in the messroom. "I could hear that shell going right over my head."

"There's nothing to be afraid of down here," Yeoman Sterling counseled. "They can't reach us here. The guys are real proud of the way you cleared the bridge."

"Yeo," Appel said, "I'm scared. I don't care what anybody thinks. I'm scared."

When the sound of shell splashes ended, Morton brought the submarine to the surface again and pursued in the dark. In the control room, George Grider thought *Wahoo*'s officers might wish, personally, that the brave Japanese captain would make good his escape. He had expended every possible ounce of boldness and daring to escape the relentless Mush Morton. But Grider realized that pursuing this line of thought would lead him eventually to a Navy psychiatrist.

Wahoo's job, Grider knew, was to dog the opponent's tracks and wait for him to make a fatal error. And at last he did.

On the horizon, a strong searchlight beam suddenly illuminated the night sky. O'Kane thought it was a Japanese warship assigned to find the missing convoy. Seeing that beacon of hope, the Japanese captain stopped zigzagging, and headed straight for the light. Mush Morton recognized that the beam probably spelled safety to his resourceful Japanese antagonist. He ordered *Wahoo* to make flank speed for the searchlight to position the submarine between the Japanese warship and the sturdy freighter. Those two decisions made quickly on a darkened ocean by sparring captains meant victory for one, and doom for the other.

Morton turned *Wahoo*'s stern tubes toward the freighter's track, and as it approached, he said, "Any time, Dick."

O'Kane responded: "Fire Nine. Fire Ten."

Below, in the conning tower, George Grider and Roger Paine believed the range was too long to secure a hit. As the seconds went by, with no sound of explosions, Grider said to Paine, "If either one of those torpedoes hit, I will kiss your royal ass."

Two blasts rent the black waters.

"Two hits," Morton yelled. "Two goddamn hits!"

On the bridge, Mush Morton exulted over his final victory over an enemy—the *Pacific Maru*—it had taken four hits from three separate attacks to sink. Below, Grider noted, "Mush Morton missed the most unusual ceremony ever performed in the conning tower of mighty *Wahoo*."

With all torpedoes expended even before *Wahoo* reached her primary patrol area, Mush Morton gave the welcome command: "All ahead, standard. We're heading for the barn."

Morton called for a radio message blank and carefully composed his report to Commander Submarines Pacific. It read: "SANK DESTROYER IN WEWAK SUNDAY AND IN FOURTEEN HOUR RUNNING GUN AND TORPEDO BATTLE TODAY DESTROYED ENTIRE CONVOY OF TWO FREIGHTERS ONE TRANSPORT ONE TANKER X ALL TORPEDOES EXPENDED."

The reply from ComSubPac was prompt: "ADMIRAL HALSEY LIKES YOU FOR GETTING DESTROYER SUNDAY X WE ALL LIKE YOU

FOR GETTING ALL FOUR SHIPS OF CONVOY YESTERDAY X COME ON HOME MUSH YOUR PICTURE'S ON THE PIANO."

The next morning, January 27, *Wahoo*'s homeward-bound rhythm was broken by the lookout's warning: "Smoke over the horizon!"

Captain Morton shifted the rudder to an intercepting course. He explained to Dick O'Kane that even though *Wahoo* had no torpedoes this would provide a good tracking exercise. Soon the topmasts of three ships appeared. A half-hour later, three more sets of masts jutted up on the horizon: a six-ship convoy. Submerged, Morton himself took a look through the periscope. It was a peculiar feeling for Mush and Dick—seeing a convoy going by without having the torpedoes to do anything about it.

"Dick," Morton said, within earshot of other officers, "we're the only ones who know we don't have any torpedoes. The enemy doesn't know that. Supposing we go to Battle Surface and make a run at them. Wouldn't they likely run off, leaving the small freighter behind for our deck gun?"

George Grider and other officers, with the promise of a return to Pearl Harbor bright in their minds, were against the idea. Even Dick O'Kane was cool to it. But Morton was adamant.

Was the captain's bravery verging on recklessness? It was a question asked about Mush. Signalman Deville Hunter passed the word: "You know what, fellows? The Old Man's going to make an attack!" One young seaman was astonished at the idea, muttering to Forest Sterling, "I think he's going stark, raving crazy. He's going to surface and fire the guns at them."

Captain Morton ordered Battle Surface and headed for the convoy. The Japanese apparently spotted *Wahoo,* for their flags fluttered up the signal halyards, and the ships began zigging. Suddenly, a new ship appeared near the rear freighter, heading *Wahoo*'s way.

"Richard, what in hell is that little thing over there?" Morton queried.

"Captain, that's a small freighter. I've noticed him all morning."

"No, that looks mighty small to be a freighter."

Five minutes later the freighter turned left, and Morton and O'Kane recognized it as a destroyer. Morton rapidly turned tail and rang up flank speed to make a run for it, but the destroyer fired up another boiler and began to overtake *Wahoo*. The tin can opened up with deck guns and sent a shell overhead.

As shell splashes bracketed *Wahoo,* Morton called "Clear the bridge." He ordered a crash dive with a 15-degree down angle—plunging the boat to 350 feet.

"Rig for depth charge," Morton said. "Now we're going to catch it."

The whack of six Japanese depth charges near *Wahoo* rattled the superstructure and rang throughout the sub. The boat was plunged into darkness until the batteries powered up emergency lighting. Stacked dishes were tossed about. Loose knives and forks flew around the messroom. Lockers sprung open spilling their contents. Patches of cork and dust swirled through compartments.

Dick O'Kane likened depth charging, known as "taking a beating," to being on the inside of an oil barrel being hit by a large sledgehammer. The "BLAM" of the explosions was preceded by a "click" that could be heard through the pressure hull. This was thought to be the detonator inside the depth charge, or possibly a preliminary shock wave. "Click, BLAM! Click, BLAM! Click, BLAM!" It was nerve-racking. The crew sweated it out, perspiring, some from heat, some from fear. They could do nothing but suffer stoically, taking their beating.

O'Kane wedged himself between the large pipe housing the radar mast and the sound operator in the conning tower. As for the crew, he let them do what was most comfortable—as long as it was compatible with their battle stations. Some sailors preferred standing in the clear, where solid objects would not bash them. Others liked to hang on tightly—for the same reason.

Yeoman Sterling reacted nervously to the beating. He

waited in terror-stricken silence, holding on to the chart table with a deathlike grip. He imagined how it would feel to have tons of water pouring through a ruptured hull into the compartments. Would death come quickly or slowly?

During a lull, O'Kane made a point of walking through the boat to check damage and reassure the men by his presence that they would come through unscathed. *Wahoo* finally weathered the beating. "Thank you, dear God," Sterling prayed, "for bringing us through safely."

When the destroyer finally broke off the attack to get back to the convoy, Morton surfaced. His sense of the ridiculous triggered, Mush sent a follow-up radio message to ComSub-Pac: "ANOTHER RUNNING GUN BATTLE TODAY X WAHOO RUNNIN DESTROYER GUNNIN." Then the skipper ordered Pharmacist's Mate Lindhe to pass out a round of depth charge medicine in miniature brandy bottles.

As *Wahoo* turned on four engines heading for home, the crew was exhilarated. On this seminal war patrol, *Wahoo* scored a number of firsts: entering a Japanese-held port; sinking a destroyer with a down-the-throat shot (though, as it turned out, the Japanese managed to beach the wrecked ship, and the *Pacific Maru* was only badly damaged); attacking and pursuing a convoy carrying hundreds of troops to fight Americans; and showing the spirit that produced the most aggressive war patrol up until then. Best of all, they were heading for the barn after the shortest Pacific War patrol, only twenty-four days estimated from Brisbane to Pearl.

Playing cribbage with his exec, Mush Morton summed up his code with a smile of satisfaction. "Tenacity, Dick. Stay with the bastard till he's on the bottom."

Dick O'Kane handed over navigation duties to George Grider for the voyage to Pearl to give the engineer experience in that arcane art. *Wahoo* crossed the International Date Line, the 180th meridian, on February 2nd, Dick O'Kane's thirty-second birthday, so he was able to celebrate it twice. Crossing the date line eastward was known as "sailing into yesterday."

O'Kane read over Mush Morton's patrol report, prepared by Yeoman Sterling. He noted that Mush was generous in be-

stowing praise on his crew—a morale-building factor which
some sub skippers neglected. In fact, Dick O'Kane, who had
been reading war patrol reports for a year, realized that it was
the first time he had seen a separate section devoted to praise
for the officers and men of the boat. Mush Morton believed
in reprimanding in private, but commending in public. It was
a concept with which O'Kane concurred.

Earlier, *Wahoo*'s exec had recommended various crewmen
to Morton for awards. "The conduct and discipline of the officers and men of this ship while under fire were superb,"
Morton wrote. "I commend them all for a job well done, especially Lieutenant R.H. O'Kane, the Executive Officer, who
is cool and deliberate under fire. O'Kane is the fightingest
naval officer I have ever seen and is worthy of the highest of
praise, an inspiration to the ship."

Of his exec's performance on the periscope in the hairy
Wewak destroyer action, Mush Morton told other officers,
"Why do you think I made O'Kane look at him? He's the
bravest man I know!"

Heading for the barn, O'Kane insisted that *Wahoo* be
made spotless and sparkling. It was a fetish among the best
submariners to make sure their boat was looking good for return to a sub base. O'Kane believed that it was the mark of
pride for a fleet boat returning from patrol to be clean on the
inside—whatever hell she had been through and whatever
the scars on the outside. Approaching the Hawaiian island of
Oahu, *Wahoo* picked up an escort destroyer and drew closer.
O'Kane sighted familiar landmarks: Diamond Head, Waikiki
Beach, and Honolulu with its Aloha Tower to the east;
Barber's Point and the naval air station to the west. In the
background above Pearl Harbor, he could see the Koolau
Mountains and sugar cane fields on the green slopes.

Captain Morton conned *Wahoo* through the channel entrance buoys into the narrow opening of the vast reaches of
Pearl Harbor, a sort of watery four-leaf clover with Ford Island in the middle. *Wahoo* slid past Hickam Field, Hospital
Point, the tall cranes of the Navy Yard and its huge Ten-Ten
Dock (1,010-feet long), and the hulls of the battleships *Arizona* and *Oklahoma,* sunk in the Japanese attack. *Wahoo*

skirted the Navy Yard piers which were jammed with cruisers and destroyers and moved into Southeast Loch—the Submarine Base with its distinctive escape-tank looming over the finger piers where boats tied up.

Wahoo's crewmen had lashed a broom—a large Australian bristle used to sweep the Brisbane dock—to the attack periscope, signifying a "clean sweep." A pennant carried the motto: "SHOOT THE SUNZA BITCHES." As *Wahoo* nosed into a slip, O'Kane ordered: "Secure the maneuvering watch." *Wahoo*'s third war patrol had ended.

At the dock, all the SubPac brass and the Navy band turned out in dress whites to congratulate captain and crew. To the deafening strains of the "Hawaiian War Chant," photographers snapped away. They caught Morton and O'Kane on the bridge sporting starched khaki shirts and black neckties under the soon-to-be-famous broom. The senior sub staffers were ecstatic at the results of the patrol. The endorsements by division and squadron commanders and by ComSubPac were glowing. Sub skippers read these senior command comments on the conduct of war patrols carefully because they amounted to an unofficial statement of submarine warfare policy.

No questions were raised by the U.S. submarine command about the transport boats incident in Morton's patrol report. Rear Admiral Charles A. Lockwood, Commander Submarines Pacific, would say, "When *Wahoo* surfaced she found about twenty of the transport's boats, landing craft of various types in the water. She approached them to pick up a few prisoners for intelligence purposes and was received by rifle and machine gun fire. There was nothing to do but sink them all, which *Wahoo* promptly did." Lockwood chose as the title of his post-war memoir, *Sink 'Em All.*

During the war, no policy guidance on shooting enemy boats in the water with troops aboard was ever given—from the top Pacific submarine commands or from Admiral Ernest J. King's headquarters in Washington. Many skippers surfaced to sink small trawlers or fishing sampans. Others decided against taking such action if and when the occasion arose.

Wahoo departed Brisbane a nonentity and returned to Pearl Harbor a celebrity. The patrol electrified the Submarine Force. Mush Morton was awarded a Navy Cross, the nation's second highest decoration for valor. General MacArthur in Australia insisted on giving Morton the Army's equivalent, the Distinguished Service Cross. Dick O'Kane received a Silver Star, the third highest decoration. *Wahoo* and her crew were awarded the much-prized Presidential Unit Citation (PUC). Each crewman was entitled to wear the PUC ribbon: horizontal red, gold, and blue stripes. In a rare departure from the security policy of the "Silent Service," *Wahoo*'s exploits were released to the press and the headlines were made to order: "*Wahoo* runnin, Japs a-gunnin," and: "One-sub wolf pack."

The legend of *Wahoo* was born.

CHAPTER FOUR

"We Were a Breed Apart"

As *Wahoo* tied up at the Sub Base at Pearl, the crew lining the deck found the naval base bustling with activity—the several lochs, or arms, filled with carriers, cruisers, destroyers, tenders, and amphibious craft. Even the damaged warships had been removed to drydock and few scars remained except for the sunken hulks of the battleships *Oklahoma* and the *Arizona,* the latter with hundreds of bodies still entombed. Looking at the anchorage, Dick O'Kane remembered when he returned to Pearl after his first war patrol aboard *Argonaut:* he was at sea during the Japanese attack. As deck officer, O'Kane had lined the crew up to view the horrific damage that seared into the memory. He and *Argonaut*'s crew wept. Dick O'Kane and other young officers who viewed the ruins of Pearl—still mostly secret to the American public—had no qualms about bitterly pursuing the war.

The Japanese devastated the U.S. Navy at Pearl Harbor. As far as O'Kane and his Annapolis friends were concerned, they would remember Pearl Harbor: it was not just a cliché. Now Pearl conveyed an upbeat feel, waiting for the new Essex-class carriers that would carry the sea war westward across the Pacific.

The Submarine Base had been undamaged during the Pearl Harbor attack, and was subsequently used by Admiral Chester Nimitz as his temporary headquarters as Commander-in-Chief of the Pacific Fleet. A submariner, Nimitz raised his new four-star flag aboard a submarine, *Grayling,* at the Sub Base. Customarily, fleet commanders flew their personal flags aboard battleships, but there weren't any left undamaged and afloat in Pearl Harbor when Chester Nimitz arrived.

During *Wahoo*'s coming home ceremonies, Morton and O'Kane welcomed aboard Captain "Babe" Brown, who had given Morton a second chance after the *Dolphin* episode. Brown informed them that Rear Admiral Robert E. English, ComSubPac, and members of his staff had been killed in the crash of a Pan American seaplane near San Francisco. Brown was acting ComSubPac until Rear Admiral Charles A. Lockwood arrived to take over as Commander Submarines Pacific from his post as Commander Submarines Southwest Pacific in Perth, Australia.

Babe Brown, Mush Morton, and Dick O'Kane watched with amusement as the crew tossed Motor Machinist Dalton Keeter overboard to celebrate his spot promotion to chief petty officer for coming up with the Wewak map. A supply officer from the Sub Base came on board to issue cash pay to the crew. Then Morton and O'Kane took off in Captain Brown's sedan to give a briefing on the patrol to senior officers at Admiral Nimitz's headquarters. Morton went to lunch with Captain Brown and then planned to drop by the Navy hospital to have his chronic prostatitis checked. Dick O'Kane was invited to dine but decided to return to *Wahoo* to make sure the boat was shipshape before handing over to the relief crew who would supervise the refit during a two-week period in drydock.

Dick O'Kane and Lieutenant Chandler Jackson, the communications officer and graduate of the University of Wisconsin, picked up Forest Sterling for the half-hour ride to the Royal Hawaiian Hotel, the submariners' rest camp. The Royal, a flamingo-pink, five-star hotel on Honolulu's Waikiki Beach, had been taken over by the Navy for the duration. It had 425 rooms for submariners and aviators.

O'Kane found a suite had been reserved for him and Mush Morton, two bedrooms, a living room, and a lanai to seaward. The refrigerator was stocked with beer. O'Kane quickly read his mail to make sure all was well at home, last letter first. Then, after long, sensuous showers, he and other *Wahoo* of-

ficers headed for the beach and an inner reef where they
gathered to bask in the sea and let the tensions drain away.

The enlisted men, too, had rooms at the Royal Hawaiian,
and delighted in the cafeteria-style food available at all
hours. They swam in the pool or ocean and sunbathed. They
sailed in outriggers and snorkled. The hotel gardens were
fragrant and dotted with coconut palm trees. There was volleyball and tennis, game rooms, and nightly movies. It was a far
cry from the cloistered life they had just left. But *Wahoo*
crewmen were not crazy about liberty in Honolulu. Compared to Brisbane, Honolulu offered ordinary sailors limited
diversions since the bars closed early, and Navy shore patrol-
men and Army MPs vigorously enforced a stiff curfew. The
town was loaded with servicemen, all looking around. There
were few available girls, except in the brothels. Enlisted
men preferred Australia for their refits, either Brisbane or
Fremantle. The sailors called Australia "Shangri-la." Their
comments about R&R at the forward Submarine Base on
Midway Island were generally unprintable. Yet two weeks at
the Royal were warmly welcomed. Yeoman Sterling liked the
hotel: to him it meant the sound of palm leaves outside his
window which lulled him quickly to sleep, knowing that he
was still alive and had a two-week guarantee of remaining
that way.

In Honolulu, submariners wearing the dolphins on their
lower right sleeve and the sub combat insignia on their left
breast seemed to be a breed of sailor apart. Sub sailors were
reserved in public and stuck together, reinforcing the image
of the "silent" service. Other sailors regarded them with a
mix of envy and awe: they had been where no one else dared.
While much of the fleet was fighting defensively, recovering
from wounds, or confined to West Coast harbors, submarines
had been to "The Empire," operating off the Japanese home
islands.

The submariner style impressed one war correspondent in
Honolulu. "They seem different," he noted. "They would come
ashore looking pale and wan, and for two or three days disappear from sight. But then by some miracle of the Hawaiian
sun, or more likely of their tough youthfulness, they would

have lost their corpse-like whiteness and with it their grave reserve. They weren't supposed to talk about themselves or their work and they didn't. Here were men who lived virtually in each other's laps for months on end, and ashore, where they had every opportunity to separate and enjoy a few hours of privacy, were seldom out of one another's company."

Chief Petty Officer Joe McGrievy, the Chief of the Boat on *Seahorse,* observed, "Submariners kept to themselves. They were reserved because they weren't supposed to talk about their work or themselves. They were indefinably different. Wearing the dolphins, and especially the combat pin, got you respect. Submariners were volunteers. They had to be since almost one man in four did not come back. One in five boats did not come back."

McGrievy was struck by the relative youth of submariners in highly technical, demanding jobs: COs were in their early thirties, chiefs were twenty-five or twenty-six and many of the crew members were nineteen or twenty. Submarine officers, too, tended to be clubby. They hung out together. There was a special table at the Officers' Club for submarine skippers. Toni Peabody, wife of Harvard-educated submarine officer Endicott "Chub" Peabody, who would become Governor of Massachusetts, thought that submarine officers had a certain something about them, very different, very attractive. You trusted them immediately, she believed. There was plenty of camaraderie among them. They were an exciting bunch to be around, and you liked them almost instinctively.

Submariner skipper Bladen Claggett observed, "In prewar days, battleship sailors thought they were the cream of the crop. The war came and we submariners were the only ones doing anything. All the wagons were swinging around their hooks in San Francisco or San Pedro Bays. But we were patrolling off the coast of Japan. So you might forgive us if we swaggered in the officers' club at Pearl. We were a breed apart."

The submariners had a sense of competition. Though they were all on the same team, each one wanted to be on a hot boat, one that had rung up a good record and had sunk Japanese ships. Wearing the dolphins and the combat pin got you noticed among your peers in Pearl.

But behind their outward swagger and insouciance, Dick O'Kane and his young colleagues knew that the year 1942 had been a bad one for the U.S. Navy and the Submarine Force. The Japanese captured Wake Island in the Central Pacific, the Philippines, Hong Kong, Singapore, Malaya, and all of the Dutch East Indies, with the vital oil fields in Sumatra, Java, and Borneo. Their troops landed in New Guinea, threatening Australia, and at Guadalcanal in the Solomon Islands. They were poised to cut vital supply lines from the U.S. and the Hawaiian Islands to New Zealand and Australia. During the year, four major U.S. carriers had been sunk in action: *Lexington, Yorktown, Wasp,* and *Hornet.* American cruisers had been badly handled and mauled in battles around the South Pacific. *Houston, Astoria, Vincennes, Quincy, Northampton, Atlanta, Juneau,* and in early 1943 *Chicago,* were sunk. Japanese warships—whose commanders employed superior naval tactics—destroyed a score of U.S. destroyers. It all came as a shock and humiliation to the U.S. Navy. Indeed, 1942 had exposed many tactical weaknesses in the way American admirals and captains handled their ships against the Japanese. Those failings, as O'Kane was bitterly aware, were apparent in the U.S. Submarine Force, whose results during the year were disappointing. Admiral Nimitz, the former sub skipper, was deeply let down by the results. U.S. subs failed to make any dent on Japanese advances anywhere in the Pacific—and sunk only 180 Japanese ships. Seven U.S. submarines were lost: *S-36, Shark, Perch, S-27, Grunion, S-39;* and *S-26,* by collision. *Sealion* was sunk in December 1941, at her berth in Cavite, Philippines, by Japanese bombers.

At the Royal Hawaiian, once the surf had been tested, the long showers taken, and the mail read, submarine officers' attention focused on shoptalk—discussing the state of the war, and Pacific Fleet submarines. Copies of *Wahoo*'s patrol report and relevant dispatches were circulated around the hotel and the Sub Base. Other skippers' patrol reports were similarly distributed. Skippers and execs dropped by the *Wahoo* suite or the officers' bar for spirited discussions. *Wahoo* officers held court in one corner, and, with a momentous patrol behind them, quickly attracted other submariners for bull sessions.

Dick O'Kane was frank in his answers to the frequent questions: on reflection, no, a down-the-throat shot was not the preferred tactic—but was rather a desperation shot. And, no, reconnoitering an enemy harbor was not recommended unless there was a compelling reason. Better to stake out a likely spot outside the harbor entrance where there was maneuvering room. If the Japanese didn't come out, you had at least stopped his commerce while he was there.

O'Kane had been through such sessions after *Argonaut*'s first war patrol, and *Wahoo*'s first and second runs. But this time it was different. Mush Morton demonstrated in one unique patrol, O'Kane told his colleagues, the very tactics some of them had been urging. While a few other boats had used these methods, it was *Wahoo* under Morton that had turned the corner completely from the pre-war submerged vessel of opportunity to an aggressive raider—even on the surface when conditions permitted. O'Kane figured that *Wahoo* had been submerged over 500 hours on Captain Kennedy's second patrol, and just under fifty hours on Captain Morton's third. This wouldn't be the norm for subs, O'Kane agreed, but it demonstrated that at times any boat could surface close to the enemy for a high-periscope search, and then dive again, without giving up the competitive advantage.

When asked, Mush Morton added his own strong view. "The best advice I can give in fighting a ship," he told a Sub-Pac officer, "you must have a strong desire to destroy the enemy. Nothing can stand in your way. You can't afford to flinch; you can't afford to give up. You must constantly keep 'rassling, and keep shooting till you destroy him."

In the course of their wide-ranging sessions, Dick O'Kane and his colleagues reviewed the overall progress of the first year of the submarine war. Operating out of three main U.S. bases—Pearl, Brisbane in Eastern Australia, and Fremantle,

the port for Perth in Western Australia on the Indian Ocean—
submarines conducted some 350 war patrols during 1942.
Most boats were deployed in Western Pacific patrols against
Japanese naval and merchant ships, but many others were
used in a variety of subsidiary missions: to evacuate key personnel from Bataan and Corregidor; to bring out gold bars
from the Philippines; to supply or rescue guerrillas and other
personnel from the Philippines and Dutch East Indies; to
land U.S. Marine commandos in the Makin Island raid; and
to support aircraft carrier raids against Central Pacific Japanese bases.

But American submarines had not been deployed according to an overall, coherent strategy. The various submarine
commands—at Pearl, Brisbane, and Perth—ordered the boats
around in helter-skelter fashion. They did not concentrate, as
did German submarines with enormous success, on sinking
merchant shipping. The Pacific boats' toll of 180 ships was
only the equivalent of what German U-boats sunk in the Atlantic in the first two months of 1942.

In June U.S. submarines had been poorly deployed to intercept the Japanese fleet attacking Midway. They were too
close to the island. They needed to be much farther away to
spot, report and attack the Japanese carriers heading for
Midway. Their hasty sighting reports were confusing to Admiral Raymond Spruance, who was directing the crucial
battle. But Spruance's aircraft sunk four enemy carriers, a
turning point in the air war.

For younger, aggressive submarine officers like Dick
O'Kane, the disappointing combat results were almost expected. As they saw it, the pre-war U.S. submarine force,
particularly the skippers and their division and squadron
commanders (two six-boat divisions formed a sub squadron),
relied on seriously flawed doctrine. Submarines were viewed
as the eyes of the fleet, scouting ahead of the battleship
force, reporting their sightings of enemy ships. Only secon-
darily did they go in to sink those ships. In peacetime maneuvers, captains were taught an exaggerated fear of escort
destroyers. They were instructed to shoot their torpedoes
from well below periscope depth at long ranges by sonic

contact in order not to risk discovery. If a sub was "sunk" during pre-war maneuvers, the captain received a black mark on his record. This produced overly hesitant thinking in the Submarine Force. And because of the slowness of peacetime promotions, sub skippers—as well as the important chief petty officers—tended to be older men who leaned naturally toward caution.

In sum, the younger officers agreed, pre-war captains were over-cautious and their admirals over-confident. U.S. submarines, by and large, had operated in a more passive role when compared to their U-boat counterparts in the European war-zone. German captains were much more at-tack-minded. Additionally, the pre-war training of U.S. com-manders had not prepared them for all-out war against merchant shipping, which had been outlawed by various peacetime disarmament conventions.

In 1920, submariner Thomas Hart, in a lecture on sub-marines at the Naval War College, summed up the curious outlook of the U.S. Navy in regard to submarine attacks: "I shall pass over the inhumane features of German submarine warfare because their ways were characteristic of their race. Any nation that attempts commerce destruction by sub-marines will tend toward certain of the same practices that the Germans arrived at." So effective tactics for anti-commerce warfare were never developed. When, on the afternoon of the Pearl Harbor attack, the order went out from Admiral Harold Stark, the Chief of Naval Operations in Washing-ton: "EXECUTE UNRESTRICTED AIR AND SUBMARINE WARFARE AGAINST JAPAN," many U.S. sub skippers were unprepared to carry out such an unfamiliar, even forbidden, task.

The submarine officers spent hours pouring over patrol re-ports to glean insights for better tactics and more effective performances. They studied the endorsements—positive and negative—by division, squadron, force, and fleet comman-ders on the patrol reports, which served as a kind of infor-mal, running, wartime doctrine for submarine officers.

The young officers exchanged ideas and, since their lives and careers were at stake, they were frank. They pulled no punches when discussing their seniors. *Wahoo*'s Roger Paine thought that gossip among officers was extremely valuable since it filled in the spaces between the lines of the patrol reports. Slade Cutter, executive officer of *Pompano,* believed discussions of tactics and the foibles of skippers were invaluable. Then, too, the officers analyzed the enemy's capabilities, the evasion tactics U.S. skippers used, the effectiveness of the Japanese anti-sub screen. Everybody tried to help everyone else, Cutter believed. George Street, a young officer on *Gar* with a bright future, jotted down observations made at the bull sessions in a notebook: things to do or avoid. What the young submariners found in the patrol reports and encountered in conversations was often disturbing.

Through his own experience on *Argonaut* and *Wahoo,* Dick O'Kane knew that it had been a difficult time for the pioneer skippers—older, slower, trained in peacetime tactics. No one realized how much pressure would be placed on a submarine commander, making critical decisions almost totally alone. Unlike a destroyer captain, there were few other officers on the bridge with whom he could share visually the tactical appreciation, nor was there a commander of a division or a task group issuing orders to follow. Only the captain had his eye on the periscope or TBT. The skipper was on his own in making life and death decisions. During submerged attacks, the CO was normally the only one who ever saw the target: he made the estimates of enemy range and angles. He personally directed the entire attack. In patrolling his area, he was allowed wide freedom of movement. He could work the hot spots or the wide-open spaces, close the coastline or patrol the traffic lanes well off shore, move surfaced or submerged. On no other ship in the Navy was the success or failure of combat operations so dependent upon the CO himself.

While a well-trained crew was essential for success, the war patrol was primarily the CO's show. Results were based on the aggressiveness and skill of the skipper, with intrepidness the more important of the two. But there was no foolproof way to select a commanding officer who would prove able and effective in combat. The only test was combat itself.

A good peacetime commanding officer did not necessarily make a good wartime one. A war patrol imposed such a mental strain on the captain that if he assumed the worries of the various departments of his ship he soon found himself cracking under the strain. Mentally the captain had the hardest job. While others could relax between watches, he had to be constantly on the alert. Many commanding officers who requested they be relieved—because of their inability to stand the strain or loss of self-confidence because of unsuccessful attacks—went on to make fine combat records in other types of warships.

Dick O'Kane had seen the problem first-hand. He was fourth officer on *Argonaut* on patrol near Midway Island when war broke out. The skipper was Lieutenant Commander Stephen Barchet, a football star at the Naval Academy. Barchet followed peacetime doctrine in remaining submerged during most of the patrol, and went even deeper at the sound of destroyers' propellers. Despite the fact that an invasion force may have been approaching Midway, *Argonaut* remained out of touch, submerged, listening only to sonar. The Japanese force of only two destroyers bombarded Midway's installations without hindrance from *Argonaut* before withdrawing. *Argonaut* was the first American man-of-war to encounter enemy warships after hostilities began in the Pacific.

A week later, Barchet lay deep while sonar suggested the approach of more warships. His executive officer, William Post Jr., asked, "Don't you think, Captain, we ought to at least put up the periscope and take a look?"

Furious with Post, the skipper on returning to Pearl Harbor after a wrenching 59-day patrol recommended to Admiral Thomas Withers, then ComSubPac, that his exec be removed from the Submarine Force. Instead, Post was transferred to the staff of Sub Squadron Six, and later went on to make a sterling record as a skipper of *Gudgeon*. In contrast, Barchet left the submarine for a division commander's job ashore.

Dick O'Kane saw the same problem in the first two patrols in *Wahoo*. O'Kane chafed under Marvin Kennedy's dilatory tactics. At the end of *Wahoo*'s first unsuccessful patrol, Kennedy admitted his deficiencies as CO in confiding to

O'Kane, "We're going to take *Wahoo* back to get someone in command who can sink ships. We're never going to win the war this way."

Dick O'Kane remembered that admission, thinking it must have been a very difficult one for a captain to make. He respected Kennedy for his honesty. Captain Kennedy changed his mind, however, and went out on an equally disappointing second patrol with *Wahoo*. During that patrol, O'Kane went so far as to consult a copy of Navy Regulations on his obligations as executive officer concerning assumption of command. He was neither the first nor the last exec to worry about his command relationship with a skipper who failed to engage the enemy. In officers' club bars at sub bases, scuttlebutt circulated about peacetime skippers who were expected to be wartime stars—and failed.

One of the nastiest surprises, and one that the young submariners took to heart, was the story of Lieutenant Commander Morton C. Mumma Jr., CO of *Sailfish* in Manila when the war broke out. *Sailfish* was actually the renamed *Squalus,* which had sunk on a routine training dive off Portsmouth, New Hampshire, in 1939. The main air induction valve had failed to shut properly. The sinking and the subsequent rescue of thirty-three of the fifty-nine crewmen and technicians aboard via diving bell—as well as the later successful salvage—captured world headlines for much of that summer. Because twenty-six men died in the after engine and torpedo spaces, the ship was considered by superstitious sailors as something of a jinx. The reconditioned *Squalus* was given a new name but submarine enlisted men and Portsmouth Navy Yard workers were apt to call the boat by the unfortunate nickname, "Squailfish."

In many ways, Mumma seemed the Navy's standard peacetime skipper: determined, dedicated, by-the-book. He told the crew: "This is what we have been trained for. You are going to sail with the coldest-blooded man who has ever captained a ship. I am going to carry you across the line. If anybody is scared, now is the time to get off." It was a tough speech. With a seemingly emboldened skipper, *Sailfish* moved north from Manila on her first patrol off Lingayen Gulf where the Japanese were expected to land forces on Luzon, the major island of the Philippines. Mumma was extremely tense. Communications officer Joseph Tucker said, "He could not relax. He walked from bow to stern almost constantly the first four or five days we were underway. So when we made our first attack, he was completely exhausted."

On the fifth day out, *Sailfish* made contact with the big Japanese landing force. Mumma ordered a dive and used sound bearings only to set up an attack. He fired two torpedoes from 100 feet at what he thought were two destroyers. The results were inconclusive. *Sailfish* received some twenty depth charges, which did no serious damage. The experience seemed to trigger some deep emotion in Mumma. He turned to his executive officer, the young, aggressive Lieutenant Hiram Cassedy and said, "Mr. Cassedy, I'm going into my cabin." He told Cassedy to lock him in the cabin and take command of the boat. The next day, with the Japanese transport force moving into Lingayen Gulf, Mumma told Cassedy he wanted to return to Manila—that he was not up to command. Hiram Cassedy sent an emergency message to Com-SubAsiatic in Manila: "ATTACKED ONE SHIP . . . VIOLENT COUNTERATTACK . . . COMMANDING OFFICER BREAKING DOWN . . . URGENTLY REQUEST AUTHORITY TO RETURN TO TENDER." On returning to Manila Bay, Mumma left *Sailfish* for shore duty.

Pearl Harbor boats had the same problem. Commanding the old *Dolphin,* Gordon B. Rainer headed for the Marshall Islands on Christmas Eve, 1941, and spent time nosing around Kwajalein. During the patrol, he learned how much pressure was placed on the wartime captain of a submarine, whose eye and nerve were so vital for the safety of the entire crew. A CO was always on call, and during long periods the skipper rarely got more than a few hours sleep at a time. Under the strain, Rainer gave way, suffering a nervous breakdown. He turned over operating control to his exec, Bernard Clarey, nine years his junior—Dick O'Kane's classmate at the Naval Academy, and a young officer who would make an enviable reputation in the war. Returning to Pearl, Rainer was relieved of submarine duty and sent back to the States.

Though kept under wraps, relieving skippers for poor performance came to be regarded as a difficult, embarrassing, but essential and all too frequent task. Several other sub captains were quickly stripped of their commands for not pressing attacks on major enemy forces sighted, particularly in the Philippines, Wake Island, and Midway areas. Some beached skippers went on to surface or shore duty—often serving with distinction, as *Wahoo*'s Marvin Kennedy did in destroyers and *Sailfish*'s Mort Mumma did in PT boats, as well as Steve Barchet in the amphibious forces. Others with valuable technical skills remained on the staffs of submarine divisions and squadrons in the Pacific. Some officers were given a second chance at submarine command. By February 1943, some 30 percent of the 135 sub skippers had been relieved of command—some at their own request, others because of poor health, combat fatigue, or poor performance. The failure of so many captains to measure up to the rigors and demands of wartime command was informally known as the "skipper problem" and it plagued the silent service throughout the war. In various post-war reports, the "skipper problem" was glossed over. It was scarcely mentioned in official Navy histories, including the detailed *United States Submarine Operations in World War II,* and Samuel Eliot Morison's monumental *History of Naval Operations in World War II.*

But execs like Dick O'Kane and junior officers who had observed their superiors in action first-hand talked freely over drinks about cautious skippers and those who avoided direct contact, while sometimes justifying their actions in their own patrol reports. Some execs went so far as to complain about their captains to division or squadron commanders. Others asked for reassignment to more attack-minded skippers. Nobody seemed able to predict what kind of officer would make the best combat skippers, but most agreed that they should be young, aggressive, with plenty of physical and mental stamina.

Speaking for the younger officers, Jack Coye Jr., a blue-eyed, fresh-faced officer destined to make an outstanding record as a skipper, observed, "Some captains of submarines when the war started were eventually relieved of command because they weren't aggressive enough. They got scared too easily, I guess. But we, the younger ones, were more aggressive. The normal procedure was if you didn't perform in one patrol you would probably get a chance at another one. But if you weren't aggressive in the second one, they would relieve you and put another guy in. So you had to do well."

He was echoed by James Calvert, another bright, up-and-coming officer, who said, "It took a good man with a tough mind—one who did not have an over-supply of imagination. There were enough real problems in the throes of combat to leave no place for a man who saw shadows. A sort of dogged, imperturbable stolidity was preferable to brilliance and imagination. But there had to be at least some of the latter, combined sometimes with an almost reckless aggressiveness to get the best results. It was a complex and somewhat rare combination of qualities. But those skippers who had them were beginning to rise above the pack by early 1943."

While there was certainly the need for aggressiveness in skippers, many submarine sailors would agree with *Pargo*'s captain, David Bell, who told his crew that his aims as skipper were: 1. To meet and defeat the enemy. And 2. To get the number one line across the dock safely back at the Sub Base.

Another intense topic of discussion was the relationship between COs and XOs. O'Kane pointed out that many submarine executive officers like himself were five years younger than their commanding officers. But the execs usually had war patrols under their belts, while the senior skippers often came from "career-broadening" shore posts. The Sub Force was in the incongruous situation, O'Kane believed, that some skippers had far less submarine time and experience than their execs. Often the execs with combat experience were put in the awkward position of nagging their older skippers into taking more aggressive action on war patrols. This produced the expected resentment on the part of the captains. As the war progressed, senior submarine officers were young, some just thirty, with their chiefs younger still.

Dick O'Kane and Mush Morton were happy to find that not all the reports spelled gloom and doom. There were up-and-coming skippers and execs making names for themselves and their boats with tough, innovative tactics, which were discussed in detail by officers at the Royal Hawaiian.

"Fearless Freddy" Warder was one of the first to patrol boldly—in *Seawolf.* Jim Dempsey in the old *S-37* and later *Spearfish* sank ships. So did Moon Chapple in *S-38* and *Permit;* Joe Grenfell in *Gudgeon;* Lew Parks and Exec Slade Cutter in *Pompano;* Mike Fenno and Red Ramage in *Trout;* Chet Smith in *Swordfish;* Gene McKinney in *Salmon;* Pete Ferrall in *Seadragon;* Lu Chappell in *Sculpin;* Dick Voge in *Sailfish;* Bob Rice in *Drum;* Bill Brockman in *Nautilus;* Bull Wright in *Sturgeon;* Burt Klakring and Herman Kossler in *Guardfish;* James Coe in *Skipjack;* Roy Benson in *Trigger;* Moke Millican in *Gar;* Joe Willingham and Barney Sieglaff in *Tautog.* The best performance in 1942 was that of quiet, self-effacing Chester Bruton in command of USS *Greenling,* with ten enemy ships down.

The submariners liked retelling the story of *Trout* with Mike Fenno at the helm: after delivering artillery shells to Corregidor, he was ordered to bring out gold bullion from Manila banks. A total 583 gold bars was loaded aboard. After sinking a couple of ships on the way, Fenno took *Trout* to Pearl. When Fenno checked the gold bars in Pearl against the invoice he had signed, he found one was missing—worth $14,500. A frantic search of the boat disclosed that the missing gold bar was being used by cooks in the galley—as a paperweight.

A rousing success story was that of *Silversides* under the irrepressible, hard-drinking Creed Burlingame, a free spirit, and his prim executive officer, Roy Davenport, a devout Christian Scientist—and teetotaler. Their relationship, unlike that of Mush Morton and Dick O'Kane, was one of opposites. It worked—though Burlingame and Davenport would never be the friends on shore that Morton and O'Kane were. The crew and officers admired and liked Creed Burlingame. *Silversides*'s first three patrols had been successful, marked by Burlingame's aggressive, hard-hitting style. In a battle surface attack against an armed trawler, Torpedoman Mike Harbin, serving as a loader for the 3-inch deck gun, was killed—the first U.S. submariner to lose his life in a gunnery action. In another attack, *Silversides* ran into a Japanese fishing net with tiny national flags attached. As *Silversides* attacked at periscope depth, trailing the flags, the captain noticed them.

"That's the first time," Exec Roy Davenport said, "an American submarine ever began an approach while flying the Japanese flag!"

The irreverent Burlingame had a small brass Buddha statue mounted in the conning tower and during depth charging, he would pat it for luck. Roy Davenport maintained that the Lord would place a shield between *Silversides* and her enemies. After one heavy depth charging, Burlingame needled his exec: "Roy, who do you think got us out of that one—Buddha or Mary Baker Eddy?"

On *Silversides* fourth patrol, a 21-year-old engineman, George Platter, was stricken with appendicitis. As Platter lay in his bunk in acute pain, Pharmacist's Mate Thomas Moore, twenty-two, a thin, sandy-haired medic, examined him carefully. Moore had taken a four-month course in nursing at the San Diego Naval Hospital with a year assisting in the operating room. He had seen many appendectomies performed and he believed he could do one himself. He approached Burlingame. "Captain," Moore said. "Platter has appendicitis pretty bad. The best thing to do would be to operate."

Burlingame spoke to the patient to see how he felt about surgery. In agony, Platter said, "Go ahead and operate." The officers' wardroom was chosen as the operating room. Moore cleaned up the place with torpedo alcohol, and placed fresh sheets on the table. He had eight hemostats, or clamps, two standard Navy surgical knives, but no retractors to hold back the incisions, so the medic improvised with a couple of spoons bent at right angles.

Moore administered a spinal anesthetic to the patient, and located Platter's appendix by rule of thumb: little finger on the umbilicus, thumb on point of hip-bone, index finger straight down, the tip points to the appendix. Moore began cutting. For two hours, the corpsman worked carefully—cutting, tying off blood vessels, locating and detaching the swollen appendix. Finally, it was removed, and the wound sewn up. The patient rapidly recovered. (During the war, two other sub pharmacist's mates performed emergency appendectomies at sea—in *Seadragon* and *Grayback*. The Navy medical establishment frowned on such improvised operations, possibly as an infringement on its turf, but the emergency procedures probably saved three lives. One senior sub staff officer even suggested that all submariners should have their appendixes taken out as a condition of going on a war patrol. In any event, the Surgeon General directed ComSub-Pac that no further appendectomies be performed at sea.)

For her fourth and fifth patrols under Creed Burlingame, *Silversides* won the Presidential Unit Citation.

Guardfish under the quiet Thomas "Burt" Klakring also turned in a successful patrol with the extrovert Herman Kossler, another O'Kane classmate, as exec. Off Honshu, Klakring shot at a freighter moored inside an anchorage at the extreme range of 7,000 yards because that was the only way open. The shot was the longest of the war that actually scored a sinking. In the patrol, Klakring sunk a total of five ships under difficult conditions.

At one point, *Guardfish*'s crew could see a train moving along the coastal rail line with the passengers seeming "all dressed up." Someone noticed that a racetrack was nearby and a sailor in the conning tower quipped, "Maybe they're going to the races." During a rare press conference after the patrol, Klakring, tongue in cheek, said *Guardfish* had been close enough to the coast to see horses running at the track— and the crew even placed a few bets among themselves. Somehow the story was taken seriously and *Life* magazine played it big. Much to his surprise and chagrin, Burt Klakring suddenly became the hero of the U.S. racing world, and was named honorary chief steward at several American racetracks.

In submarine circles at Pearl, Brisbane, Fremantle, and New London, these stories cheered the younger officers. It was men like Burlingame and Klakring and Morton and O'Kane who were setting the tone and example for the submarine war to come.

CHAPTER FIVE

The Submariner's Submariner

If the skipper problem came as an unpleasant surprise to the submarine brass, the admirals, commodores, and senior captains who directed the Force created their own special troubles. This was the "command problem." Stated simply, the admirals in charge of Pacific fleet submarines failed for years to develop a comprehensive strategy for deploying those boats. The personalities of the admirals and senior submarine force commanders played a role, too. Most had professional or personal differences with one another and their stubbornness was not conducive to devising a unified strategy.

In the Far East, neither Admiral Thomas Hart, the commander-in-chief, nor his submarine commander, Captain John Wilkes, nor Wilkes' chief-of-staff, Captain James Fife, showed any imaginative tactical or strategic use of the twenty-eight valuable submarines in the Asiatic Fleet. In the aftermath of the Pearl Harbor attack, the new Chief of Naval Operations in Washington, Admiral Ernest J. King, set priorities for targets in the Sub Force: large Japanese warships (aircraft carriers, battleships, cruisers), loaded troop transports, and then smaller warships. Merchant ships bringing valuable supplies, including almost all of Japan's oil and other vital war materials, were well down on the priority list. Admiral Hart and Captain Wilkes, as well as General Douglas MacArthur himself, neglected to plan for a realistic defense of the Philippines—or the rest of the oil-laden East Indies. As the Japanese pushed southward, Wilkes shifted his headquarters from Manila to Batavia, Java, where he continued to assign boats randomly.

The high command did not concentrate subs on the defense of the key island of Java. There were dozens of target opportunities in the Java Sea, for instance, but in one seven-day period U.S. submarines did not make a single kill. It came as no surprise when the U.S. Sub Force headquarters was forced to move south to Australia, below the Malay barrier. In Australia, Captain Wilkes, a precise, rather pedantic officer, established his submarines at Fremantle, the skimpy, Indian Ocean port for the much larger city of Perth, up the Swan River, where he himself based. Wilkes sent submarines to patrol Southeast Asia with the assistance of Captain Fife, his Chief-of-Staff. Jimmy Fife was a grim, ascetic, bespectacled submariner who was unsociable and tended to do things strictly by the numbers. The successful skipper Chet Bruton of *Greenling* observed of Fife, "Surrounded by hard-drinking submariners fresh from combat, he was a strange, solitary, almost lonely figure. He didn't drink or fraternize. He never seemed concerned about 'people.' When a submarine came in from patrol, he wanted to know all about the condition of the battery or the engines or the periscopes or electrical equipment." Submariner Eli Reich added, "Jimmy Fife was not the warmest individual in the world. He was very taciturn and when he looked at you, you always had a sense of ill feeling. You'd examine your conscience because you'd know you weren't doing something right."

On a later occasion, Bladen Claggett, skipper of *Dace,* was called on the carpet by Fife over an altercation between his exec and the officer in charge of the Sub Base Officer's Club. Fife insisted on the name of the submarine's offender. Claggett balked.

"Commodore, I am responsible for the actions of any of my officers."

Fife demanded an apology and the name of the offender.

Claggett gave Fife the name of a junior officer. Fife said he wanted the officer to appear before him.

"Commodore," Claggett said, "the officer left here by plane at five o'clock this morning for new construction in the States."

In a report to Admiral King, Wilkes and Fife seemed to recognize how subs should be best deployed. They wrote: "It was apparent that our best use of the large submarines could only be on the distant supply lines in the open sea." But they failed to act on their own advice.

One of the most closely held secrets of the war was the fact that intelligence and communications officers at Pearl Harbor had broken a Japanese naval code. This code contained priceless information about Japanese naval and merchant ship movements. It was picked up by a U.S. and British radio receiving network and relayed to the naval intelligence division, the Fleet Radio Unit, at Pearl under Commander Joseph Rochefort, an unsung hero of the war, and William "Jasper" Holmes, a brilliant former submariner who was called back from early retirement to serve in the Combat Intelligence Unit. The crack team of code-breakers translated the Japanese messages, which were given the top-secret name "Ultra."

At sea, all U.S. submarines observed strict outgoing radio silence. However, they could break that silence to transmit operational priority messages—like enemy warship sightings. Later, a whip antenna was developed for submarines. When extended, it enabled a boat to transmit with decks awash. Depending on atmospherics, boats could receive low frequency messages at periscope depth. Short-range radio communications were developed so that boats could speak to one another, and to other nearby U.S. naval ships.

Each night from Navy radio station NPM in Honolulu, the Fox (for Fleet) broadcast would go out to all Navy ships. Radiomen aboard every ship—including submarines—would monitor the nightly Fox waiting to hear their own ship's call sign, and then copy and decode the messages intended for them.

There was another bright spot in human relations: Captain Richard Voge, Lockwood's Operations Officer and skipper of *Sealion* and *Sailfish,* in the early days of Asiatic combat. Dick Voge was a brilliant analyst and a very human officer, admired by all. He included in the nightly Fox transmissions to submarines personal messages to officers and enlisted men alike. "Sometimes you got awfully lonely out there," one skipper said. "Then would come Voge's newsletter about so-and-so's wife having a baby, all's well at home, and so on. You got the feeling that he was looking out for your best interests every waking minute."

In Pearl, the Ultra team broke some rules in an unusual, unofficial manner. Commander Rochefort, the chief code-breaker, verbally passed along vital Ultra data to Jasper Holmes, head of the Combat Intelligence Unit who had close contacts in ComSubPac headquarters. Captain Holmes would walk over to ComSubPac's office and see Dick Voge, the SubPac Operations Officer. He verbally gave Voge secret information—a convoy would be at a certain location on a certain date—without revealing the source. Sometimes Holmes would write the figures on his palm to show Voge and wash his hands immediately after.

To transmit this crucial Ultra data, a special code readable only by submariners was designed by naval cryptographers. A submarine's coded messages, if intercepted by friendly surface ships, would appear to be gibberish. These Ultra messages went out over the nightly Fox schedule. Appropriate submarines would be alerted as Ultra highest priority addressees. When an Ultra was received, only the sub's communications officer could decode it, and only the captain, the exec and specially cleared officers could read the "eyes only" message before it was burned. The messages would report the passage of Japanese ships or convoys in their area, with orders to intercept.

To the sub skippers, the source of Ultra was a well-kept secret. "We didn't know where it was coming from," Slade Cutter said, "but we knew it was coming from somewhere. The dope we got was good. I didn't know where it came from and I didn't care, as long as they kept giving it to us."

The relationship between Dick Voge and Jasper Holmes was close, confidential, informal, and tremendously productive. Later, a private secure telephone line was installed between the offices of the two naval officers. Admiral Charles Lockwood, in fact, began to treat Captain Holmes as if he were SubPac's own intelligence officer. Lockwood was quick to realize his immense value to the Submarine Force. Within hours, even minutes, the Ultra information would be in the hands of a submarine captain on station.

The Pearl Harbor code-breakers followed enemy ship's movements and decoded their messages to Tokyo concerning attacks on them by U.S. submarines. As a result, top code-breakers often knew whether enemy ships had been sunk, as reported by U.S. skippers, or had survived their torpedo attacks. Ultra tip-off messages led to almost half the sinkings of Japanese ships claimed by U.S. submarines.

The distribution of Ultras was controversial: some intelligence officers thought that using the information too freely would jeopardize cracked Japanese codes. Ship sinkings could lead the Japanese to suspect their codes were compromised. But Jasper Holmes argued that Ultra information was not of much value unless it was put to use in sinking enemy ships—even if this course of action raised the danger of discovery. Hence, Holmes described the use of Ultra as a "double-edged secret." To Holmes, heavy wartime secrecy was a double-edged weapon, sometimes counterproductive.

An offbeat drawback to being privy to decoded Japanese communications was that Holmes and his staff had the unpleasant duty of dashing cold water on the reports of sinkings by U.S. submarines and American pilots. In the early part of the war, enthusiasm for missions frequently led to exaggerated claims of damage to the enemy. Holmes knew better because he was reading the Japanese messages and could assess the actual damage reports. General MacArthur's Southwest Pacific command, Holmes observed, was noted for its wild overstatements of damage to the Japanese.

Crucial Ultra information was not limited to submarines. It was an Ultra intercept, for instance, that alerted Admirals Nimitz and Spruance to the probable disposition of Japanese aircraft carriers, which resulted in the great U.S. victory in the critical Battle of Midway.

Halfway through 1942, the U.S. Navy was the victim of a security leak that could have had dreadful consequences—especially for submarines. While the Battle of Midway was still in progress in early June, the *Chicago Tribune* published a front-page story that U.S. intelligence was aware of the

strength of the Japanese force before the great engagement
began. The Navy had learned "of the gathering of the powerful Japanese units soon after they put forth from their
bases," the story said. The article listed the Japanese order of
battle in detail. Stanley Johnston, a *Tribune* correspondent
returning from the South Pacific aboard a U.S. carrier, had
learned from officers—on a confidential basis—that the U.S.
had broken the Japanese naval code. It was a stupendous
achievement.

Recklessly, he wrote the story, and his editors printed it
under the headline: "Navy Had Word of Jap Plan to Strike at
Sea." Gossip columnist Walter Winchell repeated the story in
two broadcasts—that the Navy had advance knowledge of
the whereabouts of the Japanese fleet. The Navy was aghast.
The U.S. had indeed broken the Japanese code but if Tokyo
were made aware of this, it would be changed immediately.
This would be a disaster worse than losing any sea battle.
President Roosevelt and his Secretary of the Navy Frank
Knox, a rival Chicago publisher, wanted to charge Colonel
Robert R. McCormick, the *Tribune*'s owner and an arch-
conservative, with a felony violation of U.S. security laws.
But a public trial would have drawn more attention to the
U.S. code-breaking success, so the Navy instead hushed up
the incident. However, a freshman Democratic Congressman, Elmer J. Holland of Pennsylvania, presumably to ha-
rass McCormick, rose in the Capitol to castigate the *Tribune*
for "unthinking and wicked misusing freedom of the press"
in printing the story. "Somehow our Navy," he said, "had
secured and broken the secret code of the Japanese Navy."
The speech was printed in some papers, which to the code-
breakers at Pearl Harbor seemed to be treachery compounded
by idiocy. Luckily, neither the story nor the speech caused
the Japanese to change their codes.

In Washington, Admiral King and his Chief-of-Staff, Admiral Richard S. Edwards—both of whom had served in
submarines—decided against basing all the Pacific boats at
Pearl Harbor, or even, for unclear reasons, under a single command. King left Wilkes in charge of subs conduct-

ing offensive operations in the Southwest Pacific from Fremantle–Perth. In the spring of 1942, a new U.S. sub base was set up in Northeastern Australia in Brisbane harbor under Captain Ralph Christie, a dashing, confident, peace-time torpedo specialist. He commanded two squadrons of old, leaky, uncomfortable S-boats. (They were lettered and numbered—the usual practice before submarines began to be named after fish.) Their short range would only allow them to patrol the battle zones around the Solomon Islands and the East Indies. The U.S. submarines based in Australia operated under a strange command structure created by per-sonal and professional arguments among the highest brass in Washington and in the field as to who was in charge in the Pacific: the Army or Navy. It was an argument that simmered throughout the Pacific War and involved General MacAr-thur, Admiral Nimitz, General George Marshall, Admiral King, and, ultimately, President Roosevelt, the Commander-in-Chief. It led to a divided and sometimes disastrously con-fused command structure.

The Australia-based boats at first came under the tactical command of ComSubSoWestPac, Captain Wilkes, in Perth, who in turn ultimately answered to the Naval Commander for the Southwest Pacific, Rear Admiral Arthur S. Carpen-der, also in Perth. Admiral Carpender and Wilkes reported not to Admiral Nimitz, Commander-in-Chief, Pacific, in Pearl Harbor, but instead to General MacArthur, in Brisbane, who answered directly to General Marshall in Washington. Once Ralph Christie arrived in Brisbane, the two submarine commands in Australia acted separately. This divided overall command was a source of continuing friction.

Meanwhile, all U.S. Pacific submarines came under the administrative direction of ComSubPac in Pearl Harbor. ComSubPac was responsible for the training and mainte-nance of boats in the Pacific, but had no direct, operational control over Australia-based vessels. So U.S. submarines would often shuttle back and forth, Pearl to Australia, mak-ing war patrols en route. The top commanders in Pearl Har-bor, Brisbane, or Perth assigned individual war patrol areas and directions. Major overhauls and repairs were done at

Pearl Harbor or West Coast Navy yards. The boats in Brisbane and Fremantle worked from makeshift bases with most of the spare parts and services supplied by submarine tenders tied up at dockside: *Holland* in Fremantle; *Pelias* in an auxiliary base at Albany around the southwestern knuckle of Australia; and *Griffin* in Brisbane. Captain Wilkes had only nineteen boats available, and, given transit and refit time, he could maintain only one-third on station at any time in Southeast Asia waters. Boats based in Australia had to pass through the shallow seas and many islands of the Dutch East Indies—the Malay Barrier, filled with Japanese anti-submarine forces—to get to their stations near Japanese harbors in the South China, Sulu, Celebes, Java, and Banda Seas.

Since the Australia-based boats were under the ultimate authority of General MacArthur, they were subject to his own ideas about their deployment. MacArthur ordered them on special missions, landing guerrillas or supplies in the Philippines—patrols which, while hazardous and courageous, did not utilize the submarine's potential to sink enemy ships. Most skippers believed they could provide only a meager addition to supplies needed by Army or guerrilla forces. They thought diverting submarines to such risky missions was a misuse of their main offensive advantage: putting torpedoes into Japanese ships.

The main Pacific submarine command in early 1942 was at Pearl Harbor under ComSubPac, Rear Admiral Thomas Withers, an old-school flag officer who had little insight into the deployment of submarines. From Pearl, submarines generally patrolled the Japanese-held islands in the Central Pacific and "The Empire"—the waters around the Japanese home islands. The boats were instructed to patrol off ports or track down enemy ship movements intercepted by "Ultra," rather than concentrate on deep-water chokepoints like the Luzon Strait.

Though Australia was closer geographically to Western Pacific operating areas, Pearl Harbor boats could head directly west, topping off fuel tanks at Midway Island, and reach the Chinese and Japanese coasts directly, quicker, and with less chance of detection. Submarines of both the Pearl

Harbor and Australia commands were often assigned to areas just outside ports where it was most dangerous to operate and where Japanese anti-sub forces gathered. Or they were sent to chase Japanese warships whose movements were tracked by the code-breakers—but to little effect since it was difficult to make a specific interception in the vast ocean. Few of the capital ships were found. Fewer in those days were successfully attacked.

In sum, the Pacific submarine command structure was split three ways, not from any naval or strategic logic but because that was the way the war command developed—haphazardly. At the top, this failure had to be attributed to Admiral King, the U.S. naval supremo. Brilliant as he was, King never devised a systematic plan for sinking Japanese commerce. He failed to develop a strategic vision for American submarines and their commands in the Pacific.

By mid-1942, Admiral King decided to shake up the submarine command. At Pearl, Admiral Withers was relieved and sent to the Portsmouth (N.H.) Navy Yard to direct the building and fitting out of new submarines. He was replaced by Rear Admiral Robert English, another peacetime veteran of the sub service who had fixed ideas about how to deploy his boats. In Perth, Captain Charles A. Lockwood, a career submariner, succeeded Captain John Wilkes, who was long overdue for stateside rotation. Lockwood was a cheery, avuncular man and a natural optimist with a somewhat corny sense of what was funny. He was delighted to be given a senior submarine assignment—even one as demoralized as the Perth–Fremantle command. Lockwood had commanded the antique subs *A-2, B-1, G-1,* and the early fleet boat *Bonita.* During the 1930s he had fought within the U.S. Navy for a long-range boat—instead of allowing surface admirals to use submarines only as short-range scouts for the battle fleet. At the time of Pearl Harbor, Lockwood was naval attaché in London, where he studied British and German undersea tactics. Charlie Lockwood was a submariner's submariner.

Lockwood moved temporarily aboard the venerable tender *Holland* in Fremantle to supervise submarine refitting and to be closer to his skippers and crews. He was approachable, casual but effective, and his warm personality quickly sparked kinship in the demoralized Down-under U.S. Submarine Force. Lockwood had a way of reading between the lines of a patrol report to gain a sense of the feeling aboard a boat, and to judge the compatibility of the COs, XOs, officers, and crews. The word on skippers' abilities and defects quickly got around the officers' and enlisted men's clubs. Charlie Lockwood had a good ear and eye for such things. He garnered information that didn't appear in the patrol reports. He could see first-hand whether a skipper was bone-tired, or unsuitable, and not really up to the demanding job.

Pete Galantin, commander of *Halibut,* thought Lockwood a great example of "loyalty down," and he received, in turn, the whole-hearted support and admiration of his skippers. To Galantin, Lockwood was "Uncle Charlie," the "understanding, kindly critic and taskmaster of our lonely commands."

In Perth and Fremantle, Lockwood moved quickly to improve morale and performance. For men coming off arduous patrols, Lockwood tried to rent decent rest hotels, despite objections by some brass. Strangely, some senior officers like Admiral Carpender, senior U.S. Naval commander, and Lockwood's own chief-of-staff, Captain Jimmy Fife, urged that these rest camps be located far away from big city lights. They didn't want to pamper submariners nor offer temptations to sailors. But this, of course, was the whole purpose of the two-week relaxation period: proper temptations. Indeed, Charlie Lockwood pointedly observed that Admiral Nimitz had taken over the Royal Hawaiian in the heart of Honolulu without any ideas of "monastic seclusion." Lockwood believed that submariners should be left to do as they pleased so that they could return on patrol in better physical and mental health.

Lockwood was soon promoted to rear admiral but he was second-guessed by now Vice Admiral Carpender at Perth, the overall U.S. Navy commander in the southwest Pacific. At first Lockwood welcomed Carpender's presence as a means by which he could concentrate on submarine operations. But Carpender, a nitpicker, constantly interfered, since the submarines were almost his only naval force. He criticized everything Lockwood and his staff were doing. Carpender even banned the use of the word "fish" in their patrol reports instead of "torpedo." He fought with Lockwood on the rest hotels issue, insisting they be located out in the boondocks—far away from the bars and girls of Fremantle and Perth. The two admirals soon came openly to detest one another.

During 1942, Carpender shifted his command HQ to Brisbane, where General MacArthur set up headquarters. Lockwood and Carpender would no longer rub up against each other in Perth, but Carpender, as overall U.S. Navy commander in Australia, was still Lockwood's boss.

In an unexpected move, Admiral King ordered Submarine Squadron Two at Albany to be transferred to Brisbane under Captain Ralph Christie, who was considerably junior to Lockwood. This left Lockwood upset because he thought that he, as the senior commander, should have command of the Force and that he should either move to Brisbane, or have the majority of submarines based in Fremantle. Lockwood called the transfer, which left him with only about eight subs in Fremantle, a "theft." Christie, who now had the ear of Carpender and MacArthur in Brisbane, upstaged him. In yet another perceived slight to Lockwood, Carpender chose Jimmy Fife to represent him as a "liaison" at MacArthur's headquarters. Lockwood felt bypassed by messages between Captain Fife at MacArthur's headquarters and Admiral Carpender and Captain Christie at Brisbane—some 2,500 miles away from him in Western Australia.

Though Admiral Lockwood endeared himself to his submariners in his concern for their well being, he did not come up with any more imaginative planning for his submarine operations than his predecessors had done. Like Christie and English, Lockwood placed the boats off heavily guarded ports rather than in open, well-used sea-lanes. He made no special attempt to interdict the critical oil lifeline from Sumatra, Java, and Borneo to the Japanese homeland.

In Pearl Harbor, ComSubPac English won little respect from his own troops, however well the senior brass in Washington may have regarded him. English deployed his

submarines badly during the Battle of Midway and conse-
quently they were of little use during that vital engagement.
It was questionable whether submarines with 15 miles visibility under optimum conditions should be used for the kind
of scouting that could be much better accomplished by aircraft. Admiral English did not concentrate on running his
boats to the Japanese Empire, and instead ordered many to
patrol the frigid Aleutian Islands for minimal returns.

Further, English went along with what many of his skippers considered a dangerous misuse of their boats in special
missions. Dick O'Kane's old vessel, *Argonaut,* and *Nautilus*
carried two companies of a Marine Raider Battalion, including the President's son, Major James Roosevelt, for a raid on
Makin Island in the Gilbert Islands in 1942. The raiding
party ran into stiff opposition: it had difficulty landing and
re-embarking Marines through the surf. Twenty-one men
were killed in action, and the raiders left nine Marines behind who were captured and beheaded. Colonel Evans B.
Carlson, Major Jimmy Roosevelt, the Marines, and submariners were all feted as heroes. But cooler heads pointed
out that the premature raid on Makin, which reaped few dividends, prompted the Japanese to build up their fortifications
in the Gilberts, thus insuring that the U.S. Marine landing on
Tarawa in late 1943 would be the bloodiest battle yet in the
Pacific War.

Admiral English also made a strange proposal to William
Brockman, the able captain of *Nautilus.* She was one of the
largest submarines built for the U.S. Navy, with two 6-inch
guns on deck, forward and aft of the superstructure. The Admiral said that Emperor Hirohito had his summer palace at
Hayama on the east coast of the main Japanese home island
of Honshu, near the entrance to Tokyo Bay. English thought
it would be a great morale-building exercise for *Nautilus* to
bombard the palace from offshore. *Nautilus* was about to
depart on a war patrol in Empire waters and Brockman said
he would speak to his officers about the feasibility of such
an action. Most thought it was recklessly dangerous since
the coastal area was shallow, confined, and crammed with
Japanese warships. Further, *Nautilus* was a big, old, clumsy

boat unsuitable for tricky inshore operating. It struck submarine officers that Admiral English was looking for some
spectacular feat to atone for his failure to make an impact
with his submarines at the Battle of Midway. Off Honshu,
Brockman sank a destroyer but wisely decided against carrying out his boss's idea of shelling the palace.

In a strange, narrow-minded incident, which wasted valuable submariner hours, Admiral English tried to track down
the composer of a sarcastic poem lampooning the Pearl Harbor staff called "Squat Div One," which circulated through
the Force. English ordered all higher officers in his command to find out who wrote the poem. It was finally learned
that Commander Art Taylor, skipper of *Haddock,* composed
the poesy in a fey moment. Despite Taylor's good record,
English ordered the young skipper immediately relieved of
command for composing "subversive literature." A senior
staff captain, Stoney Roper, went to bat for Taylor and a few
days later he sailed from Pearl on a war patrol, still in command of *Haddock.*

Such petty actions, together with his negative, carping
endorsements on patrol reports, engendered little respect
among Pearl Harbor skippers for their force commander.

After English's untimely death in an air crash in early
1943, popular Charlie Lockwood replaced him at Pearl.
Ralph Christie, now a Rear Admiral, took over from
Lockwood at Perth–Fremantle. Captain Jimmy Fife left
MacArthur's headquarters for the top submarine job in
Brisbane. The senior commanders continued to differ over
submarine tactics and did not get along well. Thus there
was no fresh strategic thinking in the top submarine commands in the Pacific.

Adding it up, Clay Blair, the author of the definitive *Silent
Victory,* commented, "The major reason for the submarine
failure of 1942 was not mechanical, physical, or psychologi-
cal. It was, to put it simply, a failure of imagination on
the highest levels by King, Edwards, Nimitz, Hart, Wilkes,
Withers, English, Lockwood, Christie, and Fife. All these
men failed to set up a broad, unified strategy for Pacific sub-

marines aimed at a single specific goal: interdicting Japanese shipping services in the most efficient and telling manner."

But the confusing command set-up paled in comparison with the most serious and deadly problem facing submarine skippers and their executive officers. This was the continuing malfunctioning of their torpedoes, the sub's offensive weapon. By the end of 1942, the torpedo problem had reached scandalous proportions.

In Perth, Rear Admiral Lockwood had buckled down to tackle the faulty torpedoes that plagued his skippers. Designed at the Newport Torpedo Station in Rhode Island under the pre-war supervision of the Navy's Bureau of Ordnance, the standard U.S. torpedo was the Mark 14. A mixture of compressed air and alcohol created steam, which turned the propeller turbines, and drove it. A gyroscope directed the torpedo to the proper, pre-set course. Small rudders with hydrostatic device controls set the depth at which the torpedo should run and hit the target. It left a bubbly, broad wake easily spotted in calm waters. The Mark 14 came equipped with a contact exploder that ignited its 500-pound warhead of TNT. The warhead could also be triggered by an alternate magnetic exploder, which was designed to go off when it came under the influence of the target ship's magnetic field. Ideally it would explode under the target's lightly protected hull rather than against the heavily shielded side plates. The magnetic exploder, developed under strict security, was expected to be extremely effective against enemy warships.

Because of the secrecy surrounding the magnetic exploder, and peacetime budgetary constraints, the torpedo and exploders were never actually tested live under simulated combat conditions. Instead, Newport staffers fired fish that had exercise, or "dummy," heads filled with water. Water was much lighter than TNT so the torpedoes usually ran higher in practice than they did when fitted with explosives in combat. Torpedo design was the exclusive province of naval and civilian bureaucrats in BuOrd and at Newport. They kept the development veiled in silence.

Slade Cutter, for one, was disgusted by the way the magnetic torpedo people demonstrated its effectiveness in the shop. As a torpedo officer, he watched a technician at Newport pass a charged wand over the torpedo, supposedly simulating its movement going through a magnetic field. The wand would "click" and the technicians would say "See, it works."

BuOrd did not appear to know that the Japanese had developed a much faster and more heavily armed torpedo. The U.S. torpedo carried a relatively small warhead of 500 pounds and ran at 46 knots for a range of 4,500 yards. It did not make a great impact. Rarely was one torpedo enough to sink a large Japanese vessel. The Japanese, by contrast, had in peacetime developed a submarine version of their deadly "Long Lance," a torpedo that could carry a 900-pound warhead 10,000 yards at a speed of 49 knots, powered by a wake-less, oxygen-fueled engine—far superior to Newport's vaunted U.S. version.

In its own world, BuOrd, known as the "Gun Club," reigned supreme and brooked no criticism from combat submariners using its products. Many skippers returning from early war patrols reported that their torpedoes were defective. The fish appeared to run much deeper than they had been set. Some inexplicably failed to explode when they had clearly hit enemy vessels. Still others blew up prematurely.

During one early, discouraging patrol, *Sturgeon,* captained by the hard-driving William L. "Bull" Wright, came in contact with the Japanese invasion force off Borneo. Using the deep submergence sonar approach, he fired four torpedoes at what he thought was an aircraft carrier. The sonar man reported hits and explosions. Wright sent off a message that was to become famous: "STURGEON NO LONGER VIRGIN." But Japanese intercepts indicated no loss of a warship at that time and location. Wright's claim, well meant, was typical of skippers reporting sinkings when they hadn't been able to observe the results. Their torpedoes may have been premature, or of insufficient heft to stop a large, well-armored capital ship.

The first skipper to complain officially was Tyrell Jacobs of *Sargo,* whose torpedoes in the South China Sea exploded prematurely. Jacobs, an ordnance expert, sensed that the tor-

pedoes were not functioning correctly. He thought they were
running deeper than set and that the magnetic exploder
might not be working properly. He disconnected it. In six attacks, Jacobs launched thirteen torpedoes. None exploded.
He concluded that the Mark 14 was running too deep, and
both the contact exploder and magnetic exploder were not
working. Back in port, Jacobs was severely chastised by
Captain Wilkes for deactivating the magnetic exploder. Jacobs begged Wilkes to allow *Sargo* to fire a torpedo through
a suspended fishnet to test its depth setting. The request was
denied by Wilkes and Chief-of-Staff Fife because there was
a shortage of torpedoes. A Washington expert actually flew
to Fremantle, examined the torpedoes, and announced that
the problem was the fault of submarine torpedomen and
skippers. He recommended against an actual test in Australia. A disgusted Tyrell Jacobs asked for transfer out of
submarines, prophet without respect, and the Navy lost an
excellent submarine skipper.

It was clear to other captains, if not to their superiors, that
torpedoes were defective. Skippers were reporting too many
perfect set-ups resulting in misses—or in obvious duds when
the fish failed to explode against the side of enemy ships.
There was concern over the magnetic exploder. Some skippers changed the setting from magnetic to contact, without
reporting the change—in effect falsifying their reports in the
interest of getting hits. One of the few successful skippers in
the early days was Lucius Chappell in *Sculpin,* but he was
furious with torpedoes aimed at easy targets that missed.
This valiant captain reported he was "so demoralized and
disheartened from repeated misses he had little stomach for
further action until an analysis could be made and a finger
put on the deficiency or deficiencies responsible, and correc-
tive action taken."

In Pearl Harbor, a new sub division commander, George C.
Crawford, arrived after duty in England and reported that the
Germans and British had decided that magnetic exploders,
which they also had developed, rarely worked properly.
These veteran combat submariners had jettisoned the mag-
netic in favor of the simple contact exploder. So Commander

Crawford decided to junk the magnetic exploder in the six boats of his division. He instructed his skippers to deactivate. When Admiral Withers, then ComSubPac, learned of the order he hit the roof, called Crawford on the carpet, and told him: "I know it works. I was at Newport when it was tested. I don't want to hear any more discussion about it. If I hear one more word from you on the subject, I'm going to send you to general service."

Other arriving skippers suggested to Withers that they deactivate the magnetic exploder, and set the contact Mark 14 torpedo to a shallower setting than called for. Withers was adamant. Never, he ordered. Some skippers, on reaching a combat zone, deactivated their magnetic exploders anyway and set their torpedoes to run at shallower depths. They kept their actions secret. Ironically, this understandable action was actually counter-productive: it led ComSubPac to believe he was getting sinkings with the magnetic exploder and so confirmed his faith in the defective weapon.

Withers' replacement, Admiral English, was equally convinced that Newport-made torpedoes worked: it was the skippers, he insisted, who didn't know how to shoot them. When captains with proven records recommended that depths be set to run shallower, he also refused their requests. He suggested the skippers were at fault for "their inexperience, exhaustion, and snap decisions." He ordered that commanders continue to use the magnetic exploder. When Tex Mewhenney, commanding *Saury,* reported to Admiral English that he thought some of his torpedoes were prematures, English said flatly, "SubPac has never had a premature explosion."

In Brisbane, Ralph Christie similarly forbade skippers to deactivate the magnetic exploder. As a former BuOrd torpedo officer, he had helped develop the advanced weapon. Christie insisted the boats in his command set torpedoes to standard depths and use the magnetic exploder. But things would change.

Soon after Admiral Lockwood's arrival in Australia, *Skipjack* under Commander James W. Coe put into Fremantle after an unsuccessful fifty-day patrol. A careful and brave skipper, Coe had taken meticulous notes about his poor tor-

pedo performance. He reported to Lockwood that the fish
were running deeper than set. Jimmy Coe observed pun-
gently: "To make a round trip of 8,500 miles into enemy waters, to gain attack position undetected within enemy ships
only to find that the torpedoes run deep and over half the
time will fail to explode, seems to me an undesirable manner
of gaining information that might be determined any morning within a few miles of a torpedo station in the presence of
comparatively few hazards."

Lockwood was aware that most skippers did not trust the
magnetic exploder on the Mark 14 torpedo—nor did they
trust the torpedo itself. He wrote BuOrd in Washington
about the complaints, and received a sharp response to the
effect that sub commanders were blaming the torpedo failures for their own lack of marksmanship—"alibis," the Bureau called them.

Lockwood decided to take on the problem himself.
He called Captain James Fife, now in command of the sub
detachment at Albany around the southwest tip of Australia.
They decided to hold a test there, which proved to be historic.
The exercise consisted of submerging a fishnet obtained from
fishermen at Frenchman's Bay, and firing a Mark 14 torpedo
set to run at 10 feet from *Skipjack*. The torpedo's recovered
depth recorder showed it ran at 25 feet. The hole in the net
was registered at 25 feet.

The next day, Skipper Jimmy Coe fired two more fish at
the net. Both ran deeper than designated. Fife concluded the
Mark 14 was running an average of 11 feet deeper than set.
Lockwood immediately alerted BuOrd brass in Washington,
who incomprehensibly replied that the tests could not be
considered reliable because "improper torpedo trim conditions had been introduced."

Lockwood ordered Fife to conduct another set of tests
with *Saury* firing four torpedoes from a range of 900 yards
at the fishnet. The average depth was 11 feet more than designed. He sent another pointed dispatch to BuOrd hoping
for some positive reaction. Lockwood ordered the torpedoes
on his boats set shallower, and notified other commands of
his action.

In Pearl Harbor, Admiral English, ComSubPac, who had been monitoring Admiral Lockwood's messages from Perth to Washington concerning torpedo tests, suddenly reversed his field and informed his skippers that their torpedoes were indeed running 11 feet deeper than set. He ordered the captains to set their depths accordingly shallower. However, English insisted the magnetic exploders were functioning properly and skippers were ordered to continue using them. Nevertheless, the deep running problem seemed solved.

But late in 1942, the aggressive Lawson "Red" Ramage furiously reported to Admiral Lockwood that his last patrol aboard *Trout* resulted in one premature torpedo explosion and five duds of the fourteen fish fired—or a 43 percent failure rate. This, Ramage argued, meant that a flaw existed in the magnetic exploder. Even though the errors in depth control were being worked out, it appeared that U.S. submarine torpedoes were still beset with crucial problems.

Otherwise, from Mush Morton's and Dick O'Kane's perspective, things were looking up. They had shown the way with *Wahoo*'s great third patrol. New submarines were now arriving in the Pacific, coming off the building ways at the Navy yards in Mare Island, California; Portsmouth, New Hampshire; the Electric Boat Company in Groton, Connecticut; and, of all places, Manitowoc, Wisconsin, whose dedicated craftsmen turned out well-made submarines, launched sideways into the river. The Manitowoc boats were barged from Lake Michigan, through the Chicago and Illinois rivers, down the Mississippi to reach salt water 1,000 miles away in the Gulf of Mexico.

As Mush Morton, Dick O'Kane and *Wahoo* looked forward in 1943, they put aside the failures of the submarine command and the high brass' in-fighting. The new breed of skippers believed they now had a man in Pearl Harbor after their own hearts: Charles Lockwood.

Lockwood may not have been a strategic genius and he had the occasionally wacky idea, but he was a warm, genial man who cared deeply about his skippers and crews. He fought rulebook thinking and hidebound conformity. He found time to congratulate a sailor for a job well done, to see

that good transportation and quarters were provided for incoming sub personnel.

Lockwood's presence at Pearl Harbor lifted submariners'
spirits. Unlike many senior staff commanders, he listened
carefully to his skippers and even junior officers. He trusted
them. He gave his men the impression that he was totally
on their side against the enemy—and against the bureaucrats
in the Navy Department. To his friends in the pressure hulls,
from mess attendants to skippers, Admiral Lockwood was
"Uncle Charlie." Now he was Commander Submarines Pacific, ComSubPac. Mush Morton, Dick O'Kane, and the
other frustrated submarine officers at the Royal Hawaiian
could drink to that.

CHAPTER SIX

The Great Yellow Sea Patrol

As their two weeks ashore in Pearl Harbor ended, XO O'Kane reported to Captain Morton that the officers and crew were physically and mentally ready for the next patrol. But this time they would be sailing without third officer George Grider, who was moving up to become executive officer of the elderly *Pollack*. Grider's calm, deliberative presence would be deeply missed. Roger Paine was to fleet up to the chief engineer's job. With new boats coming off the shipways, and with the wear and tear on combat submariners, about a fifth of the crew was replaced after a patrol. The veterans went on home leave, or were promoted to other boats, or reassigned to new construction, which would also provide them leave time before taking up their new duties. A submarine captain had to be prepared to fit new, often green, officers and men into the crew after each war patrol. It was a continuous, inevitable process, but it irritated skippers because just when they had a crew operating smoothly, the winning team would be broken up.

No one begrudged George Grider's becoming an exec, though he was disappointed not to get a newer boat—preferably one back in the States, which meant home leave. George wasn't crazy about switching in Pearl Harbor without a chance to visit his family. "It's a promotion," he told his shipmates, "but it isn't worth it."

Mush Morton consoled Grider. "Never mind, George, with you aboard, *Pollack* will burn up the Pacific."

"Yes, Captain, but who's going to keep you and Dick out of trouble?"

"Don't worry," Morton replied, grabbing Grider in a playful headlock. "Roger Paine is almost as big a sissy as you are. He'll take care of us."

Neither Mush Morton nor George Grider dreamed that Morton's words held a note of tragic prophecy—for there would come a time when Roger Paine, too, would leave *Wahoo*.

Roger Paine had been TDC officer before he moved up to replace George Grider as engineer. His battle station would ordinarily have been diving officer, but Mush Morton and Dick O'Kane didn't like pigeonholes: they wanted Paine to man the torpedo data computer in the attack party, so Richie Henderson took over as diving officer during Battle Stations.

Along with Lieutenant Grider, *Wahoo* was losing Chief Petty Officers Andrew Lenox and Leslie Lindhe. But the officer complement was beefed up by the assignment of Commander Duncan C. MacMillan as Prospective Commanding Officer, a makee-learn who could fill in as a watch-stander. Having MacMillan aboard was awkward because he had been originally designated *Wahoo*'s first commander before Marvin Kennedy was assigned instead. Also, MacMillan was older, a full commander without any combat experience, while Morton was only a lieutenant commander and O'Kane a mere lieutenant. MacMillan had been the exec of *Argonaut* when O'Kane was a junior officer. MacMillan was eight years older than Dick O'Kane, who was now a veteran of four war patrols, manning the periscope of mighty *Wahoo*.

One welcome arrival was Ship's Cook Paul D. Phillips, who had been left behind in Brisbane but flew to Pearl to rejoin the boat. Yeoman Forest Sterling greeted Phillips when they were assigned to share a room at the Royal Hawaiian. During a conversation, Phillips asked Sterling: "Yeo, do you get the feeling that you're gonna die in this war?"

"Naw," Sterling answered casually. "I've always had the feeling that I was going to see the year 2000. I get plenty scared at times, though, that I'm not going to make it."

Seeing the worried expression on Phillips' face, Sterling said, "Why do you ask?"

"Oh, I don't know. Just a feeling, I guess. Yeo, I just know sometimes that I'm going down on the *Wahoo*. I just can't get away from the feeling."

The talk left Sterling unsettled.

By now, *Wahoo's* bottom had been scrubbed with high-pressure hoses in a floating dock, and a new paint job added a half-knot to her underwater speed. Chief petty officers supervised the loading of torpedoes, ammunition and provisions. Food in particular had to be positioned carefully for removal on schedule so that the menu didn't run to chicken soup or Spam day after day. *Wahoo* was topped up with fuel and at 2200, just after the base movie was over, O'Kane reported to Morton: "All hands aboard and ready for patrol, Captain."

The next morning, February 23, Admiral Lockwood came down to the finger pier to see *Wahoo* off on her fourth patrol as the lines were singled up for a 1300 departure. Charlie Lockwood addressed Morton and O'Kane as "Mush" and "Dick." O'Kane had known Lockwood when the Admiral was a submarine division commander and rode aboard Dick's tin can USS *Pruitt,* which served as target for dummy torpedoes in training exercises. In a short conversation, the Admiral asked only one question.

"At what depth do you set your torpedoes?"

"As shallow as the situation permits," Morton replied. Lockwood nodded. Dick O'Kane believed the Submarine Force finally had a commander who was going to get to the bottom of the dud torpedo problems that almost all the boats were experiencing.

The diesels rumbled, their exhausts spitting steamy water from the mufflers. The lines were cast off, and *Wahoo* issued an ear-splitting, prolonged blast from her horn to signal she was backing into the roadstead. *Wahoo* departed Pearl with an escort destroyer to keep "friendly" planes from dumping bombs on the submarine as she cleared Hawaiian waters. O'Kane remembered the wise adage: once a submarine leaves the pier, it has no friends and many enemies.

Feeling more relaxed and affable, Dick O'Kane moved through the boat to make sure the new crewmembers were squared away and to check the turkey dinner being prepared for Washington's birthday. During the four-day trip to Midway Island, *Wahoo* practiced drills and trim dives, insuring that the boat would remain in proper trim, or balance, when underwater.

At Midway, the channel into the inner lagoon was tricky and treacherous, dredged through massive, sharp coral heads. The prevailing winds caused a submarine entering the anchorage at slow speed to yaw, requiring a strong hand on the rudder to keep the boat in the channel. *Wahoo*'s bridge officers approached the Midway channel, and conned her through.

At the forward Sub Base, O'Kane attended to an unusual job that had been left hanging at Pearl: *Wahoo*'s search periscope tube had become slightly pitted from friction.

"We ought to have the dentists fill the damn things," Morton said in jest. But O'Kane, ever innovative, thought it a good idea. He had sounded out the dental office at the Sub Base at Pearl Harbor, but no one believed such a solution practical.

"At Midway, 1,300 miles closer to the enemy," O'Kane told Morton, "they might think differently." They did.

A couple of dentists volunteered. Signalman Al Simonetti cleaned the pitted scope, appropriately using old toothbrushes, and a pharmacist's mate mixed the amalgam. The dentist filled in the pits. Signalman Fertig Krause polished the amalgam as soon as it had set, using fine emery paper. The patched-up periscope, O'Kane reported, was as smooth and shiny as an undamaged one.

On departing Midway, Morton announced *Wahoo*'s secret patrol destination to the crew: the East China and Yellow Seas, 4,000 miles away, south and west of the Japanese home islands. Morton believed in sharing such secret data with his men. "Hell, Dick," he remarked, "we're all in the same boat."

The area had never before been probed by a U.S. submarine, Morton said, and should be productive. The main drawback was shallow water in the East China Sea and the Yellow Sea, which O'Kane called a "wading pond." This made it inherently dangerous for a submarine to operate, since depth meant safety.

Wahoo ran across the Pacific on the surface except during morning trim dives. After ten uneventful days, the boat's arrival in Empire waters was announced by the radar sighting of Sofu Gan, or Lot's Wife, a vertical rock pinnacle some 400 feet high and 350 miles off Honshu, which served submariners as a landmark. *Wahoo* headed south to skirt Kyushu. A lookout reported, "Land ho," sighting the 6,000-foot island peak, Yaku Shima, off the southern tip of Kyushu. A quick westward transit took *Wahoo* through the Colonet Strait breasting the northern Ryukyus chain into the East China Sea. Captain Morton's aim was to cut the sea-lanes from Tsingtao, Tientsin, Dairen and Seoul—which linked the conquered Chinese coast, Manchuria and Korea to Japan.

After surfacing that evening, *Wahoo* charged batteries, dumped garbage in weighted sacks, pumped air into the compressed air banks, and ventilated the boat. The crew tuned in Tokyo Rose on the radio for amusement during their dinner hour in the messroom.

"Good evening, you wonderful American boys out there. This is Tokyo Rose speaking. Did you like our nice music? Did it make you homesick? You should be home with your loved ones: your wives and mothers and sweethearts. It is so sad that you must all die while your leaders are safe at home and the civilians who are making all the money are dating your girls. We know where every soldier's outfit is and where every ship and submarine is located. We Japanese do not want to kill you but because you are the invaders we have to."

Dick O'Kane thought her remarks were overdone, perhaps intentionally, but her records were popular ones, the same the crew would have heard stateside, so he had no objection to *Wahoo* tuning in.

The next morning, a lookout reported, "We have smoke on the horizon, Captain."

Morton and O'Kane found it difficult to identify the ship as they maneuvered closer, submerged—the atmosphere distorted light rays entering the scope lens. At first it looked like a fishing trawler. Then possibly a Q-ship—a vessel designed to resemble a harmless freighter, but armed with hidden, long-range guns for use against submarines lured into an attack ambush.

The *Wahoo* attack party dubbed her "Smoky Maru." Roger Paine remained on the torpedo data computer in the conning tower while Richie Henderson took over Roger's duties as diving officer in the control room. Captain Morton decided Smoky Maru was worth only one torpedo, not two, and ordered a single tube readied. O'Kane was at the periscope.

"Any time, Dick," Morton said.

"Constant bearing, mark!" O'Kane called out.

"Set," said Roger at the torpedo data computer.

"Fire!" O'Kane ordered.

The torpedo, watched carefully by O'Kane, seemed to be running normally, but then the fish broached and disappeared just ahead of the enemy ship. Quickly checking their estimates, the attack team realized the ship had been going slower than they thought, so the fish had run slightly ahead of target.

"What's she doing, Dick?"

"Nothing, Captain. She's still circling and smoking. Down scope." O'Kane stepped back and looked at Morton.

"Let's try it again, Captain, when old Smoky Maru comes around again."

Morton suspected an ambush from a Q-ship, armed, and loaded with ping-pong balls so that it wouldn't sink. He replied sharply, "Hell no, Dick, I'm not going to waste any more shots on what might turn out to be a trap."

Yeoman Sterling was surprised. It was the first time he had seen Mush Morton angry.

Suddenly reddening, O'Kane shot back, "Captain, we ought to sink that son-of-a-bitch. Let's don't let him get away with that."

Morton declared coldly, "That's enough, Dick. Goddamnit, when you get to be a captain in your own sub you can shoot all the torpedoes you want, at whatever you want to."

Morton turned to Roger Paine, who was watching the surprise outburst with astonishment, and ordered, "Break off the attack." Then, "Come to course two-two-five. Secure from Battle Stations Submerged."

Later, congenial spirits were revived with news that St. Patrick's Day would be celebrated aboard with a dinner of corned beef and cabbage. O'Kane pronounced the corned beef dinner the best he had tasted—outside of New York City—ranking up there with the Durgin Park restaurant in Boston.

In the Yellow Sea, *Wahoo* was now entering an area thick with fishermen in their sampans. On the bridge, O'Kane and Morton conferred. Morton said, "We'd better get some water over us. With all these sampans around we've got about as much chance for secrecy as a burlesque actress doing her act in Times Square."

As they moved into dangerous territory, the shallow waters near the Dairen Peninsula, a couple of crewmen confided their concerns to Yeoman Sterling. Krause told him, "Mush says *Wahoo* has paid for herself now, and we're all expendable."

Electrician's Mate Forest O'Brien added, "The captain gets on my nerves sometimes with that kind of talk."

Soothingly, Sterling replied, "He don't mean nothing by it. It's just his way of cracking funnies. He called this Sampan Alley we're in today."

While *Wahoo* shifted to a new position, with free time aboard, Morton and O'Kane insisted the crew keep up their studies, which would lead to their "qualifying" in submarines, and to advancement in rate in their speciality. Most crewmen were afraid of being transferred off *Wahoo* before five patrols: after completing five, they would be sent to new construction in the States and long home leave. Morton assured them they could remain aboard, but only if they qualified and finished their rating course books. So instead of the usual acey-deucey game (a popular form of backgammon), men were studying course books singly, or in groups with an officer instructing.

Mush and Dick blew off their accumulated steam by playing a popular officer's card game, cribbage. Morton dealt O'Kane a perfect hand, four fives and the requisite jack. Amateur statisticians aboard calculated the odds of getting such a hand at about 216,000 to 1. O'Kane had fellow officers sign the five cards and framed the hand. The crew took it as a lucky omen.

The next morning, lookouts spotted a large freighter, *Zogen Maru,* and *Wahoo* raced ahead on the surface to reach a suitable attack position. "AHOOGAH, AHOOGAH" on the diving klaxon took *Wahoo* down. Morton ordered two tubes readied fore and aft, and the bow doors opened. O'Kane estimated the track to target at about 750 yards.

"Any time, Dick," Morton said. "Just one torpedo."

"Stand by for constant bearing," O'Kane said, his eye to the scope.

"Constant bearing, mark!"

"Set," came Roger Paine's response.

"Fire!" O'Kane said.

The captain hit the firing plunger.

"Hot, straight, and normal," Soundman Buckley reported.

This torpedo was loaded with the new explosive, torpex, which was more powerful than TNT. The 750-yard run should have taken about 50 seconds. At a timed 49 seconds, the fish hit with a loud wallop, more resonant than any they'd heard before. The freighter's mid-section disintegrated and within moments only the bow was visible, pointing skyward. Lieutenant Chan Jackson timed the sinking from the explosion to the disappearance of the bow section at 2 minutes and 26 seconds. One ship down with two torpedoes fired, O'Kane thought, was a fine way to start off a patrol. The crew were elated: every new hand would receive the submarine combat insignia and veterans could add a star designating another successful patrol.

In celebration, Morton and O'Kane shared a hearty breakfast of bacon and scrambled eggs. Then the word came: "Captain to the conning tower."

"Here we go again," Morton said, grinning at O'Kane.

The target turned out to be a freighter and *Wahoo* began a long chase to put the boat in an intercepting position. *Wahoo* reached the desired firing point by 0900 with the attack party at the ready in the conning tower. Dick O'Kane aimed for the single stack of the freighter and fired one torpedo. He realized that the fish was heading slightly forward of the target.

Morton ordered a second torpedo readied. O'Kane fired the second. The first torpedo hit near the freighter's foremast and the second also struck, with a spray of water arcing up the ship's side. However, this was merely the torpedo's air flask exploding. The warhead itself only thudded. O'Kane groaned. It was the thud of a dud.

O'Kane fired two more torpedoes but the canny Japanese skipper managed to turn his vessel away to thread between them. The freighter then started shelling *Wahoo*'s periscope. Morton took the submarine deeper in frustration, and cleared the immediate area.

After an action, some submarine officers went about their normal duties, ate, slept, read, or played cards. But O'Kane, ever the professional, liked to hold post-mortems with the firing party around the wardroom table to see how an attack set-up could be improved. He and the officers looked up the picture of the target in the Naval Intelligence book of photographs and statistics. They checked on listed speeds and went over their plots on the torpedo data computer. They noted whether *Wahoo*'s propellers were making the proper number of turns. The idea was to do better next time.

That evening, O'Kane reported to Morton that all was quiet aboard when Lieutenant Jack Griggs yelled over the intercom: "Ship on the horizon." He sounded the General Quarters alarm. At the periscope, O'Kane identified the target as a passenger freighter, and *Wahoo* was soon in attack position, ready to fire. Morton ordered three bow torpedoes launched in a spread, so that two should hit.

Again came what O'Kane called the "welcome words" from Morton: "Any time, Dick."

The spread was almost too good—the first missed slightly astern, the second was either slightly ahead of the target or a dud, while the third hit amidships, as aimed. The force of the blast caused the ship to sink in 4¹/₂ minutes. The sunken vessel checked with the identification in the intelligence book as the *Kowa Maru*.

Later, Dick O'Kane turned in for some sack time. He could get by on a few hours rest, a habit he picked up aboard the destroyer *Pruitt*. He could fall into a deep sleep as soon as he hit his bunk. Similarly, short catnaps taken when the opportunity arose left him refreshed. As navigator, O'Kane was always on the bridge early to shoot the morning star fixes. He also liked to get a sense of what was going on in the boat before the captain did.

The next morning, after his navigational fixes, Dick sat down to breakfast with Mush. As they finished eating, another ship was sighted. The attack approach was quickly set up. O'Kane fired three torpedoes. Two hit, and the *Hozan Maru* went down. Morton surfaced *Wahoo* and ordered a sweep to try, following a long-standing instruction from ComSubPac, to obtain a copy of the Japanese Merchant Marine Code. Volunteer swimmers in the crew dove into the sea to retrieve objects from the flotsam. They found some books, but the real prize was two oversized, red-and-white house flags of the steamship's line and a large life preserver with the ship's name in both Japanese and English block letters: *Nittsu Maru*.

At this rate, with four ships down and only half her torpedoes expended, *Wahoo* was running up the best patrol of the war. That evening a 16-millimeter movie was shown in the forward torpedo room. According to custom, the show did not normally begin until the captain arrived—or indicated he would not attend. In surface ships, the crew always stood when the captain entered. In subs, this wasn't practical, but crewmen recognized the skipper's arrival by stopping conversation and nodding. For the first time in nine years of sea duty, Dick O'Kane heard a captain greeted by a spontaneous cheer and applause.

Early the next day, *Wahoo* moved westward in the Yellow Sea, closer to the Chinese coast northwest of the Shantung Peninsula. Morton wrote in his log: "There is never much water in this wading pond. We have to be careful with our angle on dives to keep from plowing into the bottom. Aircraft and patrols have been scarce because we are in virgin territory. However, she ain't virgin now, and we are expecting trouble soon. We hope to get at least four more ships and then expend our gun ammunition on the way home."

Soon *Wahoo* picked up another Japanese ship, a collier (a coal-carrier). The submarine poured on power to attain an attack position, and the smooth-running conning tower team had the set-up.

"One torpedo any time, Dick," Morton said.

"Mark!"

"Set."

"Fire!"

The warhead detonated under the coal-carrier's stack. She sunk rapidly, a huge film of bituminous dust settling on the sea around them. For a while the upended collier remained motionless.

"Her bow must be resting on the bottom and her stern is rising vertically out of the water," O'Kane said, looking through the scope. Chan Jackson took several pictures of *Wahoo*'s latest victim.

The next day, Captain Morton suggested that *Wahoo* patrol toward the Chinese port of Chinwangtao, across the Gulf of Pohai. Morton sketched out his plan—close toward the port and bombard ships tied up to piers there. O'Kane was uneasy with Morton's scheme. Till now *Wahoo*'s exec had willingly gone along with all of the captain's proposals—except that down-the-throater, but then there was no alternative. This, however, was stretching it a bit too far, O'Kane thought. They were finding ships for *Wahoo*'s torpedoes right where they were, so why accept the extra hazard?

O'Kane called Morton's attention to the obscured legend on the chart for the Gulf of Pohai—that the soundings noted on the map were in feet, not the usual six-foot fathoms. The water was laughably shallow.

"Oh, no!" Morton grinned—and called off his plan.

Operating off Port Arthur between the Gulf of Pohai and the Yellow Sea, OOD Richie Henderson located a big Japanese tanker heading *Wahoo*'s way as evening twilight set in. A spread of three fish with magnetic exploders was set up, and O'Kane fired them to hit forward, midships, and aft of the stack. The first torpedo exploded only 18 seconds after firing—almost, O'Kane thought, blowing up in his face. The second, too, ignited 18 seconds after it was launched. The third tor-

pedo was set awry by the curtain of water in the previous explosions.

"Damn the magnetic exploders," O'Kane swore. "Two
prematures and a miss. These premature explosions could
truly be dangerous." *Wahoo* soon found out how dangerous
the situation was as the mist cleared. The intended target,
now beyond torpedo range, began firing shells using flash-
less powder which the lookouts couldn't see. The shells
landed close by with a swish-swish sound, sending hunks of
shrapnel toward *Wahoo*'s bridge. Morton pulled the plug to
ponder the situation in safety. He figured if he surfaced, he
could outrun the tanker on her track to Dairen, and be there
waiting, but not if *Wahoo* dallied. Morton ordered *Wahoo*
surfaced and rang up flank speed.

It was the turn of Commander MacMillan, the PCO, to
reach the bridge first from the conning tower. He opened the
hatch part way, and reported, "They're still shooting at us!"

Signalman Hunter right behind on the ladder was blocked
by MacMillan, and looked at Mush Morton for guidance. In
the dim, red light, the skipper raised his fist with the thumb
up. Hunter goosed the Commander above him, which sent
the PCO flying to the bridge. The maneuver may not have
improved Commander MacMillan's view of the roughhouse
Wahoo crew.

With four engines on the line, *Wahoo* sped forward to
reach a firing position 4 miles from the port of Dairen. The
lookouts identified the incoming tanker and *Wahoo* submerged.

"Any time, Dick," Morton said, in the now routine order.
A spread of three torpedoes sped toward the tanker with the
third connecting under the rear-placed stack, the most vulnerable spot in such a ship. The tanker went down by the
stern within 5 minutes.

Running on the surface at night, *Wahoo* picked up another
cargo ship bound for Port Arthur. The submarine pulled
ahead of the contact, and dove. The set-up seemed good.
Morton ordered the two forward tubes readied.

"Shoot when ready, Gridley," Morton told O'Kane, al-
luding to Admiral Dewey's famous remark in the Spanish-

American War. The first torpedo exploded 48 seconds into the run that should have taken 52 seconds, tossing a huge geyser of water across the sea. The second torpedo also detonated but it was unclear whether it hit or was a premature. Yeoman Sterling recorded two prematures in his notebook.

"Goddamnit," Morton said, "it isn't hardly worthwhile to risk our necks bringing these goddamn failures all the way out here for nothing."

"She's going to get away, Captain," O'Kane warned.

"Like hell she is," Morton replied. "Make all preparations for Battle Surface."

Inside 10 minutes *Wahoo*'s deck gun was ready, with trainer, spotter, and gun captain in place on the surface, as well as loaders and ammo passers pulling 4-inch rounds from the messroom hatch. Twelve minutes after the last torpedo was fired from underwater, the deck gun opened up, with the first shell hitting the after deckhouse of the fleeing vessel. A second round knocked out the target's steering. Gunner's Mate Bill Carr concentrated fire on the ship's waterline near the engine spaces. The *Takaosan Maru* was badly holed, on fire, and sinking. An investigating small tanker was also taken under fire by *Wahoo*'s gun crew, raked with 20-millimeter bursts and set ablaze. *Satsuki Maru* then sank. Morton ordered *Wahoo* to clear the area before enemy planes could arrive.

A highly pleased Mush Morton congratulated the gun crew. It had been their day. Morton preferred gun action, though other skippers were reluctant to jeopardize their boats in a gunfight against second-rate targets. Morton noted in his log: "Anyone who has not witnessed a submarine conduct a battle surface with three 20 mm. and four-inch gun in the morning twilight with a calm sea and in crisp clear weather just ain't lived. It was truly spectacular."

During a third gun battle, with a 100-ton trawler, the 20-millimeter jammed, so Morton ordered into action his volunteer "commando" outfit. These sailors were formed as a possible boarding party and borrowed Molotov cocktails from U.S. Marines at Midway. Morton brought the nose of *Wahoo* alongside the trawler and crewmembers hurled the incendiary devices at the flaming ship. The fire and smoke gave *Wahoo*'s amateur cameramen a great shot, but the soggy trawler would not sink. Some of the Japanese crewmen even thumbed their noses at *Wahoo* and O'Kane thought them plucky enough probably to get their wounded ship back to port.

By now *Wahoo* had only two torpedoes left, both of which Morton and O'Kane considered to be of dubious value. Chronic leaks in the *Wahoo*'s battery cells, which were of a faulty experimental design, had reduced their underwater performance by 25 percent, and presented the danger of poisonous chlorine gas. So Morton headed *Wahoo* out of the confining waters of the Yellow Sea to patrol off Kyushu on the shipping lane to Nagasaki.

On station, Signalman Krause roused O'Kane early with an unusual greeting. "Lieutenant Commander," he said, "you're needed on the bridge. We have a ship—and your promotion just came in over Fox."

Morton and O'Kane tracked the new target ship, which proved to be a medium-sized freighter. The torpedomen had pulled each of the last two fish from their tubes, carefully inspected them, painted "lucky" eyes on the warheads and reloaded them. All Yeoman Sterling could think of, though, was, "Let's get these goddamn fish on their way and get out of here."

In less than a minute, the constant bearing was marked and set. The target ship's mainmast was about to touch the wire in Dick O'Kane's periscope.

"Fire!" O'Kane said. Morton hit the plunger.

O'Kane ordered the second and last torpedo launched. Roger Paine, the torpedo attack expert, began counting the seconds for the 800-yard run. A violent explosion broke the back of *Yamabato Maru*. O'Kane observed that sometimes a sinking ship makes tremendous breaking-up noises, perhaps when compartments or bulkheads collapse, the total sound like a bridge or other steel structure being slowly scrunched by a monstrous bulldozer. Such, he thought, was the case with this ship. Morton said to Jack Griggs, "Tell the crew that the noise you hear is the enemy ship breaking up."

Griggs complied over the intercom system, but in his excitement he left out the word "enemy," leaving some of *Wahoo*'s new crewmembers badly unnerved until a correction was hastily made.

Dick O'Kane began drafting a departure message for Mush Morton to dispatch to ComSubPac once they cleared the Empire. In the number of ships sunk on a single patrol, a credited nine for some 20,000 tons, no other U.S. submarine had ever come close. Satisfied, Mush Morton said, "Dick, set a course for the barn."

CHAPTER SEVEN

At the Mercy of the Cruel Sea

Wahoo headed for home. Exec O'Kane was looking for an uneventful passage across the Pacific after sinking an unprecedented nine enemy ships in only ten days. Radar spotted the checkpoint pinnacle, Lot's Wife, and *Wahoo* bounded happily into open seas.

Mush Morton took it easy. He demonstrated his dexterity with needle and thread by sewing an Indian headdress on *Wahoo*'s new battle flag. The headdress carried a train of sixteen, red-centered white feathers, one for each ship *Wahoo* reported sunk. The two huge *Nittsu Maru* house flags streamed from the broom that would be affixed to the radar mast. But soon *Wahoo* ran into quirky seas: great rollers came from behind the boat, crashing over the superstructure while the submarine rolled, pitched, and yawed. A storm was building up, and on the bridge, Lieutenant Commander Dick O'Kane knew *Wahoo* was in for heavy weather.

The Pacific Ocean takes its name from the Spanish for "peaceful," bestowed on it by the explorer Vasco Balboa when he first saw it from the Isthmus of Panama. But the Pacific can shift moods rapidly. Storms brew up quickly. The peaceful sea becomes hostile.

Navigators like Dick O'Kane watch carefully as the barometer falls, which presages rough weather. Rising winds change the sea's surface from a placid calm to a brisk swell, to pounding waves, and finally to the angry fury of a full-blown storm, ultimately a typhoon. When that happens, warship skippers no longer worry about proper maneuvering, formation keeping, or maintaining their schedule. They are concerned about survival, for they are facing the sailor's oldest enemy: the sea itself.

In a storm at sea, the stronger the wind, the higher the waves. The higher the waves, the faster they move, and the greater distance between crests and deeper troughs. When the ocean goes wild, waves lose their normal form as their tops are sliced off by the howling wind. The sky becomes a mixture of rain and spray. The waves crash down on a warship and the angry sea appears bent on destruction of those who thwart it. A typhoon is an elemental force of nature able to toss massive ships around at will. Pacific Ocean storms are marked by waves of 60 to 80 feet in height, with corresponding troughs. Near the eye of a typhoon, as in a hurricane, winds scream at more than 100 miles an hour, tearing at rigging and men alike. The screaming spindrift makes it impossible to differentiate between sea and sky. There are no visible horizons, no sun by day, and no stars by night, nothing but sheets of water and towering seas.

In a storm, a ship bucking the sea buries her bow under tons of water, putting tremendous stress on her hull. She creaks and groans and whines. The crew becomes fatigued by the constant struggle—day and night—to function, continually hanging on to keep from being thrown off their feet into steel fittings, or over the side into the roiling ocean. If propulsive or electrical power is lost, the captain cannot control the ship, which is then at the mercy of the cruel sea. A ship without operative engines and rudder will soon broach, turning sideways to the massive waves, exposing her vulnerability. A broached ship, with the seas pounding her, is in imminent danger of capsizing and sinking.

During the Pacific War, massive storms boiled up quickly, particularly in areas where U.S. submarines operated, or had to transit to reach patrol areas. The mighty Third Fleet was twice humbled. Even a renowned sailor like Admiral William Halsey underestimated the power of a storm. He failed to give his fleet adequate warning of a typhoon, or advice on how to deal with it. His smaller ships blindly struggled to keep up with the designated fleet course and speed. The typhoon slammed into warships with all its fury. Ships not merely rolled, but heeled far over, pushed by the wind past 70 degrees from the vertical. Water was taken aboard through ventilators, blower intakes, stacks, and every other topside opening. Switchboards and electrical machinery shorted and drowned out, sparking fires from short circuits. Engine spaces, fire-rooms, living compartments all suffered from flooding. Power for lighting and propulsion went out. Waves, rain, and wind tore apart topside radar, radio, and ship control equipment. Ships lost the ability to communicate internally, and with one another.

On bucking and rolling aircraft carriers, planes broke loose from their chains on flight and hangar decks and crashed into each other, starting fires from spilt high-octane fuel. On smaller ships, wind and seas carried away masts, stacks, boats, davits and deck structures, and made it impossible for crewmen to secure deck gear that had gone awry. Finally, the seas caused structural damage to hulls. In short, the storm took charge.

In two days, three modern, 2,000-ton destroyers, *Spence, Monaghan,* and *Hull,* kept rolling on their beam ends under the assault of the waves until they capsized with nearly all hands lost. The bows of huge aircraft carriers furrowed into seas and their lashed-down planes were tossed off the flight deck and men swept overboard. Serious damage was suffered by the light cruiser *Miami,* the light carriers *Monterey, Cowpens,* and *San Jacinto,* the escort carriers *Cape Esperance* and *Altamaha,* and the destroyers *Aylwin, Dewey,* and *Hickox.* Lesser damage was inflicted on a score of other warships, from heavy cruisers to destroyer escorts. The carrier force lost 146 planes, a worse toll than was ever inflicted by the Japanese.

During the typhoon centering on December 18, 1944, 790 sailors were killed or lost at sea. Many were injured. It was the greatest casualty toll suffered by the U.S. Navy in the Pacific without compensation since the Battle of Savo Island two and a half years before.

Six months later, Admiral Halsey's Third Fleet ran into another West Pacific typhoon. One hundred feet of the bow of the 670-foot-long heavy cruiser *Pittsburgh* was ripped off, the bow of the heavy cruiser *Baltimore* was badly buckled, hull plates cracked and distorted. Four big aircraft carriers suffered badly damaged flight decks. The light carrier *San Jacinto* rolled 40 degrees; deck tractors broke loose and damaged planes. In all, seventy-six planes were lost to the fleet. Thirty-two others ships received significant damage.

Admiral Halsey had not learned the lesson of the shattering damage the angry seas could wreak. A Court of Inquiry recommended he and his carrier task force commander, Admiral John McCain, be shifted to other duties. However, Admiral Nimitz in the Pacific and Admiral King in Washington decided that removing naval heroes from the Third Fleet in wartime would damage national and Navy morale. They were criticized but remained in command.

For submarine officers, handling their boats in rough weather demanded special skills. Always precariously balanced by their nature as submersibles, fleet boats were vulnerable to the fury of a storm. At times, a skipper could submerge to avoid the tempest, but that would mean running on batteries, and when these were depleted, the boat would have to surface to recharge—whatever the circumstances. Then the ship could be even more in jeopardy.

Submarines were particularly subject to "pooping," high waves striking the boat from behind and sweeping over the exposed bridge, deluging the vessel under tons of sea water. Even ordinary rough weather presented the danger of men being swept off the main deck by the sea. The bridge is so relatively low that the captain and others on duty could be tossed around or washed over the side by a large wave coming up from the stern. Lookouts had to lash themselves to their platforms above the bridge. Officers tied safety belts to stanchions. One lookout aboard *Tullibee* died of internal injuries after a huge wave crushed him against his guardrail with such force that his binoculars were jammed into his diaphragm.

Storms caused the submarine crew to become seasick. Most sailors could not eat meals. Many could not stand their watches. Beyond sickness was the sheer fatigue. The hour-after-hour struggle of hanging on to the nearest bit of metal was bone-wearying. Lookouts were battered and bruised. They climbed down, gulped hot coffee, and piled into their bunks, trying to grab what sleep the bucking vessel would permit. The usually shipshape submarine was a shambles in a storm. Everything not lashed down or wedged in place flew around, with the crash of breaking crockery. Though the sturdy cooks provided coffee, hot soup, and sandwiches, few could eat. The inability to sleep or eat made normally calm tempers run short.

Sailors cursed and rued the day they joined the Navy. They longed for the sea to abate, to once again feel normal and energetic and get on with their watches.

"I'll take a good, clean depth-charging anytime instead of this," one storm-exhausted engineman moaned.

When heavy seas engulfed the bridge, with its open hatch below, water cascaded down into the conning tower, and below that to the control room. Sea water would also pour through the main air induction opening in the fairwater. This posed the threat of a submariner's greatest worry: fire in the boat. Salt water caused electric arcs to sputter from the main power cables from the batteries. Insulation would ignite and the fire would generate choking, blinding smoke in vital compartments. Multiple short circuits grounded electrical equipment. Gyrocompass, radio transmitter, the electric steering system, engine-order enunciators, bow and stern diving planes were put out of commission. The vital air compressors were shorted out. This affected the boat's ability to dive or to surface. It left the submarine in peril.

Dick O'Kane was familiar with the ravages of an angry sea. He served for two years aboard the destroyer *Pruitt,* an old four-piper, in duty that was considered a splendid initiation for any officer who desired to become an expert ship handler. It was the sort of on-the-job training absent in larger or slower ships. O'Kane learned from reading patrol reports and listening to scuttlebutt that several U.S. submarines had nearly broached and sunk in heavy weather. *Tarpon,* he knew, was forced by a low battery charge to surface during a typhoon. A monster wave climbed over the open conning tower hatch to the bridge. Water poured down through the conning tower into the control room below, flooding out much of the equipment, and knocking out power and controls. Unable to dive, the submarine rolled and pitched wildly, barely riding out the storm. Subsequent repairs in Australia took weeks.

Now O'Kane manned the bridge of *Wahoo,* battered by rising waves and deepening troughs. The bow would plunge down, leaving the screws to break water and race wildly. The submarine trembled and shuddered, an ominous rumble sounding from the empty ballast tanks, as the sea beat at them.

The ship's radar spotted a Japanese convoy at some 7,000 yards distance. O'Kane, binoculars at his eyes, tried to spot them visually in the heavy seas. It was no use. There was nothing but yellowish grayness, rough seas, wind, and rain. The binoculars were stained with salt, useless. The spray stung his eyes, forcing him to shut them and wipe off the salt. The salt water washing over the bridge caused the radio antenna insulators around O'Kane to spark while transmitting a contact report of the convoy to ComSubPac. Without torpedoes, *Wahoo* set its course eastward, the boat bashing into the brutal seas. Great rollers from astern kept riding up the after section of *Wahoo.* Suddenly O'Kane saw a monster wave rear up astern.

"Close the hatch," he screamed to George Misch, officer-of-the-deck.

"Climb the shears," O'Kane yelled to the lookouts.

Lieutenant Misch slammed shut the hatch to the conning tower and jumped up on the lookouts' platform attached to the periscope shears. O'Kane grabbed the mounting of the target bearing transmitter, the TBT. The massive wave swept over the submarine, enveloping it. Dick O'Kane had the feeling that the boat had dived and was underwater—until the sea receded from the bridge. He checked the hatch, which was being slowly opened from below.

The word to close the huge main air induction valve under the cigarette deck had not been received by the control room. So tons of sea water poured into the air conduction line, bypassing the closed off engine rooms, and cascaded into the maneuvering room, with all its crucial electrical controls, and the motor room below. Water poured into the after torpedo room. The salt water in the maneuvering room shorted out electrical connections. All power was lost. *Wahoo* wallowed perilously without steerageway.

As acrid smoke sputtered up, torpedomen dragged semi-conscious electricians from the maneuvering room, across the combing and into the after torpedo room. Captain Morton ordered the batteries shut down to stop more electrical fires. He, Dick O'Kane and Chief Electrician's Mate Ralph Pruett donned smoke masks and entered the stricken maneuvering room. There they found Chief Electrician's Mate Norman Ware and Motor Machinist Richard Goss nearly suffocated while trying to rig electrical jumpers to reestablish power in the submarine. Ware and Electrician's Mate Joe Vidick tried to fight the fire but were choking badly. Morton and O'Kane with their smoke masks managed to get the injured men out of the compartment. Other crewmen moved in and began pumping water out of the motor room below.

Captain Morton scrambled into the engine room and asked Chief Motor Machinist's Mate Keeter, "Do you think we can go ahead on one engine now?"

"I think so, Captain."

"We'll try it then. The electricians have got a mess to square away in the maneuvering room."

Morton called for one diesel engine started up so that the suction of air into the engines would clear smoke from the after part of the ship. The boat could move barely enough to keep from broaching in the heavy seas. With the smoke cleared, electricians began replacing burned motor and generator parts with spares. The main induction system was cleared of water and the after torpedo room pumped dry. A second engine was put on the line and *Wahoo* was able to creep ahead and charge batteries.

The worst was over, but it was a close-run thing, a near-fatal ordeal. Dick O'Kane considered the fight to save the ship a truly remarkable performance by dedicated petty officers who knew their jobs. The next day the storm abated, but it had showed O'Kane what an angry ocean could do to a fleet submarine, even one that had just racked up the war's best patrol so far.

On leaving the Yellow Sea, Mush Morton purposely delayed sending a departure report to ComSubPac until well clear of the Empire. Now, with the storm behind, he sent the message listing the astonishing number of enemy ships sunk. Morton added a note about the torpedoes: "ONE SURFACE RUNNER X ONE DUD X FOUR PREMATURES."

Dick O'Kane knew that a submarine usually doesn't air its soiled laundry in a war patrol departure message, which was monitored by boats guarding the Fox frequency. But Morton was not a usual skipper and he had sufficient prestige to put *Wahoo*'s poor torpedo performance on the line for all to read. O'Kane thought Lockwood would thank Morton for doing so, since it provided immediate ammunition to support the Admiral's efforts to deactivate the magnetic feature of the exploder.

Admiral Lockwood quickly replied: "CONGRATULATIONS ON A JOB WELL DONE X JAPANESE THINK A SUBMARINE WOLF PACK OPERATING IN YELLOW SEA X ALL SHIPPING TIED UP."

Dick O'Kane had Radioman Young fix the message to the bulletin board in the crew's mess for all to see. Because *Wahoo* had sunk one and a half times as many ships as any previous U.S. war patrol, O'Kane knew the crew was looking forward to refit and relaxation at Pearl Harbor. Instead, *Wahoo* was assigned by radio to Midway Island for the rest period—great disappointment. O'Kane believed that the forward base was fine for use as a fuel stop and emergency repairs but hardly qualified as a relaxation area for exhausted submariners.

During quiet periods aboard ship, Mush Morton attended to getting his men promoted, even though the boat might not carry a complement for a particular rating. He believed Gunner's Mate First Class William Carr, for instance, should be made a chief petty officer—and so ordered.

Yeoman Sterling cautioned, "We don't have any authority to do that, Captain. There's no allowance for rating a chief gunner's mate while on a submarine. The only way I know it can be done is to transfer him to the Squadron staff with a recommendation for promotion—and to get him back after he's been rated."

"Go ahead and make out the papers," Morton instructed. "Leave the space for authority blank and after I see Admiral Lockwood, I'll have authority for you. This business of trans-

ferring men to the Squadron to get them rated is the bunk.
When I decide I want a man rated, I'm going to rate him."

"Aye, aye, sir," Sterling said, "but I'm afraid the Bureau of
Personnel will frown on it. They won't like it."

"To hell with the Bureau," Morton snapped, "and their antique methods. We're the ones fighting this war, and I'm
going to reward my men when they deserve it."

When "Guns" Carr checked later with Sterling, he asked,
"Did the captain get an authority?"

"Yep," Sterling said, "I'm to fill in that you were rated by
reason of meritorious conduct on *Wahoo*'s war patrol."

"Really?" Carr asked, suddenly full of pride.

"That's right," Sterling said. "If Mush says he's gonna pull
a rabbit from a hat, I'm gonna start looking for a carrot."

On arrival at Midway, tying up near the sub tender *Sperry*,
Wahoo proudly displayed Mush Morton's hand-sewn battle
flag. Though there was less brass in attendance for this most
successful patrol, the welcome was even warmer in the isolated
forward base. Morton and O'Kane headed for the Gooneyville
Lodge, which was originally the single-story, wooden Pan
American passenger hotel used during stopovers of the trans-
Pacific China Clipper in pre-war days. A sign now proclaimed:
"The best submariners in the world recuperate here."

It was set among the trees, and officers relaxed there while
the enlisted men had their own club. They could swim in the
lagoon, sunbathe on the atoll's beaches, play softball, volleyball, or poker and other card games—and eat and drink. Or
they could watch the antics of the thousands of gooneybirds,
a species of albatross. But that was it. The "Midway Hymn"
went: "Beautiful, beautiful Midway, Land where the gooneybirds grow. Beautiful, beautiful Midway, the goddamnedest
place that I know."

Yeoman Sterling turned over his duties to relief crew yeoman William White. White confided that he envied Sterling's
job aboard the famed *Wahoo* and would dearly like to make
a war patrol because he wanted to tell his grandchildren he
had made a run. Before heading off for the rest hotel, Sterling supervised the enforced transfer off *Wahoo* of one young

seaman who had disturbed the crew with his nightmares about being depth-charged.

Lieutenant Commander O'Kane made a point to issue only ten dollars a day to the crew because building contractor workmen gambled frequently on the island, fleecing the eager young sailors who were enticed into the game.

"Attempts to stop it are futile," O'Kane explained to Morton. "They are waiting like leeches for our crew to come ashore, so each sailor draws his pay but surrenders all but ten dollars to Pappy Rau who puts the balance in an envelope in the ship's safe. The lads can learn the easy way by losing only ten dollars, and if they want to try again, Pappy will disburse daily."

As a lark to relieve the monotony, Yeoman Sterling and Ship's Cook Juano Rennels caught a motor launch for the Naval Air Station at Sand Island across the lagoon and bummed a joyride aboard a PBY Catalina patrol plane. It turned out to be a full day's trip over the empty Pacific—uneventful and boring. But it served to give the two adventurers special status with their fellow crewmen who were treated, as Sterling gleefully put it, "to an embroidered tale of a great aerial saga."

At the Gooneyville Lodge, Mush Morton, Dick O'Kane and their colleagues learned of the tragic fate of a fellow submariner, Howard W. Gilmore, captain of *Growler.* Gilmore's first patrol took him to the cold, inhospitable waters of the Aleutians. Patrolling near Kiska Island, he encountered three anchored Japanese destroyers. Gilmore fired torpedoes at all three tin cans. One was sunk and two were badly damaged, earning Gilmore a Navy Cross for his aggressive patrol. On his second patrol, in the East China Sea, he sank four freighters for another Navy Cross. After an unsuccessful third run, Gilmore left Brisbane for the Southwest Pacific area to patrol between Rabaul and the Western Solomons. He quickly sank a sizeable passenger-cargo ship. He then shot at a gunboat, but the torpedo appeared to run deep under the target.

On the night of February 7, 1943, Gilmore prepared to attack the *Hayasaki,* a patrol ship. *Growler* went to Battle Surface, but *Hayasaki* charged at the submarine head-on, intending to ram. On the bridge, Gilmore ordered, "Left full rudder," to avoid being rammed, as he sounded the collision alarm. The sub was making 17 knots and the port turn carried *Growler*'s bow into the enemy ship with a loud, rending screech. The gunners on the damaged *Hayasaki* opened fire with machine guns, raking *Growler*'s bridge, killing a young ensign, Bill Williams, and a lookout, engineman W.F. Kelley.

Gilmore was badly wounded. He clutched a bridge frame with one arm, the other shoulder shattered and bloody, and shouted to the topside crewmen, "Clear the bridge." The OOD, the quartermaster, and two wounded lookouts hustled down the hatch, pulled by willing hands below through to the conning tower. They looked up at the badly bleeding Gilmore who ordered, "Get below." At the foot of the bridge ladder, the executive officer, Lieutenant Commander Arnold F. Schade, peered up waiting for Skipper Gilmore, alone on the bridge with the bodies of his men.

He heard Gilmore shout, "Take her down."

Bullets were striking *Growler*'s superstructure, punching holes in the bridge and striking the conning tower. Gilmore did not appear at the hatch. In the conning tower, Schade hesitated briefly. It was a terrible decision to make—to try to get back up on deck and rescue the wounded captain in the fusillade of bullets, thereby jeopardizing the ship or to follow his orders. "Flood negative," Schade ordered. "Flood safety. Take her down."

The collision had smashed *Growler*'s entire bow leaving an 18-foot section at a 90-degree angle with the forward torpedo tubes useless. Bullet holes in the conning tower allowed seawater to pour in. Schade held *Growler* steady while emergency repairs were carried out. Somehow, Schade managed later to surface, away from the destroyer, and conn his crippled ship back along the treacherous, 2,000-mile voyage through Japanese-patrolled islands and waters, returning to Brisbane. Exec Schade's patrol report was widely read. In his endorsement, Admiral Halsey, South Pacific Commander, wrote: "the Force commander is proud to extend his congratulations and commendation to this valiant ship and her courageous crew."

Commander Gilmore had sacrificed himself for his ship.

He was awarded the Medal of Honor, posthumously, the first submariner in the war to win the nation's highest decoration for heroism. Howard Gilmore's last words were enshrined in naval history: "Take her down."

At the Gooneyville, officers found that a big room had been set aside for submariners to meet and talk shop, corner tables for each submarine. Refrigerators along the wall were filled with bottled beer. O'Kane spotted Fritz Harlfinger, who had participated in the wretched Aleutian Islands campaign in the old *S-35,* and more recently as exec of *Whale* in patrols off the Mariana Islands and the main Japanese island of Honshu. Harlfinger was soon to establish a great record commanding *Trigger* with Ned Beach as his exec. Dick and Fritz were old friends, and quite alike in talent and temperament. Recounting his sub's Aleutian duty, Harlfinger told O'Kane, "The conditions those boats endured up there are simply indescribable. It was God-awful. Cold. Dreary. Foggy. Ice glaze. The periscopes froze. The decks and lifelines were caked with ice. Blizzards. You could never get a navigational fix." O'Kane was thankful that he had not been assigned any Aleutian patrols.

O'Kane was swapping stories with Harlfinger when Fritz jerked his thumb in the direction of an adjacent table where Commander MacMillan, the *Wahoo*'s recent PCO, was rattling on in an extended criticism of the patrol. MacMillan belittled most everything that *Wahoo* had accomplished on this record-breaking patrol. He included some disparaging remarks about Morton and O'Kane. MacMillan disapproved of the informal manner in which *Wahoo*'s conning tower was run during attacks, and added that he made a negative report to the squadron commander on *Sperry* on arrival. MacMillan's frustration at seeing officers several years his junior commanding *Wahoo* and expertly firing torpedoes seemed to O'Kane to have built up resentment in the older officer. MacMillan still appeared aggrieved that he didn't get command of *Wahoo* on commissioning as expected. There was bound to be some clash between the strong personalities of

Mush and Dick on one side and Commander MacMillan on the other.

Mush Morton, flipping the pages of *Life* magazine, was within earshot of MacMillan and heard some remarks. He beckoned to O'Kane.

"Let's get out of here, Dick, before we get into a fight," Morton said. In furious silence, the pair headed for the dock where *Wahoo* was moored. Once there, Mush Morton changed his mind.

"Let's go back and square this away," he said. O'Kane felt he could read Mush's thoughts: "Say what you want about me, but don't lambaste my ship and crew!" They headed back for the Gooneyville, but, possibly in anticipation, the corner tables had been cleared, and the place was shutting down. O'Kane, who had been up most of the previous night, said he was headed for bed.

Morton went to the officers' club and got into a crap game to let off steam. O'Kane may have changed his mind about hitting the sack. He was furious with MacMillan. The next morning, he ordered that Commander MacMillan's leftover belongings be placed on the dock and the ungrateful PCO not be allowed back aboard.

Meanwhile, Morton had received an urgent summons from Admiral Lockwood to fly to Pearl Harbor to discuss *Wahoo*'s brilliant patrol personally. O'Kane took over their corner suite, which during late afternoons and early evenings became an informal war patrol seminar. The officers exchanged ideas derived from their own and other's patrols, often in great detail at O'Kane's prodding. Dick thought he learned much from these bull sessions, especially from Fritz Harlfinger.

A few days later, Yeoman Sterling noticed that O'Kane showed up on *Wahoo* with a shiny black eye, which led to widespread speculation that the executive officer might have had it out with Commander MacMillan. Roger Paine speculated that Mush and Dick had serious personality conflict with Commander MacMillan and that sparks could easily have flown. O'Kane remained silent on the subject. "It turned out to be the best-guarded secret the Navy ever had," Yeoman Sterling said.

CHAPTER EIGHT

"There is Something Wrong with These Torpedoes"

At Midway, word reached Morton and O'Kane that in addition to Dick's old boat *Argonaut,* three other submarines had recently been lost operating out of Brisbane under the overall command of Captain Jimmy Fife. Ralph Christie, though now a rear admiral, lost a bureaucratic fight to base in Brisbane. He was sent to Perth–Fremantle to be in charge of submarines there—even though Brisbane usually had more boats under its command. Captain Fife in Brisbane decided that many skippers were over-cautious and should be quickly relieved if they didn't measure up on a war patrol.

Because of the code-breakers' efforts intercepting Japanese maritime traffic, sub force commanders were privy to a steady flow of reports on enemy ship movements. Fife decided to use the approach German Admiral Karl Doenitz had employed with his U-boats in the Atlantic and placed his submarines on a kind of ocean checkerboard, tightly controlling their movements from Brisbane. But this meant frequent messages back and forth—instructions and acknowledgements— which risked enemy detection. It was not a good policy.

Fife had sent Dick O'Kane's old boat, the elderly *Argonaut,* which carried the Marines to Makin Island, on a war patrol— a mission for which she was no longer suitable. In the dangerous area between Bougainville and New Britain Islands, the big, clumsy boat was set upon by Japanese destroyers and went down with 105 men aboard. Three other boats were lost: *Amberjack, Grampus,* and *Triton.* They were battle-tested, but Fife moved them around often with frequent radio traffic issuing to and from Brisbane. They achieved little, and failed to return.

"Tough luck," the cold-blooded Fife wrote in a letter to Lockwood, "but they can't get Japs without taking chances . . . don't think the time has arrived to inject caution into the system because it is too difficult to overcome again."

An informal investigation was begun to determine how to avoid such losses. The probe exonerated Fife, but his rival, Ralph Christie in Perth, believed that there was altogether too much radio traffic to and from the submarines, which the Japanese could monitor and act accordingly. Christie made his feelings known; bad blood developed between Christie and Fife in the Australia command.

The officers at Midway and other sub bases continued to worry about the war patrol reports of defective torpedoes. Mush Morton and Dick O'Kane had just experienced the frustration of firing erratic or dud torpedoes on *Wahoo*'s dangerous Yellow Sea patrol. In Fremantle, Red Ramage returned on *Trout* after his third patrol. One of the best skippers in the Force, Ramage was furious that his torpedoes had malfunctioned during his run off Indochina. As he readied for a fourth patrol, which included an unpopular mine-laying mission, he called on his boss, Admiral Christie, a developer of the magnetic exploder.

"How many torpedoes have you got?" Christie asked.

"I've got sixteen torpedoes and twenty-three mines on board," Ramage answered.

"Well, I want you to get sixteen ships with those torpedoes," Christie replied in a misplaced jest.

Ramage replied curtly, "Admiral, if I get twenty-five percent reliable performance on your torpedoes, I'll be happy. By the same token, you will be overjoyed because there is something wrong with these torpedoes and they can't be relied on."

This deliberate needle infuriated Christie who was quick to condemn anyone who complained about the magnetic torpedoes. The meeting grew heated.

"This is just small talk and people are trying to berate these torpedoes and there's nothing to it," Christie insisted.

Staff officer Tex McLean grabbed Ramage and pulled him out of Christie's office. On the drive from Perth to Fremantle, McLean said, "You know, Red, you're very lucky to be going to sea."

Ramage shot back, "I think you've got that turned around a little bit. I think what you mean to say is we are very lucky to be coming back from sea. You can just grab your bag and come along with me. I'll be glad to show you first hand how the torpedoes don't operate."

That stopped the conversation.

On his next patrol, Ramage's torpedoes again did not function well, but Christie blamed the skipper's set-ups and shooting. He sent Ramage back to the States for new construction. Ramage left believing that Admiral Christie inspired little confidence among his submariners. He would be heard from again.

The difficulty in tackling the torpedo problem was that they often worked, as was the case during *Wahoo*'s third patrol. In a successful Fremantle patrol, William "Wild Bill" Post, former exec of Dick O'Kane's *Argonaut,* commanded *Gudgeon* with Exec Mike Shea—both of them had been surfaced after a negative performance at the Battle of Midway. In this second chance, Christie credited Post with sinking four ships. Because Skipper Post commended the magnetic exploders, Admiral Christie was doubly happy.

Post's performance tended to confirm Christie in his belief that it was sloppy performance on the part of a submarine crew that led to poor bags of enemy ships. On his next patrol, Post invented the "up-the-kilt" shot by firing four fish directly at the stern of a huge passenger ship, the *Kamakura Maru,* as it moved away from *Gudgeon*'s bow. He heard three hits and when he surfaced he saw the ship sinking, the largest vessel sunk by a U.S. submarine to date. For his successful patrols, Bill Post was awarded two Navy Crosses.

In Fremantle, submariners continued to complain about the dud fish. They liked to quote the message of *Thresher*'s Moke Millican, reporting on hits with dud torpedoes: "I clinked him with a clunk."

Firmly settled in at Pearl Harbor, Admiral Lockwood addressed again the perplexing torpedo matter. His incoming sub captains believed the magnetic device was prematurely exploded by the target's magnetic field, and that the explosions and splashes seen through periscopes were often mistaken for genuine hits. Some captains were now deactivating the magnetic device and firing their fish with simple contact exploders, though this was still against Sub Force policy.

Unfortunately, Lockwood believed—and pointed out—that Mush Morton had used the magnetic exploder on his famous first patrol from Brisbane. Morton's results on his first two patrols were so spectacular that they continued to influence Lockwood's assessment of the efficacy of the magnetic exploder, but Morton had changed his mind and so would Lockwood.

Lockwood's view reversed when he received the full patrol report of *Tunny*'s encounter with a Japanese carrier force. *Tunny* was commanded by John A. Scott, who on his first run sank two large freighters and damaged an even larger transport—an excellent performance. On *Tunny*'s next patrol, Scott was tipped off by an Ultra from Pearl and got into position in the middle of the carriers and escorts. It was a rare opportunity offered to few skippers during the war. Scott set the depth of his torpedoes to run at 10 feet to make sure there was no trouble with the magnetic exploders. He figured that if the target's magnetic attraction did not function the contact exploder would. Scott launched ten torpedoes at the close range of 800 yards at the ships. As he dived to avoid escorts, he heard seven hits. Scott and his crew were jubilant when they returned to Pearl—as was the welcoming brass. The skipper received glowing endorsements from division, squadron, force, and fleet commanders. Then came the bad news from code-breakers: intercepted Japanese messages indicated that one carrier had been damaged, but four torpedoes aimed at a second flat-top were premature, exploding 50 yards from target. Here was direct testimony from the enemy that American torpedoes were duds; not from excited U.S. skippers, but from the Japanese themselves.

Lockwood was mystified. In a conversation with Admiral Nimitz, the Pacific Fleet commander told him, "Lockwood, either our torpedoes are defective or the Japs have some secret defense which triggers them prematurely." Did the

Japanese have a device to cause premature explosions? Whatever the case, ComSubPac was now convinced that the magnetic torpedo was somehow defective. In messages to Ralph Christie in Perth, Lockwood expressed his concern. But Admiral Christie still swore by the magnetic exploder he had helped develop. Christie, in fact, continued to insist his skippers use them, against their own much better judgment. Christie's uncompromising position was creating a serious breach between him and Lockwood—and between policies guiding the submarines of the two Pacific sub commands.

Lockwood thought the *Tunny* incident was positive proof of the unreliability of the magnetic torpedo. While Mush Morton and Dick O'Kane readied *Wahoo* for a fifth patrol in Midway, Lockwood after debriefing Morton in Pearl Harbor flew to Washington to raise the torpedo question personally.

The Westinghouse Corporation had promised an electric torpedo, the Mark 18, to be delivered to the submarine force by the middle of 1942. This was an ideal weapon, developed by both the Germans and the Japanese, which would provide a wakeless torpedo run to the enemy target.

The bright young combat submariner, Eli Reich, a native New Yorker, was executive officer of *Lapon,* a newly commissioned submarine assigned temporarily to assist in the test firings of the electric Mark 18 at the Newport Torpedo Station. Reich, his skipper Oliver Kirk, and *Lapon*'s own torpedomen nosed around the secret factory area on Gould Island. They soon found that the Westinghouse technicians in charge of the electrics were not receiving any help from the Newport Torpedo Station regulars, who were developing their own, rival electric torpedo, the Mark 2. "The Westinghouse people were getting kicked around," Reich reported. "We very quickly got that feeling that there was something wrong at Newport and not just the torpedo. The atmosphere and the situation was simply sickening."

Reich and Kirk thought the Mark 18 was a potentially fine weapon. They tested many torpedoes, firing from *Lapon* at dockside and in Narragansett Bay. They found that the torpedoes were running erratically because the torque generated by the large motor brushed the tail of the fish against the tube

and shutters during launch. This caused them to run erratically. Working with Westinghouse engineers they devised a
way to get the torpedoes to clear the tubes properly and move
into the water correctly.

After Reich and Kirk spent six weeks helping to develop a
workable electric torpedo, *Lapon* continued on a shakedown
run to Panama and Pearl Harbor. While underway, Reich
wrote a report of the difficulties at Newport, which Oliver
Kirk signed. They referred to the "devious workings of this
queer place." They presented it to Dick Voge, Lockwood's
operations officer. Voge told the young officers that Lockwood had suspected all along that something was fishy at
Newport and was glad to have a first-hand report. Lockwood
sent personally for Kirk and Reich and asked for written details. They added material they had left out of their memo to
Voge. Lockwood promised quick action.

The memo suggested a combat submariner be assigned as
an "expediter" to the Torpedo Station. Word of the Kirk–Reich
memo eventually worked its way to Admiral King who assigned the Navy's Inspector General to look into the matter.
This admiral reported back that Newport had failed to work
closely with Westinghouse, partly because Newport had its
own electric torpedo, the Mark 2, in development, and treated
the Westinghouse model as an unwanted competitor. At a
meeting of a regular Submarine Officers' Conference in
Washington, which he attended, Charlie Lockwood was blunt.
"If the Bureau of Ordnance can't provide us with torpedoes
that will hit and explode," he pleaded, "then for God's sake,
get the Bureau of Ships to design a boat hook with which we
can rip the plates off a target's side."

Rear Admiral William P. "Spike" Blandy, Chief of the Bureau of Ordnance, was furious with his old friend Lockwood. He told him heatedly, "I don't know whether it's part
of your mission to discredit the Bureau of Ordnance but you
seem to be doing a pretty good job of it."

Lockwood replied, "Well, Spike, if anything I have said
will get the Bureau off its duff and get some action, I will
feel that my trip has not been wasted."

Lockwood's outburst resulted in Blandy's agreeing that

something had to be done pronto. Blandy wrote Lockwood: "Send me a damn good officer who knows torpedoes as well as submarines and you will get results."

With the faulty torpedo situation still unresolved—almost a year and a half into the war—Mush Morton and Dick O'Kane finished preparations for *Wahoo*'s fifth patrol, and Morton's third as skipper. Ensigns Jack Griggs and John Campbell were given home leaves. A new junior reservist, Ensign Eugene E. Fiedler from Brooklyn, with a background in radar operations, came aboard as low man on the ward-room totem pole. His qualifications, O'Kane thought, made him a welcome addition to *Wahoo*.

Increasingly, reserve officers were playing a major role in filling out submarine wardrooms, just as they were in other ships of the fleet. While sub skippers and execs at this stage of the war were inevitably Naval Academy men, sometimes known as "trade school" graduates, many junior officers were reservists—civilians until they entered the Navy in wartime. They were often called "ninety-day wonders," be-cause of their three-month midshipmen school courses that turned them into new ensigns.

Though some regular Navy officers looked down on re-servists, that attitude rarely existed on submarines, espe-cially *Wahoo*. Academy graduates on *Wahoo* like O'Kane, George Grider and Roger Paine actually welcomed reservists because they often had a fresher and more innovative ap-proach to their duties than regular officers. Grider and Paine thought their initiative wasn't blinkered by traditional con-cepts of naval warfare learned at the Academy and rigor-ously followed. On submarines, young officers were given much more responsibility than on capital ships like carriers, battleships, and cruisers.

The old pro, Chief of the Boat Pappy Rau, was transferred to the Submarine School at New London. Promoted Chief Gunner's Mate Bill Carr replaced him, the young pro. In all, there were sixteen new hands aboard. And *Wahoo* carried an-other PCO, Lieutenant Commander Johnny Moore, a bright, appealing young officer.

Mush Morton returned from his flight to Pearl Harbor

with medals for the crew issued by Admiral Lockwood. Mush received his second Navy Cross, and Dick his second Silver Star. Other officers and crew were rewarded accordingly. Lockwood was delighted by *Wahoo*'s performance. Morton's second patrol as CO had resulted in nine ships sunk. By contrast, the other twenty-eight war patrols departing Pearl during the first three months of 1943 downed only twenty-five ships in all.

Medals were important for the prestige and standing they gave the officers and men of a submarine, but awards also enhanced promotion chances for officers. When time came for selection to a higher grade, promotion boards took serious note of decorations won in combat. Earlier in the war, the awards process took an inordinate amount of time; recommendations had to be reviewed all the way up the chain of command. By the time the awards came through, the submarine might be sunk, the crew lost. O'Kane didn't believe that posthumously awarded medals served as much of an incentive. The new policy was much quicker and was based on the number of ships sunk.

As exec, Dick O'Kane was central to getting the officers and crew recommended for the valuable awards. Mush Morton was generous to the crew and wanted to reward them for their combat performance, but he hated paperwork, and was slow to draft and sign the necessary submissions for awards. Roger Paine was grateful to Dick because he brought individual citations to Morton's attention and then followed up the paperwork to insure that a man got his medal. In Roger Paine's case, it was a Silver Star, the third highest award for gallantry in action.

Without fanfare, *Wahoo* slipped her lines at Midway at 1500, April 25, 1943, off on her fifth patrol, this time for the Kuril Islands, the chain that runs north from Japan to the Soviet peninsula of Kamchatka. *Wahoo* was ordered to check a report that a Japanese surface force was heading for the Aleutians. On reaching the Kurils, O'Kane was unhappy to learn that *Wahoo*'s cranky main battery, of experimental design, was still not able to build up a full charge despite repairs at Midway. This meant Mush and he would have to be careful about how long *Wahoo* remained underwater during attacks and evasions.

Passing through hail and snow, the crew found the North Pacific climate weird after previous patrols in tropical waters. The latitude was about the same as Newfoundland. *Wahoo* gingerly approached through fog banks and ice chunks, and reached a landfall at snowcapped Onekotan Island covering the Sea of Okhotsk.

Yeoman Sterling, standing bridge watches, had to add another piece of clothing to go on lookout. On watch, it had begun to sleet and snow, and he stood by helplessly trying to peer into a darkness that was not penetrable with the human eye. He came off watch shivering, teeth chattering, with his nose and ears so cold he was afraid to touch them for fear they would shatter into crystallized fragments.

As *Wahoo* eased ahead, Sterling had the impression that there was no ocean to be seen but instead a vast thin ice plain. Jagged rock islands pierced this ice at irregular intervals. *Wahoo*'s nose cleared a pathway through the 6 or 8 inches of ice so smoothly that the surface seemed to part at her approach. It gave the illusion that *Wahoo* was standing still and the ice was moving.

Mush Morton headed south to reconnoiter Matsuwa, a Japanese island with an air base. PCO Moore at the conn spotted a Japanese ship, and the attack party took over with O'Kane at the periscope. The target was a choice one: a big seaplane tender with aircraft on deck, *Kamikawa Maru*.

The familiar instruction came from the relaxed Morton: "Any time, Dick."

O'Kane waited for a few tense moments to bring the periscope wire aligned to the forward mast of the target.

"Fire!" O'Kane said, and Morton pushed the firing plunger three times.

The first torpedo exploded with an enormous detonation between the stack and the bridge. The ship rolled to port, but kept moving. The second torpedo headed directly for the engine room. It was a dud. The third missed. The ship was listing about 5 degrees, but was still making 11 knots and heading back towards the western side of the Kurils.

Wahoo's failing batteries did not permit her to follow under-water for a daylight attack. In a surface attack, an alerted tar-get ship could outgun the submarine.

Mush Morton was furious that a torpedo shot which shouldn't—couldn't—have missed turned out to be either erratic or a dud. The torpedo problem was again affecting *Wahoo* and Mush Morton personally.

The next morning, after the daily trim dive, a tangle of fish was found on deck. Jesus Manalesay, the officers' steward, proudly brought below two handfuls of squid.

"Do you know how to cook them?" O'Kane inquired.

"Yes, sir," Manalesay answered, and scurried aft. O'Kane anticipated something crisp and fried, but the squid came back boiled and with a peculiar sour taste. After eating a cou-ple, O'Kane asked about the taste.

"Oh, you have to boil this kind of squid in vinegar to take out the poison," the steward replied.

As soon as Manalesay disappeared, O'Kane and the offi-cers deep-sixed the remainder of the squid.

Wahoo's operation order called for the submarine to patrol off the main Japanese island of Honshu. Arriving near the northern coast, the lookouts sighted one large freighter and a smaller escort with gun mounts. The attack party quickly fig-ured out a set-up.

O'Kane fired two torpedoes at the larger ship and a spread of four at the escort. The first torpedo loaded with torpex hit the freighter *Toman Maru* and broke her back. However, the escort managed to thread the four-fish spread without dam-age, so *Wahoo* rigged for depth charge. Indeed, depth charges rained down, but *Wahoo* was able by silent running to get away from the main drop zone. Those that followed seemed less severe, O'Kane thought, though falling depth charges were never a laughing matter. Though the escort got away, O'Kane was happy that at least new *Wahoo* sailors would get their submarine combat pins and had been introduced to depth charges dropped in anger.

Morton sidled by O'Kane's room and said, "Dick, I've been thinking about this morning, our diving 12 miles off the coast. When the two of us get involved, it's like a committee decision. We are each tempered by our thought of what the other is considering, and we don't come down with the quick, aggressive decision either of us would make if alone. After thinking it over, I realize that you wanted to make a dash for the coast. Now as navigator, you have to be up there anyway. So starting in the morning, I want you to take *Wahoo* in and plunk her down, and then call me when you've got a ship."

The captain, O'Kane mused, reflected his own thinking. His response was a hearty: "Aye, aye, sir."

O'Kane laid out a route for Kobe Saki Bay farther down the coast and *Wahoo,* with a third of the crew on watch, settled into a comfortable routine: a battery charge, good meals on time, movies, hot rolls, and bread from the oven. O'Kane liked the way the new operating procedure worked, with the captain arriving refreshed, sizing up the situation, and then returning to his cabin or the wardroom. Under Morton, *Wahoo* had become a fast-moving boat and left the enemy anti-submarine forces far behind—or guessing. Many of *Wahoo*'s newer hands volunteered for *Wahoo* because Mush Morton was their idea of a great wartime skipper—one who would lead his crew into battle and swiftly get them out. Now this was made more difficult by a high ratio of escorts, *Wahoo*'s failing battery, and a very confining operating area.

That evening, *Wahoo* found a three-ship convoy—a large auxiliary and two freighter-types—moving down the coast only 1,500 yards from the beach. The set-up was near perfect: O'Kane fired three torpedoes at the big vessel aiming for her foremast, midship, and mainmast. The first torpedo exploded after 50 seconds, only halfway to the target. The second fish running down the same track was deflected by the premature blast and it failed to explode. The third hit the point of aim, sending a column of water about 10 feet into the air, but this was only the air flask rupturing: the warhead was a dud.

Morton ordered *Wahoo* to dive deep and clear the area. That burst of speed placed the resulting depth charges well astern. In the wardroom that night, *Wahoo*'s officers engaged in a heated discussion about the faulty torpedoes. O'Kane pointed out that both sound operators reported the thud of the dud at the same time that a column of water about 10 feet high was observed at the target's side, abreast of her foremast as the air flasks exploded. Thus Dick O'Kane put his finger on a troubling mystery: the exploding air flask appeared to the eye at the periscope as a legitimate hit, but was actually a dud warhead. Once again, the officers went over potential reasons for the magnetic exploder failures.

O'Kane argued that targets could have irregular magnetic signatures that triggered the delicate exploder before it reached the ship—or not at all. Or the earth's magnetic field in this area might affect the exploders. O'Kane thought that this had led to the firing of large salvos when a single, reliable torpedo and exploder would have sufficed. On the last two patrols, *Wahoo* had carried this combination of unpredictable exploders and unreliable torpedoes, but Mush obtained results by hammering away with what *Wahoo* had.

Early the next morning, *Wahoo* picked up a large tanker and freighter, without escort, hugging the coast. The submarine dived 5 miles ahead of the enemy ships. O'Kane fired three torpedoes at the tanker and three more at the large freighter. The first fish hit the tanker *Takao Maru;* the fourth and fifth blasted the freighter, *Jinmu Maru.* Through the second periscope PCO Moore watched both ships sink.

That evening, the men on *Wahoo*'s bridge reported smoke on the horizon. Mush Morton closed on the contact, which developed into two ships—a large and a small freighter. Morton pushed *Wahoo* on the surface forward of the freighters' track. After the evening meal, he ordered the boat submerged for an attack in the moonlight.

Dick O'Kane fired two torpedoes at the largest freighter of the *Anyo Maru* class, and two more at the second cargo vessel. Dick heard the zing, felt the shudder, and the poppet pressure from all four torpedoes. Soundman Buckley called "All hot, straight, and normal." But only the first torpedo aimed at the large freighter's mainmast detonated. Morton ordered *Wahoo* surfaced for an end-around and a night surface attack. The top lookouts spotted smoke again. *Wahoo* caught up with the *Anyo Maru.*

O'Kane ordered the last bow torpedo fired. But no phosphorescent wake was sighted. Morton maneuvered for a stern shot and O'Kane fired *Wahoo*'s last torpedo. The fish struck between the target's stack and bridge with an explosion audible on *Wahoo*'s bridge, but it lacked the "whack" of a true detonation. Morton figured it was a low order explosion. The *Anyo Maru* turned away with sparks flowing about the deck above the hit, but still under control. The second ship began firing at *Wahoo,* so Morton ordered a dive.

Several minutes later, *Wahoo* surfaced again, and with no more torpedoes, Morton called for Battle Surface, intending to destroy *Anyo Maru* with *Wahoo*'s deck gun. But the sister ship opened fire again, and Morton ordered the gun crew below.

"That whole lousy maru's not worth one of my crew," Morton said. Feeling helpless, Mush Morton ordered *Wahoo* to clear the area, moving off to deep water. With all torpedoes expended, Morton continued heading *Wahoo* eastward for the barn.

Eight days later, on arriving at Pearl Harbor, SubPac brass turned out at the pier. Morton and O'Kane were disappointed that more ships had not been sunk, even though *Wahoo* accounted for three ships down and two damaged. But compared to the other Pearl Harbor boats' patrols, *Wahoo*'s was the best. Dick O'Kane believed the other boats had experienced similar troubles with torpedoes.

Wahoo's fifth patrol, while somewhat disappointing, had a positive effect. Once ashore, Mush Morton roared into Admiral Lockwood's office in a rage. In rough sailor's language, he castigated the Mark 14 torpedo, listing his prematures, duds and erratics. After all, Mush Morton was Lockwood's star: he and O'Kane had conducted a brilliantly aggressive patrol. *Wahoo* had one of the best torpedo attack teams in the Force. Had the torpedoes functioned properly, *Wahoo* would have sunk six ships, not three.

Both Mush Morton and Dick O'Kane were angry and frustrated with *Wahoo*'s experience. The report by Morton and O'Kane—following similar accounts from proven skippers like Vernon "Rebel" Lowrance in *Kingfish,* John Scott

in *Tunny,* and Willis Thomas in *Pompano*—at long last convinced Lockwood that something was drastically wrong with
the magnetic exploder. He decided it should be deactivated,
but he wanted one last consultation with Admiral Spike
Blandy at BuOrd.

Deferring to the powerful Bureau of Ordnance was an
ingrained custom for senior navy commanders, including
Charles Lockwood, so he did not immediately order tests
at the Submarine Base—which was his and Dick Voge's
inclination—but waited for Blandy to come up with answers.
They waited in vain.

In Pearl, PCO Johnny Moore went on to command his own
boat, *Grayback,* running up a splendid record. By this time,
Wahoo's officers and crew were worn down. *Wahoo* was
worn, too. She had established the best record in the Sub
Force in a few short months under Mush Morton. Lockwood
decided the boat needed a major overhaul at Mare Island.
Mush Morton, though he never mentioned it to the crew or to
the brass, was suffering from a chronic prostate infection,
which needed treatment during and between patrols. The ail-
ment was bothering him again. So, having rung up an unpar-
alleled record, *Wahoo* and her crew were happy to depart
Pearl for the Golden Gate and San Francisco Bay.

Dick O'Kane had won three Silver Stars and a Commendation Ribbon in six war patrols. He added much toward
making *Wahoo* the star of the Pacific Fleet Submarine Force.
He was admired by the crew who realized how much their
exec had contributed to Mush Morton's success. They knew
O'Kane could be stern, but he was always fair. If disciplinary problems came up, he settled them quietly without
bothering the captain. The word went around the crew how
coolly O'Kane comported himself during their attacks. When
O'Kane made the rounds, he instilled quiet confidence.

"Dick O'Kane was a brilliant man," James Lavine, a
boatswain's mate from the Chicago area, said of his exec.
"He had to be one of the best officers in the Navy."

Walter Heiden, an electrician's mate who lived in Thiens-
ville, Wisconsin, believed that "O'Kane had a difficult job

under Kennedy, being an exec to a skipper who was afraid to shoot torpedoes. O'Kane was gung-ho. But he didn't hound the men on the boat. You could see him developing on *Wahoo*. You could see that he was determined to sink a lot of ships."

Dick O'Kane and Mush Morton had become the closest personal friends. They were two mavericks who had worked out well together, but this would be Dick's last voyage aboard mighty *Wahoo* with Mush the Magnificent. In a message received at sea, Lieutenant Commander O'Kane was ordered to the U.S. for new construction. In Mare Island he would be detached from the most famous submarine of the Pacific War. He would get what every serious submarine officer yearned for: his own command, USS *Tang*.

CHAPTER NINE

"From Knowledge, Sea Power"

On the speedy run from Pearl to San Francisco Bay, Dick O'Kane turned the navigator's duties over to Roger Paine, who would be his replacement as executive officer. *Wahoo* rendezvoused off the Farallon Islands with the escorting destroyer *Lawrence*. The tin can messaged *Wahoo*: "FROM COMWESSEAFRON [Commander Western Sea Frontier] CONGRATULATIONS AND WELCOME TO THE STATES."

The customary morning fog was dissipated by a weather front, and *Wahoo* sailed beneath the rust-red Golden Gate Bridge with a glorious sunrise over the East Bay hills. O'Kane thought the bridge was man's most beautiful creation in steel. Moving slowly through the bay, past Alcatraz and Angel Islands, *Wahoo* turned north and slowed to a creep to allow the crew to breakfast and dress themselves and the ship in proper homecoming style. A special yardarm was rigged atop the radar mast with the captured large house flags of the *Nittsu Maru* flying to port and starboard. The halyards carried small Japanese flags marking the ships *Wahoo* had sent to the bottom.

Mush Morton personally arranged a special pennant that remained furled, attached to the attack periscope. *Wahoo* moved past Berkeley, with its landmark University of California campanile, and Richmond on the right, into San Pablo Bay. She swung east toward Carquinez Strait, then executed a sharp turn north to enter the Napa River, between Vallejo and Mare Island.

The Mare Island waterfront was packed with well-wishers and a band played, "California, Here I Come." As *Wahoo* prepared to tie up, Captain Morton nodded to Signalman Simonetti who broke the pennant free from the scope, the breeze snapping the same message it delivered in Pearl Harbor.

On the crowded dock, the wife of Rear Admiral W.L. Friedell, the Navy Yard Commandant and chief greeter, peered through her glasses and asked her husband what the pennant said.

"Madame," the Admiral replied, "that reads, 'Shoot the Sons of Bitches!' "

Now, nearly a year after she had left, *Wahoo* was back at her Mare Island birthplace. O'Kane was grateful that the Submarine Detail office in Washington had picked a new construction boat at a yard near his family. His wife, Ernestine, and his young children, Marsha and James, lived in a rented apartment in Ignacio, 20 miles across San Pablo Bay from Mare Island and Vallejo. He stepped off *Wahoo*'s gangplank to greet his family. He was delighted to be home, knowing he would have plenty of time with his wife and children while he put *Tang* into commission. But he was still exec of *Wahoo* and had to attend to many final details. The next morning O'Kane was back aboard.

Yeoman Sterling had drawn up thirty-day leave papers for the entire crew. O'Kane divided the list into two sections. The first was those who had been on *Wahoo* the longest. They would take off immediately. The second section would shove off when the first returned. *Wahoo*'s lines had hardly gone over the side, when the first half of the crew was on their way. Of the men left behind, those who didn't have the duty were given liberty ashore in Vallejo. Yeoman Sterling was on the first leave list but he had clerical details to clean up before departing, so he telephoned his girlfriend in Los Angeles asking her to marry him. She arrived within two days for the wedding.

Forest introduced his bride Marie to Mush Morton and Dick O'Kane. Morton, about to depart on his own thirty-day leave to see his wife Harriet and two children in Los Angeles, offered hasty congratulations.

Dick O'Kane remained on board as acting commanding officer of *Wahoo*. His first action as CO was to conn the boat into dry dock. His second was to order immediate leaves for every crewman who could be spared. Then O'Kane called Sterling aside.

"Yeo, if you want to make out your leave papers now, I'll sign them."

"It won't take five minutes, sir."

"If you want to take the time," O'Kane added with a smile, "you can make out the papers rating you to Yeoman First Class. Let's call it a wedding present."

"Yes, sir," came the happy response. In a few minutes, Sterling returned topside: he was a first class petty officer with thirty days' leave, and a pretty wife to take on honeymoon.

Dick and Ernestine O'Kane were invited to stand up for the wedding of *Wahoo*'s Lieutenant Chandler Jackson and his bride, Iona, a Navy WAVE, at the Mare Island chapel. The O'Kanes gave a reception for the new couple at their place in Ignacio with guests including *Wahoo* officers who lived in the Vallejo area.

A month later, Mush Morton returned from leave, refreshed after a spell in a naval hospital in Long Beach for treatment of his cranky prostate gland. *Wahoo* crewmembers began returning. Some sailors were transferred. New men joined the ship.

Dick O'Kane had a farewell lunch with Mush Morton in *Wahoo*'s wardroom. Then he left *Wahoo* for the last time, heading for *Tang*. He carried an oblong, silver cigarette box, engraved to him from the officers and crew of *Wahoo*. It was a bittersweet farewell. Dick had become a close friend of his mentor, Mush Morton. He had won the respect of *Wahoo*'s crew. He was considered tough but fair and the men had come to see him as a natural leader of men. He went to bat for them when they got into trouble. That counted.

The silver gift box left Dick O'Kane with misty eyes as he waved good-bye to *Wahoo* from dockside. He was entering a new phase in his life and career.

Richard Hetherington O'Kane was born within the salt smell of the sea, on February 2, 1911, in Dover, New Hampshire.

Dover is a manufacturing city at the falls of the Coheco River where it meets the Piscataqua, just northwest of the big Portsmouth Navy Yard at Kittery, Maine, which built fine submarines. Dick was the son of Walter Collins O'Kane of Irish extraction and his wife, who had the unusual name of Clifford Hetherington. He was the youngest of four children. Walter O'Kane was professor of entomology at the University of New Hampshire at nearby Durham on the Oyster River. The family lived on a farm just outside of Durham, where Richard learned early on to perform daily chores, and developed a knack for fixing things mechanical. The many waterways in the area made sailing a popular sport, and young Dick was an enthusiast. He combined his interests by building a sailboat with a Maytag washer engine.

Inculcated by his parents in the value of education, young O'Kane won a part-scholarship in 1925 to Phillips Academy in Andover, Massachusetts, a posh prep school which numbered among its students Humphrey Bogart, artist Joseph Cornell, Dr. Benjamin Spock, photographer Walker Evans, Judge Gerhard Gesell, authors James Ramsey Ullman and Ring Lardner Jr., and Presidents Bush, senior and junior. Andover was a boarding school with about 650 students when O'Kane entered. It was a conservative place, white and elite, but prided itself on having scholarship students. Young Richard waited on tables and worked in the cafeteria for his part-scholarship.

There was a prominent old-boy network and many graduates went on to Ivy League colleges and then into Wall Street, East Coast law firms, big business, or government. Very few chose the Navy for a career. Andover's curriculum was an academic one with Latin, Greek, math, and science among the courses. Graduates remember that Andover was fairly strict then and not a particularly happy place, for there was a certain amount of regimentation. The students mainly worked hard: the goal was to get into a good college, not to have fun.

O'Kane studied diligently for four years at Andover. He committed to memory poems by New Englanders Ralph Waldo Emerson and Robert Frost. Unlike most of his classmates, he had a naval bent and yearned to get into Annapolis after leaving Andover. While waiting for an appointment to the U.S. Naval Academy, he enrolled at the University of New Hampshire.

In the late summer of 1930, nineteen-year-old Richard O'Kane entered the Naval Academy as a lowly plebe, member of the Class of 1934.

Then, as now, the Naval Academy was a special place. It was founded in 1845 by President James Polk and Secretary of the Navy George Bancroft and was graced by a spacious, neatly trimmed campus known as "The Yard." Set a few blocks from the Maryland State Capitol, the Academy had its own landmarks: towered Mahan Hall Library, center of the academic group; the copper-sheathed, baroque-domed chapel, which holds the remains of the Navy's Revolutionary War hero, John Paul Jones (Jones, submariners noted, was essentially a commerce raider, captain of *Bon Homme Richard,* whose goal was to take valuable prizes, not unlike the sub captains of World War II), and a baptismal font made of wood from USS *Constitution;* the sprawling Bancroft Hall dormitories; the parade grounds and sports fields—all on land-fill where the Severn River enters Chesapeake Bay.

Many Americans' view of Annapolis in the Thirties was formed by the romantic Hollywood movies made about the Naval Academy. It was a natural setting: beautiful grounds, dances, football weekends, and marching midshipmen. Movies like *Annapolis Salute* and *Navy Blue and Gold* conveyed a sense of glamor, spotless uniforms, elegant parades, with handsome young men undergoing a rite of passage as they vied for the favors of pretty debutantes. The plots were often laughable: Hollywood depicted a sanitized version of life at the Naval Academy, emphasizing warm sentimentality and true-blue patriotism in the process by which the Navy produced its warrior-officers.

The Naval Academy of O'Kane's generation was a tightly knit community of students and faculty with an enrollment of about 1,800 in the four classes: plebes (freshmen), youngsters (sophomores), second classmen or oldsters (juniors), and exalted first classmen (seniors). Dick O'Kane fit the conventional pattern of students: mostly from genteel, white, middle-class backgrounds. Like its opposite number, the U.S. Military Academy at West Point, Annapolis in the early Thirties was reasonably, although not totally, sheltered from the Great Depression. Midshipmen from Annapolis and cadets from West Point had a certain social cachet with the belles from New York, Baltimore, and Washington. It was a time when some college boys drove roadsters and convertibles and drank mint juleps with their dates. In the Academy's annual yearbook, *Lucky Bag,* Brooks Brothers ran ads for officers' uniforms, ready-made or to measure. The Shredded Wheat ads declared: "Brawn and bravery come from food as well as training." And the Hotel Astor in New York City advertised rooms with bath at $3 up. But midshipmen rarely left the campus.

At Annapolis, Dick O'Kane, like other incoming plebes, found a special society with its own laws and language. Plebes were ordered around by the staff and by senior midshipmen. They were subject to hazing by upperclassmen, officially outlawed but a common practice. In many ways, it was difficult for a plebe to maintain any personal dignity when he was treated as a low recruit. The tough regimen, like boot camp for enlisted men, was designed to impart discipline— learning to take orders before giving them.

The schedule was full. One of Dick O'Kane's classmate friends recalled that the middies' day was highly regulated: reveille at 6 a.m., formations at 7 a.m., first class at 8 a.m., and so on. The only private time middies had was an hour before dinner, and a half hour before lights out at 10 p.m. Students marched from their main dormitory, Bancroft Hall, to various classrooms. It was a crowded life with little contact with the outside world.

Midshipmen were generally conscientious students in the 1930s. After all, they were volunteers who worked hard to get appointed to the Naval Academy. At government expense during hard times they were getting a free education with a highly saleable degree: Bachelor of Science in Engineering.

Many plebes were given nicknames that stuck with them through their careers, such as "Mushmouth" Morton. O'Kane was known simply as "Dick." His classmates were amused that he used an old-fashioned, straight razor.

Each first classman was given a thumbnail description in the annual yearbook. The Class of 1930, for instance, described Mush Morton: "A famous smile. Ever ready sense of humor and charming personality has made him admired. A heart of gold and a fast appreciation and understanding of others made Dudley beloved of those who are so fortunate as to really know the man behind the smile." George Grider was said to be: "Genial, yet unassuming, courteous, yet cordial, with a rich sense of humor displayed by his ability to tell a good story."

During the year, middies in the Regiment of Midshipmen were separated into four battalions, each comprising men from all four classes. While the Annapolis student body was fairly close, Dick O'Kane and his fellow midshipmen were so busy that they only got to know others in their own battalion. They marched to class together. They did everything with their own companies and battalions except for the summer cruises on the old battleships USS *Arkansas* and USS *Wyoming*. Then battalions were thrown together and a middie widened his range of acquaintances.

Midshipmen's free time was circumscribed. They had only eight days leave at Christmas, no spring breaks, only Saturday afternoons in Annapolis, which they called "Crabtown." Permission was needed to dine out. The midshipman's spending money allotted at the time, as a classmate of O'Kane remembers, was $2 per month for plebes, $5 for youngsters, $7 for second classmen, and $10 a month for first classmen. A midshipman's pay was $78 a month and a 15 percent budget cutback reduced it to $66.30. They paid for their uniforms.

The students were largely insulated from the severe economic conditions that existed nationally, and they did not see the bread lines, except through newspapers. They read about General MacArthur and the bonus marchers. Yet the Depression left a mark on the Naval Academy. Salaries of staff and midshipmen were cut 15 percent. A number of civilian professors were discharged. The budget-minded Congress decreed in 1932 that only the top half of the graduates of the

Class of 1933 and subsequent classes would be automatically inducted into the Regular Navy as young ensigns, the lowest officer rank. Those in the bottom half of the class would not receive immediate commissions. They would have to leave the Navy, join the reserve, and wait until officer-ensign openings occurred—by attrition or by Congress enlarging the size of the officer corps.

When the Class of 1933 graduated, President Franklin D. Roosevelt personally handed a diploma to each graduate, but those in the bottom half did not receive commissions. Among the members of the Class of '33 affected by the cutback were John Bulkeley, destined to become a wartime PT boat hero and win the Medal of Honor, reaching the rank of Vice Admiral; and Draper Kauffman, who would become an underwater demolition team commander and later Rear Admiral specializing in deep diving operations. After leaving Annapolis, John Bulkeley complained of being beaten as a plebe with broom handles for minor infractions by a small number of upperclassmen. Some of the hazing, he insisted, was cruel and even sadistic. Bulkeley's memory of the Naval Academy was so bitter that he never attended a class reunion. But he also believed that after reforms Annapolis was the finest institution of its kind in the world.

Uncertainty hovered over Dick O'Kane's Class of '34. The possible fate of landing in the second half of the class caused indifferent students like Charles Elliott Loughlin, Class of '33, to pull up their socks in their last two years in order to make the top half. An all-American basketball and tennis player, Elliott Loughlin hit the books hard. That practice carried over to the Class of 1934; they wanted to make sure of their commissions on graduation. But President Roosevelt's expansion of the "two-ocean Navy" needed all the young ensigns Annapolis could provide. In May, 1934, Congress authorized the President to commission Dick O'Kane's entire Annapolis graduating class and to offer commissions to the discharged members of the Class of 1933.

It took a wise superintendent to realize that while midshipmen had to comply with rules, some leeway had to be extended to the energetic young men who were expected to be aggressive, imaginative, and courageous in combat. The senior officer-instructor's job was to teach middies that they must cultivate high personal standards of integrity, professional skill, and the ability to make decisions with imperfect information. But Academy superintendents over the years oscillated between being too slack, which led to erosion of morale and standards, or becoming martinets—with similar results. There was always a pull between duty-conscious midshipmen and the ones with a maverick streak. Dick O'Kane himself spent a certain amount of weekends restricted to the *Reina Mercedes*. This was an Annapolis institution, a Spanish vessel captured in 1898, which served as an Academy barracks ship and punishment quarters for midshipmen serving various periods of time for committing minor infractions of rules. To most midshipmen, a spell or two aboard the *Reina* was thought to be a minor mark of independence and distinction.

Like other exuberant middies, O'Kane was torn between cutting up a few touches and adhering to the strict discipline imposed on a government-funded student body training for war. The Academy's regulations decreed that midshipmen were "not only required to abstain from all vicious, immoral or irregular conduct, but to conduct themselves with the propriety and decorum of gentlemen."

While Annapolis' reputation rested on its "trade school," engineering-oriented credentials, it had the occasional scholarly side. It boasted two Nobel laureates, including Albert A. Michelson, the first American to win one, in 1907 for physics. He was the son of immigrants from Poland, like another middie, Hyman G. Rickover, Class of '22, the father of the modern nuclear navy. When Michelson was handed his diploma in 1873, Admiral John L. Worden, then Superintendent, offered him the tart advice: "If in the future, you'll give less attention to scientific matters and more to your naval gunnery, there might come a time when you would know enough to be some service to your country."

In 1930, the year Dick O'Kane entered the Academy, graduating midshipmen won six of America's twelve allotted Rhodes scholarships. That same year's graduating class was pleased to find that the Association of American Universities approved the move to award officially accredited Annapolis graduates the degree of Bachelor of Science.

Dick O'Kane's four years, in fact, witnessed dramatic and controversial change. In 1931, a new superintendent was named. He was Rear Admiral Thomas Hart, a strict disciplinarian and submariner who was to be the ill-fated Commander-in-Chief of the U.S. Asiatic Fleet when the Japanese attacked the Far East. Hart was a conservative naval officer, but had an open mind, and proved to everyone's surprise to be a progressive educator. In his second year, he introduced the most liberal curriculum since the Naval Academy was founded. Admiral Hart created a Department of Economics and Government, as well as a course in comparative literature. He increased the proportion of time devoted to the humanities from 21 to 32 percent. In O'Kane's time at the Academy, the faculty departments were: Seamanship and Navigation, Ordnance and Gunnery, Marine Engineering, Mathematics, Electrical Engineering (Physics and Chemistry), English and History, Modern Languages (French, Spanish, Italian, German), Economics and Government, and Physical Training.

Superintendent Hart was cold but even-handed. He insisted that middies in full dress have exactly one-eighth inch of their collar showing, and exactly a quarter inch of the cuffs. Slade Cutter in the Class of 1935 and his mates cut off their shirtsleeves and sewed cuffs inside the coats. They put a button inside their collars in back of their coats and two buttons in front to hold their full dress collar in place.

Hart's liberal reforms were short-lived, however. His successor, Rear Admiral David F. Sellers, a past Commander-in-Chief of the U.S. Fleet, reversed Hart's program in 1934 on the grounds that the new liberal curriculum was "an unacceptable sacrifice of professional education." Sellers insisted the Naval Academy had one, and only one, justification for existence: "To educate and train officers to fight the fleet." The new Superintendent added: "Any element introduced into the Naval Academy curriculum which takes its place at the expense of professional training and development should be excised forthwith."

The motto on the Naval Academy's coat of arms was: "Ex Scientia Tridens" (From knowledge, sea power). The argument over finding a proper balance between professional subjects and the liberal arts at service academies—the choice between Athens and Sparta, as one submariner described it—continues to this day.

Outside of classes, Academy life was livened by traditional social functions and athletic events. Participation in sports—varsity and intramural—was encouraged. Dick O'Kane didn't take part in varsity sports though he was a good swimmer, skier, ice skater, and tennis player. He could hold his own on a dance floor, too, and played the field with the ladies.

Cheering the Navy football team was a must for middies: it would remain so throughout their careers. The annual Army–Navy football game attracted nationwide interest. The Navy's team mascot, Billy the Goat, was famous and "Beat Army" was the watchword. Middies found accommodation for their "drags," dates for football games and proms, in nearby, quaint old homes. They danced in their spanking white trousers with blue tunics and white hats, then raced home to Bancroft Hall "to beat the clock" at midnight. In the Yard, they flipped pennies at the statue of Indian warrior Tecumseh as an offering for obtaining passing grades, and as first classmen they contributed a dollar apiece to the fund awarded to their class anchorman, the man at the bottom.

Midshipmen looked forward to summers, which consisted of a two-month cruise aboard one of the men-o'-war of the fleet followed by a month's vacation. O'Kane spent one summer cruise with a middie who would become a friend, Roy C. Smith III, aboard the battleship *Arkansas*. Smith considered O'Kane outgoing, solid, intelligent, and fairly modest, a young man who listened to others, but tended to go his own way. Dick didn't go by the numbers. He was an innovator, a pragmatist who liked to try out new ideas.

On the summer cruises to foreign ports, students got to know middies from other Academy battalions. Roy Smith believed the Academy experience established a bond be-

tween classmates much stronger than among friends at other
colleges. The bond strengthened as you went through the
service. Young officers never went to any port—Panama,
Shanghai, Guantanamo Bay, San Diego—where they didn't
know someone from their class at Annapolis.

As an upper classman, Dick O'Kane declined to haze
or pick on the younger students. As a first classman, he
presided over a dining table of midshipmen. George Street,
Class of '37 who would win fame in command of submarine
Tirante, sat at the table. "He asked the plebes at his table serious questions about the Academy," Street said, "naval history, battles, naval heroes, very good questions, and insisted
we look up the answers and recite them at table. We learned
a lot. He never sent plebes off on wild-goose chases for his
own amusement, as upper classmen often did. The point was
he treated us seriously. He was humane."

The emphasis at Annapolis was on grades: the daily
grade, the weekly grade, the semester grades. The weekly
grade, called weekly "trees," were posted publicly and
showed which midshipmen had failed to do satisfactory
work that week. In the Academy's grading system—and the
Navy's at large—a mark of 4.0 was perfect, while 2.5 was
the minimum passing grade. Throughout the Navy, "four-
oh" was the standard expression for excellence.

Final Academy class standing was based on a combination
of academic grades and less tangible qualities such as good
conduct, military bearing, evidence of leadership, and the
overall judgment of the regular Navy instructors. "Grease
mark" was slang for a midshipman's grade in military apti-
tude and comportment. High grades were sought. As a member of Dick O'Kane's class noted, "There was a lot of study,
a lot of personal effort, and mutual self-help among your
roommates and your classmates."

A midshipman's academic standing was much more than
a matter of prestige, or making a dean's list, or applying to
graduate school—as in civilian colleges. One's ranking in
his Naval Academy class determined a new officer's "signal
number," or seniority within the naval service. Officers' signal numbers ran from No. 1, the Chief of Naval Operations,

down to the lowliest ensign with the last number in the Naval Register for that year. In the junior officer ranks, an Academy class tended to be promoted all on the same day, from ensign, say, to lieutenant junior grade. Officers of equal rank were given seniority by their date of rank. If many were promoted on the same date, as was the usual case, the senior man was deemed the one with the highest signal number. He would take precedence over a lesser-numbered officer in any situation involving command. An officer could lose numbers in the overall Navy signal standings as a result of a disciplinary hearing, or, conversely, gain numbers for meritorious achievement.

In the submarine service, this numbering system had important consequences, for a sub skipper had to be senior to all his officers, even of the same rank. As younger officers assumed command, their officers had to be correspondingly junior in signal number. Because of the relative youth of officers in submarine wardrooms in the latter part of the Pacific War, this sometimes led to complications. Annapolis graduates therefore were always aware of their position in their class. They also were aware that the midshipmen chosen to be regimental, battalion, and company commanders—those who wore the thin stripes on their uniforms, the "stripers"—and placed near the top of their class, were presumed to be on the fast track in their Navy careers. For example, the regimental commander of Dick O'Kane's class was Edward J. Fahy, who became a submariner and though he sank no enemy ships as skipper of *Plunger* he was eventually promoted to rear admiral.

Marriage was forbidden for midshipmen. Even fresh ensigns had to wait two years before getting married, though some were wed secretly. *Wahoo*'s George Grider, for instance, quietly married his wife, Anne, when he was fresh out of the Academy. After two years, he remarried her publicly and in style. It was important for a young officer to get a posting where his wife could be comfortable. The saying went: "Marriages aren't made in heaven; they're made by Bupers" (the Bureau of Personnel in charge of assignments).

Midshipman O'Kane adjusted relatively easily to life at

the Naval Academy, perhaps because he was used to the strict regime at his boarding school. His plebe class began with 645 middies. Dick was in the broad middle of his class: he graduated 264th out of 464 midshipmen.

Most midshipmen, unlike John Bulkeley, enjoyed their time at the Naval Academy though life was tough and disciplined. Dick O'Kane revered the Academy. Submariner Slade Cutter, a year behind Dick O'Kane, loved everything about it. "It was during the Depression," he said, "and everybody was so doggone happy to be there. We had a lot of hazing and stuff like that, but it was all done in good spirit. I thought it was great."

Dick O'Kane's class of 1934 was one of the few that would provide the backbone of the officers who commanded destroyers, submarines, and aircraft squadrons in World War II. In the massive build-up of personnel during the war, only 5 percent of naval officers were Annapolis graduates. Much credit for the eventual, hard-fought victory was thus due to those many thousands of reserve wartime officers who made up the other 95 percent of the officer corps. Yet the "trade school" officers formed the professional core around which the wartime Navy expanded. They supplied a sense of continuity—as well as holding down the senior positions of command.

Of the Annapolis graduates who served in the war, 6 percent were killed in action, but the ten classes that graduated in the 1930s averaged twice that figure. Dick O'Kane's Class of '34 suffered a 12 percent loss rate; the highest was the Class of '36 with 16 percent of its members killed in action. Twenty-seven Annapolis men won the Medal of Honor—fourteen posthumously—their ages ranging from fifty-seven to twenty-three.

As he left the Naval Academy, Dick O'Kane's independent personality was reflected in the *Lucky Bag*'s brief description of him: "Any attempt to describe Dick adequately in a few words is bound to be futile and to result in being insufficient to do him justice. Dick's a Yankee and proud of it."

When Dick O'Kane tossed his white middie hat in the air on graduating as a brand new ensign, he felt the responsibility of living up to the traditions of the Naval Academy. He was loyal to those traditions. He knew his education was designed toward one end: ultimately to win battles at sea. As Dick O'Kane would find, some Academy classmates were destined to win those battles; others would fail.

On graduation from Annapolis, Ensign O'Kane was assigned to the heavy cruiser *Chester* as a junior gunnery officer. A few months later, he was given duty as signal officer. Service aboard a heavy cruiser in the 1930s, with 700 men aboard and a four-striper as captain, tended to be a spit-and-polish assignment, with protocol rigorously observed. But big-ship assignment—battleships and cruisers—was deemed essential to a line officer's career, so O'Kane was contented. After a year aboard *Chester*, he was transferred to a destroyer, the *Pruitt*, one of the last of the World War I vintage "four-pipers," with their distinctive quartet of stacks.

Tin can duty was more to Dick O'Kane's liking. There were only a half-dozen officers on the ship so he had plenty of responsibility and duties. Life aboard a "can" was rough and ready, a demanding school in all basic shipboard assignments—gunnery, torpedoes, communications, navigation, commissary, tactics—and aspects of seamanship usually denied young officers in larger or slower ships.

During his time at sea, Dick O'Kane corresponded and kept company with a girl he first met as a teenager in Durham, New Hampshire: Ernestine Groves. Their professor parents had lived in neighboring houses for a time in Durham during the 1920s. Ernestine attended summer school in Durham when she first went out seriously with Dick. On June 1, 1936, during the destroyer *Pruitt*'s overhaul at the Mare Island Shipyard—and one day after the mandatory two-year waiting period expired—Dick O'Kane married Ernestine Groves at the Episcopal Church in Berkeley, California.

Pruitt was then home-ported in San Diego, but soon after, the ship rebased in Pearl Harbor, and Ernie joined Dick in Hawaii. There they enjoyed a near-idyllic life. In 1937, O'Kane decided to put in for submarines: he was attracted to the easy-going style aboard the boats and to their fascinating machinery, but he was also lured by the higher hazardous duty pay, and the opportunity for early responsibilities and advancement. An officer had to serve two years in the fleet before being considered for Submarine School. Lieutenant (j.g.) Richard O'Kane was accepted for the January class of 1938 in New London, Connecticut.

The O'Kane family returned to the mainland. Dick and Ernestine with their infant daughter Marsha drove from Mare Island through torrential rains across the continent to the Sub School. (Actually, the Submarine School is situated across the Thames River from New London just upriver from Groton, but has always been known as "New London," home of American submariners.)

Ernestine was introduced to the tight-knit world of the Submarine Force, an inner circle within a larger Navy community, where the wives were supportive of one another. Everybody knew everybody else. Their kids all went to school together and even married one another. The officers were Naval Academy graduates, many of them classmates. You didn't go out of your way to make waves, or embarrass people. In the pre-wartime period, this could lead to an overly clubby atmosphere, where people knew their rank and their place.

The wives and children watched husbands' and fathers' training boats sail down the Thames River every morning. They knew that a chance accident could mean the submarine and the men aboard would not return. They knew that when a submarine submerged, it might not come up. (Some months later everyone would be shocked by the accidental sinking of *Squalus* off Portsmouth in 1939, which captured world headlines when thirty-three crewmembers were saved but twenty-six lost.)

O'Kane was in a remarkable class, as events would show: Ed Fahy, regimental brigade commander in O'Kane's Class of 1934; John Eichmann, a four-striper; Slade Cutter, an Academy football hero; Robert "Dusty" Dornin, another football great; Elliott Loughlin, basketball and tennis all-American; Norvell "Bub" Ward; Joe Enright; and Keats Montross. Most were married and all were serious-minded young officers. They got together for lively Friday and Saturday nights.

Submarine School was tough but rewarding for Dick O'Kane. Everyone worked furiously during the six-month course. Enlisted men studied a six-week basic sub course and then specialized in their ratings for advance training. Slade Cutter believed they learned more about the technical aspects of ships and electrical engineering in six months at New London than during four years at the Academy. The students had a heavy schedule: they studied diesel engines, electric batteries, torpedoes, and torpedo fire control at the attack teacher console. Students were trained to escape in a 100-foot water tank, going from bottom to top in a Momsen lung, an underwater breathing device. Some in Sub School didn't take the Momsen lung training very seriously: the general feeling was that if your sub went down in 2,000 fathoms of water, you weren't going to have much use for the escape device.

Twice a week, for a morning or afternoon, the students boarded tiny old R-boats, "school boats," sailed down the Thames River, and spent the day diving in Long Island or Block Island Sound. "Everybody liked everybody else," Slade Cutter said. "We were there to do the best we could and learn as much as we could. We knew war was coming, and that's what we were training for. It was serious, very serious business."

Dick O'Kane worked especially hard in Sub School. He knew the top third of the thirty-man class had their pick of assignments; the bottom third was usually assigned to duty in the Asiatic Fleet, or Panama, where wives could not join their husbands.

After the six-month course, Dick O'Kane wound up in the top ten, and at his request was assigned to Pearl Harbor, joining *Argonaut,* the largest submarine in the Navy, which had been designed to lay mines as well as fire torpedoes.

The O'Kane family moved back to Hawaii in the summer of 1938. If New London was the home of the U.S. Submarine Force, the Sub Base at Pearl Harbor was its most important overseas extension. Honolulu then was still a small, resort-like town—the first traffic light was not installed until the late 1930s on Beretania Street. It was semi-tropical and sleepy, and naval and military officers had long weekends with their families, at the beach or on the golf course. Fully furnished apartments cost $45–$55 a month. Most officers were married and resided in town. Enlisted men lived in barracks just off the base or took apartments in town.

Being a young officer on *Argonaut* and moving up the ladder was a valuable experience for Dick O'Kane. Mere graduation from sub school did not immediately "qualify" an officer for submarine duty: he needed to spend at least a year aboard a submarine before being eligible for the prized twin golden dolphins insignia worn on the breast. He had to pass a tough qualification exam.

After a year aboard *Argonaut,* O'Kane qualified for submarine duty and was awarded the dolphins. In late 1941, he passed the arduous tests to be rated "qualified for command" of a submarine, and was promoted to full lieutenant. By then a son, James, had joined Marsha in the O'Kane family.

Among *Argonaut*'s wardroom officers were William "Wild Bill" Post, the fiery executive officer, and Ignatius "Pete" Galantin, who would become skipper of *Halibut,* and eventually a four-star admiral. Even then, Pete Galantin recognized in Dick O'Kane a maverick figure, an innovator who got things done, not always going by the book. Dick O'Kane didn't seem to care what people said, Pete thought, but only what it took to get a job done.

Argonaut was a huge, unwieldy ship to operate, with ten torpedoes forward and seventy-eight mines in the after torpedo room. The sub carried two 6-inch guns, which could throw a shell almost 20 miles. O'Kane adapted readily to his various assignments, though he was appalled at the way the tired submarine's electrical equipment broke down on patrol. In late November 1941, with war warnings flying, *Argonaut* was ordered to patrol near Midway Island. She was on station when the Japanese attacked Pearl Harbor. In defending Midway, *Argonaut*'s only action was sighting two Japanese destroyers scouting the island. O'Kane, like Bill Post, thought

Skipper Steve Barchet was much too cautious, remaining submerged all day long and diving deep at the hint of a Japanese escort in the area. The all-day dives, then considered doctrine, were a severe strain on *Argonaut*'s equipment, with high humidity contributing to the small fires that broke out in electrical connections.

Returning from *Argonaut*'s first war patrol, O'Kane witnessed the devastation wreaked by the Japanese air raid. He was in charge of the deck force and faced the ranks to each side of *Argonaut* to stare at the various scarred and sunken ships—in which many older *Argonaut* hands had served. The battleship *Nevada* was beached at Waipio Point, masts of sunken battleships were askew along "battleship row," *Oklahoma* was upside down, fleet flagship *Pennsylvania* was bombed in dry-dock, *Arizona* lay crumpled with 1,177 of her complement killed in action, most entombed, oil still thick on the waters.

Dick O'Kane found Ernestine and other Navy families on two-hour notice to evacuate Hawaii. He also picked up orders to report for duty as executive officer of *Wahoo,* which was being completed at the Mare Island Navy Yard. *Argonaut* was scheduled for overhaul at Mare Island, so Dick O'Kane sailed to San Francisco aboard her, while the family took the Matson liner *Lurline.* He found rental quarters for his family in Ignacio near Hamilton Air Field in Marin County across the bay from Mare Island about 20 miles north of San Francisco. O'Kane commuted to Mare Island, as he and the CO, Commander Marvin Kennedy, spent weeks supervising the final fitting out, commissioning, shakedown, and readying of *Wahoo* for war. *Wahoo* sailed for Pearl Harbor on August 12, 1942.

Now, a year later, *Wahoo* was receding into Dick O'Kane's past. As he strode past shipbuilding ways with his silver cigarette box, heading for *Tang,* O'Kane looked forward to whatever the future would bring. He had begun his career as a raw ensign. He rose through the ranks as a sometimes brash junior officer, with a few rough edges. But his personality had matured as exec of *Wahoo.* He had changed in combat from the impatient, impetuous junior officer into a more thoughtful one—though he had lost none of his warrior's audacity. He had kept his Irish temper in check. He had developed a reputation as an officer who kept his word. He could be stern when needed, but the crew thought him fair.

Dick O'Kane was eager to command, and he had been probably the most successful exec in the Submarine Force, but O'Kane had observed topflight executive officers that didn't make it as commanding officers. He was confident, however. After all, he had fired more torpedo war shots than most skippers. On *Wahoo,* his role was that of the tough guy to Mush's good guy. Now he had more latitude. He could be his own man.

Lieutenant Commander Richard O'Kane prepared to face the most demanding test of his career: command in combat. As he had seen in action, it is one thing to be the exec, the number two, but quite another to be number one, the captain—carrying the burden of submarine combat command alone.

CHAPTER TEN

"There's Going to be Ice Cream on *Tang*"

Dick and Ernestine were content with their modest two-bedroom apartment in a housing complex called Ducel Court near Ignacio in Marin County, a fairly rural place in those days. Other Navy families lived in there too and the residents all shared a nearby Victory Garden. The period ahead, during which Dick outfitted *Tang,* was as close to normality as the family would experience in wartime. O'Kane spent many evenings at home after an early morning 20-mile commute to Vallejo, a full day at work with *Tang,* and the return drive to Ignacio. He complained that both drives on Highway 37 were into the sun, eastward into the rising sun, westward into the setting sun, which was hard on his pale blue eyes.

Most mornings Dick listened to the Don McNeil radio breakfast show with Ernie and Marsha, sometimes joining in a sing-along. Usually six-year-old Marsha walked from home to a one-room schoolhouse in Ignacio along Highway 101 where she attended first grade. Dick thought it formed Marsha's character to study in such a stimulating environment. It also increased her appreciation for the value of education, he believed, just as he had inherited those values from his own academic parents. In the evening, the father read the Uncle Wiggly comic stories to her and James. At home, O'Kane relaxed by working on auto engines. Dick also built a doll's house for Marsha in the shape of their own duplex apartment. He liked fixing things around the house—Ernestine never had to call in a repairman when Dick was around.

Often Dick worked at Mare Island on Saturdays, taking

Marsha along. A base barber would cut her hair. He would take Marsha aboard *Tang* with him, or on errands to San Francisco and other localities. She remembered one excursion to San Francisco music stores where her father was looking for a metronome, which the inventive O'Kane planned to use aboard *Tang*. He found one at Sherman Clay & Co., which he figured could be used to devise a way to count the propeller turns of enemy escort vessels, thus determining their speed.

On Sundays, the family listened to classical music programs, opera or symphony on the radio, then took drives in Marin County's beautiful hills and seacoast. The highlight of the Mare Island stay was a family trip by car, with borrowed gasoline ration coupons, to Yosemite National Park. Dick O'Kane loved hiking and fly-fishing, which his father had taught him.

Dick was no military martinet of a father. Young James thought he seemed quite an ordinary dad. Some officers ran their households as if they were military units, but not Dick O'Kane. Around the house, he relaxed in his old civilian clothes, leaving his military style and uniforms at Mare Island. James felt no sense of loss when his father was away. When Dick was ashore, he was around the family, giving his children his full attention. He was very caring, very dedicated to the family. At sea, well, his absence was no different from hundreds of thousands of other fatherless households in the war. To his children, Dick appeared to be modest even reticent about his exploits. He didn't spin sea tales. If a fellow submariner like Fritz Harlfinger dropped by they would swap stories, but otherwise, Dick was happy to devote his thoughts and time to his family, so his children had difficulty with the concept that he was a naval hero. Their father was just Dad to them, but everyone in the naval community had heard about *Wahoo*.

Ernestine took it all in stride. Strong-spirited, she knew she had married a naval officer and a submariner as well. She accepted his career without complaint. She knew that in his life, in wartime, the Navy had to come first.

The submarine community was a small one. Submarine

families were concentrated in only a few areas: Mare Island and Vallejo, San Diego, New London, Portsmouth. The sense of shared danger made them even more cohesive than other service arms. While *Wahoo* was at war, Ernestine O'Kane busied herself raising her children. She was happy with their location. Ernie liked residing some distance from Vallejo where many submarine wives lived, because there were always many rumors circulating that this or that sub was down. She and the other wives were very careful not to talk about submarines in public: they didn't want to give any aid to the enemy, and believed that the Japanese would know anything reported widely in the U.S. within twenty-four hours.

The wives were aware of the high rate of losses in submarines. They all felt that they had to be extra lucky to get through the war with their husbands still alive. They lived in dread of the yellow Western Union telegram beginning: "The Navy Department deeply regrets to inform you . . ."

Curiously, submarine officers seemed to make pretty good husbands; at least the divorce rate among them was not any higher than among other Navy officers. Though enlisted men sometimes returned from patrol to find a "Dear John" letter, or learned through other means that their wives or girlfriends had run off with other men, this rarely happened in the submarine officer community. Slade Cutter thought that at home his officer friends spent a lot of time with their wives and children because they missed them when at sea and wanted to be good fathers.

For the crews, men and officers alike, rest and refit in Australia was considered a kind of Shangri-la. "Everyone wanted to end a patrol in Australia," one *Wahoo* crewmember said. A promising young officer, James Calvert on *Jack,* thought that the threat of death posed a problem for young officers and crewmen, especially those temporarily based in Australia where young women were more than plentiful. Some officers believed that once you crossed the international date line and the equator all bets concerning infidelity were off—vows and pledges were put in temporary abeyance. In Australia, Jim Calvert sensed that the war mentality and psychology were prevalent among younger officers, although rarely among the skippers. Every few weeks they would hear that another U.S. submarine had been lost. Would they be next? Was their two-week leave the last period on earth they would be able to enjoy? Such thoughts affected a young officer's viewpoint.

Slade Cutter thought there was an unstated understanding among some submariners' wives. They could accept that their husbands might need some release in Australia—as long as it was for the moment and did not involve love, commitment, or permanence. One group of Australian women set up house on Paradise Beach near Brisbane and entertained officers from a particular submarine. When the sub went back on patrol and another came in for a two-week refit, the newly arrived officers inherited the beach house and the ladies. But, Cutter said, when you went back to the ship, that was it—the end of the relationship. Toni Peabody believed there were surprisingly few divorces among submarine officers and their wives, given the tensions that many were under.

In the Vallejo area, wives in the submarine community all shared the loss of friends. There was a quiet acceptance and a sharp awareness of the special nature of submarine duty: that the ship and crew were a single entity, that in submarine warfare, crews died with their ships, rarely were there survivors. Normally, sub personnel were described as missing rather than killed in action. One young wife whose husband's submarine was reported overdue said desperately, "I don't know whether I'm a bride or a widow. If only I knew for sure."

At 3:59 p.m. on Tuesday, August 17, 1943, the Mare Island whistle sounded loudly, a bottle of champagne was smashed across the bull nose of the submarine, the sponsor intoned, "I christen thee *Tang*," and USS *Tang* slid down the slipway into the Napa River at slack tide. The launching ceremonies over, Dick O'Kane took command of *Tang* while the fitting out process took place alongside the dock, freeing up the building way for the construction of yet another new submarine to fight in the war against Japan. O'Kane worked out of a wooden office on the dock beside *Tang*, surrounded by power, air and welder lines snaking like Medusas over the side to the submarine. Yard workmen scurried back aboard to finish their work on the new submarine before the ship would be ready for commissioning as a formal part of the U.S. fleet.

At this stage, Dick O'Kane was pleased with what he saw. *Tang,* hull number SS-306, was 312 feet long, 27 feet in beam, and 1,525 tons displacement. He liked the name: *Tang,* a small, tropical, fighting fish with needled fins. Importantly, *Tang* was provided with a new, thicker pressure hull, fashioned out of welded carbon steel, that would enable her to go deeper than *Wahoo* and the boats of the earlier class. *Wahoo*'s test depth was only 300 feet. The stipulated—and secret—test depth of *Tang* was to be just over 400 feet, but Dick O'Kane thought *Tang* could do much better. He believed the hull could probably take double that pressure and depth—but tests would have to prove whether the sea fittings through the hull could hold up.

A submarine was fitted out in stages. While yard workmen adhered to the basic general design—hull, torpedo tubes, engines, batteries—a new skipper could cajole from the yard team many impromptu improvements in the final version of the boat's equipment. For example, the target bearing transmitters, the TBTs, could be rejiggered to suit the captain, who had to use them in combat. All sorts of creature comforts could be installed with willing yard workmen, and a crew that knew what it wanted and how to cut corners.

Dick O'Kane's first order of business was to welcome and assemble his officers and crew as they arrived individually in Mare Island, assigned to *Tang* by the Bureau of Personnel. First came his new executive officer, Murray Frazee, a Naval Academy graduate from Gettysburg, Pennsylvania. O'Kane knew from his own experience how important a fine exec was to a well-functioning combat submarine. O'Kane considered himself fortunate in getting Frazee, who had served as a junior officer pre-war aboard the carrier *Lexington* and the destroyer *DuPont.* After Sub School, "Fraz" made seven war patrols aboard *Grayback,* which was awarded the Navy Unit Commendation for her seventh patrol. He knew what a depth charging was like. Curiously, Fraz was one of the few submariners not to have volunteered. He was an officer on a destroyer when the ship received a message: "The Bureau of Personnel contemplates ordering Ensign Frazee to Submarine School for the September class. Have him take a physical exam and report the results by dispatch." Frazee had no objections to the preemptory orders and went.

Fraz was a quiet, confident officer of medium height with a winning smile and easy manner. His first skipper on *Grayback,* Willard Saunders, was something less than aggressive, so he and O'Kane had similar experiences of the war's early days. Frazee thought at first that his new CO on *Tang* was somewhat uptight. For a few weeks, they felt each other out, sizing each other up, wondering how they would interact. The ideal skipper, Frazee knew, let his XO run the ship. Fraz soon came to realize that O'Kane agreed with him: Dick put him in charge of the internal workings of *Tang,* liaising closely with the Chief of the Boat. Disciplinary problems were to be solved internally, as they had been on *Wahoo.* Fraz realized that O'Kane's intensity came from his overriding desire to get *Tang* ready for sea and for sinking enemy ships.

Between the two of them, they had made thirteen combat runs, quite a record. As the weeks wore on, Fraz warmed up and became friendly with the captain and they developed a bantering relationship. Frazee was pleased to be *Tang*'s exec, and he believed that O'Kane's insistence that all his officers and chiefs work flat out was a positive force for everyone, including himself. As the weeks went rapidly by, he thought that Dick O'Kane was looking like a well-cut skipper with a commanding presence.

The most important figure among the enlisted crew of a submarine is the Chief of the Boat (COB), who serves as kind of assistant executive officer. He is the equivalent of an Army top sergeant. No enlisted man in the U.S. Navy has more responsibility than the COB in a submarine. In consultation with Murray Frazee, Dick O'Kane looked over the chief petty officers assigned to *Tang* and decided to offer the COB's post to Chief Torpedoman's Mate William Ballinger. A COB was not necessarily the most senior chief aboard—some older chiefs didn't want the responsibility—but one who was a natural leader of the crew and could act as a go-between with the exec and skipper. Bill Ballinger hailed from Rosemead, California, and had been given a high recommendation by his former skipper, John Scott of *Tunny,* whom both O'Kane and Frazee knew and admired. Ballinger readily accepted their offer.

The basic quality of a Chief of the Boat was his ability to lead, not just his rating, though most COBs were torpedomen. On board *Jack,* for instance, Jim Calvert, the exec, replaced a highly regarded Chief Gunner's Mate, who was killed in an auto accident in San Francisco, with, surprisingly, a Chief Commissary Steward, D.W. "Rebel" Watson. No submarine had ever made a cook the Chief of the Boat. But Jim Calvert and Skipper Al Fuhrman decided that Watson had that magic ingredient called leadership ability, which was so hard to define and yet so immediately recognizable aboard a combat submarine.

Other officers arrived at *Tang:* Lieutenant William Walsh, who was to be third officer and engineer, had made two patrols on *Tautog;* Lieutenant Frank Springer, tall, with a serious look, was the torpedo fire control officer; Ensign Hank Flanagan, a tall rangy "mustang," was a former enlisted man who had fleeted up from chief torpedoman's mate after seven war patrols aboard *Tambor* and one on *Thresher;* Lieutenant Bruce "Scotty" Anderson, a big solid man from San Francisco, had been in the Merchant Marine; and Ensign Fred Melvin "Mel" Enos, or lowly "George," was a medium-sized, green, ninety-day-wonder from Vallejo and the University of California.

On *Tang,* a valuable addition to the attack team was Chief Quartermaster Sidney W. Jones, who would serve as assistant navigator and member of the battle attack party. Another petty officer, Boatswain's Mate Bill Leibold came aboard. Known as "Boats," Leibold looked like a character from a Navy recruitment poster, and came from Los Angeles. Though there was no complement for a boatswain's mate—a deck specialist on larger ships—Boats got on board because of a good word put in by Murray Frazee. He would serve as an all-round petty officer. O'Kane was happy to hear Leibold had once served aboard his old destroyer *Pruitt.* Other key enlisted men arrived at Mare Island to join *Tang:* Floyd Caverly, who came from Hill City, Minnesota, a smart, well-liked sailor, who was a radio technician but served as the number one soundman during battle stations; Clayton Decker, a cool, quick-thinking motor machinist from a ranch in Western Colorado; torpedoman Hayes Trukke, always a valuable man on a sub; and Pete Narowanski, another seasoned torpedoman.

At O'Kane's insistence, Chief Ballinger managed to find an ice cream maker, a luxury item that was considered regulation for only battleships, cruisers, and carriers. Shipyard officials vetoed the idea of installing one: ice cream makers had to be approved by the Bureau of Ships. But O'Kane told Ballinger, "There's going to be ice cream on *Tang*." Somehow, *Tang*'s Chief of the Boat managed, by hook or crook, to wangle the machine an hour before officers from the battleship *Tennessee* turned up to claim the precious item as theirs.

O'Kane demanded the best food possible aboard *Tang*. The captain liked to eat, though maintained a trim waistline. He knew that good cooks were the best morale builders on a boat. He mentioned that he would prefer a real baking oven to the warming oven in the officers' pantry. Once he had indicated his wishes, O'Kane turned his back on how the job was accomplished. The chiefs found a proper oven somewhere and the installation was quickly completed.

Dick O'Kane also supervised the rejiggering of the target bearing transmitter (TBT) on the centerline of the bridge for night surface attacks. He rigged up a fitting to which binoculars could be mounted to insure accuracy in night sightings. O'Kane and the machinists and electricians supervised the aligning of diesel engines, motors, generators, and batteries. Then each element was rigorously tested, separately and as a functioning whole.

Captain O'Kane was all over the place, pushing yard workmen and crewmen alike. He was bent on doing everything he and his crew could to speed *Tang*'s completion and get her out to the Pacific. Sometimes he seemed rough-edged, even overbearing, but it was never personal. It was in the interest of perfecting *Tang*. His standard was: don't complain unless you are going to come up with a solution. O'Kane pushed his officers to raise their level of performance. Fraz welcomed that extra shove. He thought it made a difference. O'Kane placed trust in his officers. Once when a yard storekeeper told a *Tang* officer that he needed the presence of "the officer in charge," a ticked-off O'Kane told the storekeeper, "Every officer on my ship represents me."

Dick O'Kane had one more major change on his mind. He wanted to convince the shipyard to reposition *Tang*'s deck gun aft rather than forward of the superstructure and bridge. This was considered a major alteration since the placement of a deck gun in new subs was left to the shipyard, using its own blueprints. Some submarines came out of the shipyards with the gun forward, some with the deck gun aft; a few others with guns fore and aft.

The subject of deck guns and their use had become a matter of disagreement in the Submarine Force. Some big pre-war fleet boats were equipped with 6-inch diameter guns, as large as a light cruiser's, but they were deemed too cumbersome for realistic combat. Subsequent submarine classes had 3-inch guns, and then 4-inch. *Tang* was designed with a 4-inch gun placed forward. Later subs would be given a short-barrelled 5-inch weapon, which was thought to be the best of the war. Skippers like Mush Morton swore by deck guns and tried to use them whenever it was feasible. "Surface and sink the bastards," was one of his mottoes. After *Wahoo*'s fourth patrol, Morton told a SubPac staff interviewer that *Wahoo* liked to shoot her guns on every occasion presented. "We shoot our guns with two purposes," Morton said. "One is to destroy enemy shipping, the other to keep the morale of the *Wahoo* crew tops."

Admiral Lockwood, ComSubPac, seemed to share Morton's penchant. "There was no better morale builder than a well-planned gun action," he commented. "There were those in high places who said subs used their deck guns too much—took too many chances. I was not among those critics. The guns were tremendously useful for targets not worth a torpedo." Yet Lockwood seemed to want it both ways. In his endorsement to *Wahoo*'s fourth patrol, after congratulations for the surface gun attacks, he noted: "It is well to re-member that our submarines are very valuable and, at the same time, vulnerable targets when gunfire is used as the at-tacking weapon."

Not every skipper or staff officer agreed with their Force commander's enthusiasm for gun attacks. Pete Galantin, *Halibut*'s skipper, thought that a submarine on the surface was too vulnerable to make the use of its deck gun a reason-able risk—except in very special situations. Skipper Charles Nace of *Rasher* believed that a submarine should be pre-pared for a surface gun action, but that it should engage in such an action only as a last resort.

Other officers observed that a deck gun never proved to be much of an asset other than to raise the morale of a crew, whose war patrol had failed to find proper torpedo targets. On the way home, the crew might think a quick island bombard-ment or sinking of some enemy small craft was a worthwhile use of the deck gun.

A senior Pacific Fleet intelligence officer, Jasper Holmes, pointed out that a submarine is a poor gun platform. One good enemy hit could destroy a boat's ability to dive, and thus evade, and could mean the loss of the sub. A comman-der who deliberately sought a surface engagement with an enemy ship of equal gun power was foolhardy rather than courageous. Holmes acknowledged that a submarine crew often preferred a gun action, full of sound and fury in the bright sunlight, to a stealthy torpedo attack while submerged. But still, he thought, American submarines were probably better off without using a deck gun.

While the Navy Yard determined the original placement of deck guns, Admiral Lockwood took a permissive view toward later overhauls: a skipper could decide where to place the weapon. Sometimes officers got into heated discussions in meetings called by SubPac to fix a standard location for a submarine deck gun. After listening to the arguments in such a meeting, one anti-gun captain declared, "Put it forward or put it aft, or stick it in your ear. I'm not going to use it." An-other skipper added, "I don't care whether the gun's forward or aft, but put it on wheels. When we're beyond the 3-mile limit, we'll push it over the side!"

Though actively involved in gunfights on *Wahoo,* Dick O'Kane had come to share the skeptics' view that a deck gun was of little value to an attack submarine. He wanted the 4-inch deck gun on *Tang* moved from the designed forward position to the rear of the superstructure. O'Kane argued that if *Tang* had to surface to fight it out, he would be running from a Japanese ship and the gun would be better placed aft in order to fire astern at a pursuer. Otherwise, *Tang* would have to change course to get off a shot, which would present a better target to the enemy and slow down the boat. Further, the aft positioning of a gun would help *Tang's* streamlining underwater, cutting down drag. O'Kane may have won the argument in theory, but the shipfitters still installed the gun forward.

When everything was shipshape as far as Mare Island and Dick O'Kane were concerned, his boat was ready for commissioning. On October 15, 1943, USS *Tang* became a warship of the U.S. Fleet. Chief Quartermaster Sidney Jones attached a commissioning pennant to her stub mast, and the crew began drawing 50 percent added pay for submarine service. Commander O'Kane read to the crew his charge from Secretary of the Navy Frank Knox: "Immediately after her shaking down period the USS *Tang* will be assigned to duty wherever she is then most needed. It is entirely possible that you will proceed directly into combat. Your first action may be by day or night, against any type of vessel or aircraft possessed by our able and ruthless enemies.

"Your future Fleet, Force, and Unit Commanders must rely on USS *Tang* as an effective fighting unit from the hour when she reports to them for duty. It is your task to justify their confidence."

Then the assistant shipyard commander presented Dick O'Kane a formal $7 million receipt for one submarine: USS *Tang.* He signed it as he had so many other chits in the past few weeks, official and unofficial.

      *   *   *

While O'Kane was fitting out *Tang,* Admiral Lockwood continued to address the torpedo problem in Pearl Harbor. ComSubPac finally lost his patience with the Bureau of Ordnance over the torpedo mechanism. His skippers' bad experiences with the magnetic exploder convinced him that the device should be deactivated from the Mark 14 steam torpedo. The final straw was the report by a fine skipper, Roy Benson, aboard *Trigger,* that he had scored four hits on the carrier *Hiyo* near Tokyo Bay. (Actually, one fish prematured, but Benson hit *Hiyo* with three torpedoes.) One was a dud; only two exploded. Lockwood knew from the Pearl code-breakers that only one torpedo had done real damage and the carrier was afloat. After consulting with Skipper Benson on his return to Pearl on June 22, Lockwood decided to deactivate the magnetic exploder. Admiral Nimitz agreed and the order went out to SubPac submarines on June 24, 1943.

The Bureau of Ordnance and Admiral Christie in Fremantle promptly questioned Admiral Nimitz on the reasons behind his order. Nimitz explained that it was "because of probable enemy countermeasures, because of the ineffectiveness of the exploder under certain conditions, and because of the impracticability of selecting the proper conditions under which to fire." But Ralph Christie, who had helped develop the magnetic exploder, decided that his submarine command would not go along with the Pearl Harbor order. This decision widened the breach between the two Pacific submarine commanders, and put sub skippers in an awkward position. When a boat was sent on patrol from Pearl with orders to continue to Brisbane or Fremantle, a skipper deactivated the magnetic exploder while under SubPac's command. But passing into the jurisdiction of Southwest Pacific, the skippers had to reactivate the magnetic exploder. The reverse was true for submarines departing Australia for patrols ending in Pearl Harbor.

The naval element of MacArthur's command, meanwhile, changed in title to Seventh Fleet, and the subs in Seventh Fleet split into two task forces, Christie in Perth and Fife in Brisbane.

In Pearl Harbor, Admiral Lockwood's problems with torpedoes were mounting. On July 24, *Tinosa* reported a startling experience. Skipper Lawrence Daspit came across an unescorted Japanese whaler, which had been converted into an important, 20,000-ton tanker, the *Tonan Maru III;* it was a choice target. In a perfect set-up Daspit fired two torpedoes with contact exploders. He saw the splashes indicating hits and the tanker stopped dead in the water, but it did not appear to be sinking. Still, it was a sitting duck. Under nearly ideal conditions, with no anti-sub vessels around, Daspit carefully fired a total of fifteen torpedoes. He observed that thirteen hit the target squarely without exploding. Daspit's team took careful notes.

Furious at the duds, he saved his one remaining torpedo for examination and returned to Pearl Harbor. Daspit was livid, practically speechless, when he reported to Admiral Lockwood. Lockwood was confronted with indisputable proof. The contact exploder was not working properly either. This had previously been disguised because of the other malfunctions: the deep running torpedoes, and the faulty magnetic exploders.

Lockwood received further support on defective torpedoes when Mush Morton came storming back to Pearl Harbor after an exceedingly dangerous but unproductive patrol with *Wahoo* in the Sea of Japan.

Mush Morton was eager to go to sea again after *Wahoo*'s seven-week overhaul in Mare Island, and his own brief stay in Long Beach Naval Hospital. Because of his prostate problems, he was offered a shore job if he wished and his wife, Harriet, pleaded, "Mush, please stay home."

"Harriet," Morton replied, "don't ever ask me that again. I have a job to do to get this war over with. It's for our children and all children."

Before Mush left, he instructed his wife on what to do if he failed to come back: how to handle his pay, insurance, and government benefits.

So battle thirsty had Mush Morton become that some friends worried he might have become overconfident, perhaps thinking himself and mighty *Wahoo* invincible. *Wahoo* departed San Francisco on July 21 for Pearl Harbor and the submarine's sixth war patrol. Lieutenant Roger Paine fleeted up to become Morton's executive officer replacing Dick O'Kane—a jump in a single year that would have taken five years in peacetime.

Chief Gunner's Mate Bill Carr was now Chief of the Boat. The efficient yeoman, Forest Sterling, ran the ship's office and helped with administration. The other officers included Richie Henderson, John Griggs, John Campbell, George Misch, and Eugene Fiedler.

In Pearl Harbor, *Wahoo* was scheduled for ten days of refresher training before setting off again for the Empire, but then the unexpected happened. Roger Paine came down with acute appendicitis and was sent to the hospital. Chief Carr became sick with a respiratory problem and he, too, was hospitalized. Lieutenant Commander Verne L. Skjonsby, who was in O'Kane's Naval Academy class, replaced Paine as XO. He had completed postgraduate studies in ordnance and like O'Kane, he was selected by Morton to man the periscope at Battle Submerged, but Skjonsby hadn't made a war patrol. The junior officers thought the new exec simply did not have Dick O'Kane's weight with Mush Morton. One officer thought that when Mush said, "Charge!" O'Kane could say, "Let's double-check." There was a big difference.

For his part, Roger Paine hated to depart *Wahoo*, but with an emergency appendectomy necessary, there was little he could do about it. He viewed hazardous submarine duty stoically: "the idea was that it couldn't happen to you, but it could. All that noise and banging during depth charging tells you so. When it turns out to be you, it's too late. The feeling is always present. We are fighting a war. This was our part of the war, a job to be done, and we would do it. There was a compulsion to do your duty."

Mush Morton's orders were to patrol the Sea of Japan, where few U.S. submarines ever dared venture since it was almost landlocked, accessed by only three narrow straits. *Wahoo* entered through the northernmost La Perouse Strait. Mush Morton planned to fire one torpedo per ship target, and perhaps rack up a new record—fifteen or so ships—for the

Submarine Force, but he no longer had Dick O'Kane and Roger Paine as his crack firing party. Worse, his torpedoes wouldn't work. In nine attacks, ten torpedoes fired at six ships with easy set-ups either broached, made erratic runs, or were duds—hitting ships' sides with only a dull thump. Morton suspected a defective exploder mechanism.

"Damn the torpedoes," he wrote in *Wahoo*'s log.

Furious, Morton broke radio silence to report the disastrous torpedo performance in the dangerous Sea of Japan and requested that he bring the remaining fourteen fish home for examination. He transited La Perouse Strait on the surface at night. In the Sea of Okhotsk, *Wahoo* surfaced to sink three sampans with her 4-inch gun. Morton continued to Midway, where he dropped off ten torpedoes and returned to Pearl with four. Yeoman Sterling thought the crew seemed gloomy.

Morton was understandably frustrated and angry. For the first time, he returned to the barn empty-handed. His division and squadron commanders questioned whether it was wise to fire only one torpedo per target, rather than a spread of two, three or four. Admiral Lockwood concurred, remarking: "Failure to use torpedo spreads during most of the attacks undoubtedly contributed materially to the lack of success." In his endorsement, Lockwood added: "This patrol is not considered successful for the Combat Insignia Award." These were bitter words for Mush Morton.

Given his star skipper's experience in the Sea of Japan, Admiral Lockwood was determined to get to the root of the exploder problem. First he assigned *Muskallunge* supervised by Captain C.B. "Swede" Momsen, inventor of the Momsen escape lung, to fire Skipper Lawrence Daspit's remaining torpedo and two others at a submerged cliff at the deserted island of Kahoolawe, a Navy bombing range. The Mark 14 torpedo was recovered by divers and returned to Pearl for examination. Experts found that the exploder mechanism released the firing pin, but the pin hadn't hit the primer cap with sufficient force to set it off.

Lockwood ordered backup tests at the Sub Base. Technicians loaded torpedoes with concrete rather than torpex, and equipped them with exploders. They lifted the fish with a cherry picker crane to a height of 90 feet and dropped the weapon nose first on a steel plate. This duplicated a direct 90-degree hit in combat. Of the first ten warheads dropped, seven failed to explode! The impact test corroborated the experiment by *Muskallunge* at Kahoolawe.

Further tests were made with the cherry picker. It was found that when the torpedo hit the steel plate set at an angle, a glancing blow, the exploders worked. This explained why less than perfect hits resulted in explosions while deadeye shots were duds. Lockwood asked his technicians to devise a stronger exploder mechanism, which would function as designed. They readily did so.

Lockwood alerted Spike Blandy at BuOrd. The Newport Torpedo Station then conducted tests. They confirmed Pearl Harbor's findings and a new exploder mechanism was designed in Newport. Meanwhile, Lockwood advised his skippers to try for glancing blows against targets rather than right-angle hits. During this period, a famous message went out to the submariners at sea recommending they try to hit their targets "on the turn of the bilge," so that the unimproved exploder had the desired glancing contact. Without doubt, Jim Calvert on *Jack* thought, this message caused some blue language in the wardrooms of the Sub Force. With no sure way of estimating the draft of targets, and with all the other problems an attacking firing party has, asking for hits on the turn of the bilge seemed a bit much. It was a message Calvert was sure that Admiral Lockwood and his staff would rather forget.

Admiral Lockwood believed he had finally solved the torpedo crisis, one problem disguising another, in the face of resistance from BuOrd. But Admiral Christie still insisted that boats attached to his Southwest Pacific command must use the magnetic exploder. Many skippers remained confused over the strange and irritating lack of coordination at the Force command level.

Submariners might have been cheered had they known that the German submarine force ran into its own problems with defective torpedoes, but Grand Admiral Doenitz, Germany's chief submariner, insisted on getting to the root of the issue, and when he did, ordered four ordnance officers and officials court-martialed and jailed. If only the U.S. Navy's arrogant Gun Club had been dealt with so summarily.

In October 1943, Charlie Lockwood was made vice admiral. He promptly notified the men in SubPac: "The Force Commander desires to tell the Submarine Force that he considers his spot promotion to Vice Admiral not as a personal honor but as a commendation of the officers and men of the entire submarine organization by the President for the splendidly aggressive spirit displayed in action against the enemy and for the severe punishment inflicted on him."

So while the submarines in Southwest Pacific remained operationally independent, Charles Lockwood as the only three-star admiral in the Submarine Force became the type of commander who set the pace, and established policies and doctrine. That suited U.S. submarine skippers just fine. Dick O'Kane looked forward to bringing *Tang* under the command of Uncle Charlie Lockwood.

CHAPTER ELEVEN

The Deepest Dive

Dick O'Kane began the long-awaited sea trials of *Tang* in San Francisco Bay. In practice exercises, he was delighted to find that *Tang* functioned without the bugs usually found in new ships fresh out of the yard. O'Kane soon made shallow test dives in the Bay and supervised the firing of dummy torpedoes to check out the operation of *Tang*'s ten tubes. O'Kane drove his crew hard. He believed deeply in training: only constant training could bring a submarine up to the level where it could function well in combat. But he was not a stickler for spit-and-polish stuff. "Boats" Leibold thought that while some crewmen complained about the rigorous training, those with more experience at sea knew that O'Kane's methods and tactics would pay off. Still, some older chiefs aboard grumbled at the intensity of the exercises. But Dick knew he had to train the crew for the trying times ahead in combat. Though some were veterans, they had never operated as a team aboard *Tang*. Nor had he proved himself as a skipper.

Mush Morton had entrusted him with the periscope on *Wahoo*, but O'Kane decided to man it himself on *Tang*. It was not that he hadn't faith in Murray Frazee; Dick just saw no reason to let his own periscope experience go to waste. O'Kane was aware of the dangers of being a martinet: he had seen how morale of crews suffered under such skippers, and had himself served under one or two. But he did strive to maintain a tone aboard *Tang*, which could best be described as professionalism. He had faith in Fraz as an exec who did more than his share in holding the crew together during the sometimes difficult shakedown period.

In another innovation, O'Kane rotated his officers around. He didn't follow normal procedures. Instead, he picked officers for the jobs they were most comfortable in. Ordinarily, an engineer doubled as the diving officer, but O'Kane would let everyone take turns diving the boat and determine which officer seemed the best at that job.

Tang's last sequence out of Mare Island was to establish her behavior at test depth, 400 feet, much deeper than the older boats Dick had served aboard. Test depth meant a 100 percent safety factor at that level. In theory, a submarine could dive to twice her test depth without the pressure hull imploding, but that was theory and few skippers purposely tried it.

The deeper dives took place outside the Golden Gate where the Continental Shelf dropped off precipitously. O'Kane ordered the boat under, and took her down in stages with shipyard machinists aboard equipped with micrometers to test the hull's compression. At 400 and then 438 feet, O'Kane and the workmen found that *Tang*'s hull deflection was negligible. Dick O'Kane felt a confidence in *Tang*'s hull at a test depth he believed few skippers could share.

Tang was ready for her next exercise: a high-speed endurance run to San Diego with representatives from Fairbanks-Morse and General Electric monitoring the diesel engines, generators and motors. This would be the first phase of *Tang*'s shakedown cruise that would train the crew to function as a deadly team at sea. It would also enable O'Kane to perfect his own skills as a ship handler. Submarine officers prided themselves on their ability to maneuver a ship well, but O'Kane wanted his officers standing the OOD watches to enhance and develop their own expertise at the helm. He made sure everyone excelled in seamanship.

On the run south, *Tang* was escorted by the destroyer *Patterson,* the same tin can that had accompanied *Wahoo* from Brisbane earlier in the year. But *Patterson* suffered problems with her fuel oil system and had to return to San Francisco. Since *Tang* was well into her 24-hour endurance run, O'Kane had no wish to break it off. He informed Commander Western Sea Frontier, who controlled coastwise shipping, that *Tang* was proceeding alone.

As a former tin can sailor, O'Kane wisely plotted a course that passed well clear of Point Arguello and the Santa Barbara Channel Islands. Twenty years before, he remembered, a fourteen-ship destroyer squadron en route from San Francisco to San Diego in column formation at night in heavy fog was travelling at high speed, similarly on an engineering run. The destroyers were of the same class as his old ship, *Pruitt*. The flagship's navigator misjudged the turn to the eastward following the California coast and steamed straight onto the rocky shore at Point Pedernales near the town of Lompoc. In follow-the-leader fashion, eight more destroyers piled onto the rocks. Seven of the nine ships were total wrecks; two managed to pull free of the rocks and remain afloat. Twenty-three sailors lost their lives in what was considered the worst navigational disaster in the history of the U.S. Navy.

Along the way, O'Kane put another of his ideas into practice. He believed that *Tang* would be more effective operating on the surface when possible: it gave the ship more mobility and made target-finding easier. So O'Kane crowded the superstructure with lookouts, more than other submarines, all equipped with the big 7×50 binoculars. He believed that with sharp-eyed lookouts *Tang* could spot enemy planes or ships before being sighted, and act accordingly. Murray Frazee agreed: below the surface a submarine was almost blind. Fraz believed Dick was introducing ideas for spotting enemy ships before they found you and without resorting to radar, which could be intercepted. He thought the main worry of a submariner was that a target could get by because the submarine didn't see it.

On schedule, *Tang* arrived at the huge San Diego naval complex, and was greeted by Commodore Byron McCandless, the base commander with whom O'Kane had served in the destroyer *Pruitt*. At dawn the next day, *Tang* began a week of intense training exercises. O'Kane decided to continue *Wahoo*'s practice of aiming single torpedoes at a target ship rather than simply firing automatic spreads of fish. O'Kane split the 79-man crew into three shifts, as would be the case on a war patrol. He trained each watch in diving *Tang* and firing dummy torpedoes at the destroyer targets. Then the fire control team practiced night approaches, submerged and surfaced, with the escort destroyers. *Tang* came through with flying colors.

In yet another innovation, O'Kane borrowed a tape recorder from the naval base and copied all the conversations in the conning tower and control room during practice approaches. He replayed the tape, illustrating to his officers and the crew how much extraneous conversation went on during the simulated attacks. "Hey, there's too much talking here," he commented.

The captain liked to get all his officers' input around the wardroom table when discussing anything connected with *Tang*. When the points were made, O'Kane would say: "Okay, that's enough." And everyone was quiet.

Ashore in San Diego, Dick O'Kane showed an equally decisive, if unusual, authority. One evening Boats Leibold, recently married, borrowed a Navy jeep assigned to *Tang* without permission. After several drinks, he ran into Commander O'Kane at the U.S. Grant Hotel. Leibold sounded off in O'Kane's presence and O'Kane ordered him back to the ship with some sharp comments.

The next day Exec Frazee said to Leibold, "I heard you had words with the captain."

An apprehensive Leibold admitted he had been out of line. Frazee saw O'Kane.

"Do you want to see Boats for a talk?" Fraz asked.

"No," O'Kane said. "That's the end of it."

Much later, Leibold asked O'Kane why he was not disciplined. O'Kane replied, "I had faith in you, Boats."

With his customary thoroughness, O'Kane had kept track of Japanese advances in anti-submarine activities. Early in the war the Imperial Japanese Navy had generally ignored anti-submarine warfare (ASW) on the grounds that it was defensive: their ships were offensive, with offensive-minded officers. The rapid early victories of the Japanese Navy and the ineffectiveness of U.S. submarines reinforced that view. Two major mistakes characterized Japanese anti-sub strategy: they failed to organize an Empire-wide convoy system and they failed to build large numbers of small, effective, anti-sub escorts.

Their early convoys were usually small and lightly escorted, and some civilian merchantmen wanted to sail independently, unescorted. Near terminus points they would be met by local anti-sub patrols, but on the open sea legs, they relied on strategic routing and zigzagging. In U.S. submarine circles, there was an axiom: for every ship saved by a fortuitous zig, another is lost by an unfortunate zag.

The Japanese Navy organized a small escort force in 1942, covering the Japan–Singapore sea-lane. A second group was formed to patrol the Japan–Truk route. Not until the fall of 1943 did the Japanese high command organize the Grand Escort Fleet, along with an air escort squadron specifically designed to protect convoys against submarines.

Earlier in the war, Japanese tactics had been weak. U.S. submariners at the sharp end, like Dick O'Kane, learned that Japanese skippers often failed to press attacks to a conclusion, assuming a U.S. submarine had been sunk by a desultory effort. Escort captains appeared to be anxious to get back to their convoys. Japanese limitations were recognized by U.S. skippers and exploited: their depth charges were set too shallow, they broke off their attacks too soon, and they indulged in over-optimistic estimates of results.

The Japanese Navy had no shipboard radar in the early stages of the war. When radar became available, it was used sparingly, usually at night or in low visibility. The Japanese were afraid their radar signals would be detected—they themselves used radar detector equipment on their ships. However, the enemy's radio direction finder network was well developed. They were able to intercept almost all U.S. radio transmissions, except for very low or very high frequencies. Thus the Japanese could fix the position of a submarine transmitting on the surface within an area of about 100 square miles. This provided a means of keeping tabs on the number of U.S. subs in various areas, the number on patrol, and the general distribution in the Pacific. Luckily, the direction finders could not pinpoint exact locations of American vessels to help Japanese ASW escort vessels. Japanese underwater listening gear was also excellent, and echo-ranging destroyers were a constant threat to U.S. boats. But no hunter-killer teams were sent against submarines, and the Japanese never assigned small carriers to that vital task as the Americans and British did in the Atlantic.

A key weakness of the Japanese anti-sub efforts in the first part of the war was the fact that their depth charges had a surprisingly light punch: only 200–300 pounds. More importantly, the charges were rarely set to detonate below 150 feet. This was precious knowledge and an invaluable asset for U.S. sub skippers. To evade serious damage from "ash-cans," captains would descend to 200 feet or deeper. The Japanese did not know how deep even the older American submarines could submerge. This was a closely held secret during the war. U.S. skippers realized that if they crash-dived soon enough and deep enough they could avoid the worst of a depth charge beating.

But almost overnight that built-in safety factor vanished. The Submarine Force was hit by the worst security breach that befell it during the war. Admiral Lockwood was always publicity shy for his service, except for rare exceptions, like *Wahoo,* when he thought news about a submarine's exploits was important for Navy or national morale. "We operated under such secrecy and anonymity," Lockwood explained, "that only the barest mention was made of these men of lonely heroism, who fought the war not in the newspaper headlines, but sealed off beneath the sea, in great steel hulls that sometimes became their tombs. We preferred to publish nothing at all, not even the score of enemy ships sunk by returning submarines. We wanted no part of the Navy Department's campaign for play-by-play account of the war. We wanted the Japanese to think that their existing methods were highly effective, that another of our subs had gone to Davy Jones' locker."

Despite these precautions, the most mindlessly damaging security blow to the Silent Service occurred in Congress. Japanese propaganda had been making claims of massive sinkings of American submarines, which, while not true, were fine with the U.S. undersea sailors—let the Japanese be complacent over their alleged sinkings. Incredibly, Congressman Andrew Jackson May, a 68-year-old member of the House Military Affairs Committee, returned from a junket to the Pacific in the summer of 1943 and held a press conference. He pointed out that the Japanese claims of sinking U.S. subs were overstated—because their depth charges were set to go off too shallow. U.S boats could avoid them by diving deep, perhaps deeper than the Japanese thought them capable. The newspaper reports of this catastrophic blunder reached Japan and its navy reset depth charges accordingly.

Privately, Admiral Lockwood blamed Congressman May's bombast for the loss of U.S. submarines and lives. An incensed Lockwood wrote a colleague: "I hear Congressman May said the depth charges are not set deep enough. He would be pleased to know [they] set them deeper now." Later Lockwood wrote, "I consider that indiscretion cost us ten submarines and 800 officers and men."

While on the West Coast, Dick O'Kane learned that the Submarine Force was finally winding up patrols in the European Theater of Operations. American submarine activities in the Atlantic and European theaters of war proved to be something of a bust. Many old S-boats were sent out on local patrol from Panama but they never sank any Japanese or German warships. The Panama Canal was, curiously, never the target of an enemy submarine or surface bombardment. At the behest of the British, U.S. submarines were sent to the British Isles in 1942 and early 1943. However, there were few Nazi targets for them to shoot at, and the British boats were better designed for operating in the constricted waters of the Mediterranean Sea.

U.S. submariners in the Atlantic were sometimes the targets for friendly aircraft, which often bombed first and asked questions later. Three submarines were lost: *S-26* rammed by a U.S. escort vessel off Panama; *R-12* sunk off Key West by a flooded torpedo room; and *Dorado,* a fleet boat running from New London to the Panama Canal and Pearl Harbor. *Dorado* was believed sunk—when it temporarily changed course to avoid heavy seas—by a U.S. patrol plane flying out of Bermuda. In all, eighty-eight patrols were conducted in 1942 with no confirmed sinkings. There were seventeen patrols in the first half of 1943 with no confirmed results. So the boats, which were under the command of Commander Submarines Atlantic, and operated out of Panama, Bermuda, and Roseneath, Scotland, were sent to the Pacific via the Panama Canal.

In San Diego, Dick O'Kane was finishing *Tang*'s rigorous training schedule, firing dummy torpedoes at destroyer targets off the Southern California coast. O'Kane welcomed another addition to the wardroom, Lieutenant Ed Beaumont, a radar specialist. Beaumont's arrival meant that O'Kane had the luxury of having an Officer of the Deck and an Assistant OOD on each of the three watches. Though O'Kane had undergone depth charging, as a captain he was interested in the effect prolonged underwater bombardment would have on the crew. He and other skippers read with fascination the special report circulated in the Submarine Force concerning the underwater ordeal of *Puffer* on her first patrol in October 1943.

With Lieutenant Commander M.J. Jensen as her skipper, *Puffer* was patrolling the northern waters of the Makassar Strait between the large islands of Borneo and Celebes just after dawn. Jensen hit a Japanese merchant ship with two torpedoes. The target listed but did not sink. Jensen fired two more torpedoes: one was premature, the other a dud. As Jensen maneuvered for another shot, an enemy Chidori escort came out of nowhere and dropped half a dozen depth charges. They exploded close aboard. *Puffer*'s conning tower hatch and door lifted off their seats causing water to pour in. A number of sea valves began leaking. *Puffer*'s rudder and stern planes suffered damage. The submarine went deep, but the destroyer hung on: it may have sighted escaping air bubbles or diesel oil. Five more depth charges were dropped nearby.

From then on, the Chidori continued to drop depth charges, at greater range. They were not set deep enough to crush the submarine, but the crew was unnerved by the apparent ease with which the Japanese vessel seemed to return and find *Puffer,* a few hundred feet down.

Puffer's air conditioning was shut down to conserve power and prevent noise. After the submarine had been down for twelve hours, carbon dioxide absorbent and oxygen were used to purify the stultifying air. A second vessel joined the Japanese ship in the early evening and the depth charging continued into the night, though it did no further damage to *Puffer.* The last depth charges were dropped just after 0100.

The two ships continued making dry runs over *Puffer* until shortly after noon. Thirty-one hours after submerging and twenty-five hours after the first attack, the enemy broke off, but *Puffer* stayed down until 1900 when she finally surfaced in bright moonlight after thirty-seven hours below.

As the extensive report indicated, *Puffer*'s depth charging was not one of the worst of the war, nor had her machinery suffered serious damage. What was of special interest to the Sub Force command was the reaction of *Puffer*'s personnel: how the crew stood up, how they behaved. The staff wanted to discern how the human mind reacted to the ordeal. It was SubPac's first attempt at "psychoanalyzing" a crew.

The first salient fact noted was the almost unbearable heat. Once the air conditioning was shut off, the temperature inside the sub rose to 125 degrees in some compartments. The steam room atmosphere affected the crew almost like a drug. Men gasped for breath and slipped on the greasy decks. Sweating crewmembers thirsted for cool drinks, but with refrigeration off everything liquid soon reached sweltering room temperature. Men drank, vomited, and then drank again. Profuse sweating and their inability to keep down liquids produced severe dehydration in the crew.

Despite the addition of oxygen and carbon dioxide absorbent, the air was totally foul toward the end. An officer making the rounds of the compartment had to pause several times to rest. He found some men in a state of physical collapse. Others were in a stupor and unable to be roused to stand watch. As the hours went by, volunteers manned stations. Some men seemed past caring what happened.

The main emotion shown by the men was anger: anger at the enemy, and at themselves for having been caught in such a predicament. They fantasized about what they would do to the Japanese vessels, even suggesting such crazy ideas as discharging acid around the enemy craft to eat holes in the hulls.

The officers generally held up better than the men, mainly because they were privy to what was happening: the movement of the enemy vessels, the state of *Puffer*. The men were left in a void. The suspense kept feeding their imaginations. The officers tried to go through the boat explaining the situation. The crew did not like listening to the loudspeaker system because they thought it was too noisy and would be heard by enemy sonar men, so the conning tower talker began passing the word quietly through the battle circuits to talkers in other compartments.

Men who were idle were subjected to the suspense of hearing the approaching Chidoris pinging as the sub was sought out, followed by the sound of approaching propellers, and then the explosion of the depth-charge salvo. Sometimes there were no explosions. The constant round of build-up and climax strained sailors' nerves severely.

Importantly, the commanding officer seemed listless and his morose behavior caused the crew's morale to plummet. He toyed with the idea of surfacing. He allowed an informal vote among the crew to be taken. Most said they would rather sweat it out. One crewman said he didn't care whether they stayed under or surfaced but he would not commit himself in a vote.

Some officers and men expressed a desire, in their frustration, to surface and fight the Chidori with *Puffer*'s deck gun, which would have been hopelessly outmatched. As spirits sagged, one man suggested flooding the submarine and getting it over with. The most depressing aspect of *Puffer*'s plight was the apparent ease with which the Chidori could locate the submarine. Toward the end, some officers believed they would not come out alive. An order to don life-jackets in case the sub had to surface quickly produced a deeply negative reaction among crewmen. They thought it meant the end was near. Later, officers agreed that the crew should have been alerted for the order to put on life-jackets. They concurred that running the air conditioning would have been preferable to the oppressive heat and humidity, which so sapped the crew's physical and mental strength.

After *Puffer* surfaced, the crew rapidly recovered. In twenty-four hours, they were restored physically, but the symptoms of mental strain lasted for some time.

The Force Command concluded that when a submarine had been through such an ordeal the crew should be broken up; otherwise newcomers would be considered "outsiders" by those who went through the depth charging. For his own lack of leadership, the captain was relieved of command.

The *Puffer* report pointed out that some of the sailors who remained at their stations were not those who had been considered the "leaders" of the crew. Many who held up best were the quieter, more phlegmatic types, who weren't much in evidence when things were running smoothly. The report said succinctly: "The worriers and the hurriers all crapped out, leaving the plodders to bring home the ship."

Dick O'Kane spent hours training his crew in crash dives. As a result, *Tang* could eventually dive from the surface to periscope depth, 60 feet below, in a remarkable 30 seconds. Clay Decker on the bow planes thought that was pretty damn good. As a final training fillip, Dick O'Kane was determined to show the crew what *Tang* could do in a really deep dive. He was keen to find out which hull fittings might show signs of weakness, even though the pressure hull itself was holding firm. O'Kane knew that plenty of water overhead was the greatest possible insurance against Japanese depth charges.

In planning his deep dive in San Diego, Dick O'Kane was aware that Admiral Lockwood never issued precise rules on how far down to take a boat, leaving that to skippers as the tactical situation dictated. O'Kane's idea was to dive deep so that *Tang*'s officers and crew would have a special confidence in her. With engineer Bill Walsh as diving officer, O'Kane ordered *Tang* down by deliberate stages. Senior petty officers manned phones in all compartments reporting on leaks or any other signs of stress. *Tang* sank deeper. The submarine went past test depth with the crews' eyes on the large round depth indicator. At 450 feet, a gauge line parted, and the hose to the Bendix speed log, which projects outside the boat, broke. A crewman jammed a raw potato into the gauge line plugging the leak until the valve could be closed. The speed log's shutoff valve was in sight and was quickly shut, too.

At 525 feet, the rollers that held the sound heads in the lowered position cracked. O'Kane ordered *Tang* to surface. Overnight, with the backing of Commodore McCandless, Navy Yard ship fitters installed a strengthened type of roller for the sound heads. A machinist soldered a new fitting on the gauge line. A welding hose was substituted on the Bendix speed log.

The next free afternoon, O'Kane ordered another deep dive. *Tang* slipped past the 525-foot level with no problems. At 580 feet, a flanged joint in the vent risers sprung a leak. O'Kane ordered *Tang* once again to surface and headed back to the Navy Yard. Ship fitters worked half the night tightening the bolts on the flanges and fashioned a special wrench for the crew to use in case they leaked again.

The next morning at dawn, Dick O'Kane ordered *Tang* down again. The crew remained tense as their captain coolly brought the ship down. *Tang* creaked and groaned but held together. The ship slowly went deeper. The depth gauge needle slipped past the 575-foot mark. O'Kane called for reports from the compartments. The crew seemed nervous but no major leaks were reported. The depth needle hit 600 feet and stopped on the holding pin. That was the last figure on the depth gauge. Despite the air conditioning, many of the crew were sweating. What was the captain up to? What was he trying to prove? *Tang* slipped lower, about 625 feet. This had never been done before.

Dick O'Kane instructed Bill Walsh to level off. He called for reports from the boat: there were a few minor leaks and some watertight interior doors didn't seal properly. Some crewmembers were uneasy: it was like coming to the edge of the ocean. They thought it time to head back up. But Dick

O'Kane insisted on maneuvering at various speeds to test and illustrate how well the undersea propulsion plant functioned at that great depth. As a final feat, O'Kane ordered *Tang* to maneuver in reverse!

Dick O'Kane was satisfied. Fraz knew that nobody in the submarine had ever been that deep—accidentally or on purpose—or even close to it. Some crewmen, even chiefs, were scared.

The captain ordered the submarine to rise slowly in stages to the surface, and returned to San Diego. It was the deepest recorded dive that a U.S. submarine ever made—and returned to tell about it. That fact seemed to spook some of the men, but the unique test dive, Exec Murray Frazee thought, showed the crew that Dick O'Kane was a different kind of skipper. Fraz had a lot of faith in Dick and the officers had a sense that their skipper knew exactly what he was doing.

For the last week of shakedown, Captain O'Kane requested that *Tang* be permitted to operate independently. He and Murray Frazee decided to take her south along Mexico's coast. O'Kane planned to treat the coastline as if it were Honshu in Japan, using combat recon techniques, approaches on shipping, observing harbors, everything except firing torpedoes. Mexican fishing boats substituted for Japanese marus as O'Kane shifted all his officers around so that each had a turn at performing all the duties aboard.

On return to San Diego, the submarine division commander learned that O'Kane had gone south. He was aghast, though O'Kane pointed out that his orders had not prohibited *Tang* from operating off Mexico.

"You could have caused an international incident if you had been sighted," the commander warned.

"Sir, if *Tang* can't avoid the Mexican fishing fleet," O'Kane replied, "she doesn't have any business going on patrol."

Tang was given overall high marks for the shakedown and was ordered back to Mare Island for a final check. The rigorous schedule had irritated a few of the crew, not used to Dick O'Kane's ideas that only tough, constant training would eventually save lives in combat. Nerves were on edge. Boats Leibold thought O'Kane was pushing the crew to the last degree, though he could understand why, and approved. O'Kane drove himself harder than anyone.

The day before departure from San Diego, the chief commissary steward told the exec he was shook up by the deep dive and wanted off *Tang*. Frazee knew a chief cook was essential and that a replacement couldn't be supplied immediately. Frazee told the chief he couldn't get off right away. The commissary man replied, "Well, if you're not going to do anything about it now, I just won't show up tomorrow morning."

Frazee remarked to Chief of the Boat Ballinger, who was standing next to him, "Chief, you heard what he said, didn't you?"

"I sure did," Ballinger replied.

Frazee grabbed the chief cook by the front of the shirt and said, "Listen, you son-of-a-bitch, if you're not here tomorrow morning at 0800 when we sail, I'm going to have you shot for desertion in time of war! Now, have you got that straight?"

The chief blanched. Frazee's approach was not according to Navy Regulations, but it worked. When *Tang* departed for San Francisco Bay, the chief was aboard.

Two days later, O'Kane brought *Tang* into dock at Mare Island. To instill a sense of commitment in the crew, the captain read the "Articles for the Government of the Navy," commonly known as "Rocks and Shoals." Article 19 was the bottom line: it said a commanding officer was culpable if he "does not do his utmost to overtake and capture or destroy any vessel which it is his duty to encounter." This was Dick O'Kane's version of Mush Morton's address to *Wahoo*'s crew on taking command in Brisbane. The reading of the articles, which listed punishments including execution for a variety of offenses, seemed to rattle some crewmembers. Others, too, had been shaken by the deep practice dive off San Diego. Chief Ballinger informed Murray Frazee that a few other sailors had expressed a desire to get off *Tang*. O'Kane told Frazee and Ballinger to tell the reluctant sailors that their requests for transfer would be granted, but only when *Tang* reached Pearl Harbor. Nothing further was said about the matter.

At the last minute, *Tang* was ordered to Hunter's Point Shipyard in San Francisco for the installation of new, low-cavitation propellers which were much quieter running underwater. So with these, and knowledge of the depth to which *Tang* could dive, Dick O'Kane believed that the boat was ready for action. He thought his crew and officers formed a finely tuned team, and took to heart Commodore Arleigh Burke's dictum that "the difference between a good officer and a fine officer is about 10 seconds."

O'Kane's own personality still had some rough edges, for he could be irritable and impatient, but those around him sensed a new maturity in command. He was a cool and confident captain. Now he might have another ship personally to avenge. Rumors were circulating that Mush Morton was overdue on *Wahoo*'s seventh war patrol.

With a crew of seventy-nine aboard, O'Kane and *Tang* observed New Year's Day, 1944, by sailing out from San Francisco headed for the Hawaiian Islands. As *Tang* passed through the Golden Gate, Ernestine O'Kane, Marsha and James were parked at the observation point at the end of the great suspension bridge. They waved from beside their car as *Tang* with Dick at the conn passed below them. Ernestine O'Kane wore a bright red coat so that her husband would notice her as he again sailed westward to war.

CHAPTER TWELVE

"Fook 'Em, Boys, Let's Go"

En route to Pearl Harbor, Dick O'Kane posted his Captain's Standing Night Order to the Officer of the Deck and the phrase would remain *Tang*'s watchwords:

"Report any changes in weather or other circumstances.

"If in doubt, call me to the bridge. If in doubt about being in doubt, call me immediately or dive.

"Remember, no officer will ever be reprimanded for diving, even though it prove unnecessary."

During a brisk six-day run, O'Kane poured over copies of war patrol reports of other submarines to bring himself up to speed on the latest tactics, results, and experiences of the Sub Force.

Tang sighted landfall at Molokai Island, picked up an escort, and sailed past Diamond Head on Oahu. O'Kane increased the deck detail so that crewmen who had never been in Pearl Harbor could see the famous anchorage and naval complex. There were few remnants now of the Japanese attack, except for the hulls of *Oklahoma* and *Arizona*. *Tang* tied up at the Submarine Base on January 8, 1944, scheduled for two weeks of training. Her skipper paid a courtesy call on Admiral Lockwood, ComSubPac. After a cordial welcome, Dick O'Kane reported to the Commander, Training Command, who turned out to be his and Mush Morton's old friend, Captain Babe Brown.

Babe Brown was Admiral Lockwood's right-hand man and close friend, a good-natured, outgoing officer who had saved Mush Morton from being surfaced a year before. He was a former squadron commander. A submarine squadron, commanded by a four-stripe captain, consisted of a subma-

rine tender, twelve boats in two divisions, and a submarine
rescue ship. Aboard the tender or based ashore were two relief, or refit, crews for each division. Exclusive of ships'
crews, the squadron complement was about 415 officers and
men. Squadron and division commanders, though their actual rank was captain or commander, were given the courtesy
title of "Commodore." Because they were older, some commanders had not made a war patrol, while their skippers had.

Squadron and division commanders were administrators,
supervising the upkeep and training of subs assigned to
them. They also wrote endorsements on the patrol reports of
incoming submarines. Admiral Lockwood and his operations officer Captain Dick Voge directly assigned all war patrols. Once a skipper departed on patrol, he was in charge
of his boat's operations, though ComSubPac might direct
him from time to time to a specific task. The endorsements—
positive or negative—by division, squadron, and Lockwood
on submarine patrol reports became the closest thing to submarine doctrine during the war.

When a new boat like *Tang* arrived in Pearl, or a veteran sub needed a refresher, it was taken out by Training
Command officers—often those in charge of squadrons or
divisions—for an exercise patrol lasting several days. "They
worked your tail off," grumbled Slade Cutter, "twenty-four
hours around the clock: numerous torpedo exercises, attacks
by ASW craft, destroyers or aircraft. You had a very tough,
senior training officer on board who was looking over your
shoulder. If in their view you were ready to go, they certified
you. But if in their view you were still rusty, they would either prescribe another practice patrol or you might find that
you had been recommended for relief. It was very realistic,
very hard on all and sundry."

Babe Brown, who was an admirer of Dick O'Kane, said,
"Dick, now what would *Tang* like to do, and does she need
anything?" O'Kane gave Brown a proposed eight-day schedule for training exercises.

"That looks good to me," Brown said. "Will you have
Frazee work it up with operations?" O'Kane was surprised

but pleased that Babe Brown knew the name of *Tang*'s executive officer.

At their meeting in SubPac headquarters, it fell to Babe Brown to confirm to Dick O'Kane that his beloved *Wahoo* was indeed "overdue and presumed lost" with Mush Morton and all hands.

When *Wahoo* departed Pearl Harbor for her seventh war patrol, Mush Morton was in an ugly mood. The submarine command endorsements on his sixth patrol—suggesting his poor torpedo performance resulted from taking single shots rather than from defective fish—infuriated him. He was determined to redeem his honor and *Wahoo*'s reputation. Morton quickly readied *Wahoo* in a fast turnaround for her seventh patrol. Mush requested a return to penetrate the dangerous waters of the Sea of Japan for his patrol area. Lockwood gave some thought to beaching his favorite skipper to allow him to cool off, but he decided he couldn't deny Mush Morton his request for the war patrol.

By now most of Captain Morton's officers were fairly new: only Richie Henderson, George Misch and John Campbell had made more than two patrols on *Wahoo*. The steadying influence of officers like Dick O'Kane, George Grider, Roger Paine, and Chandler Jackson was gone. They were replaced by officers who were possibly awed by Morton's towering reputation. George Grider thought Mush had been surrounded by officers who knew him well enough to suggest to him what *not* to do. Roger Paine believed that Morton's new exec, Verne Skjonsby, did not yet have Dick O'Kane's authority in terms of advising or cautioning the captain.

Yeoman Sterling, after the fourth patrol, had put in for advanced stenography school in San Diego, since that would be a requirement for further advancement in rating. At Pearl, shortly before *Wahoo* was scheduled to depart, Sterling was delighted to receive notice that his request was approved, with an authorization for transfer to San Diego to join the next steno school class in November. Excitedly, Sterling showed Captain Morton the letter.

"That's great news, Yeo," Morton said. Then he added, "Yeo, I'm going to ask a favor of you."

Sterling's heart sank. "Yes, sir."

"How's about you making one more patrol with me? We'll be back in October. I'll get you plane transportation back to the States."

"Captain," Sterling replied, downhearted, "your word is good enough for me. I'll get back to work."

"Thanks, Yeo, I knew you wouldn't let me down."

Another sailor, Fire Controlman Robert Logue, was on the tender USS *Orion* awaiting reassignment and bumped into Mush Morton. He informed Morton he had experience with the new electric torpedo and said, "I'd like to make a war patrol with you." Morton invited him aboard. Every sailor in the Submarine Force wanted to be on *Wahoo*.

On her first leg to Midway, *Wahoo* gained a special transit passenger: Commander Gene Tunney, the legendary heavyweight boxing champion, now a physical education specialist. On the four-day jaunt to Midway, Tunney proved to be a popular addition to the wardroom, but he turned off the crew when he advocated that rest periods at the Royal Hawaiian should include early reveille followed by calisthenics before breakfast, and running drills before lunch. For the afternoon, Tunney recommended organized softball and volleyball tournaments between submarine crews.

At one point, Mush Morton asked Commander Tunney, "What do you think of submarines, Gene?"

"I have been giving it a good deal of thought, Captain, and have developed a plan for their welfare."

Puzzled, Morton asked, "What is that?"

"Men aboard submarines don't get enough exercise. I'm in favor of letting them have two or three days in which to do whatever they please when they come off war patrol. After that there will be daily exercises and hardening drills. Their liquor and cigarettes will be taken from them. By the time they are ready for sea again, they will be in excellent physical condition to withstand the rigors of undersea life."

Sterling, who was present, thought: "Oh, brother. This is the great Gene Tunney! No wonder he became a world's champion boxer. But he sure doesn't know anything about submariners."

Morton smiled at Sterling. "The commander has a fine idea, don't you think, Yeo?"

"The men will receive it with great enthusiasm," Sterling replied straight-faced.

Commander Tunney looked pleased.

During a six-hour refueling layover at Midway, *Wahoo* tied up alongside the tender *Sperry,* with the Squadron Ten Commander aboard. Sterling noticed Ship's Cook Juano Rennels looking unsettled.

"Yeo," Rennels said, "I got a terrible feeling that something is going to happen to us on this trip."

"Aw, snap out of it. I feel bad, too, but nothing's going to happen to *Wahoo* while I'm on here and don't you forget it."

Motor Machinist's Mate Olin Jacobs, wiping his greasy hands on a rag, broke in, "I have a feeling that we're going to catch hell this trip out."

"Forget it, Jake," Sterling replied. "The only thing that will catch hell will be the Japs. How's the wife and that prospective baby doing?"

Jacobs brightened. "Last letter I got, the wife told me not to worry none. They're just fine."

"Another trip or two," Sterling said, "and you'll be back there bouncing him on your knees."

"I hope so." Jacobs looked doubtful.

Sterling returned to the tiny ship's office. He was puzzled that Torpedoman Oscar Finkelstein was still aboard. Finkelstein suffered from chronic seasickness and was due to be transferred off *Wahoo* back at Pearl Harbor. Without checking with Sterling, a relief crew yeoman mistakenly transferred Seaman John August instead.

Suddenly, Sterling felt a huge hand slapping him on the back. Angered, Sterling turned with his fists clenched, ready to swing at a crewman. It was Mush Morton who pointed to the silver oak leaves on his collar, his badge of rank. Meaning don't swing on your skipper. "You still want to go back to the States? Got your orders made up, Yeo?" Morton asked, referring to the steno school authorization.

"No, sir, but I could sure make them up in a damn quick hurry if you gave the word."

"We've got an hour before we sail," Morton said. "Let's go up to the squadron and get you a relief."

Sterling thought Morton was joking.

"If you mean it, Captain, what are we waiting for?"

Aboard *Sperry,* Morton told the squadron commander, "I'm giving up the best goddamn yeoman I ever had working for me. He's got orders to go back to stenography school. Have you got a relief yeoman you can give me?"

"I think it can be arranged, Mush."

A replacement, Yeoman 2nd Class William T. White, who had served as a relief crewman aboard *Wahoo* before, quickly volunteered for duty aboard the famed sub. It was Yeoman White who originally suggested to Sterling that he apply for steno school. Within a half hour, White was hauling his seabag aboard, while Forest Sterling typed out the transfer orders. Sterling said good-bye to his pal, the nervous but expert cook Paul Phillips, a veteran of all six *Wahoo* patrols.

"So long, be seeing you stateside," Sterling said jauntily.

"I hope so, Yeo."

Phillips looked pale. Sterling felt as though he had let him down, since he promised that he wouldn't leave *Wahoo* before Phillips. Standing on the Midway dock, Sterling cast off *Wahoo*'s last line. Mush Morton shouted, "Take care of yourself, Yeo."

"Good hunting," Sterling called back.

Forest Sterling sat on his seabag and watched as *Wahoo* moved off, out into the harbor toward the horizon, disappearing into a rain squall. Forever. No one heard from *Wahoo* again.

Sterling often pondered his stroke of good fortune, but he never figured out what caused Mush to change his mind and release him from *Wahoo* at Midway.

Mush Morton's last patrol was highly successful. He roamed the Sea of Japan, sinking a large transport, and three other ships.

As he attempted to exit La Perouse Strait on October 11, 1943, *Wahoo* was spotted on the surface by an enemy ar-

tillery battery on the northern tip of Hokkaido. It opened
fire, driving the sub down. *Wahoo* was trailing oil. It was unclear why she was on the surface in daylight, but Japanese
records indicate the boat may have hit a mine earlier. Dick
O'Kane thought a circular torpedo run might have damaged
it. After the first sighting on the morning of October 11,
enemy planes converged and dropped bombs and depth
charges. They were followed by three anti-submarine vessels
dropping depth charges as *Wahoo* headed east to clear the
Sea of Japan. They sighted a submarine's conning tower
amid a long oil streak. This was followed up by an attack
by Japanese sub chasers which dropped dozens of depth
charges in the Strait. More diesel oil appeared with bits of a
submarine's propeller. *Wahoo* had barely transited La Perouse
into the Sea of Okhotsk when she went down.

The loss of *Wahoo* and Mush Morton shocked and saddened the entire Submarine Force. "It just didn't seem possible that Morton and his fighting crew could be lost," Admiral
Lockwood said. Lockwood immediately shut down the Sea
of Japan as a patrol area. Morton posthumously received a
fourth Navy Cross for the patrol, and his sinkings made him
the highest-scoring sub skipper in the Force in late 1943.
After all the results were in, Mush the Magnificent, the fighting warrior, would be one of the top three scoring American
sub skippers. For the Submarine Force in the Pacific, he had
shown the way and set the standard.

George Grider heard the bad news about *Wahoo* as newly
assigned executive officer of *Hawkbill*. He thought it a great
shame that Mush had lost two experienced execs in a row:
Dick O'Kane and Roger Paine. Grider believed that Mush
had subconsciously come to rely on O'Kane and Paine to tell
him what not to do. They had the personal authority to advise him on the difference between the calculated risk and
foolhardy chance.

Roger Paine was still recovering from his appendectomy.
He, too, suspected that *Wahoo*'s fire control team might not
have been seasoned enough under Mush's impetuous leadership. Roger did not want to dwell on the last hours of the
valiant crew, slowly suffocating. There was an armory under

the control room, Paine remembered, with .45 caliber hand-guns. Those who wanted to go quickly could choose to do so.

Entombed forever with Mush Morton were eighteen crew-members that had made all seven *Wahoo* war patrols, along with Chief "Guns" Carr, Chief Keeter, and Forest Sterling's nervous friends, Forest O'Brien and Paul Phillips.

When Dick O'Kane received confirmation in Pearl about *Wahoo*'s loss, he was deeply grieved. He thought that sub-mariners would always remember Mush Morton, the captain who shook off the shackles and set the pace. O'Kane re-solved to avenge *Wahoo* with *Tang*—as he had avenged *Argonaut* with *Wahoo*.

On the brighter side, in Pearl Dick O'Kane learned from of-ficers' scuttlebutt that a Sub School classmate, Slade Cutter, had completed a terrific patrol with *Seahorse*. Cutter was an all-American tackle at the Academy who had won the Army–Navy game by kicking a field goal in 1934. Slade re-sembled Mush Morton in that he was big, likable, athletic, and aggressive in combat. Cutter admired O'Kane and the feeling was reciprocated. On the first patrol, Cutter's relations with the skipper of *Seahorse,* Commander Don McGregor, resembled those between O'Kane and Marvin Kennedy on *Wahoo*. They were not good.

McGregor was an inept and cautious skipper who had done poorly on *Gar* earlier and been relieved. He was given a second chance with *Seahorse,* but remained hesitant during the boat's first war patrol. Cutter urged McGregor to be more aggressive, citing his own previous experience as exec under Lew Parks aboard the successful *Pompano*. (Roger Paine was a junior officer aboard *Pompano* on her first war patrol before being assigned to *Wahoo*.) *Seahorse*'s first patrol, de-spite the large number of enemy ships sighted, was a bust. Cutter was furious with McGregor's poor performance, and a chill set in between the captain and exec. On the return trip to Midway, Skipper McGregor ordered Exec Cutter relieved of his duties. McGregor's first action at Midway was to rec-ommend that Cutter be expelled from the Submarine Force, but when Admiral Lockwood went over the record, he ordered Don McGregor to be beached, and Slade Cutter was given command of *Seahorse*.

Cutter was blessed with a fine executive officer, John "Speed" Currie and a popular Chief of the Boat, Chief Quartermaster Joe McGrievy. Because morale under Captain McGregor had slumped alarmingly, *Seahorse* needed an injection of confidence. For his first patrol as *Seahorse*'s skipper, Cutter asked for the assignment of Lieutenant Ralph Pleatman for one run. Pleatman had been a junior officer on *Pompano* when Cutter was exec. He had a shock of black hair and a deceptively smooth, rosy complexion, but he was hard as nails. *Pompano*'s skipper Lew Parks, tall and leathery, was also tough—as well as being an ambitious, opinionated but effective captain. Ralph Pleatman was a reserve officer, a ninety-day wonder, who placed first in his Submarine School class. Captain Parks told Lieutenant Pleatman he would force him off *Pompano* inside two months because he didn't like reserve officers and he didn't like Jews. Slade Cutter couldn't believe Parks would say such a thing, but Pleatman repeated the conversation verbatim to Cutter.

Ralph Pleatman turned out to be a brilliant, aggressive submarine officer on *Pompano*. He was Cutter's assistant on the torpedo data computer during attacks. Cutter thought Pleatman had a mind as sharp as any he had seen, and caught on quickly to the complexities of the TDC in the fire control party. Pleatman was, in fact, so proficient in combat that even Captain Parks came to admire the young reserve officer. Strangely, they became good friends. Slade Cutter was pleased to see that Pleatman's performance and personality ended Lew Parks' anti-Semitism.

Cutter was eager to get Pleatman aboard *Seahorse* when he heard that his former shipmate was unhappily attached to SubDiv 42 staff. Cutter thought he was doing Pleatman a favor by requesting him on *Seahorse,* but the Lieutenant came aboard in a fury. The free-wheeling Pleatman opened Cutter's door at the Gooneyville Hotel and threw his briefcase at his new commanding officer.

"You son-of-a-bitch," he said. It was not the usual way to address a commanding officer.

"What the hell is wrong?" the startled Cutter replied.

Pleatman heatedly explained that he had just gotten orders for new construction; that he had been married for only three months before shipping out on *Pompano;* and that he was looking forward to returning to the States and a reunion with his wife.

"Good God," Cutter said. He was deeply apologetic. "Well, anyway, Ralph, here you are."

Cutter thought Pleatman was a marvelous addition to *Seahorse*'s wardroom. He was as attack-oriented as himself, and got along well with the crew. Pleatman was irreverent, a fire-brand. His attitude toward the enemy, which Cutter loved, was always: "Fuck 'em all, boys, let's go."

Cutter, however, told Pleatmen, "Look, Ralph, you can't say 'fuck 'em' in front of the enlisted men."

"Then I can say, 'Fook 'em,' goddamnit," Pleatman replied.

Cutter agreed. "Okay, you can say 'fook 'em.' "

So Pleatman continued to urge the attack party: "Fook 'em, boys, let's go."

Pleatman's exuberant attitude, even at the most trying times, proved to be the spark plug needed aboard *Seahorse*.

Chief Joe McGrievy said, "Ralph Pleatman was a hell-raising, mathematics genius on the torpedo data computer. Pleatman and Cutter when together were like ham and eggs—bread and butter. He brought to the boat youth, vigor and confidence."

Seahorse returned to Pearl Harbor to be greeted by Admiral Lockwood and his staff. Cutter sank five ships, a brilliant first performance for which he received the Navy Cross. In honor of Pleatman, the crew fashioned a flag with the words "Fook 'em" on it, and attached it to the periscope. Cutter made up for the injustice to Ralph Pleatman's marital life by getting him flown back to the States. He contacted a friend in the Navy Department's Submarine Assignment office who sent Ralph to new construction, where Cutter knew he would be assured several months ashore with his wife before the boat was commissioned and he was sent to sea again. Ralph Pleatman shared in the Presidential Unit Citation for *Seahorse*'s great second patrol.

There was a storied aftermath to *Seahorse*'s first patrol under Slade Cutter. The boat had been operating in the same area as *Trigger,* commanded by Robert E. "Dusty" Dornin. Both Cutter and Dornin were from the Naval Academy Class of 1935 and both attended Sub School in the same class with Dick O'Kane. They had been teammates on the Navy's winning football team and were close friends—and competitors. Both subs picked off targets in a Japanese convoy, unaware of each other's presence. Both skippers were a bit surprised when they saw ships hit with torpedoes they knew they didn't fire.

The two captains radioed their contact and action reports to Pearl Harbor. There, a staff officer, who thought they might have been claiming the same ships down, with a misguided sense of humor returned messages: "The first liar hasn't got a chance." It was stupid and insulting. Dornin's exec, Ned Beach, among the finest young officers in the Sub Force, brought his captain the message, expecting him to blow his stack. Dornin laughed it off. But Cutter on *Seahorse* fired back an explosive reply arguing that the message questioned their veracity. The next day Admiral Lockwood apologized by radio message to both skippers. The radio exchange, avidly read by all submarines at sea, gave rise to the myth that Dornin and Cutter were great personal rivals, stealing Japanese ships from one another.

This rivalry set the stage for the great lauau dustup. In Honolulu, Cutter planned a Hawaiian lauau party for his *Seahorse* crew and managed to garner a traditional roast pig from civilian friends. Dornin, now a veteran of nine patrols and due for reassignment, planned a similar feast for *Trigger*'s crew, but he failed to find a pig. Cutter offered to share a joint party with *Trigger.* The crews of the rival submarines showed up for plenty of good food, Hawaiian poi, and drink. A chief quartermaster from *Trigger,* worse the wear from alcohol, started harassing a young officer from *Seahorse.* Cooler heads pulled him away but a fight broke out among the crews and a bit of bedlam ensued. Cutter and Dornin managed to halt the brawl and with their officers got the crews separated, but not before the shore patrol arrived with two tractor-trailers hauling wire mesh cages. They dumped

Seahorse sailors in one, and *Trigger* sailors in the other. End of lauau party.

Slade Cutter was furious that a *Trigger* sailor would threaten his officer and start a brawl. Dornin was just as angry at his own crew for precipitating the fight. He ordered Ned Beach to sort it out, but on patrol Beach had depended heavily on the chief quartermaster at fault: he was an excellent sailor and assistant navigator at sea, but a screwup on shore. When Beach visited Cutter at the Royal Hawaiian to apologize, the quartermaster showed up drunk again, appearing to threaten Cutter. Somehow Ned Beach managed to restrain Slade Cutter from extreme violence. He hastily conveyed Dusty Dornin's apologies and made sure his quartermaster was duly punished, if somewhat less than Skipper Dornin had demanded: boiled in oil and put on bread and water for a year.

In Pearl, the skipper problem continued to plague the Sub Force. Admiral Lockwood had to relieve captains who failed to deliver—about 15 percent of sub commanders were replaced in 1943, half the 30 percent of the previous year. ComSubPac needed qualified captains with the proper Academy credentials and seniority to replace them. There was still no way for Lockwood to determine in advance who would make an effective combat skipper and who would fail. Often athletes, like Mush Morton, Slade Cutter, and Dusty Dornin in *Trigger,* did well. Benny Bass, an Olympic gymnast, was a star in *Plunger,* and Elliott Loughlin, an all-American basketball player, was a natural in *Queenfish.* Yet O'Kane's Academy classmate Walt Griffith was a studious type with a kindly look, but fearless in his command of *Bowfin.* Eli Reich, an intellectual, would compile an outstanding record, as would Dick O'Kane's old shipmate, pipe-smoking, ruminative George Grider.

In various conversations, Dick O'Kane heard that younger skippers and execs had made names for themselves and their boats during the previous year: Herb Andrews in *Jack;* Donc Donaho in *Flying Fish* with his exec, O'Kane's classmate Reuben Whitaker; Sam Dealey in *Harder;* John Tyree in *Finback;* Roy Benson and Dusty Dornin in *Trigger;* Roy Gross in *Seawolf* with another O'Kane classmate, Bob Risser, as exec. O'Kane's Sub School classmate Bub Ward in *Guardfish* was running up a fine record. Another classmate, Lieutenant John Eichmann, was lost aboard *Triton* in 1943. In one unique shift, William Stevenson had relieved his successful older brother, Harry, in command of USS *Aspro* when Harry's eyesight weakened and he was disqualified for sea duty. William Stevenson would prove to be no less successful than his brother.

In December 1943 out of Brisbane, Lieutenant Commander R.J. Foley, skipper of *Gato,* was depth charged by enemy destroyers. He surfaced later to find an unexploded ash can still on Gato's after deck. His inventive solution: with enemy ships still pursuing in the distance, he lashed the depth charge to a rubber boat, punctured to produce a slow leak, submerged the deck, and left the depth charge in the path of the enemy before charging away at high speed.

At the Pearl Harbor bull sessions in January, 1944, Dick O'Kane found differing views over the use of U.S. wolf packs in the Pacific War. Admiral King in Washington ordered U.S. submarine commands to devise wolf pack formations similar to those the Germans employed with such success in the Atlantic Ocean, but it was mid-1943 before Admiral Lockwood had enough boats available at Pearl to attempt to deploy them as a team. Unlike Admiral Doenitz who controlled all his submarines from headquarters ashore, Lockwood felt the vast reaches of the Pacific needed a pack commander on board one of the subs.

Admiral Lockwood ordered Captain Babe Brown to set up a wolf pack training system at the Pearl Harbor Sub Base. His program was dubbed "Convoy College." The campus was the open-air dance floor of the Submarine Officers' Mess at Pearl, once used by officers and their ladies for peacetime galas under the stars. The dance floor was covered by a black-and-white checkerboard pattern, each section one-foot square. The students at Convoy College would try to work out practical tactics under "Dean" Brown. They formulated a plan employing three submarines with a squadron or division commander in charge of the wolf pack embarked in one of the boats. The instructors thought that radio communications and security had improved enough to maintain contact among the pack, but skippers themselves were still leery of using their radios frequently in areas where the Japanese could intercept transmissions.

The tactics called for one "attacker" boat against a convoy and two "flankers," each following the point submarine in hitting the enemy formation. After firing, the attacker would drop behind to reload and become a "trailer" to finish off damaged ships. Under this system, unlike Admiral Doenitz' tactics, there would be no central direction from shore headquarters. The pack commander would contribute advice only when needed or available.

In training, each of the three boats in the wolf pack was assigned a corner of the game board. Each CO with his torpedo fire control party remained behind a screen and simulated an attack purely on the basis of signals sent between the boats. Staff instructors, the "faculty," maneuvered the convoy itself. After contact was established, wolf packers were allowed brief sightings of the convoy, as in real action. When the doctrine was worked out, the tactics were tried at sea off Oahu. The subs practiced against incoming U.S. convoys from the West Coast.

The first U.S. wolf pack left Midway on October 1, 1943, assigned to the East China Sea. It comprised *Shad, Grayback,* and *Cero,* with the commander, Captain Swede Momsen, riding in *Cero.* Momsen followed the College's concept that one sub would attack a convoy forward with the other two hitting from the port and starboard flanks. After the initial boat fired its fish, one of the flankers would move in, while the point boat would drop back to finish off a damaged Japanese ship. But communications difficulties prevented the three submarines from operating effectively together. It was difficult for Momsen to remain in radio contact with the other boats without giving their position away to skilled Japanese interceptors. The three submarines scattered in chasing their prey, so that the wolf pack became more a joint search unit than a joint attack group. The pack sank only three enemy ships, which was not a great testimonial to the concept. Momsen decided that a commander ashore should control the wolf pack.

The next wolf pack under Commander Freddy Warder fared little better—with *Harder, Snook,* and *Pargo,* commanded by three seasoned skippers, Sam Dealey, Chuck Triebel, and Ian Eddy. Though they sank seven enemy vessels, all three skippers thought the concept was a waste of time. Submarines could do better operating on their own without trying to stay in touch with one another. The *Snook's* captain was inhibited because he feared that a torpedo he fired might hit *Pargo,* which could easily happen in a confused night battle.

Freddy Warder reported to Admiral Lockwood that he thought a separate wolf pack commander riding along was a supernumerary, possibly even a detriment. He recommended that the senior submarine commander be in charge of the pack. But Lockwood was keen on the wolf pack idea and pursued it intermittently through the rest of the Pacific War—sometimes with separate commanders, more often with the senior skipper in charge. Some observers thought Charlie Lockwood liked the idea of a separate pack commander because it provided him the chance to give older staff officers a highly prized shot at a war patrol and a submarine combat pin.

After the first few anonymous wolf packs, SubPac staff officers began giving them alliterative names pegged to the commander, like "Blair's Blasters," "Wilkins' Wildcats," and "Sandy's Sluggers," assigned to geographical areas called "Hit Parade," "Marus' Morgue," and even "Convoy College." Sometimes wolf pack skippers would get testy with each other because they failed properly to inform pack-mates soon enough about contacts or details on course and speed of targets in their brief reports.

Shortly before *Tang* arrived in Pearl Harbor, a wolf pack suffered a serious setback. Lockwood decided to send a pack to support the invasion of the Gilbert Islands and Tarawa by patrolling off the Japanese bastion of Truk. He chose Captain John Cromwell, commander of Submarine Division 43 who had never made a war patrol, to ride aboard *Sculpin* along with *Searaven* and *Apogon*. On the night of November 19, *Sculpin*'s skipper Fred Connaway on his first patrol as CO sighted a Japanese convoy. He submerged for a dawn attack. But the sharp-eyed, enemy convoy commander spotted *Sculpin*'s periscope and turned the entire convoy toward the submerged submarine, presenting a difficult bow-on target. Connaway went deep and later surfaced to chase the convoy. However, the canny Japanese commander left behind the destroyer *Yamagumo*. It attacked *Sculpin*. Connaway dove again, suffering depth charge damage, which knocked the sub's depth gauge out of whack, though this wasn't immediately evident. *Sculpin* remained down for several hours. She suffered a rough depth charging, and then a couple of hours of quiet. Possibly, Connaway thought, the destroyer was gone. At noon, he ordered a move up to periscope depth for a look around.

Ensign W.M. Fiedler, a reservist making his first war patrol, was temporary diving officer. He ordered the ballast tanks blown. The boat rose—200 feet, 190 feet, 150 feet. At 125 feet, the depth gauge needle stuck. But Fiedler didn't notice and continued expelling water to make the boat rise. With no warning, *Sculpin* inadvertently surfaced, its bow rising high out of the water before splashing back into the sea. *Yamagumo* charged, hurling depth charges at the diving submarine. Damage was extensive and the pressure hull was breached. The steering mechanism failed and the diving planes were stuck.

"We've done our best," Connaway told his officers. "We'll have to surface while we can still bring her up. Battle Stations! Gun action!"

In bright sunlight, *Sculpin* labored to the surface. No torpedo tubes had been readied. The crew ran topside to the guns, but the destroyer opened up with its entire armament, raking the submarine and killing Skipper Connaway, his exec, the gunnery officer, and gunners. The senior surviving officer was a reserve, Lieutenant George E. Brown, who saw that *Sculpin* could not survive and gave the order to abandon and scuttle the ship.

Captain Cromwell decided he knew too much about current plans involving not only the Gilberts invasion but also the future Marshall Islands attack. Worse, he feared he might give away Ultra secrets under torture. The Japanese would change their code. Inestimable information would be denied the United States. Some officers like Slade Cutter promised themselves—and their wives—they would not be taken prisoner. Captain Cromwell decided to go down with *Sculpin.* He sat on an ammo case gazing at the small photo of his wife he carried with him. Ensign Fiedler, who seemingly blamed himself for the diving error, joined him. Sitting with Filipino steward Eugenio Apostol in the wardroom, Fiedler told a chief petty officer who urged him to hurry off the boat, "We do not choose to go with you. We prefer death to capture by the Japanese." Ensign Fiedler began dealing a hand of solitaire.

Lieutenant Brown yelled to the remaining crewmen: "Abandon ship and God have mercy on your souls."

Then Brown and Chief Motor Machinist Philip Gabrunas opened the vents to the sea and *Sculpin,* still pressing ahead, began her last ride down.

Captain John Cromwell was eventually awarded the Medal of Honor. He died to protect the Ultra secret.

In a tragic postscript, *Sculpin* survivors were picked up by the Japanese, taken to Truk, and transferred in two groups to two aircraft carriers to be carried to Tokyo. *Sailfish* sank the carrier *Chuyo* with half the survivors—all of whom died. When *Sailfish,* then *Squalus,* went down off Portsmouth in 1939, she had been located by her sister ship, *Sculpin.* *Squalus* survivors owed their lives to *Sculpin*'s finding them.

At the Sub Base, Dick O'Kane and Murray Frazee heard about the political infighting that worsened submarine command problems in the Pacific. In the Southwest Pacific, the unpopular senior naval officer, Vice Admiral Arthur Carpender, who had alienated General MacArthur, was farmed out to Great Lakes, Illinois, to command the Ninth Naval District. His replacement, Vice Admiral Thomas Kinkaid, was a battle-tested Pacific task force commander. Assessing the conflicting orders on using the magnetic torpedo exploder,

Kinkaid ordered Rear Admiral Ralph Christie to deactivate the magnetic torpedo for Southwest Pacific boats—as Admiral Lockwood had done seven months previously in Pearl Harbor. Christie had to accept the decision, though he privately sulked because his invention had been discarded as deficient. He still sought some way to make it work properly.

Jimmy Fife in Brisbane was assigned to Admiral King's staff in Washington as a planner, and Christie moved to Brisbane. But Christie's high-handed style offended both Kinkaid in Brisbane and Lockwood in Pearl. Christie awarded medals to incoming submariners before any action by the Decorations Review Board. This practice, however complimentary to subs and skippers, could let the Japanese know that the instant awards signified sinkings had been confirmed by American intelligence, the code-breakers. Kinkaid forbad Christie to award dockside medals. He also stopped him from recommending Army medals, suggested by General MacArthur, to U.S. Navy personnel. Trouble was brewing between Admirals Christie and Kinkaid, as it had between Christie and Lockwood.

As a Vice Admiral, the only one in the U.S. Submarine Force, Lockwood was regarded as the type of commander who set the established policies, but he was never officially designated as such. The submarine command in Australia continued to go its own way under Rear Admiral Christie, who answered only to Vice Admiral Kinkaid and General MacArthur.

Strategically, in 1943 both Lockwood and Christie had shuttled boats around randomly, rather than concentrating on vital supply lines between Japan and its Greater East Asian Co-Prosperity Sphere. So the Submarine Force entered 1944 with no unified doctrine on where and how best to employ the boats.

The Force was further troubled by another fiasco: a whole squadron of twelve new fleet boats was fitted with diesel engines, manufactured by the HOR (Hoover-Owens-Rentschler) Company. The HOR boats were called "whores" by angry enginemen because they were badly designed, failed to work properly, and continually broke down on patrol. They should never have been installed in the first place, let alone allowed to remain in boats going into combat. When *Gunnel,* under John "Junior" McCain (later four-star admiral), broke down in the Yellow Sea, Lockwood wrote Washington the area "was a damned bad place for a lousy set of engines to demonstrate their unreliability." One by one, the HORs were all replaced by the reliable General Motors or Fairbanks Morse diesels. "The breakdowns of the HOR engines saved the Japanese thirty or forty ships," one skipper commented.

In Pearl, Admiral Lockwood thought the defective torpedo problem had been largely solved with Admiral Kinkaid's order to Ralph Christie to discard the magnetic exploders. Electric torpedoes powered by batteries that left no wake were belatedly arriving in Pearl, but the new electric fish were slower than steam torpedoes and still full of bugs. The Newport Torpedo Factory had dragged its heels in helping expedite development and delivery of the electrics because they were labelled "Not Invented Here." Admiral Lockwood began sending boats on patrol with both the steam torpedoes and the electrics.

Many skippers were still complaining about erratic torpedo performance, especially the dreaded "circular runs." *Sargo, Perch, Flying Fish, Guardfish, Growler, Seawolf, Barb, Trigger, Tench, Seahorse, Grouper, Dace, Harder, Redfish*—all fine subs—reported firing torpedoes which ran erratically in a circular pattern, heading back toward the submarine and endangering it. Because of its neutral buoyancy, a submarine struck by a torpedo—the enemy's or its own—was inevitably destroyed. The most aggressive skippers boring in on the surface ran the greatest risk. Nobody seemed to deal with the problem of circular runs, though the British had a rudder control mechanism that kept the torpedo on a straight path.

However, all in all the submarine picture was very much looking up at the beginning of 1944. True, there were problems with skippers and with torpedoes, but increasingly U.S. submarines were performing as they should on patrol. Boats were probing waters deep in the Empire with a boldness that had not been apparent in 1942. Younger, blooded submarine officers were moving into positions of command. Ultra was providing information that was simply priceless. Lockwood had become the guiding admiral in the submarine war. But the U.S. had lost submarines: in 1943, *Argonaut, Amberjack, Grampus, Triton, Pickerel, Grenadier, Runner, R-12, Grayling, Pompano, Cisco, S-44, Dorado, Wahoo, Corvina, Sculpin,* and *Capelin. Corvina* was sunk by a Japanese submarine, the only American boat lost that way.

Toward the end of *Tang*'s indoctrination period, Captain Babe Brown, the senior training officer, sailed aboard for a day and night exercise. He pronounced *Tang* ready for combat, readier than any new boat he had inspected—and after a shorter training period. But over coffee in *Tang*'s wardroom, Babe Brown warned Dick O'Kane, "I would caution you that you are way ahead of much of your crew, and you'll do well to temper some of your tactics for a time."

With a smile, Murray Frazee reported to Captain O'Kane that Chief Ballinger confided none of the crewmen seeking to get off *Tang* in San Diego had decided to accept O'Kane's offer for transfer ashore at Pearl. O'Kane was pleased and credited his executive officer with handling a delicate situation with skill. *Tang* crewmen spent the last couple of days in Pearl reloading torpedoes, refuelling, taking aboard stores, attending briefings, and preparing the details for getting underway for war. On the last evening, the crew came back from a movie at the Sub Base. Murray Frazee knocked on O'Kane's door. "All hands are aboard and *Tang*'s ready for patrol, Captain," he said.

The next morning, January 22, 1944, Uncle Charlie Lockwood and his SubPac staff came down to the finger pier to wish *Tang* Godspeed. Everyone took a special interest in *Tang*. Would Dick O'Kane prove a worthy successor to Mush Morton? How well, they wondered, would Dick do on his own, as captain?

CHAPTER THIRTEEN

A Sensational First Patrol

With a loud blast of the horn, Captain O'Kane backed *Tang* away from the finger pier at the Submarine Base, spun neatly around in Southeast Loch and moved through Pearl Harbor to the channel entrance. *Tang* cleared the last sea buoy and followed her destroyer escort along the prescribed course for the open Pacific. Finally O'Kane and *Tang* were on their own, a great feeling for a man as confident as Dick, though a lonely one, too.

O'Kane's orders for *Tang,* with her load of twenty-four modified Mark 14 steam torpedoes, were to patrol the Caroline Islands with the Japanese bastion of Truk at the center. But first he was instructed to act as a beacon and lifeguard for a U.S. Navy bomber strike on the airfield at Wake Island, taken by the Japanese in the first weeks of the war. The air strikes by Navy four-engine Coronados would interdict enemy air support for the Marshall Islands, which were being invaded by U.S. Marines and Army soldiers supported by the mighty Fifth Fleet under Admiral Raymond Spruance. The code name was Operation Flintlock.

The long-awaited U.S. Pacific offensive was on the move. Admiral Halsey's troops in the South Pacific theater were climbing up the Solomon Islands chain; General MacArthur was launching his leapfrogging operations on the northern coast of New Guinea; and the U.S. Marines took Cape Gloucester on New Britain Island, bypassing the big Japanese base at Rabaul. Admiral Nimitz had begun his Central Pacific campaign with the assault on Tarawa and Makin in the Gilbert Islands. The big, new aircraft carriers were coming off the ways and appearing in the Pacific under Admiral Marc Mitscher.

During *Tang*'s voyage, Yeoman Ray McNally placed patrol reports on the captain's desk, which O'Kane read avidly. O'Kane liked a competent yeoman on board like Forest Sterling on *Wahoo* to keep administrative concerns up to date. But he, like Slade Cutter, realized there were times when skippers worried more about a yeoman being a good bow planesman or sonarman, their Battle Stations, than an expert typist.

Dick O'Kane approached Wake atoll cautiously. He relied on Murray Frazee's expert navigation to bring *Tang* to the island rather than possibly giving away his position with a radar search. For two days, *Tang* circled Wake noting activity ashore but encountered no target ships entering or departing.

On the second night, O'Kane moved *Tang* 10 miles east of Wake to serve as a beacon by using her signal searchlight. To screen the glare from the light so that it could not be seen on the atoll, someone came up with the idea of using the yeoman's circular wastebasket, which fitted neatly around it; the wastebasket was secured with adhesive tape supplied by the Pharmacist's Mate.

The bombers staging out of Midway Island were picked up on *Tang*'s radar and, flying low over the dark water, they saw the submarine's searchlight and homed-in on the target. Their bombs lit up the atoll with flashes and flames. O'Kane remained on station until the bombers departed, and then circled the island looking for downed aviators. After midnight, *Tang* was radioed that none of the planes had been shot down. The submarine was instructed to remain in the area for a second bombing strike. There was plenty of Japanese air activity but no ships to be sunk. After the second Coronado strike, *Tang* was released and ordered to continue to her patrol area in the Carolines. Flintlock had been a success, with Kwajalein and Entiwetok taken by Marines and soldiers. The Marshall Islands could now serve as U.S. advance bases for the march across the Pacific.

O'Kane was vexed because the long detour to Wake would mean less fuel to patrol for targets in the Carolines. However, during the fitting out at Mare Island he had devised a way to store extra fuel aboard: he offered night shift Navy Yard workmen a baked ham in exchange for their quietly installing a waterproof, neoprene lining—holding fuel in the safety tanks until needed. This bright idea had increased *Tang's* cruising range, and from O'Kane's point of view, an extra enemy ship sunk because of it was well worth the price of a ham.

Tang arrived in her designated patrol area, some 120 miles west of Truk. Dick O'Kane welcomed his freedom, being on his own with the boat and no instructions on how to conduct his patrol. All he had to do, he thought, was to find the enemy. But O'Kane departed from standard doctrine, which was to keep the ship moving at all times. He thought that doctrine could be overdone. He believed it was useful as a guide to a set of procedures, established through experience, but doctrine should be flexible not rigid. That was the situation here: they were in an open sea, with the enemy on any possible track, and no amount of running around would increase the probability of a sighting. It would only make *Tang* a target for enemy submarines and the noise of the boat's screws would blank out enemy sounds. Further, he wished to save fuel and wear and tear on the crew. So *Tang* lay to on the surface, raising her search periscope, which would reach out past the bridge's horizon. Each evening, O'Kane shifted *Tang's* patrol position about 20 miles.

At 1130 one morning, the cry came over the intercom speaker: "Fire in the galley!" Fire: a submariner's nightmare! The fat in a large fryer installed to sate the crew's appetite for French-fried potatoes and chicken had caught fire. The heating element had fused and could not be turned off. The heat caused the paint and cork on the bulkhead to blaze, too. A member of the damage control party went into action. He swung the spike of an old-fashioned ax and ripped the electrical cable out of its junction box, which shut off the heating element. The fire was dying when a crewman opened the small compartment ventilation flap to let the smoke out of the galley, but the rush of air rekindled the fire and acrid fumes spread through the boat. The fire fighters had to don smoke masks and use fresh water hoses to douse the blaze. Everyone not wearing masks was forced to scramble out the hatches topside to the deck. They were armed with every kind of small weapon aboard in case of Japanese air attack.

O'Kane reached the control room where he found sailor Homer Anthony still glued to the radar screen, gasping. He ordered the radar shut down, and Anthony topside. Finally with the fire out, O'Kane ordered the boat aired out, then buttoned up, and gotten underway again.

As was his custom, O'Kane held a post-mortem, which resulted in a revision of the fire bill for emergency stations. He, Frazee, and Chief of the Boat Ballinger agreed on improved measures for the damage team. They posted the fire bill notice in every compartment—including the proviso that ventilation flappers were to be kept closed unless ordered otherwise. Ballinger also checked the fryer, a commercial model, designed for operation on an AC circuit. It had been rejiggered to fit *Tang*'s DC system, but the relay mechanism had fused when the fryer was going full blast. Ballinger discussed the suitability of the equipment with key crew members.

"Captain," the Chief of the Boat reported, "the troops would like to get rid of the goddamned thing." That night the deep-fat fryer was deep-sixed over the side to Davy Jones' locker.

Tang spent the next twenty full days without spotting an enemy ship. The crew was getting tense and nerves were taut. The men wanted at least one enemy ship down to qualify for combat insignia.

ComSubPac sent *Tang* an Ultra message that a convoy was heading eastward toward the big Truk base. The crew sensed action ahead. O'Kane ordered *Tang* on an intercepting course and then took a quick stroll through the boat. In the engine room, where no one could speak above the roar of the rock-crushing diesel engines, the motor macs gave him the okay sign. O'Kane was determined to do his damnedest to live up to the crew's trust and expectations.

Dick O'Kane told Murray Frazee to brief the crew over the intercom. Then *Tang* began searching for the convoy. In the conning tower, O'Kane had a crack team: he manned the search periscope and Chief Quartermaster Sidney Jones the second scope. At the wheel, forward, was Quartermaster Robert E. Welch, who also handled speed changes and called out log speeds. To the starboard was Lieutenant Scotty Anderson who supervised the Quartermaster's notebook, the detailed log recording all commands and changes. Behind him was Chief Signalman Earl Ogden at the chart desk, which tracked all *Tang*'s movements. Next came Radio Technician Floyd Caverly and Radioman Fred Schroeder, manning the sonar gear. To the port side, forward to aft, were Radioman Edwin Bergman, who raised the radar mast when needed; Lieutenant Ed Beaumont on the firing panel; and Lieutenant Frank Springer and Ensign Mel Enos handling the torpedo data computer and the angle solver. Exec Murray Frazee stood by to supervise, readying the torpedo tubes and informing O'Kane of the chosen firing track.

All was ready when the radar sighting came the next night, February 16: "Bearing three zero five true, range thirty-one thousand yards."

As navigator, Murray Frazee figured out the convoy's base course despite its zigzags, and its speed of 8½ knots. O'Kane ordered a northeast course to intercept the convoy. As *Tang* came closer, radar separated the pips into two large vessels and a smaller one. There were escorts ahead and on each side of the formation, and two wider flanking craft.

But an additional escort destroyer coming up on *Tang*'s stern surprised them and two blasts took the submarine down. O'Kane paused at periscope depth for a quick sighting of the ship's course, so that *Tang* could turn away. The destroyer continued dead ahead and O'Kane dove deep, heading toward the convoy. O'Kane worked under a temperature gradient showing on the bathythermograph. As they passed 450 feet, five depth charges were dropped. *Tang* was rattled but not hurt. Under the gradient, *Tang* continued tracking the convoy as the escort pulled away. Then O'Kane began a long climb back to the surface. A quick search with the raised radar mast showed *Tang* was ahead of the convoy at 9,000 yards. The convoy moved closer, and on a zig crossed *Tang*'s stern. The escorts crossed *Tang*'s track. She was inside the screen. It was early morning, February 17.

"Open the outer doors, aft," O'Kane snapped.

"Constant bearing—mark!" Quartermaster Jones read the bearing.

"Set," called Frank Springer on the torpedo data computer.

"Fire," O'Kane commanded.

Murray Frazee hit the firing plunger. A slight shudder, a sound of the torpedo's screws, the pressure of the poppet valve venting residual air from the tube into the boat.

"Fire," O'Kane ordered, sending off another fish. He launched two more torpedoes at the big freighter.

"All hot, straight, and normal," Floyd Caverly called on the sound gear.

"What's the time of the run?" O'Kane asked Frazee.

"Fifty-eight seconds, Captain."

Jones began a count: "Thirty-five . . . forty . . . fifty . . ." O'Kane raised the periscope. "Fifty-five . . ." WHACK!

The stern of the 7,000-ton freighter *Gyoten Maru* vanished. Two more torpedoes hit, and the ship practically disappeared before O'Kane's eyes. With her went 1,000 Japanese army troops of the 52nd Imperial Division. *Tang* had drawn her first blood. The skipper ordered the boat deep to 575 feet to get under any depth charges. He had no fear of going so far down. *Tang* could take it.

O'Kane and Frazee took a break for cups of coffee, but then Caverly reported another contact on sound. O'Kane ordered periscope depth. He spotted a ship at 14,000 yards and surfaced *Tang*.

To reach an attack position, O'Kane asked the engineers to push the diesels to the limit. He knew this pained the men but they, like him, saw an engine casualty as a calculated risk in sinking a multi-million dollar enemy ship. The throbbing Fairbanks Morse engines carried *Tang* forward of the target into an attack position. O'Kane dived again, but the target turned away, leaving *Tang* out of position. O'Kane was crestfallen that *Tang* had been left empty-handed.

The boat was ordered to head for Saipan in the Marianas

to seek out ships that might be fleeing the Japanese base after a Fifth Fleet carrier air strike. The radar picked up pips on the screen, which as *Tang* closed the range, turned out to be five ships with another group of vessels ahead. Visibility was low. Dick O'Kane thought of two methods of attack: barrel in, fire a full spread of six torpedoes, and then retire; or shoot at individuals. The first was the German approach against the huge American convoys crossing the Atlantic, but it could be wasteful of the torpedoes, which *Tang* had carried 5,000 miles into battle. Japanese convoys were generally skimpy, usually as few as two or three ships, while the ratio of escorts was increasing, so Captain O'Kane decided to single out targets and try to make each torpedo count.

Hank Flanagan, the torpedo officer, suggested to O'Kane that he use the forward torpedoes in the next attack. He wanted to keep peace between the competing torpedo gangs, and the after torpedo room had made the first kill. O'Kane agreed, but mainly because he didn't want to fire four more stern tubes and be empty of stern torpedoes in an emergency, a one-ended boat.

On the surface, near Aguijan Island south of Tinian and Saipan Islands, *Tang* approached a target that turned out to be a patrol boat. O'Kane preferred to ignore this dangerous small fry in pursuit of a larger, more important target. He soon found it—a big, armed merchantman, identified later as the *Fukuyama Maru*. As *Tang* closed, the target ship turned toward the submarine on a zig, too close for the torpedoes to arm. So O'Kane ordered a "dipsy-doodle" maneuver: the submarine turned, pulled away from the target, and then swung back, with the range now suitably opened. It was close to midnight, February 22.

On the bridge, O'Kane, looking through the binoculars on the target-bearing transmitter, called: "Stand by for constant bearings. Mark."

"Set," reported Frank Springer in the conning tower.

"Fire."

O'Kane fired three more fish, and ordered a turn with "right full rudder."

As *Tang* veered away, all four torpedoes hit the freighter, which virtually disintegrated. An escort gave chase. O'Kane ordered, "All ahead, emergency." Five million watts coursed through *Tang*'s motors, driving the twin shafts. The smoke from the engines and spume hid *Tang* as the submarine made a fast getaway.

After evading, O'Kane let the fire control party track the other enemy ships. He ordered the crew to secure from battle stations to give the men a rest while *Tang* caught up with her next quarry. As the range narrowed, Chief Ballinger sent up a new set of lookouts. They spotted a large naval auxiliary with an escort astern and another ahead. Exec Frazee reported from the conning tower: "We've got her on course two seven zero, speed eight, Captain. Range twenty-eight hundred. We're twelve hundred yards from her track. It looks good from here."

O'Kane maneuvered for a shot straight ahead with a near zero gyro angle. A sudden squall hid *Tang* from the escort astern. Quartermaster Jones was tracking the bow escort.

"She's turned back, but she'll never make it," Jones said.

"Constant bearing—mark!" O'Kane ordered on the bridge.

"Set," came the reply from the conning tower.

"Fire!"

O'Kane fired three more torpedoes in 8-second intervals.

The spread would insure that the 600-foot target could not maneuver to avoid a hit. Three torpedoes hit and a huge shockwave engulfed *Tang*. The large ship, the naval tender *Yamashimo Maru,* twisted and was wrapped in flames. It flipped like a spoon on end, and sank quickly by the stern on February 23.

The explosion was so tremendous that O'Kane called down, "Are you all right below?"

"We're okay," Frazee reported. "We're checking the compartments. What the hell was it?"

O'Kane realized the auxiliary must have been carrying munitions, the equivalent of many torpedo warheads, which generated the enormous shock wave. Though Dick O'Kane didn't realize it, the shock had jarred loose the gasket in *Tang*'s Number 5 torpedo tube door.

The captain now ordered the forward tubes reloaded. The

closest three pips on the radar screen were escorts, which O'Kane wanted to avoid. He set off after the second group of ships originally spotted. Then he turned into his bunk for some sleep.

When O'Kane arose, he went to the wardroom for coffee and found his officers in an analytical session. Young Mel Enos argued that each of the three ships down could have been sunk with three torpedoes rather than four.

"You're right, Mel," O'Kane admitted. "But they're on the bottom and that's what counts."

O'Kane had been tempted to fire spreads of only three torpedoes, but he believed that firing the fourth fish sealed the destruction of the target and let him concentrate on evasive measures from angry escorts.

O'Kane and Frazee began a cribbage game. Dick repeated what Mush Morton had told him on *Wahoo*: "Tenacity, Fraz. Stay with 'em till they're on the bottom!"

So far Dick O'Kane was satisfied with the patrol. He realized that targets weren't exactly falling in his lap, but *Tang* was finding ships and, most importantly, the torpedoes were working right. Radioman Floyd Caverly had a camera and developed films of sinkings in O'Kane's stateroom.

By now, Frazee's star fixes showed *Tang* some 150 miles west of Saipan. On the morning of February 23, Scotty Anderson noticed a tiny wisp of smoke on the horizon. O'Kane ordered *Tang* to pursue. On the surface, he raised the periscope to fullest height—"high periscope"—to identify the target from long range. But he preferred to rely on Sidney Jones wedged in the periscope shears as a lookout with his 7×50 binoculars that were stronger than the scope lens and had a wider field.

"I've got 'em now," Jones called down. "A big tanker, a freighter, and a destroyer."

O'Kane motioned Jones down from his lonely perch and they plotted a course toward the convoy, with an end-around to get ahead and then dive for the submerged attack. Frequent rain squalls and defective radar allowed *Tang* to follow the convoy only intermittently. O'Kane suspected the wild zigs and zags were due to *Tang*'s being spotted. Finally he

began trailing the freighter, *Echizen Maru,* which was bringing up the rear of the convoy. With much patience, O'Kane
and his team continued doggedly tracking the ship and then
an unexpected zig brought the target into a shooting set-up.

Dick O'Kane fired his now standard spread of four torpedoes, and three hits brought the freighter quickly under the
waves. The escorting destroyer fired wildly in all directions,
a sign that she hadn't spotted *Tang.* O'Kane was amazed that
after all the frustration, the target set-up turned out to be
close to ideal. He moved away from the sinking and to
5 miles off the beam of another ship in the convoy, a tanker.

O'Kane consulted with Frazee and they decided on positioning *Tang* ahead of the target for a submerged dawn attack. O'Kane hit the sack. At morning twilight, he was back
on the bridge. Frazee had worked *Tang* forward of the naval
tanker *Choko Maru* at 10,000 yards. The target was heading
in *Tang*'s direction, as planned. But O'Kane worried that the
light from the morning star, Venus, as bright as a quarter
moon, might illuminate *Tang.* He gritted his teeth: this was
no time for wavering. He ordered *Tang* submerged and went
ahead full speed for 20 minutes. Soundmen obtained bearings on the naval vessel.

"We're right on," O'Kane reported over the loudspeaker
system to the crew. "Now standby for a set-up."

The sea was glassy. O'Kane didn't want to risk the periscope
being sighted. At his command, Chief Jones raised the scope
briefly.

"Bearing—mark! Range—mark!" O'Kane's voice was
quiet; *Tang* was a bit close. He ordered a slight turn away to
increase the range: a last look at the tanker and at the escort
destroyer. The destroyer was heading *Tang*'s way. O'Kane
thought of the similarity to *Wahoo* at Wewak, but he refused
to waver. A last periscope sighting showed the destroyer
turning and running down the tanker's side. The loaded
tanker dwarfed the destroyer. O'Kane's report on the intercom let the crew breathe easier. *Tang*'s turn unmasked the
sub's stern tubes. O'Kane recognized white-uniformed sailors
along the decks confirming the vessel was a naval tanker.

The firing set-up was right.

"Fire!" O'Kane commanded.

Murray Frazee hit the firing plunger, then three more times at O'Kane's command.

O'Kane glued his eye to the periscope. The tanker's crewmen were pointing at the torpedo wakes. The torpedo run was only 23 seconds. Four hits! The explosions threw debris and Japanese sailors into the air above the belching smoke. The tanker headed down by the stern. In 4 minutes, *Choko Maru* was gone. The time was 0643 on February 25. Five ships down!

O'Kane ordered a crash dive to avoid the escort destroyer. He wanted *Tang* under the protecting gradient at 475 feet before the destroyer, which was dropping depth charges in the distance, got organized for a more systematic search. Diving officer Bill Walsh brought *Tang* down past 450 feet. O'Kane ordered: "Level off at 500, Bill."

Torpedo officer Hank Flanagan suddenly reported: "We're taking some water in the forward torpedo room, but can hold it for a while." The gasket that had been sprung by the previous explosion of *Yamashima Maru* was now leaking badly.

O'Kane noticed that instead of levelling off at 500 feet, *Tang* kept slipping down, to 600 feet where the needle stuck at the limit of the depth gauge. *Tang* was still going down!

The captain scuttled down the ladder from the conning tower to the control room. Diving officer Walsh was working the pumps and diving planes and called for more speed to level off. O'Kane knew that additional speed with a down angle would only drive *Tang* deeper. O'Kane ordered Walsh to blow the safety tank with a massive charge of compressed air. But when Walsh gave the order, O'Kane saw that Chief Motor Machinist De Lapp gave it only a small shot of air. Not enough. *Tang* continued to drop. Much more would be needed. The ship was in danger!

"Blow safety!" Dick O'Kane ordered. "Blow bow buoyancy!"

De Lapp twisted the manifold levers to send 3,000 pounds of air pressure roaring into the tanks. The diving bubble showed *Tang* slowly taking an up angle. The boat should have been rising but it was impossible to tell whether it was.

Like astronauts in a space vehicle, submarines found it difficult to judge from the feel alone just which way the ship was
moving. The hand on the depth gauge still rested at the 612-
feet stopper.

O'Kane considered blowing the main ballast tanks. This
would send the submarine upward, but it would also release
huge air bubbles, which would rise to the surface betraying
Tang's location to an anti-sub vessel. That was a last-chance
solution.

O'Kane knew *Tang* was as deep as she had ever gone. The
captain and crew tensely waited and listened. Was she sinking or rising? Would propulsion and diving planes take hold?
The minutes seemed to drag by, O'Kane thought—the longest
in his life. But the ship was not leaking further. The torpedo
room problem with incoming water hadn't reported worsening. Finally Dick O'Kane heard the lovely words from Bill
Walsh: "We've got her."

The depth gauge needle fluttered and moved off the pin.
Tang was under positive control again. And the bilge pumps
in the forward torpedo room were working.

O'Kane strode to the torpedo room where he found the
torpedo gang knee-deep in water working on the Number 5
tube which was below the mesh decking. Water was spewing
from the tube door, showering everything in the room.

The skipper knew that to deal with the leak, *Tang* needed
less outside sea pressure. He would have to bring the boat
higher. So *Tang* moved up through the temperature gradient:
staying below it for safety was irrelevant now. Bill Walsh
vented the bow tanks slowly so that the bubbles would be
smaller as they rose to the surface.

Tang levelled off at 100 feet and everyone breathed easier.
Hank Flanagan reported that the bilge pumps were gaining
on the incoming sea water through the torpedo tube leak.
Then Floyd Caverly on sonar picked up an escort's screws.
The destroyer was heading *Tang*'s way. Dick O'Kane's knew
he would have to use every evasive tactic in his bag of tricks.

"Stop pumping," O'Kane ordered.

Tang was quiet, except for her slowly turning screws. The
noise of the destroyer's screws stopped. She had slowed

down to listen closely, O'Kane decided. But he needed to look—and to confront the destroyer if necessary.

"Bring her up to 80 feet," he said. "Open the outer doors forward."

O'Kane planned to fire only in an emergency: only if the destroyer began to drop depth charges. Bill Walsh brought *Tang* up very slowly because the free-standing water surface in the torpedo room might have sloshed around, upsetting the submarine's delicate balance. O'Kane thought the maneuver was like balancing an ice tray full of water. At 60 feet, he ordered the scope up and spotted the destroyer at 700 yards, but it was not a good enough angle for a torpedo shot. So he decided to slither silently away. With the pumps off to decrease noise, water began rising in the forward torpedo room again. Taking more water aboard would increase the danger of shorting out *Tang*'s electrical listening equipment, located in the rear of the torpedo room. O'Kane ordered limited pumping resumed.

By now the entire crew shared the captain's concern. Word spread that the boat was locked in a duel with a destroyer, so Dick O'Kane relayed through talkers that *Tang* would only fire in defense. The destroyer remained idling as if in no rush. O'Kane continued evading, pumping, just waiting. It was a trying time for all hands, and for the captain: he had to be ready to shoot at any moment. Meanwhile, improvising torpedomen stuffed batting into the defective torpedo tube to help plug the leak. This reduced the need for noisy pumps. But the destroyer continued to hover in the area. O'Kane assumed the Japanese skipper thought *Tang* was deep—as any submarine would normally have been. He didn't realize *Tang* was close to the surface observing him at intervals. Possibly, O'Kane thought, the Japanese captain had not put to sea with a full load of depth charges. He might be shorthanded, having depleted his store on early fruitless depth charging near the ships *Tang* sank. He could be waiting for the perfect fix before dropping his last ash cans.

It was a nerve-wrenching contest of will between the two captains. Sunset was approaching. With dark, *Tang* might surface and slip away to repair the damaged torpedo tube.

O'Kane kept sneaking looks through the scope. Finally, sightings showed only pitch-blackness. O'Kane thought the destroyer captain must be equally anxious about what *Tang* would do in the dark. At 2030 the destroyer suddenly speeded up, her screws churning. The sound, swish-swish-swish, echoed through *Tang*'s hull. O'Kane tracked the destroyer through Floyd Caverly's sonar. In a daring tactic, he set *Tang* on the opposite course, so the two ships would pass each other at the best possible speed. The destroyer passed clear to the rear as *Tang* increased speed. Suddenly the boat was shaken by eight heavy depth charges. The crew waited for the worst, but when the detonations faded, the destroyer's screws faded, too. Captain O'Kane concluded that the destroyer charged overhead by chance. He dropped his last depth charges on speculation, before heading back to his base. Whatever the case, *Tang*'s crew breathed a collective sigh of relief. O'Kane had won his tense mano-a-mano fight with the destroyer captain.

He took a quick swing through the compartments and found there were some in the crew who believed that the destroyer, having lost the ships in her charge and not sinking *Tang,* blew herself up in humiliation.

With three blasts, victorious *Tang* surfaced to the crew's cheer, and quickly aired out the boat. As torpedomen prepared to fix the damaged tube, Ship's Cook Frederick Wixon broke out steaks for a late dinner. Wisely, he had had them thawing since noon, foreseeing a special meal might be required that evening.

Seeing calm and empty seas, O'Kane ordered divers over the bow to inspect the forward tubes. They worked in the dark, and replaced the gasket on the outer tube door. They manhandled the gasket into the groove, closed the outer door tight, and drained the tube from the inside. Then the inner door gasket was also replaced. *Tang* continued to clear the area, which Dick O'Kane suspected would soon be alive with anti-sub patrols. At the same time, Floyd Caverly repaired the faulty surface search radar with spare parts spread out around the conning tower deck. O'Kane told the crew to take a break from the arduous routine leaving only watch

standers on duty. There was plenty of sack time for everyone.

   Tang still had four torpedoes and O'Kane meant to fire
them. It wasn't long before the word came from a lookout:
"Smoke on the starboard bow!"

   "Here we go again," said Murray Frazee.

   O'Kane ordered *Tang* to turn right on an intercepting
course. The boat remained slightly over the horizon from the
target, which was identified as possibly two major ships. Occasionally, he poked the periscope up to its full height to
keep an eye on the distant vessels. As *Tang* pulled ahead and
closed range, O'Kane identified the first ship as a large, coal-
burning transport, the *Horai Maru* class. Three other masts
were sighted, probably escorts. O'Kane thought the best
solution would be to wait for a dawn attack. He consulted
Murray Frazee. His exec's opinion was blunt.

   "Oh, Christ, Captain, then it's so damn long till dark."

   What Frazee meant was that they might have to spend another long day underwater avoiding depth charging if they
waited until dawn to sink an enemy ship. O'Kane was quick
to realize that Frazee was reflecting the crew's feelings—that
it was awfully soon to go through another full day of evading
enemy destroyers. O'Kane took Frazee's views to heart.
When Ed Beaumont reported the radar was back on the line,
O'Kane decided *Tang* would attack that night.

   After the moon set at 2130, O'Kane singled out the *Horai
Maru* to attack in the convoy, which now appeared to com-
prise five ships. On the bridge, he maneuvered for a shot,
taking repeated bearings on the ship's course. O'Kane ordered four torpedoes fired. Almost immediately, he knew
something was wrong. Through his binoculars, O'Kane saw
that the wake of the first torpedo racing toward the center of
the ship, rather than leading the bow. The other torpedoes
seemed to be heading too far to the *Horai Maru*'s rear. The
firing party had underestimated the target's speed.

   O'Kane waited expectantly as *Tang* passed by the transport's stern. The seconds crawled by. There were no explosions. To Dick O'Kane's deep disappointment, *Tang* had
missed. No more fish.

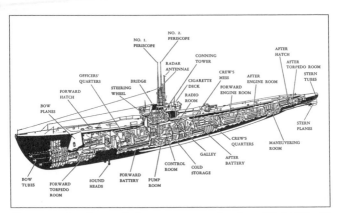

Cut-away showing typical compartmentation in a World War II U.S. fleet submarine like *Wahoo* and *Tang*.

Lt. Cdr. Dudley "Mush" Morton (right) on the bridge of USS *Wahoo* with his exec Lt. Richard H. O'Kane, returning to Pearl Harbor from the third war patrol, February 7, 1943. *(U.S. Naval Historical Center)*

Wahoo arrives at Pearl Harbor, early February 1943, with Mush Morton on the bridge and Dick O'Kane to the left with his foot up on a fitting on the cigarette deck. The broom on the periscope indicates *Wahoo* made a clean sweep on its historic third war patrol. The pennant bears the slogan "SHOOT THE SUNZA BITCHES" and one Japanese flag flies for every vessel sunk. *(U.S. National Archives)*

The last photograph taken of *Wahoo* as she departs on her sixth war patrol. *(U.S. National Archives)*

Crewmen bring aboard three of twenty-two Navy airmen rescued on *Tang*'s second patrol, lifeguarding off the Truk atoll in April, 1944. A Kingfisher float plane from the battleship *North Carolina* assisted in the rescue of nine downed aviators by towing their rubber rafts to *Tang*. The rescue was unprecedented and at the war's end, *Tang* ranked second in the number of airmen plucked from the sea. *(U.S. National Archives)*

Tang returns to the Sub Base at Pearl Harbor from her 11,500-mile second patrol and the unprecedented feat of rescuing twenty-two naval aviators. The huge crane at the Navy yard is in the background. *(U.S. National Archives)*

A montage of Japanese vessels sunk by U.S. submarines in the Pacific. *(U.S. National Archives)*

Lt. Cdr. Murray B. Frazee receives the Silver Star aboard *Tang* in May, 1944. Frazee was O'Kane's highly valued exec on *Tang*'s first four war patrols. He made eleven combat runs in the war. *(U.S. National Archives)*

Lt. Cdr. Creed C. Burlingame, commanding officer of the *Silversides*, the hard-living, highly successful skipper who patted Buddha's belly for luck. *(U.S. National Archives)*

Cdr. George L. Street III, commanding officer of the *Tirante* and Medal of Honor winner, pictured with the Navy Cross. *(U.S. National Archives)*

Slade D. Cutter, audacious skipper of *Seahorse* relaxing with crew in the torpedo room. *(U.S. National Archives)*

Capt. John P. Cromwell, who elected to go down aboard *Sculpin* in order not to give away vital secrets, November 1943. He was posthumously awarded the Medal of Honor. *(U.S. Naval Historical Center)*

Vice Adm. Lawson P. Ramage, Medal of Honor winner as daring Captain of *Parche*. *(U.S. National Archives)*

Cdr. Samuel D. Dealey, "destroyer killer" skipper of *Harder* and posthumous winner of the Medal of Honor. *(U.S. Naval Historical Center)*

Cdr. Eugene B. Fluckey, hard-charging and innovative Captain of the *Barb*. He was awarded the Medal of Honor. *(U.S. National Archives)*

Lt. Cdr. Howard W. Gilmore, after winning the Navy Cross in 1942. He was awarded the Medal of Honor posthumously after saving *Growler* by ordering "Take her down" without him. *(U.S. National Archives)*

Rear Adm. Ralph W. Christie, the jaunty, confident Commander Submarines Southwest Pacific. His controversial actions led to conflicts with Admirals Kinkaid, Lockwood, and Fife. *(U.S. National Archives)*

Rear Adm. James Fife, Jr. replaced rival Ralph Christie as Commander Submarines Southwest Pacific. His cold-blooded manner and tactics did not please all his skippers. *(U.S. National Archives)*

Vice Adm. Charles A. Lockwood, "Uncle Charlie," the submariner's submariner, well regarded by his captains, and senior submarine authority as Commander Submarines Pacific. *(U.S. National Archives)*

George W. Grider, diving officer of *Wahoo* and later successful CO of *Flasher*. *(U.S. National Archives)*

Edward L. Beach, the brilliant young exec of *Trigger* and *Tirante*, and CO of *Piper*. *(U.S. National Archives)*

President Harry S. Truman congratulates Cdr. Dick O'Kane following the presentation of his Medal of Honor at a ceremony on the White House lawn in March, 1946. *(U.S. Naval Historical Center)*

Skipper O'Kane rang full power on the Fairbanks Morse diesels, which were able to rev up immediately. As *Tang* pulled away from the convoy in the dark, O'Kane promised himself that he would visit the Fairbanks Morse plant in Beloit, Wisconsin, to deliver his personal thanks. He had Mel Enos transmit a contact report to ComSubPac for the benefit of other U.S. submarines.

Once out of danger and heading for Midway Island with empty torpedo tubes, Dick O'Kane and Murray Frazee chatted over a cribbage board, discussing the last attack. O'Kane knew a submarine was not held accountable for every torpedo miss, any more than a quarterback was for not connecting with every pass. Most submarines, in fact, fired spreads of torpedoes at targets, knowing that one or two might miss, forward or aft, in order to insure one or two hits. Dick had no intention of assessing blame, but he held his usual postmortem into what went wrong. He didn't want to fire four torpedoes vainly again. The officers in the firing party gathered in the wardroom over coffee. O'Kane believed they had soon found their error. They had been firing on convoys making 8 or 9 knots, and the afternoon tracking of this one had shown roughly the same speed. But the radar had been out of action, and because of some fancy zigzagging, the target's speed was underestimated by 1 1/2 knots. Further, a shower of sparks O'Kane noticed coming from the stack meant the transport was speeding up, which could cause a larger error—up to 6 knots—in the estimated speed. O'Kane's maneuver in swinging *Tang*'s bow quickly for the shot may have factored another knot into the firing equation. O'Kane knew that sometimes such errors cancelled themselves out in a firing set-up but this time they were compounded.

O'Kane grimly figured it out: 6 knots misjudgement in the transport's speed is 200 yards a minute. The torpedo run was about 70 seconds. The ship would have been 650 yards further along its track than the set-up indicated. The torpedo aimed just forward of the target's bow must have just missed the stern. All the other fish necessarily ran further astern. O'Kane accepted another home truth. This was the first attack when he did not personally know the solution for speed when firing. He was surprised to find that the computer's input was for 8½ knots. His seaman's eye had pegged the ship at moving about 13 knots. In the future, O'Kane resolved, he would keep himself completely informed and impose his own judgment, if necessary. Having discovered the reason for their mistake, the officers in the wardroom felt the better for it. They had a great patrol under their belts.

Tang was assigned for refit at Midway, a disappointment since the gooneybird island had not improved much as a rest and recreation center. En route, *Tang*'s crew concentrated on their study courses: new members to qualify for submarines and others to move up in their rates. O'Kane believed that study for advancement and keeping the vessel clean made for a taut but happy boat. The cooks broke out their best cuts of meat, knowing they would be soon replenished, so the crew ate heartily.

Entering Midway on March 3, gingerly as usual, O'Kane saw the masts of the sunken *Macaw*, the submarine rescue vessel that had gone down in a storm a few weeks previously while trying to pull the grounded submarine *Flier* off the rocks of the atoll. *Flier* had hit a coral reef while trying to enter the harbor in rough weather. Six days later, after the blow subsided, a heavy crane came out of the harbor and succeeded in lifting *Flier*, but *Macaw* was badly holed and sunk in deep water with the loss of her commanding officer and four crewmembers. Another submarine, USS *Scorpion*, earlier went aground on an offshore reef at Midway. She was stuck for five hours—an unfortunate action that resulted in the removal of the captain and executive officer. Both went to surface duty. The wreck of *Macaw* remained as a grim warning to captains entering the tricky channel. *Tang* slid through and tied up at a new submarine dock to a warm welcome by base officers.

It was a well-deserved welcome after a sensational patrol. This was the first time a U.S. submarine had sunk five enemy ships—more than 30,000 tons—on her first war outing. Dick O'Kane had scored sixteen hits with his twenty-four torpedoes, a remarkable feat of marksmanship for a U.S. submariner. Dick and Murray Frazee had developed the night surface attack into a polished tactic. ComSubPac Lockwood was delighted with *Tang*'s performance. O'Kane was awarded the Navy Cross, and he recommended Murray Frazee and Bill Walsh for Silver Stars, and two enlisted men, Chief of the Boat Bill Ballinger and Chief Quartermaster Sidney Jones, for Bronze Stars.

Tang had made a splendid mark as a new, aggressive boat in the Submarine Force, with a finely honed crew and a fighting skipper. Dick O'Kane had shown himself a worthy successor to Mush Morton. He returned from his first patrol more assured—a proven submarine captain.

CHAPTER FOURTEEN

"Rendering Gallant Lifeguard Service"

Dick O'Kane was the first to admit that Midway atoll was no Isle of Capri. Some crews wanted to speed up their refit at Midway and get back to sea, hoping their next rest period would be in Australia. For the men of *Tang*, it was the chance to turn over their duties to a relief crew and do nothing for the next several days. They lined up for their pay. As he had on *Wahoo*, O'Kane ordered Chief Ballinger to instruct the disbursing officer to hand over only $10 per man. The rest was put in an envelope bearing the sailor's name and went into *Tang*'s safe. That would keep a young sailor's paycheck from falling into the hands of the civilian workmen, who were pros at cards and dice. O'Kane would rather his crew learn the facts of gambling life for $10 rather than $150. If a sailor wanted to send a money order home, he could draw his entire pay, but he had to return with a postal receipt. Murray Frazee and Chief Ballinger agreed.

As the crew dashed off to relax with beers, baseball games, swimming, and poker, O'Kane still had some ship's business. Murray Frazee was finishing up the patrol report. Division commander Chet Smith complimented O'Kane on the pristine condition of the boat. The hull would need some work, however. O'Kane noted that the glossiness of its black paint had faded and bleached to a splotchy slate gray, looking almost camouflaged. He thought that the faded look was perhaps more suitable at sea than getting a new black paint job.

Captain C.D. Edmunds, the senior submarine officer, invited Dick and Fraz to his quarters. The two *Tang* officers were given a drink by the steward and informed that Edmunds was at the airstrip seeing off a guest, Eddie Peabody, the jazz banjo artist, who was entertaining troops in the Pacific. The plane had engine trouble so Edmunds returned with Peabody and invited O'Kane and Frazee to dinner—a big boned rib roast. O'Kane prevailed on Peabody to stay an extra day and entertain *Tang*'s crew.

Though *Tang* was turned over to the relief crew, O'Kane and Frazee knew that responsibility for their submarine rested with them alone. They made sure new gaskets were locked into the torpedo tube doors.

O'Kane had an idea: he wanted to create a "crow's nest" lookout platform above the bridge. The sub tender installed a steel plate connecting the periscope shears, and welded it in place so that a lookout could stand well above the bridge, but have a railing at chest height to protect him. At the command "Clear the bridge," he could swing down from a line connected to newly installed pad eyes and cleats. The additional height would give *Tang*'s lookouts a much better perch, while still allowing them to scuttle below before a crash dive.

Dick and Fraz spent their evenings at the Gooneyville, where a large corner room was still reserved as a meeting place for submarine officers. There were tables with green baize cloth for poker games and big reefers full of cold beer. It was here, O'Kane believed, that officers really learned what went on during submarine war patrols. There were things discussed here that were deemed too trivial or personal to include in official patrol reports, but they often provided better insights into submarine problems than the reports themselves. Further, the informal atmosphere and drinks helped break down barriers between junior and senior officers and encouraged frankness in conversations.

Murray Frazee was saddened to pick up the unofficial report that his former submarine, *Grayback,* on which he had made seven patrols, was overdue in late February in the Western Pacific. Dick O'Kane shared Frazee's sorrow since *Grayback*'s skipper, Commander Johnny Moore, had been PCO on *Wahoo*'s fifth patrol with Mush Morton. Moore had

run up a splendid record, sinking ten Japanese ships on three
war patrols.

After a few days at Midway, O'Kane was surprised when
Frazee and Chief Ballinger asked to see him. They said the
crew had had enough of life on the gooneybird island and
would just as soon leave on their next patrol a couple of days
early. That would mean getting back from patrol sooner, and
having more time in Pearl Harbor, or better yet, Australia.
O'Kane agreed and speeded up the training schedule. On the
last evening in Midway, all hands remained on board for dinner: no one asked permission to go ashore. It was the fastest
refit, training, and turnaround the Submarine Force had seen.

"Ready for getting underway, Captain," Frazee reported.

"Let go the spring lines," O'Kane ordered. "Slack the
stern line. Take a strain on the bow line." *Tang*'s stern swung
away from the dock.

"Let go all lines," the captain said. "All back two-thirds.
Port ahead two-thirds, starboard back one-third." *Tang* lost
sternway and spun around, pointing toward the channel entrance.

"All ahead two-thirds." The boat was on her way past the
jagged coral heads and into the deep Pacific.

Tang's orders were to patrol around the Palau Islands,
3,500 miles away. O'Kane and Frazee had been hoping for a
patrol in Empire waters where the pickings might be richer,
but orders were orders. Sailing to the Western Pacific, O'Kane
tried out the new crow's nest. Both Dick and Fraz had
climbed up during the training period and approved: it
lengthened the horizon. But to O'Kane's surprise, Chief
Ballinger seemed somewhat skeptical. O'Kane asked why.

"It's just such a goddamned long way to the hatch, Captain," Ballinger said.

O'Kane thought his answer short and to the point from a
top-notch COB who had an ear to the crew. Exec Frazee
manned the crow's nest for part of a watch. He reported to
O'Kane that in the open sea with the wind whistling past, a
lookout might have difficulty hearing the command "Clear
the bridge" and get left behind during a fast dive. O'Kane

decided to make this a volunteer spot for the elite and agile few. To give them added confidence, the OOD would yell his first "Clear the bridge" at the man high in the crow's next.

Speeding to Palau Island, *Tang*'s lookouts spotted the masts of a ship hull down on the horizon. Dick O'Kane conned *Tang* closer in and carefully looked over the target with 7×50 binoculars. That inspection revealed the enemy ship was merely a trawler. Some sub skippers attacked trawlers, particularly earlier in the war, on the grounds that they were cutting down Japan's food supply, but O'Kane believed the contrary. Having patrolled Empire waters he thought attacking small fishing boats was equivalent to swatting mosquitoes on the New Jersey shore. Further, a lucky hit by an armed trawler could needlessly endanger a submarine. *Tang*'s business at sea was sinking warships and merchantmen.

O'Kane explained to his officers that the main reason they were to patrol the Palau area was that much of the Japanese fleet had evacuated Truk and was based in harbors farther west. *Tang* and other U.S. submarines in a patrol line were to watch for vessels leaving Palau. Dick O'Kane was unhappy with the deployment of U.S. subs in scouting operations, backing up the fleet. He thought boats should operate independently, using their ability to reach Japanese home islands to strike with surprise. He believed that a submarine trying to chase an Ultra and make contact with a fast-moving warship was of limited value. The enemy ship would have to pass within 15 miles of the sub to be spotted. And even if *Tang* or the other subs on the patrol line spotted an enemy, a warship would be moving at high speed, with alert escorts using sonar gear, all racing past like an express train.

O'Kane and Frazee thought true surprise came from the submarine's long voyage to an area where the enemy least expected surprise attack—not in the middle of a fleet action. In any event, O'Kane preferred that U.S. subs be positioned at intervals along the legs of a V covering the probable path of fleeing enemy warships. The submarine at the apex of the V could send a contact report with echo-ranging equipment, allowing the other boats in the formation to move into an attack.

It was all rather moot for now. O'Kane was surprised that there was so little enemy activity, either surface or air, around the major base that now constituted Palau atoll. *Tang* spent a couple of days watching an air strike on the Palau group by pilots from Task Force 58, but neither the lookouts nor the radar found any enemy ships. Unexpectedly, ComSubPac ordered *Tang* to move 500 miles to the west to patrol near Davao Gulf at Mindanao Island in the Philippines where four Japanese cruisers were sighted. En route, Murray Frazee urged all the crew to work on qualification for the next higher rating and the messroom tables looked like a schoolroom with the men diligently perusing manuals and copybooks.

O'Kane received a message to position *Tang* in a circular screen with other submarines around Davao Gulf, the very tactical disposition he thought ineffective. With equal suddenness the next message from Pearl Harbor ordered *Tang* to return immediately to the Palau Islands area. O'Kane did not relish the idea of sailing back to an unproductive area, particularly when four enemy cruisers were supposedly still anchored at Davao port. As they headed back to the Palaus, Floyd Caverly delivered an ominous report. "The radar's just crapped out, Captain." Caverly, Lieutenant Ed Beaumont, and Edwin Bergman began round-the-clock efforts to repair the SJ search radar.

To make up for the lack of radar in enemy waters, O'Kane ordered additional lookouts to man the forward machine gun deck. In the event of a crash dive, they would have to scuttle into the gun access trunk, an uncomfortable but watertight locker. O'Kane didn't like the set-up, and neither did the lookout, but he told them that's the way things sometimes have to be. He hated sailing back and forth in a boat used to scouting out targets. It wasn't so much that the crew got bored—the waters were too dangerous—but that they might lose that edge that kept *Tang* at fighting pitch.

Tang closed the Palaus. The skipper issued orders urging the crew to remain alert, the sharp eyes of lookouts making up for the lack of sea search radar, which was still being repaired. O'Kane preferred to keep the air search radar off because enemy direction finders could zero in on *Tang*'s bearing and send planes out on that vector.

"A patrol or ship can come from any direction," he ordered.

"Keep me completely informed. Call me at any time. If in doubt, dive!"

Tang received an order to rendezvous with *Trigger*, commanded by Dick O'Kane's old friend, Fritz Harlfinger. *Trigger* had undergone a severe depth charging and needed replacement parts to stay on station. A rendezvous between submarines in enemy waters was a very tricky operation, but O'Kane had prepared the radiomen, sound operators, and deck gang for the meeting at sea. The two boats found each other and closed. O'Kane, who had been skeptical of *Tang*'s new paint job, became a believer. Without his binoculars, he couldn't spot *Trigger*—her sides painted a light gray haze and decks black—at 500 yards. *Trigger* was only sighted visually by the water pouring from her limber holes, the vents where superstructure decking meets the ballast tanks in the hull. She needed spare parts but a squall delayed a transfer until well after nightfall. The second rendezvous was arranged by blinker light. A rubber dinghy was launched from *Trigger* and it carried over movies her crew had seen. It picked up spare radar tubes, a battery ventilation motor, and compressor valves. The night exercise seemed to lift *Tang*'s morale, which was suffering from the lack of enemy targets.

Because of the dearth of ships, O'Kane and Frazee suspected that U.S. aircraft might have mined the main channels into western Palau lagoon. But why didn't ComSubPac's staff assign *Tang* or another boat to the eastern passage? O'Kane set up another rendezvous with *Trigger* to discuss the situation. Harlfinger was equally puzzled, but those were the orders. Three more fruitless days followed until the highly frustrated Dick O'Kane received word to head back to Truk to stand by for a major U.S. air strike against the Japanese bastion.

While O'Kane believed that sinking enemy ships was a

submarine's highest priority, he understood the rationale behind putting the boats on lifeguard duty. It was a new insurance for carrier pilots—having submarines loiter in areas
targeted by the task force. It was, however, dangerous duty
because the subs operated under the guns on Japanese atolls,
while all the time being threatened by anti-submarine air and
ship patrols.

On an earlier strike *Skate* picked up six aviators from the
carrier *Lexington,* the "Fighting Lady," including the air group
commander. *Skate* lost one ship's officer mortally wounded
when a Japanese plane strafed the sub during the rescue
operation. When *Skate* returned the airmen home by an
at-sea transfer, *Lexington*'s grateful captain messaged the
sub's skipper, Gene McKinney: "ANYTHING ON LEXINGTON IS
YOURS FOR THE ASKING X IF IT IS TOO BIG TO CARRY AWAY WE
WILL CUT IT UP IN SMALL PARTS."

Tang's crew would be up to the difficult task of lifeguarding. Off Wake Island, they had developed a bridle to attach
to a downed floatplane and tow it out of range of Japanese
gunners. O'Kane believed that standing off an island at
30 miles waiting for lifeguard instructions—as per some orders sent from SubPac—was wrong. *Tang* would move into
the reef as soon and as close as possible. While Dick O'Kane
did not like using the deck gun, en route to Truk he ordered
Bill Leibold to conduct practice firing in case *Tang* had to
use the 4-inch weapon against Japanese shore batteries. Sailing past Fais Island, *Tang*, as *Wahoo* had done, fired thirty-
three rounds at the phosphate plant. O'Kane congratulated
all hands.

O'Kane hurried to take position south of Truk for the air
strike, harassed by Japanese planes that kept *Tang* diving and
surfacing. He was philosophical, his motto: "If your dives
and surfaces come out even, no day is a total loss."

Tang's radar picked up incoming planes: they were aircraft
from U.S. carriers shuttling between Task Force 58 and Truk.
O'Kane thought it was the most encouraging sight he'd seen
in the war. The boat guarded a special radio frequency used
by U.S. aircraft reporting to their task force. In late morning,
April 30, *Tang* got the word: an aviator's raft was in the water

about 2 miles from the Truk atoll's reef. O'Kane rang up flank speed ahead. He was now free to leave his holding pattern and use his own imagination.

Close to Truk, the sight stirred Dick O'Kane. U.S. planes were diving through a hole in the clouds at the Truk anchorage and the atoll's shore facilities. Planes were being hit with flak. If the aviators could brave the anti-aircraft fire, *Tang* could get a survivor 2 miles off the beach. Sidney Jones was in the crow's nest. "Thar she blows," he yelled. The rubber raft was spotted at 1100 hours about 4 miles west of the reported position. No matter. O'Kane rang up emergency speed, a blistering 22 knots, and *Tang* was there in 10 minutes.

O'Kane maneuvered the submarine with the raft upwind and then turned to snake in close aboard, slow and straight. Lieutenant Hank Flanagan headed the rescue party. They tossed lines overboard and pulled the raft alongside. Lieutenant (j.g.) Scott Scammell, Aviation Machinist's Mate Joseph D. Gendron, and Aviation Radioman Harry B. Gemmell were hoisted aboard *Tang*. O'Kane ordered a shot of Lejon brandy, depth charge medicine, for the aviators.

The captain assigned the three men to what he dubbed his new AIC, aviation information center—guarding the fleet aircraft radio frequency next to the radio room, with a Hallicrafter set specially rigged up in the crew's messroom. *Tang* now had a pilot and radioman in the AIC who recognized all the call signs and knew many of the airmen personally. They manned the Hallicrafter and *Tang* provided a large-scale chart of Truk Atoll.

Through its newly installed AIC, *Tang* received a report that two more planes were down, with the crews in life rafts. The closest raft could be reached around nightfall. The other was outside the reef and its airmen could paddle through the night, and wait for rescue the next day. As *Tang* approached the first raft, O'Kane ordered the deck gun crew to pump shells into the gun emplacement on the atoll to cover the rescue mission. The Japanese returned fire but *Tang* pulled out of range toward the aviators. In the dark, the boat commenced a zigzag search for the raft, sending up a green Very star shell every 15 minutes. These were not prearranged and O'Kane hoped the aviators would answer back with their emergency flares in the raft. It was a difficult time for navigator Frazee as they moved through the shallow water and reefs. The search proved to be in vain. The airmen would have to wait for first light.

As the sky lightened, *Tang*'s lookouts were manning the bridge and the fully extended periscopes.

"Submarine conning tower bearing zero three five," Signalman Ogden reported. There were no other U.S. subs in the area. O'Kane ordered a quick but quiet dive to attack the target, the first in forty-eight days of patrol. He maneuvered for position. "Up scope," he said. Chief Quartermaster Jones moved the handles of the periscope up for O'Kane and then followed him up from a squatting position marking bearings.

"Bearing," O'Kane said. "Mark! Down scope."

The set-up was almost perfect: a Japanese submarine on the surface departing Truk's southern channel at a speed of 10 knots. O'Kane ordered the outer torpedo tube doors opened. He raised the scope for a last firing bearing. "Lost his screws, Captain." It was Floyd Caverly on sonar. No sign of the enemy on the scope. The submarine had dived!

A fast sweep of the radar indicated the probable reason: U.S. planes were on their way to Truk. But there was also the possibility that the Japanese sub had picked up *Tang*. Was this a case of the hunter mixed up with the hunted, like a duel in a darkened room?

Tang rigged for silent dive and moved silently to 150 feet. If the enemy had picked up the boat and guessed O'Kane was at periscope depth, he would be wrong. Sound could hear nothing. The enemy submarine seemed to have disappeared. *Tang* waited. O'Kane went to periscope depth for a look. Nothing. He couldn't hold up his rescue mission any longer and ordered *Tang* to surface—moving away from the submarine contact and toward the downed American airmen. O'Kane resurfaced and sent off a contact report to Task Force 58 on the Japanese sub sighting, course and probable submerged speed at time of diving.

Lieutenant Scammell, the aviator, suggested to Captain

O'Kane that *Tang* lash down American flags fore and aft of the bridge as a safeguard against attack. It would come as some irony for U.S. pilots to attack a sub with U.S. aviators aboard. Hardly had the flags been secured when the first contact report came to *Tang*'s impromptu Air Information Center at 0828. Downed fliers were in a raft a short run away near Ollan Island off the southern reef of Truk.

When *Tang* arrived, O'Kane found that one U.S. Kingfisher float plane attempting a rescue had half-capsized in the choppy seas. A second Kingfisher landed in the water and was trying to tow the first plane as well as the rubber raft clear of the island to the open sea. *Tang* pulled alongside the raft and rescued Lieutenant (j.g.) Robert F. Kanze and his crewman Aviation Radioman Robert E. Hill. These were the men on the raft that *Tang* couldn't reach the night before. They had paddled toward the Southern Cross all night long and cleared the atoll. Then *Tang* picked up the pilot of the wrecked Kingfisher, Lieutenant John J. Dowdle. The second scout plane, piloted by Lieutenant (j.g.) J.A. Burns, off the battleship *North Carolina,* managed to get airborne and flew off. O'Kane ordered *Tang*'s 20-millimeter gunners to sink Lieutenant Dowdle's plane.

A topside lookout in the crow's nest warned that a torpedo bomber was smoking in a long glide across the atoll. O'Kane rang up speed to head for an intercepting course, although it looked as if the plane wouldn't make it across the lagoon to the safety of the sea. But with a last effort the pilot gunned the engine and pulled up over the strip of the atoll and past the reef into the Pacific. He ditched perfectly and within 20 minutes, *Tang*'s crewmen were hauling on board Air Group Commander A.R. Matter, and his crewmen Aviation Radioman James J. Lenahan and Aviation Ordnanceman H.A. Thompson. The aviators' rubber raft served as a bridge from plane to boat and the fliers were wet only to their knees. O'Kane offered his cabin to the pilot, a full commander. The aviators were given the usual sedatives by the smiling pharmacist's mate.

The AIC was functioning smoothly. With the additional airmen aboard, the team knew all the pilots by name and most by voice alone. They were intercepting reports from the airmen overhead to the task force commander and saving precious time in aiding *Tang*'s rescue operation. Ever the innovator, O'Kane devised a new tactic by breaking voice radio silence to request the carriers to put up air patrols overhead while *Tang* rescued downed airmen.

As *Tang* headed for newly reported downed airmen in three rafts near each other on the eastern side of the atoll, Dick O'Kane got a first-hand look at the huge air strike at Truk. Dive-bombers were peeling off at 3,500 feet and zooming their bombs home on enemy ships and shore installations. O'Kane was proud of the way the carrier pilots pressed their attacks in the face of heavy anti-aircraft fire.

However, Lieutenant Burns, *North Carolina*'s Kingfisher pilot, had beaten *Tang* to the airmen in the three rafts. Burns taxied near the reef and took some men aboard on his single float, and was towing the other rafts to seaward. They were out of immediate danger so O'Kane chose to push *Tang* toward another raft somewhat to the south. In case *Tang* was forced to submerge, Boatswain's Mate Bill Leibold had rigged the towing bridle to *Tang*'s radar mast with a long line and a life ring at the end. *Tang* could now tow a plane, raft or swimmer from a submerged position to safety. Meanwhile, the squadron mates of the downed airmen flew a combat air patrol overhead, strafing any Japanese gun position that tried to open up on *Tang* and her brood.

Tang pulled aboard Lieutenant Harry E. Hill. Then another report to the AIC sent the boat a bit more to the south looking for a swimmer in the water. She reached him at 1300. Luckily, an aircraft had dropped a rubber raft to the downed pilot who was exhausted and had barely managed to get half his body into it. The raft was dangerously close to the reef. O'Kane ordered *Tang*'s sound heads rigged in and nosed close to the rocks. A *Tang* swimmer with a line was poised at the bow to leap into the sea if necessary, but the boat's crew managed to get close enough to pull in the wet and tired airman, Lieutenant James G. Cole.

O'Kane ordered *Tang* to return to the Kingfisher float plane and raft left behind earlier. They found the Kingfisher down by the stern with her tail surfaces bashed by the choppy waters. O'Kane could see that the plane would never fly again so he didn't worry about bumping the Kingfisher as he brought *Tang* alongside. Nine airmen quickly tumbled aboard, like a pack of hounds, O'Kane thought, scrambling out of a kennel. The new arrivals were Lieutenants Burns, Robert S. Nelson, Robert T. Barbor, and Ensign Carroll L. Farrell; Aviation Radiomen James L. Livingston, Joseph Hranke, and Aubrey J. Gill; and Aviation Machinist's Mates Robert W. Gruebel and Owen F. Tabrun.

O'Kane ordered the 20-millimeter gun crew to destroy the Kingfisher. As Murray Frazee wryly observed: *Tang* destroyed the entire USS *North Carolina* air group, and rescued all the personnel of the battlewagon's aviation department.

Tang moved quickly out of gun range of the atoll. Word came of another downed raft some distance away, toward the southwest of the atoll. The report was not encouraging because *Tang* could not reach the position before night settled in. Further, the current there could blow the raft back on the atoll during the hours of darkness. Dick O'Kane went below to consult with the aviators in the AIC.

"There are the new night fighters," Lieutenant Barbor offered. But Commander Matter, the senior officer aboard, interrupted.

"Only the task force commander could authorize that."

Night fighters were the answer, O'Kane decided. He told the airman to contact Vice Admiral Marc Mitscher, Commander of Task Force 58.

O'Kane's airman had the wizened Admiral on the voice radio within minutes. "We'll need two night fighters to locate the last raft, Admiral," the aviator said.

"You'll have three," Mitscher replied.

Dick thought that Commander Matter seemed appalled that they didn't go through the chain of command, perhaps with him in the chain, but Mitscher seemed to like the way *Tang* addressed the matter, and that was fine with O'Kane.

Three black-winged night fighters from *Enterprise* joined up with *Tang* at sunset. *Tang*'s bridge and periscope shears

bristled with lookouts in the fading light and began its down-
wind search pattern, as did the night fighters. Abruptly, a
U.S. aircraft dove, firing red star rockets, or tracers, creating
a shower of sparks on the sea off *Tang*'s starboard bow. The
raft was located and the fighters sent home with Godspeed
and thanks. *Tang* took aboard Lieutenant Donald Kirkpatrick
and Aviation Ordnanceman Richard L. Bentley, who had
planned to set sail for the Solomon Islands, 1,200 miles
away.

Throughout the rescues, *Seahorse* patrolled a nearby atoll,
lifeguarding during a strike on Satawan Island. Slade Cutter's radiomen cut into the voice transmissions between *Tang*
and the carrier planes and he piped in the broadcast over *Seahorse*'s loudspeaker system. Cutter thought the play-by-play
was more exciting than any football broadcast. He should
know: he kicked the winning field goal in Navy's 3–0 win
against Army in 1934.

To keep the aviators busy, O'Kane and Frazee agreed to
put them to work as watch-standers and had Chief Ballinger
provide them with bunks, doubling up with the crew and
Tang's officers. O'Kane had offered his own bunk to Commander Matter for the moment, but did not consider this a
permanent arrangement. The captain was not expected to
move out of his own cabin. Chief Ballinger solved the problem by knocking on O'Kane's door and telling Commander
Matter: "Your bunk is ready, sir." Matter was given the top
bunk in the Chief's quarters, a privilege because it was out of
the way of men climbing in and out of their sacks.

The aircraft radiomen helped guard the special 4475
frequency the AIC was using. They learned that Admiral
Mitscher congratulated all units on a splendid performance:
sixty enemy planes had been shot down, another thirty were
destroyed on the ground. But the task force reported twenty-
six U.S. planes downed, with only eight airmen rescued and
"some others" on *Tang*.

Obviously, O'Kane reckoned, Task Force 58's air opera-
tions had not monitored Freq 4475 as closely as *Tang* had.
O'Kane deliberated whether to report the aviators aboard to
Mitscher but decided against it. It would be hot enough in

the area without giving Truk's radio direction finders a chance to zero in on *Tang*.

As navigator, Fraz thought it a miracle that *Tang* didn't go aground in those three days of nosing around reefs. But Dick O'Kane didn't mind if he knocked off an underwater sound head on the way to rescue an aviator.

With the airmen aboard and safe, Captain O'Kane could see that *Tang* was a happy ship. After the evening meal, the wardroom and crew's mess became a lounge for the visiting airmen from the carriers. The new crewmembers were not accustomed to drop-in movies or hot, fresh-baked bread and rolls throughout the night, served with *Tang*-made ice cream. They volunteered for lookout duty and the pilots serving as assistant OOD were delighted to look through *Tang*'s periscopes, for the boat was still on patrol and seeking enemy shipping. At the end of a submerged period, *Tang*'s captain played a submariner's joke on his guests. He announced that the smoking lamp was lit, meaning crewmembers could smoke. The airmen tried to light up, but the lack of oxygen in the submarine's compartments would not keep a match burning or a cigarette smoldering.

Tang stood by for another lifeguard mission, this time for an Army air force Liberator strike, but there was no call for help. The boat was held for a few more days until a relief submarine arrived on station, and then moved out from the Truk area. O'Kane and Fraz prepared their message for ComSubPac. They decided on something simple: "FOLLOW-ING AIRMEN ABOARD ALL HEALTHY." It listed the twenty-two aviators alphabetically. Dick O'Kane was disconcerted to find that Commander Matter had drafted his own message. It read: "REQUEST RENDEZVOUS EARLIEST FOR TRANSFER AIRMEN AND EFFECT THEIR RETURN TO PARENT AIR GROUPS." Murray Frazee thought the CAG was trying to take charge, communicating directly with Pearl Harbor. "If there's any communicating," O'Kane snapped, "I do the communicating."

Dick O'Kane knew that Task Force 58 was scheduled to return after additional bombardments to Majuro in the Marshalls for replenishment. He knew the aviators, after their ordeal, would not be looking forward to R & R on Majuro, which had no more charms than Midway had for exhausted submariners. The flyboys wanted to stick with *Tang*'s crew and head for Pearl Harbor, the joys of Honolulu and the Royal Hawaiian at Waikiki. O'Kane decided that if the Air Group Commander's dispatch was sent, some damned fool at Pearl or Task Force 58 would see to it that the request was carried out—at Majuro or at sea. O'Kane turned to Lieutenant Dowdle, an aviator who was filling in as coding officer in the radio room. He suspected Dowdle was a fun-loving type who would know what to do with Commander Matter's message.

"Will you take care of these?" O'Kane inquired, with a knowing smile, handing the Lieutenant the two messages. He added, "Will you read them now?"

Dowdle read *Tang*'s message with a broad smile. Then he went over Matter's request and scowled.

"Why that son-of-a-bitch!" Dowdle mouthed the words.

O'Kane nodded. The aviators would know how to take care of this.

After supper both dispatches were sent through the transmitter, but Dick O'Kane strongly suspected that during Commander Matter's message transmission, the lead to the antenna was mysteriously disconnected.

As *Tang* headed for Pearl, the evening Fox radio schedule brought multiple congratulations from everyone up the line. O'Kane hadn't planned to delay news of rescuing airmen in seven daring maneuvers. It was just a common-sense security precaution. But the delay had served to build up suspense, in the task force, in Pearl Harbor and in Washington. The message reached Pearl with maximum impact. To rescue twenty-two aviators who were believed lost or captured was an enormous achievement for the Pacific Fleet.

At breakfast, Commander Matter told O'Kane, "I can't understand why they haven't set up the rendezvous—or at least answered my message." The wardroom fell silent.

"Well," O'Kane improvised, "it looks like they want you all back at Pearl for a little publicity. It isn't every air group commander that gets out and carries the mail!"

O'Kane's compliment seemed to smooth Matter's ruffled

feathers. As *Tang* headed for the barn with its airdale passengers, O'Kane was pleased to learn that thirty-five crewmen had become qualified submariners on the patrol, and eighteen men were advanced in rating. Further, in his report Dick O'Kane made recommendations for lifeguarding—including standardization of identification flares, and coordination of carrier and submarine radio operations—that would become Pacific Fleet doctrine. Based on O'Kane's recommendations, Admiral Mitscher organized a special combat air patrol to protect submarines during rescues of downed airmen. The patrols located downed fliers, defended submarines, and guided ditching aircraft to the submarine's position.

There was only one setback for the crew. *Tang* had failed to sink an enemy ship, the normal requirement for a "successful" patrol meriting the submarine combat pin. Those crewmembers who had joined *Tang* at Midway for her second patrol would be deeply disappointed. O'Kane was sympathetic: he knew that some of the most difficult and dangerous war patrols resulted in no ships sunk.

On the way back some of the pilots revealed that carrier planes had dropped mines around the Palaus, which reaffirmed O'Kane's view about the lack of Japanese shipping from the atoll channels. This, he thought, would have to be taken up with Admiral Lockwood in Pearl: ComAirPac ought to inform ComSubPac as to where his planes were sowing mines.

On arrival at the Submarine Base, *Tang* was assigned to Pier One and found a royal welcome awaiting. Fleet Admiral Nimitz, Admiral Lockwood and senior members of their staffs were on hand to greet the submarine with its airmen aboard. The pier was crowded with press and photographers. They snapped pictures of Dick O'Kane surrounded by the twenty-two airmen rescued in the dangerous pick-ups off Truk, the Japanese Gibraltar of the Pacific.

Admiral Lockwood decided to make an exception to his general rule of minimum publicity about submarines. This unprecedented rescue of downed pilots was a tremendous morale booster for the carrier task force. As Uncle Charlie Lockwood shook hands all around, Lieutenant Burns, the heroic, upfront pilot of the Kingfisher, unexpectedly stepped forward.

"Admiral Lockwood," he said. "There are some new members of *Tang*'s crew who joined her at Midway. Is this patrol going to be designated as successful for combat insignia?"

Slightly surprised, the Admiral said, "Why, uh, why, yes, indeed."

Lieutenant Burns thanked the Admiral as *Tang*'s crew broke out in broad smiles. The endorsements on *Tang*'s second war patrol called it as "outstanding" as O'Kane's first. *Tang* was commended for transferring supplies to *Trigger*, which resulted in a highly successful trip for Fritz Harlfinger's boat. It was a rare patrol without any ships sunk that actually added to a boat's reputation in the Submarine Force.

The pictures of the rescued airmen and story of O'Kane, *Tang* and the aviators made the front page of the *Honolulu Advertiser* and many others. *Life* magazine devoted a whole page to the shot.

As *Tang*'s crew piled off to take buses to the Royal Hawaiian, 12 miles away. Dick O'Kane stayed aboard long enough to sign a recommendation that Lieutenant Burns be awarded the Navy Cross for placing himself in grave jeopardy to save his fellow fliers. O'Kane himself was later awarded the Legion of Merit, which at the time outranked the Silver Star, and his junior officers also received decorations.

The citation for *Tang* read: "Rendering gallant lifeguard service during air strikes against enemy-held atolls by United States forces, the *Tang* braved the treacherous reefs off the coast of a powerfully fortified enemy stronghold to rescue twenty-two Naval aviators in seven pick-ups, completing this perilous mission within close range of hostile shore batteries. The brilliant and heroic achievements of this vessel reflect the highest credit upon the courage, seamanship and determination of her officers and men and enhance the fine traditions of the United States Naval Service."

O'Kane's lifguarding tactics were made the basis for training other subs in the techniques. Admiral Lockwood commended *Tang*'s patrol report to be studied by all commanding officers as a guide for future lifeguard duty.

Lockwood had no qualms about devoting valuable submarine efforts to lifeguarding and lifesaving. As he put it, "The value of lifeguarding cannot be measured alone in terms of lives saved, important though that factor is. Actually, its effect on the morale of the air force was of much greater moment. No one relished the thought of making a one-way flight. The thought that if shot down, he might be tortured or murdered by a barbarous enemy or serve as live bait for sharks or barracuda, could not be comforting to an aviator. So the lifeguarding had a great and beneficial effect on the fighting spirit of the aviators."

Lifeguarding became big business as long-range carrier air strikes grew more frequent, and the B-29 bombers started flying from Saipan and Tinian against the Japanese home islands. In all, eighty-six submarines rescued a total of 504 downed fliers. Taking a leaf from Dick O'Kane's book, one skipper—Commander Robert R. Williams of *Finback*—rescued a pilot in a raft by towing him with a raised periscope out of range of enemy shore gunners. The same sub also picked up a young carrier pilot by the name of Lieutenant (j.g.) George Bush—shot down north of Iwo Jima. *Finback* sank two cargo ships before returning to his carrier, *San Jacinto,* the future President of the United States.

CHAPTER FIFTEEN

Good News and Bizarre News

Dick O'Kane found life at the Royal Hawaiian relaxing as usual. He and Murray Frazee shared a suite with a balcony overlooking Waikiki Beach and Diamond Head. Their mail was arranged by a sub division officer on an outside table with the most recent letter from home on top, which they read with a cold beer. And then they and their fellow officers unwound by lolling around the reef off the beach. *Tang*'s crew spread out along the beach or headed into Honolulu. The frustrations and satisfactions of the second patrol faded from their minds.

On the fourth day, Dick O'Kane received a summons from *Tang* at the Submarine Base. They had left Bill Walsh and Scotty Anderson aboard to work with the relief crew, since both were to be transferred: Bill to postgraduate engineering school, and Scotty to the Submarine Base staff. While awaiting official transfer they volunteered to keep an eye on *Tang* as the list of materiel requisitions and minor alterations got underway.

Lieutenant Walsh pointed out to Captain O'Kane that two new radio antennas were being installed by workmen to get better short-range VHF and UHF frequencies, but they were unretractable, towered above the periscope shears, and were mounted side by side on the conning tower, thus cutting off access to the *Tang*'s unique crow's nest. The antennas added to *Tang*'s width. They would interrupt the streamlined superstructure and contribute to underwater drag, slowing the boat when submerged. They would increase the turbulence at the periscope shears, and this might be spotted by Japanese planes.

O'Kane immediately ordered the work stopped. *Tang*'s

submarine division commander was William Irvin, ex-skipper of *Nautilus,* who was angry at O'Kane's order.

"What's this about your stopping the VHF–UHF installation?" he demanded.

"Not stopping, Commander," O'Kane replied calmly, "just delaying until we arrange the installation best suited for *Tang.*"

"Well, what's so damned special about you and *Tang* that the antennas can't be installed exactly as on the other boats?"

O'Kane explained the crow's nest would be put out of action by the location of the antennas and suggested that if they were placed fore, aft and a bit lower they would be much more effective. "Only the Force commander can authorize any change!" Commander Irvin was adamant.

Where had he heard that theme before? O'Kane wondered. Would Admiral Lockwood be as flexible as Admiral Mitscher?

O'Kane reported to Lockwood, who wanted to set up a meeting to discuss carrier task force-submarine cooperation in future Pacific operations.

"Admiral," Dick began, "there is one thing you can do for *Tang.* We're about to lose access to our crow's nest unless the new VHF/UHF antennas are installed fore and aft of the shears. Will you authorize it?"

Lockwood was interested in the crow's nest concept though he didn't inquire how *Tang* came to have one. He quickly grasped how the side-by-side installation of the antenna could limit the lookouts and the radar gear.

"It's your boat," Lockwood told O'Kane. "Have them installed anywhere you want."

With Admiral Lockwood's imprimatur, Commander Irvin quickly approved O'Kane's request and peace was restored with *Tang*'s division commander. Dick and Fraz went back to the Royal Hawaiian to complete their rest period.

O'Kane and Frazee discovered that while they were busy on their first two patrols, by mid-1944 the submarine war had taken a gigantic turn for the better. New boats coming off the ways at Mare Island, Portsmouth, Groton, Manitowoc, and

Philadelphia were arriving in Pearl every week and sent out on patrol to the Western Pacific. There were many more submarine successes than failures. A new advance sub base was established at Majuro in the Marshall Islands, with the tenders *Sperry* and *Bushnell* moved into the lagoon to look after the boats. The first, *Kingfish,* arrived for refit on April 7. The torpedo problem had been largely solved through the efforts of Admiral Lockwood—though many skippers still complained of occasional misfires, duds, and erratic or circular runs.

Several submarines had returned from patrol so the bull sessions at the bar of the Royal were in full swing. As at Midway, O'Kane believed there was much to be learned during such sessions when captains and their officers filled in the spaces between the sparse lines of patrol reports. O'Kane concluded they all learned much about fighting their submarines and the tactics of the Japanese enemy as well.

The submariners heard good news about submarine exploits. Jack Coye had taken over *Silversides* from Creed Burlingame and was running up an even better record. Reuben Whitaker continued his sterling performance as skipper of *Flasher.* Herb Andrews in *Gurnard* sank three large ships laden with troops and equipment heading to reinforce Japanese forces on New Guinea. Tom Baskett had taken over from Barney Sieglaff in *Tautog* and maintained that submarine's reputation as a leading scorer in the Pacific War. Don Weiss in a brilliant action with *Tinosa* sank four ships on his first patrol. *Trigger* was now under the command of Dusty Dornin, who had moved up from exec, to be replaced by the indefatigable Ned Beach. Together they kept *Trigger* a terror of the seas. Sam Dealey operating *Harder* out of Australia had become another top skipper in the Submarine Force.

A crack submarine that won a Presidential Unit Citation for her first two war patrols was *Sandlance* under Skipper Malcolm Garrison. He sank nine ships on his first two patrols, but one of them was a Russian vessel near Kamchatka, which Garrison misidentified as the *Florida Maru.* It turned out to be the *Bella Russia,* which was not travelling in a safe conduct lane nor had any Soviet markings. Three other U.S.

skippers would sink Russian ships by mistake in the war: Eugene Sands in *Sawfish,* Moon Chapple in *Permit,* and William Germershausen in *Spadefish.*

Walt Griffith had a splendid first patrol in command of *Bowfin.* From Fremantle he went out on his next, *Bowfin's* third, into the South China Sea. In heated action Griffith fired off most of his torpedoes, sinking one confirmed ship and damaging several others. Griffith, having been at sea only fourteen days, returned on January 29, 1944, to Darwin for a new load of torpedoes and to refuel. Unknown to him, his boss, Rear Admiral Ralph Christie, had decided to make a war patrol. Christie's request to make one had twice before been turned down by Admiral Carpender, but Carpender was replaced by Vice Admiral Thomas Kinkaid. Christie decided not to make a formal request, and simply acted on his own. "If I came back," he said, "I would be congratulated—if I did not—well, frankly, that was never seriously considered although many of our splendid ships did not return to port." The high-handed Ralph Christie overlooked or ignored the danger of a force commander being captured by the Japanese. He also ignored the pressure put on a lowly submarine commander when an admiral was looking over his shoulder on patrol, especially during the second half of an arduous run. Christie flew from Perth to Darwin and boarded *Bowfin* on January 29, instructing Skipper Griffith to drop mines off Borneo and then seek out enemy shipping. Christie volunteered to stand OOD watches to earn his passage in what he considered the thrill of his life—the first flag officer to make a combat run.

Admiral Nimitz in Pearl firmly refused Admiral Lockwood's request to make a war patrol. Nimitz decreed that senior commanders, privy to top-secret operational plans, had no business going on combat patrols—no matter how worthy the motive. But Christie wasn't under Nimitz's central Pacific command. So seeds were planted for high-level discontent by what some submarine officers considered Ralph Christie's showboating.

When *Bowfin* returned, having fired thirty-five torpedoes for sixteen hits in the double-barreled patrol, Christie got off at the refueling depot at Exmouth Gulf in northwest Australia. He received a message from General MacArthur: "Congratulations! I cannot tell you what a thrill the magnificent service of your submarines gives me. Nothing in this war, or any other for that matter, can surpass it."

Admiral Christie awarded Walt Griffith a Navy Cross for his first patrol on *Bowfin*. He unusually recommended Griffith to General MacArthur for a further award, perhaps the Medal of Honor. Christie hadn't heard from MacArthur about the award—but he would hear heatedly from Admiral Kinkaid who disapproved of Army awards for Navy officers, particularly for the same action for which they had already received a Navy decoration.

Tommy Dykers, a popular, elegant officer from New Orleans, sank three ships off Honshu on his first patrol with *Jack*. On his second he sailed from Pearl Harbor to Fremantle via the South China Sea. He conducted an aggressive patrol, sinking four tankers in one day and expending all torpedoes. When *Jack* reached Fremantle, Christie met Dykers at the dock with a Navy Cross. Ultra had confirmed the sinkings.

Art Krapf, a classmate of Dick O'Kane, succeeded the highly able Tommy Dykers after he rode along as a PCO makee-learn on *Jack*. Jim Calvert, the third officer, noticed that the captain seemed especially tense. Krapf conducted attacks with coolness and determination, but something was still eating at him: the skipper chain-smoked cigars in the wardroom and sat staring into space. During evening card games, he kept to his room.

On the ride to the barn after a successful patrol, he confided to Exec Miles Refo and Jim Calvert, "I intend to be relieved of command after we return to Fremantle. Although I don't believe I have given any outward signs of it, I am just worn out. I can't take the responsibility for all these lives unless I feel that I am in tip-top condition. And I'm not. Frankly, Miles, I just don't think I could do it again without you, and I'm not going to hold you back just so that you can bolster me up on patrol. I believe there are other things I can do to help the war effort, and I am going to do my best to do them."

Miles Refo replied, "I've served with a number of skippers by now, and I've never known a finer or more dedicated man than you, sir."

"Thanks, Miles," the captain said.

Calvert and Refo left feeling deep admiration for the manly way in which Art Krapf had handled a terribly difficult matter.

The officers at the Royal Hawaiian also learned of an unusual command move. Joseph Enright was the popular skipper of the new *Dace*. Enright had been in the Sub School class with Dick O'Kane and Slade Cutter. Like some other boats, *Dace* had obtained a slot machine, which the crew set up along dockside in the U.S. and on occasional other stops. The machine could pull in as much as $150 a day in profit which was used for the *Dace*'s slush fund, paying for ship's parties, booze, beer, cigarettes, cigars, and exotic canned goods to bring along. *Dace* was a happy ship.

Off Honshu on *Dace*'s first patrol, Enright received an Ultra reporting an enemy aircraft carrier moving through his area. He made contact with the carrier and its escorting destroyers. He then attempted a tentative approach but with daylight approaching he dived, and the carrier sped away. Later, Enright mounted an attack on a large tanker, but again its escorts drove him down and pummelled *Dace* with depth charges. Enright was shaken by the experience, and blamed himself for not being in the right position to nail the carrier. On his return to Pearl, he asked to be shorn of command of *Dace*. "I feel I was responsible for the unproductive patrol and request to be relieved by an officer who can perform more satisfactorily," he said. Enright was assigned to duty with the relief crews at the Midway sub base. He thought this would be a dead-end from which there would be no escape. *Dace* would be heard of again, and so, in another way, would Joe Enright.

*   *   *

One of the more bizarre stories circulating around the Royal
Hawaiian in mid-1944 concerned the sudden relief of Wayne
Merrill as captain of *Batfish*. Another Naval Academy classmate of Dick O'Kane, Merrill was notorious for his antics
once he hit the beach. He delighted in having a good time
ashore, perhaps too good. He seemed to thrive on a minimum amount of sleep and was a night owl. A compact, handsome and highly social man, he enjoyed drink, the company
of women, and the conversation of shipmates. On her first
patrol, *Batfish*'s radar picked up pips for what eventually
turned out to be the battleship *Yamato*, the world's largest,
and her escorts. Merrill thought that *Yamato*'s radar could
also pick up *Batfish* and decided to submerge when the submarine came within range of the warship's 18-inch guns.
The Executive Officer, Lieutenant Peter Molteni, Jr., urged
the captain to stay on the surface, because *Batfish*'s 6 knots
underwater speed would not be enough to set up a proper attack. Merrill refused to reconsider. *Batfish* went under but
never got close; *Yamato* and escorts sailed over the horizon.

Batfish's luck changed and Merrill sank two Japanese
freighters before returning to Midway for refit, but there a
strange incident occurred. Captain Merrill stayed up half the
night drinking with anyone who would provide company. He
even gravitated toward the enlisted crew who felt uncomfortable drinking with their captain. He seemed to dwell on the
loss of *Grampus* on which he had served as exec. The night
before departure for *Batfish*'s second patrol, a slightly drunk
Merrill went to the room of his executive officer, presumably to repair their damaged relations over more whiskey.
Molteni, who was rooming with the diving officer, Jim Hingson, said he needed sleep. The captain persisted and the
torpedo officer was called into the room. The three officers
decided it was necessary to end the evening. Two of them
lifted the captain up bodily and dropped him outside the window for a soft landing on a sand dune a few feet below. Merrill got up, took the broad hint, and repaired to his room.

On *Batfish*'s second patrol, Merrill drew a blank. Partly
because of heavy seas, *Batfish* made no attacks. The sub was
ordered to Pearl for refit. Merrill seemed emaciated, worn

down by a highly frustrating patrol, but he retained his flamboyance. *Batfish*'s crew, too, shared Merrill's frustration. They looked forward to the third patrol as an opportunity to restore the boat's pride.

The exec, Peter Molteni, was transferred off *Batfish,* and diving officer Jim Hingson moved up to XO. *Batfish* departed Pearl for Midway with Merrill looking, to some of the crew, in terrible physical shape. Exec Hingson more or less took over command and reported that fact to ComSubPac. When *Batfish* arrived at Midway, the crew sensed something unusual was afoot. ComSubPac had gotten wind of Wayne Merrill's escapades ashore. *Batfish*'s division commander came aboard and inquired whether Skipper Merrill was in shape for another patrol.

"I'm willing to go out now, even though I don't feel quite up to it," Merrill said.

Commander John K. Fyfe, who had survived Dizzy Rainer's ill-fated first patrol in *Dolphin* as engineer, came aboard *Batfish* temporarily to "proceed, report, and relieve" Captain Merrill. Fyfe gave no explanation for the procedure. Through the grapevine, the crew learned that Lew Parks, now a captain and in charge of submarine activities at Midway, was to conduct an inquiry into Merrill's activities ashore that earlier evening. He interviewed all the officers including Lieutenant Molteni, who was at Midway.

The investigation focused on the window incident at the Gooneybird Hotel.

"It was all done in good fun," Merrill testified.

A stern-minded Lew Parks disagreed. "This is a terrible thing to have happen," Parks stated in his report. "Any commanding officer who allows himself to be thrown out of any window by his subordinates has lost his usefulness to his ship. The indignity of this conduct can only be interpreted as a lack of respect which will affect the entire crew and seriously undermine their morale." Parks recommended to Lockwood that Merrill be relieved of command of *Batfish.* Fyfe was designated the new skipper. Thus Merrill was ordered out of submarines at the same time that he was awarded the Silver Star for his first patrol.

In taking over *Batfish,* Jake Fyfe, who was O'Kane's Academy classmate, paid an oblique tribute to Wayne Merrill by telling the crew that *Batfish* was a "damned fine boat." Fyfe took the situation in hand and ran up a sparkling record in four war patrols, culminating in the sinking of three Japanese submarines in three days, which Lockwood called a brilliant performance. Jake Fyfe got the Navy Cross and *Batfish* the Presidential Unit Citation.

Another episode, reminiscent of *The Caine Mutiny,* involved the competent but volatile Henry G. Munson, thirty-four, in *Crevalle.* Hank Munson was an aloof, intense, brooding figure who stood third in his Academy Class of 1932 and was a Rhodes scholar. He had a good combat record, making six patrols aboard the rusty *S-38* in the first year of the war. In *Crevalle's* first patrol, Munson turned in a strong performance, but on the second patrol he seemed to Executive Officer Frank Walker and third officer William Ruhe to show signs of vacillation. He would attack vigorously on the surface, but not follow through to dispose of damaged ships. His tactics seemed dilatory, especially when submerged. Using the Morton–O'Kane system, Walker manned the periscope while Munson supervised the overall attack. At one point in the patrol, Walker and Ruhe discussed their skipper's behavior. Ruhe pressed Walker to encourage the captain to be more aggressive.

"You can't let the Old Man stop now," Ruhe said. "Even if he is tired."

Walker demurred. "He's off the beam again."

When a convoy was sighted on the horizon, Ruhe suggested to the exec, "Let's just steer *Crevalle* north [toward the target] while he's up on the bridge. He'll never notice the difference."

Frank Walker was dispirited. He didn't want to try to put one over the captain. He told Ruhe, "This whole business is hopeless. The captain is in no mood for further attacks."

"But we can't quit now," Ruhe insisted. "You've got to go up to the bridge and get the captain off the dime." Walker sighed, "It's hopeless."

At that moment a shadowy figure emerged from a corner

of the darkened conning tower. It was Captain Munson, who had slipped unnoticed down the ladder from the bridge.

"All right," he said sarcastically, "you fellows go ahead and conn my boat wherever you damn well please. You seem to know exactly what I should do. Now you do it."

Captain Munson climbed the ladder back to the bridge. Ruhe was too shocked to respond, but Walker ordered the helmsman to steer a course to pursue the convoy. With the captain looking on, Frank Walker fired six torpedoes, sinking a Japanese naval auxiliary.

The next day, Captain Munson told his third officer, "You know, Ruhe, that was mutiny you pulled on me last night. I've felt all along the dissatisfaction of both of you about how I've been running this boat. I'm going to court martial you and Frank for insubordination when we get back to port."

The next day, Munson switched signals. He praised Bill Ruhe for putting up with his "vacillations" and helping hold *Crevalle* together as one of the best fighting ships in the Navy. Later, returning home, Captain Munson changed his mind yet again. "You think I've forgotten about how you and Frank tried to take over my command," he told Ruhe. "That's mutiny, you know!" Bill Ruhe protested that the captain had just praised Frank Walker and himself for making the patrol a success. Munson was adamant. "You'll never go back to sea on my submarine," he said, "and I'll see that you're bounced out of the Navy."

On *Crevalle*'s arrival in Fremantle, Admiral Ralph Christie pinned a Navy Cross on Captain Munson. That seemed to change the skipper's attitude still once more.

"I told Christie about how I had periods during the patrol when I wasn't putting it all together," Munson told Ruhe, "and even blanked out at times. Then I told him about how you two, taking a big risk, carried me through those periods, and did a superior job despite my problems."

Munson recommended Frank Walker and Bill Ruhe for Silver Stars. The latest Munson about-face made Ruhe feel "like a heel."

Christie decided to honor Munson's request for a rest and

put him in charge of relief crews in Fremantle. Frank Walker was given command of *Crevalle* with Ruhe moving up to exec. Walker and Ruhe in *Crevalle* made two successful patrols together in the South China Sea, winning Frank Walker two Navy Crosses. During one patrol, a Japanese anti-sub vessel dropped a grappling hook, caught *Crevalle*'s cigarette deck railing, and actually dragged the submarine underwater for some minutes before it could break free. *Crevalle* was awarded the Navy Unit Commendation under skippers Munson and Walker.

After a couple of months ashore, Munson was given command of *Rasher.* He turned in an outstanding patrol, sinking five ships including a light aircraft carrier, and winning his third Navy Cross. With 52,600 tons of enemy shipping down, Hank Munson's patrol was the second best of the war in total tonnage. *Rasher*'s fifth war patrol was included in the Presidential Unit Citation for the submarine. Hank Munson seemed to have recovered total equilibrium.

Tang was ready to go, with all hands set for the third war patrol. Dick O'Kane had a final conference with Admiral Lockwood at SubPac headquarters. Lockwood was still trying to perfect the wolf pack tactics, but he knew that his ace submariner preferred to operate independently. He issued orders to O'Kane that he would patrol in the East China and Yellow Seas. He would be accompanied to the patrol areas by *Sealion II,* commanded by Eli Reich (*Sealion I* was sunk by Japanese bombers at the dock at Cavite in 1941) and *Tinosa,* under Don Weiss. But the three submarines would operate independently. U.S. submarines were assigned to a numbered area in the Western Pacific. They were ordered not to stray into adjacent operating areas assigned to another boat. Skippers could search for their own targets, unless specially instructed from ComSubPac to go after an Ultra intercept or participate in some special mission like lifeguarding.

O'Kane explained to Lockwood he believed grouping U.S. submarines in a circular disposition near enemy ports was not as efficient as his favored layered-V formation. Lockwood took notes. Then O'Kane pointed out that if a senior submarine officer were assigned to the staff of Admiral Mitscher or carrier group commanders, and if the carrier group commander was in direct communication with U.S. subs, *Tang* and *Trigger* would not have wasted days guarding mined Japanese channels that enemy shipping avoided. Lockwood thanked O'Kane for expressing his frank views and Dick left for *Tang* with renewed confidence in a commander in whom a skipper could confide.

There was only one blip. O'Kane received a sealed letter from the Sub Force medical officer, Commander Walt Welham. He pointed out that the master-at-arms assigned to the crew's wing of the Royal Hawaiian reported finding the remains of a tin of alcohol in *Tang*'s area. O'Kane suspected that the crew had obtained pure ethyl alcohol, which was used on board for cleaning and drying optics and electronic connectors. He was right. Floyd Caverly had put in a requisition for the alcohol, but he actually used plain soap and water to clean the delicate equipment. O'Kane and Dr. Welham worried that the crew could be sickened or even killed by drinking the undiluted chemical. However, Caverly and the crew were smart enough to cut their alcohol at the Royal with plenty of pineapple, grapefruit or orange juice to soften the blow—so that the kick of the "gilly" was more like a strong screwdriver. Another source aboard was the straight methyl alcohol used as combustion fuel in the torpedo chambers. This was known as "torpedo juice," though both forms of alcohol were often called by that name. Methyl alcohol was poisonous and was purposely tinted pink to warn sailors away from drinking it. Some learned, however, that filtering torpedo juice through bread could drain off the methyl, leaving the residue mostly ethyl alcohol. This, if they were lucky, was drinkable when correctly cut. But often the filtering was not done properly. While incidents were not publicized during the war, American sailors were blinded or even killed by drinking methyl alcohol.

Though Dick O'Kane was unaware of it, Floyd Caverly, who was a prized member of *Tang*'s crew, had installed a tiny portable still in the radio storage space deep in the submarine next to the bilges. During a patrol he would brew alcohol a

drop at a time, for eventual drinking at a rest camp. "Boats"
Bill Leibold knew what was going on and believed Caverly
did it to keep busy during long patrols, and to beat the system with his own alcohol at the rest camp, rather than to get
high on board. "We all knew that if the Old Man found out
about it," Leibold said, "we would get our asses kicked out of
submarines."

For the third patrol Dick O'Kane and Murray Frazee were
losing two experienced officers in Lieutenants Walsh and
Anderson. However, they were happy to welcome on board
two replacements. One was Ensign Richard Kroth, a large,
likable Naval Academy graduate from Hamtramck, Michigan, who became "George," or low man on the totem pole, as
Mel Enos moved up a step.

Tang's rest and refit period passed quickly. O'Kane was
aware he could stay in Pearl Harbor for a further few days, but
this would mean entering their patrol area well after *Sealion*
and *Tinosa*. Arriving third, *Tang* might find the Japanese
stirred up and on special alert. Dick O'Kane discussed the
timing with Chief of the Boat Ballinger. Speaking for the
crew, Ballinger said *Tang*'s sailors would prefer to shove off
earlier and take advantage of entering the Yellow Sea before
the other two vessels. *Tang* spent the next three days in training exercises, breaking in the two new officers and twelve
new crewmen. Returning to the finger pier, *Tang*'s crew formed
a bucket brigade to pass commissary stores down below for
future consumption. *Tang*'s training at sea was supervised
by the squadron commander, Captain C.B. "Swede" Momsen (inventor of the Momsen Lung), who pronounced *Tang*
ready for patrol.

She also carried a Prospective Commanding Officer
makee-learn in the person of Lieutenant Commander Morton H. Lytle, from Tulsa, Oklahoma. He had been exec of
Porpoise, with war patrols under his belt, and would have a
place on the watch list and help take the burden off O'Kane
and Frazee.

Before departing Pearl, O'Kane and Frazee were brought
up to date on Japanese anti-submarine warfare efforts.
Though the Japanese were late in building escort craft, they

eventually designed two capable classes. The Chidori class was highly maneuverable and of shallow draft. At 500 tons, it was a particularly dangerous adversary, designed for the express purpose of hunting and killing submarines. It was equipped with good sonar and listening gear and armed with a large complement of depth charges. Just as effective were the slightly smaller Kaikobans, or coast defense vessels, which could be produced in ninety days. They came into service in strength in 1944. They were 250 feet long, diesel-powered, a speed of sixteen knots, with two 4.7-inch guns, and at least 120 depth charges. Those depth charges posed a wicked threat to U.S. submarines. A Kaikoban was not to be trifled with.

Until 1943, the standard Japanese depth charge was a cylinder containing 242 pounds of high explosives. It could be set to detonate at 100, 200, or 300 feet. Later depth charges, after Congressman May's incredible blunder, were similar in size but carried 357 pounds of explosives, and more importantly could be set to go off at depths of 100, 200, 300, 400, or 500 feet, a serious menace to U.S. submariners.

In 1944, the Japanese anti-submarine effort was growing more effective each month and the enemy perfected a superior weapon: the efficient radio-detection system. Admiral Lockwood was worried about the Japanese ability to pinpoint a U.S. boat through radio transmissions. Monitoring sub traffic, the enemy learned much about American boats. They were particularly good at intercepting communications between the subs in a wolf pack. The Japanese naval experts scoured their universities and business firms and put together officers who were conversant in American vernacular speech. They obtained more information about U.S. operations by monitoring voice broadcasts than U.S. submarine officers suspected.

Further Japanese anti-submarine vessels were now equipped with electronic devices that could sense U.S. radar beams coming their way, and could therefore detect American boats in the vicinity. That was the key reason Dick O'Kane planned to keep his radar searches to a minimum and then only in short bursts.

Overhead, the enemy posed a new threat: in submarine operating areas like "Convoy College," the Japanese were using a new airborne radar in night searches. U.S. subs were often subjected to air attack as they recharged their batteries on the surface. Japanese planes carried standard bombs modified for use as an ASW weapon. Small planes were loaded with 150-pound bombs and larger aircraft dropped 625-pound ones. The bombs were equipped with delayed-action fuses, which were set to explode at a predetermined depth. In 1944, the Japanese organized special anti-submarine air squadrons, and while their pilots might not be as proficient as carrier aviators, they sharply increased the risk to U.S. submariners. The pilots were ordered to keep pursuing suspected submarines and not break off the attacks.

There was still another major new hazard: extensive antisubmarine minefields planted in the hundreds in many areas where U.S. boats were likely to operate. During much of the war, the only way to learn of the existence of a new minefield was the hard way: to lose a submarine. And even then it was difficult to know whether a boat's loss was due to a mine, a depth charge, or an aircraft bomb. Captured enemy maritime documents helped Admiral Lockwood determine the location of minefields, but they could not keep up with the newly planted underwater weapons. The Japanese were mining areas all the time. Admiral Lockwood attempted to fight the threat by encouraging the development of a new frequency modulated device—a kind of FM sonar—that could detect mines outside the submarine's hull.

In sum, O'Kane learned that Japanese anti-submarine tactics were more effective and the enemy was more aggressive. So the battle between hunter and hunted was to become more spirited and dangerous in mid-1944. He and *Tang* were ready to go. The crew was cheered by the news of the Allied invasion of Normandy, June 6, half a fighting world away.

CHAPTER SIXTEEN

A Clean Sweep

On June 8, 1944, with a crew of eighty and a load of sixteen new model steam torpedoes, the Mark 23, and eight new Mark 18 electrics in the after torpedo room, *Tang* backed away from the pier into Southeast Loch, swinging around as she went. She sailed smartly out of the vast Pearl Harbor naval complex at two-thirds speed, kicking up a spray in her wake.

Dick O'Kane was keen to patrol the waters that *Wahoo* had exploited so successfully sixteen months earlier—turning in what was still the top patrol of the war when she sent nine enemy ships to the bottom. On *Tang*'s wardroom table was the well-thumbed report of *Wahoo*'s fourth patrol. The radio operators copied the nightly Fox broadcasts with brief updating on the Normandy landings, and the transcriptions were posted on the crew's bulletin board.

The stop at Midway Island alongside tender *Holland* to top off fuel was routine, though Captain O'Kane noted that sailors turned up in the early dawn to gape at the ship, like train watchers in small town America. *Sealion II* followed *Tang* into Midway. The two skippers agreed to rendezvous off Japan before heading for individual patrol areas.

Several days later, *Tang* spotted the familiar Sofu Gan, Lot's Wife, which marked their entry into Empire waters. O'Kane used the uninhabited rock as a check for his sea search radar. He gave the torpedo tracking party practice zeroing in on the rock as if it were a stopped enemy ship. He wanted to use the air search radar as little as possible since it was easily detected, and he would employ it only when necessary in short bursts, preferably when underwater with the radar mast raised. This would reduce the possibility of discovery by the many enemy shore radar stations. O'Kane again ran drills with seven lookouts and determined they could all clear the bridge without delaying the dive. He would keep all seven topside during daylight hours.

The captain was supplied with frequent cups of coffee by his trusty steward's mate, Howard M. Walker, a black sailor. At that stage of the war, blacks aboard Navy ships almost all served as stewards in fighting ship's wardrooms. But they manned battle positions on the controls in submarines, and on anti-aircraft guns on larger combatant ships.

On July 15, radioman Ed Bergman brought in news that the massive Fifth Fleet and Fifth Amphibious Force had invaded Saipan in the Mariana Islands. Dick O'Kane hoped that the ships *Tang* sank on her first patrol had helped a bit to weaken Japanese defenses on Saipan. Now the Central Pacific offensive was in full swing. The Marianas would be used as naval bases, but more importantly, as air bases for the B-29 aerial assault against Japanese cities.

Dick O'Kane's first priority was not being spotted by the Japanese as he moved *Tang* through the Nansei Shōtō Island chain into the East China Sea. *Tang* was back in shallow water where few places allowed him to dive below a temperature gradient. He would be fortunate to find depths of 100 feet for an attack, or 200 feet in which to hide. So his tactics in seeking out ships among the many offshore islands off southern Japan and South Korea, and the waters between them, would involve hit-and-run attacks, fast surface speeds at night, and above all announcing *Tang*'s presence only when her torpedoes hit the hulls of Japanese ships.

O'Kane was on the bridge when the speaker announced: "Hot Ultra from ComSubPac, Captain." O'Kane climbed down to the control room to read the deciphered message: "DAMAGED BATTLESHIP PROCEEDING FROM RYUKYUS THROUGH NANSEI SHOTO THENCE TO KOBE OR SASEBO NEXT THIRTY HOURS X POSITION SUBMARINE TO INTERCEPT SASEBO PASSAGE." O'Kane was happy to see that ComSubPac was telling a skipper what to do and not how to do it.

Tinosa with the senior skipper, Don Weiss, radioed *Tang* requesting a rendezvous to consult on tactics. This was not a coordinated wolf pack but a group designated to work adjacent areas close together, and pass contacts from one to the other. O'Kane instructed Murray Frazee to advise Don Weiss that the three American submarines should be placed near the Kyushu coast on a likely approach route for traffic heading for Sasebo or Nagasaki. *Tang* met *Tinosa* and O'Kane sent Frazee out in a yellow rubber boat, rowed by Gunner's Mate Darrell Rector. This young sailor was something of a celebrity: he was the man operated on aboard *Seadragon* for an emergency appendectomy. Young Rector survived in style.

In the meeting aboard *Tinosa,* Frazee reported back that Commander Weiss wasn't keen on O'Kane's suggestions for tactical disposition, but he allowed *Tang* to patrol closer inshore while the other subs were out in the open sea. He thought the others should have taken his suggestions to patrol closer to the offshore islands. He moved *Tang* at full speed into position to intercept any ships heading toward Sasebo.

"Radar contact," reported Dick Kroth on *Tang*'s bridge, "bearing one five zero, range 20,000 yards."

O'Kane stared at the chart. Ed Bergman at the radar reported, "A mess of ships, range still 20,000."

O'Kane took a look at the radar screen. There were indeed many pips. Though none seemed as big as a battleship, O'Kane was satisfied that it was a convoy with plenty of vessels to target. He ordered a contact report to *Tinosa* and *Sealion II*. The picture clarified. There were six large ships in two columns, with a dozen smaller escorts in a circular formation around them. "Christ!" said Quartermaster Sidney Jones, speaking for the entire bridge watch.

O'Kane thought it a formidable formation. He began the tricky surface maneuver of bringing *Tang* inside the escorts with the help of the sharp-eyed Jones and Boatswain Bill Leibold and their 7×50 binoculars. Dick thought Boats Leibold was proving to be a natural leader: he planned to promote him to chief boatswain's mate and make him COB when Bill Ballinger eventually transferred.

O'Kane worked *Tang* to the rear of the big ships and between the following escorts. Jones concentrated on the position of the escort to port, Leibold to starboard, each escort a mile away from *Tang*.

"Our bow's inside their sterns," Frazee reported from the conning tower. His voice was barely above a whisper.

O'Kane asked Mort Lytle, the PCO, to take the conn as he dropped down into the conning tower for a glance at the action chart with Fraz. He then climbed back to the bridge. The lookouts had identified the two big ships nearest *Tang* as a tanker and a big freighter. Behind these were other ships in column. O'Kane planned to fire his six forward torpedoes, three at each forward target. He peered through the binoculars on the target-bearing transmitter.

"Make all tubes ready for firing," he ordered.

Frazee in the conning tower replied, "All tubes ready. Right on."

"Come left to two seven zero," O'Kane said. "Open outer doors forward. Slow to one-third when steady."

O'Kane asked Fraz to double-check the convoy's speed. He didn't want to repeat the mistake of *Tang*'s first patrol.

"Speed ten knots," Frazee said. "Any time, Captain."

"Constant bearing," O'Kane said. "Mark!"

The TBT binocular's wire was on the leading freighter's after mast.

"Fire!" O'Kane said.

O'Kane sent two more torpedoes at 8-second intervals at the leading ship. Then he shifted targets. He ordered three more fish fired at the tanker. So quickly were they launched that all the torpedoes were in the water at the same time during the run of 1 minute and 47 seconds.

"Thirty seconds to go, Captain," Frazee said, reaching the bridge.

All six torpedoes hit! Enormous explosions were seen and heard. The two targets were sinking. Other ships appeared to be damaged. Escorts raced, wildly dropping depth charges, but on the surface *Tang* quickly cleared the immediate area for deeper water. O'Kane and company finally pulled up about 7,000 yards from the remains of the convoy. It was midnight, only 7 minutes after *Tang* had fired her last torpedo. O'Kane ordered a reload. Then he went below for a long-delayed visit to the head.

In the wardroom, Steward's Mate Walker had a cup of coffee waiting for the skipper.

"How many'd we get, Captain?" he asked.

"Both of them, Walker. We saw them go."

"I think there was more, sir," Walker replied.

O'Kane replied that with all the explosions, it might be hard to tell what was going on.

"Oh, I wasn't down here," Walker said, surprising O'Kane. "You were topside so long I brought your coffee to the bridge. It was so exciting, I dropped your cup over the side."

O'Kane smiled. Leave it to Walker, he thought, he'd get into the act one way or another. Frazee cleared a message to *Tinosa* and *Sealion,* reporting the attack on the convoy, its location and course, and that *Tang* was tailing.

Though Dick, Fraz and the crew did not know it at the time, they had sunk four Japanese ships in the convoy: the large cargo ship *Tamahoko Maru* at 6,780 tons, the tanker *Nasusan Maru* at 4,400 tons, the freighter *Tainan Maru,* 3,175 tons, and the cargo ship *Kennichi Maru,* 1,937 tons. Dick O'Kane sank four ships with six torpedoes, making it the single best U.S. submarine attack of the entire war.

O'Kane picked up a remaining pip on radar and began tracking it toward Nagasaki. Suddenly he noticed the range shortening rapidly. A closer look verified the target was a dangerous destroyer escort heading *Tang*'s way. Opening up to flank speed—*Tang* reached an unprecedented 22½ knots—and changing course to get out of harm's way, O'Kane was thankful that the new camouflage paint job made the submarine nearly invisible on a dark night.

Sensing that Nagasaki would be crawling with anti-submarine ships at dawn, O'Kane ordered *Tang* turned away and headed south. There, Dick O'Kane calculated, the seas would be deep if not friendly.

PCO Lytle did not relish fighting in such shallow water. "If the object is to sink ships and avoid depth charges," he told O'Kane, "then I guess this is all right, but I'd hate to think it was going to be my steady diet. I'll take a few depth charges out in deep water any old day."

Dick O'Kane moved *Tang* from the shallow waters around Nagasaki farther south into deeper water but still close to the Kyushu coastline. He believed that the Japanese would not soon run nighttime convoys because of the damage *Tang* inflicted. O'Kane was satisfied this would cut down on the overall movement of cargo essential to the enemy war effort.

On the misty morning of June 26 lookouts spotted a Japanese freighter, which surprised O'Kane, because it was travelling alone, close to shore. He conned *Tang* to a firing position ahead of the freighter, and dived to await its arrival. Then *Tang* turned to bring her four stern tubes to bear. "All ahead one-third," O'Kane ordered. "Open the outer doors aft."

There were four new Mark 18 electric torpedoes in the tubes. They would run at only 27 knots, rather than the steam torpedoes' speed of 47 knots, but they would leave no telltale wake that gave away *Tang*'s firing position. With a last periscope sighting, Dick O'Kane ordered the four stern torpedoes fired. It was a perfect set-up.

"Christ," muttered O'Kane at the scope. Instead of running smoothly, undetected, underwater, two torpedoes broached the surface, then porpoised. As they settled on their runs, they kicked up a huge plume of water behind them, clearly visible to the enemy lookouts. The time for the 2,100-yard run was a full 2 minutes. The enemy skipper had ample time to turn his ship sharply, inside all the torpedo tracks. The torpedoes continued on to the beach and exploded.

Well, O'Kane thought, at least the detonators worked— if that was any consolation to anyone. The Japanese ship sought refuge in a cove, inaccessible to *Tang*. O'Kane ordered his submarine to retire into deep water and go under for an examination of the torpedoes. It was a dispiriting day-long process, reminiscent of the war's earlier days when crews puzzled over malfunctioning torpedoes. O'Kane was determined that the four remaining electric fish be made to function properly.

The torpedomen tackled their task: they examined each

torpedo, checking hydrostatic devices, depth engine, differential valve, and the air flasks. They hung the individual torpedoes with a chain fall from the overhead, and swung and tilted them, checking the operation of the vertical and horizontal rudders with the gyros running. The fish appeared to be in good working order. The following morning *Tang* was ready for action but was kept under by Japanese patrol planes.

A message came from ComSubPac to rendezvous with *Sealion II* and *Tinosa,* and fan out under the command of Don Weiss to attack vessels along a specified shipping lane in the area. O'Kane thought the rendezvous a waste of time; the three subs would do better working on their own since there was plenty of shipping in the area between Japan, Korea and the China coast. Arranging a meeting of the subs was just precious time lost. It was an example of what O'Kane abhorred in staff officers thousands of miles away: telling commanders how to do their jobs. But he put Murray Frazee over the side in *Tang*'s rubber boat to consult with Weiss, the senior skipper.

Fraz returned with a smile. *Tang* was to be the northernmost boat near the shipping lane. Weiss didn't specify the northern boundaries of *Tang*'s operational area, and Frazee did not press for a limitation. As Dick and Fraz saw it, *Tang* could operate as far north as desired. This meant all of the Yellow Sea. O'Kane was delighted.

Lookouts picked up a freighter heading west near the islands that speckle the sea south and west of the Korean peninsula. O'Kane needed to remain close to the freighter so as not to lose it, while overtaking the target. He ordered *Tang* surfaced in a strong, choppy sea. After an hour and a half trailing the freighter, *Tang* pulled abeam about 15,000 yards distance. O'Kane fretted. A stern chase, the saying went, is a long one, and time seemed to drag throughout the boat. Finally *Tang* drew ahead of the ship, the *Nikkim Maru,* and the ship made a long zig toward *Tang.* O'Kane ordered another dipsy-doodle, turning *Tang* away from the target's course and then circling around for the best set-up. "Up scope," he ordered. He fired two torpedoes at the cargo ship. Both headed directly for the target, but there were no explosions. They had passed under the enemy ship.

O'Kane was furious. He ordered *Tang* under, since he knew he could not immediately reattack an alerted target. He felt a little silly since the ship was not a destroyer, but he was surprised when the freighter managed somehow to drop two depth charges, close aboard. "They weren't supposed to do that!" O'Kane thought. The shoe was now on the other foot.

The freighter moved away and *Tang* surfaced again. O'Kane and his officers mulled over the situation. It seemed like the bad old days: bringing torpedoes 5,000 miles to the Yellow Sea only to have them run erratically. Of the last six torpedoes fired, four were faulty and interfered with the run of two others. But Dick was not given to brooding about what had gone by. Opportunity lay ahead.

"What was that last sound bearing?" he asked Floyd Caverly.

"Three five zero true, Captain," Caverly said.

"All ahead full," O'Kane ordered. "Come right to three five zero."

Tang was back on the trail. The cook set out steaks for the crew to cheer up their spirits.

In the wardroom, O'Kane, Hank Flanagan, and Mel Enos pondered the problem. They checked the draft of the ship in the intelligence book of Japanese ships and decided that she was most likely empty, and thus her draft was only 8 or 10 feet. The torpedo setting should have been a couple of feet shallower. That settled, O'Kane could concentrate on the attack. "Knowing rather than fretting is half the battle," he thought.

The steward brought the skipper a cup of coffee. "We're going to get her this time, Captain?"

"That's right, Walker, one right in her middle."

O'Kane called for Battle Stations and ordered the tubes and the torpedoes set to run at only 6 feet. He planned to fire one "feeler" fish first, and if that missed, to fire a spread. He peered through the scope.

"Constant bearing—mark!" The target was coming on strong.

"Set." Her stack was in the periscope.

"Fire." A steam torpedo cut through the whitecaps.

"Torpedo run 30 seconds," Frazee reported.

The torpedo wake headed for the stack in the middle of the freighter. It hit with 500 pounds of exploding torpex. The force of the explosion broke *Nikkim Maru*'s back, both halves of the vessel slipping under in a hissing cloud of smoke, steam, and fire. It was 0130, July 1, 1944. Dick O'Kane decided he was more than satisfied with the light gray camouflage paint, which made *Tang* very hard to sight at any distance and in any sea.

The next day was to be one of rest. The crew took it easy and tended to their personal kit, read, or worked on qualification exams. But the Japanese didn't get the word. "Smoke ho!" the high lookout reported from the crow's nest.

The smoke soon developed into a two-ship convoy, and *Tang* began tracking in a long end-around maneuver. In another O'Kane innovation, he did not call the crew to Battle Stations but allowed watch standers to conduct the basic tactical approach. This gave the other two-thirds of the crew the chance to relax. O'Kane knew the pressures put on crews who were kept continually at Battle Stations for twelve hours or more, often unnecessarily. He trusted his officers of the deck to conduct the maneuver, and of course, he, Fraz, or Mort Lytle were available for instant backup.

O'Kane had his special way of dealing with the running problem of losing senior men, officers and enlisted, after each patrol. He knew many were due for rotation after a patrol, for shore duty or new construction, so he had each key man turn his duties over to an understudy, while keeping an eye on things. Those moving into the senior jobs would carry out routine duties and participate in firing the thirteen torpedoes left. O'Kane believed that boats like his own *Argonaut* and *Wahoo* tended to hang on to key personnel for one or two patrols too long, and then were forced to give them up all at once. This left the boats without veteran officers and petty officers and led to trouble. On-the-job training was his way of insuring that the loss of a quarter of the ship's complement after a patrol would not affect *Tang*'s efficiency.

With high periscope observations, O'Kane saw that *Tang* was moving in front of the two target ships, which turned out to be a small tanker, *Takatori Maru,* and a freighter, *Taiun Maru,* zigging and zagging. Only an air patrol could prevent *Tang* from getting into place for an attack. She submerged and lay in wait during the afternoon.

With a good set-up, Dick O'Kane fired two electric torpedoes at the first target, the tanker. The torpedo run seemed long, and O'Kane was about to curse, when the words were backed up in his throat by a terrific explosion, which blew the stern off the tanker. It sank quickly. In the confusion, the freighter turned away, interrupting O'Kane's torpedo set-up. A shot on the fly would have little chance. He planned another night's chase to bag the cargo ship, but first he told Chief Ballinger to allow crewmembers to peer through the scope at the sinking *Takatori Maru* before the ocean closed over her.

Tang tracked *Taiun Maru* during the afternoon, underwater at 6 knots. O'Kane took a turn through the boat to chat with the crew, particularly the new hands who were not used to back-to-back, day-and-night attacks. His confidence in his men was bolstered by a chart they had stuck in the messroom with the track of the enemy ship carried almost to the coast—where it ended in a large black X.

At sunset, *Tang* surfaced, with three engines on line and the fourth charging batteries. The surface chase was a long one, for the freighter had managed to ring up 11 knots from her coal-burning plant, which emitted much smoke. Moonrise would be soon, so the night would be fairly bright. *Tang*'s rock-crusher diesels brought her into position ahead of the cargo ship just south of Ko-To, sometimes called Quelpart Island.

Tang dove. The moonlight silhouetted *Taiun Maru* against the horizon. O'Kane followed the ship's stack with his periscope lens. He fired twice.

"Both hot, straight and normal," Caverly, on sound, reported.

Then an enormous blast shook *Tang*. The first torpedo had apparently set off a cargo of munitions, for only a short section of the bow was left visible when Murray Frazee peered through the scope. The second torpedo exploded against the detached bow, adding to the mess of flotsam. Awed by the finality of the attack, O'Kane set *Tang* on a course round the island, and into the Yellow Sea.

The captain was pleased with the way the patrol was going, every crewmember doing his part, and the understudies fitting in naturally to the jobs they would take over on the next patrol.

The 4th of July was approaching. O'Kane checked the menu and found it to a New Englander's liking: salmon loaf and peas. July 3 was a rest day. The men, sensing that the patrol was more than half over, broke out their course books to work on qualification.

Tang's schedule called for another rubber-boat rendezvous with *Sealion II,* and skipper Eli Reich. O'Kane told Fraz to offer Reich an informal invitation to accompany *Tang* counter-clockwise around the Yellow Sea, scouting for targets. They would operate independently but in mutual support. On his return, Frazee reported Reich had decided to turn down the offer in order to patrol around the Shanghai area instead. Dick thought that Eli, too, would prefer to roam unhindered by another boat: they were both of an independent cast of mind. Reich reported that *Sealion II* and *Tinosa* patrolled on the surface with their air-search radars on—and unlike *Tang* were frequently driven underwater. *Sealion II* had only one ship down to show this far.

O'Kane's invitation for a circular tour of the Yellow Sea had been well thought out. After *Wahoo*'s great fourth patrol, Japanese shipping tended to move along the coast rather than directly across the sea. So *Tang* would nose along the edges, beginning with the Korean coast, looking for such Japanese merchant traffic. O'Kane intended to meet the enemy head on.

Tang bade farewell to *Sealion* with a blinker light "Godspeed" and headed off early on July 4. Her radio operators monitored Fox newscasts from Pearl so the crew followed the Battle of Normandy and the securing of the Marianas, and caught up with the results of the great carrier air victory in the Battle of the Philippine Sea.

O'Kane and Frazee were discussing plans over early morning coffee in the wardroom when word came from the bridge: "Ship bearing zero four five." The time was 0408: first light. *Tang* was in an easy position to intercept. Dick O'Kane thought the solution simple: open the range for secure high periscope observations, shift the boat to the enemy's forward track, and shoot when the Japanese ship came by. The problem was that the sea near the Korean shore was dotted with small islands. Between *Tang* and the target was a small fleet of drifting, fishing sampans, which *Tang* would have to thread through at 13 knots on the surface. Luckily, there seemed to be no sign of activity aboard the fishing craft, which surprised the captain since he thought that fishermen like farmers were reputed to be up and active before dawn.

Tang executed some broken-field running to get into position, with the target and sampans in view. O'Kane ordered a quick dive under power, which under the circumstances, felt to him like the kickoff of a football game. He took a brief look through the scope and saw a really big tender, or cargo ship, up close. But it had zagged away from *Tang,* so O'Kane decided on an underwater chase through the sampan fleet.

Tang closed with the choice target, *Asukasan Maru.* O'Kane worried that raising his periscope might damage the lens or shaft if it hit a sampan. The water was getting dangerously shallow. Two fathoms under the keel. Then one fathom. The echo merged with the outgoing signal. This was the bottom. *Tang* had run out of water.

"All engines stop," O'Kane ordered. "Up scope."

"Ten degrees to go," Frank Springer reported. "Outer doors are open forward."

O'Kane glanced at the depth gauge. It was 58 feet.

"Hold her down," O'Kane said.

"I can't. We're aground!"

"All back full," O'Kane said. "Up scope."

Quartermaster Jones brought the periscope handles up to the skipper's fingers.

O'Kane spotted the target.

"Fire!"

Three torpedoes were on their way, heading for the stern, middle, and forward part of *Asukasan Maru*.

"Hot, straight, and normal," Caverly reported.

Suddenly, O'Kane had a disturbing thought. Would firing the torpedoes from a submarine temporarily resting on the mud bottom damage their delicate depth or exploder-impeller mechanisms? Before he could brood on what he might have done, two tremendous explosions elated him. He watched through the scope as the 6,886-ton cargo ship sank on an even keel beneath the sea.

It was an amazing torpedo shot, firing while backing off the bottom. Torpedoman Donald Sharp who kept a secret, forbidden diary, noted: "Well, we did it again, and once more no shit cans [depth charges]. I say this is the way to fight the war. With as little as four fathoms under the keel, we'll have to put skids or roller-skates on our bottom. If ever Hollywood could make a scene like it, any sub man would laugh and say, that's a hell of a lot of bull."

O'Kane headed due west into deep water, three engines driving *Tang,* the other charging batteries. He ordered the counter-clockwise search of the Yellow Sea resumed. Over breakfast coffee in the wardroom, the officers discussed the last attack. O'Kane pointed out that a submarine was not truly aground until she was high and dry. Murray Frazee said it must have been a first: backing full speed from being aground while firing. O'Kane had no apologies for going after *Asukasan Maru* almost to the end. He remembered Mush Morton's dictum to him, which he adopted as his own: "Tenacity, Dick. Stay with the bastard till he's on the bottom."

The day passed quickly. The crew feasted on Independence Day lunch, which the cooks took special care in preparing. With the wardroom relaxed, and evening approaching, the phone rang from the conning tower. Mort Lytle picked it up, from Ensign Kroth.

"Here we go again, Captain. We've got smoke."

O'Kane glanced at a chart. The situation was not really to his liking. The sighting showed the ship was moving close to the islands off shore. The moon would be full so a submerged attack was in order, but O'Kane wanted somewhat more depth than he had had for the last attack. The OOD reported the wispy smoke of another ship had been sighted.

This could be confusing. The rule on *Wahoo* and now *Tang* was: stick to one ship at a time; don't change targets until you've sunk the first one. Still, for every rule, there was an exception. And Dick O'Kane was, if nothing else, flexible in doctrinal matters. The second ship's position would allow for an attack in deep water. O'Kane immediately changed plans and the attack team focused on the second vessel, the 7,000-ton *Yamaoka Maru.* O'Kane had one goal: to sink this ship with just two of his four remaining torpedoes.

On *Tang*'s bridge, O'Kane closed the range on the target then ordered, "Clear the bridge." In the moonlight, he counted the lookouts scrambling down the hatch. *Tang* went under at 2041 hours and levelled off at 47 feet. Frank Springer cranked in the latest figures on the torpedo data computer. Floyd Caverly manned the sound gear. Ed Bergman shifted from the radio room to radar for a sweep of the target. O'Kane felt his crew was confident and ready for *Tang*'s ninth attack of the patrol.

Floyd Caverly caught the change of sound a rudder makes when shifting: he was a true professional, not just someone listening in.

"She's zigging, Captain," Caverly said.

"Right full rudder," O'Kane responded. "All ahead standard. We'll fire on this leg."

"Up scope," O'Kane said.

Quartermaster Jones lifted the periscope and set it to the proper bearing as registered on his side of the scope.

"Ten degrees to go," O'Kane said calmly. In his lens was a huge freighter, the largest target *Tang* ever had in her scope.

"Fire!" O'Kane commanded, twice.

Frazee, looking at his stopwatch, announced the time of run: 30 seconds. Jones was well into the count. At "thirty-one," a massive explosion ripped the freighter apart. *Yamaoka Maru* broke up and dropped into the sea. Quartermaster Jones took a look through the scope. "She's gone! Christ, all of her!" Grinding, breaking-up noises echoed through *Tang*'s hull, relayed over the intercom system. O'Kane thought the sickening sounds were a grim warning to lookouts to be constantly alert.

Tang surfaced and nosed through the wreckage. O'Kane spotted a survivor hanging on to a lifeboat and ordered Bill Leibold to bring him aboard. It took a while for Boats to pull the raft over with a grappling hook and drag him aboard. The sailor was reluctant—but he was destined for a better fate than a grave in the Yellow Sea. Captain O'Kane thought that the extra time taken in picking up a seaman provided activity for the crew, and in a strange way, fulfilled a sense of obligation for them, sailors all.

Dick O'Kane ordered *Tang* to continue north, with two torpedoes in the after tubes—and a fine sense of Independence Day well spent. His view of the 4th was seconded by Torpedoman Don Sharp who recorded in his private diary: "If I hadn't been on this ship and experienced it with my own eyes, I would never have believed it—the way we celebrated the 4th of July out here today. I can say not many people had the fireworks we did. Today we sank two ships, both damn big ones. I'll stick with Dick!" Later, Sharp added: "July 4: Went topside as a lookout. The ship was still visible going down slowly. I could see Japs jumping from the bow and about ten swimming away from the ship. One Jap in a sampan was mad as hell and damn near fell out of the boat, he shook his fist so hard. At the time it was a sight I've been wanting to see ever since I've been in subs—to see a ship go down."

The seaman prisoner was dubbed "Firecracker." He was petrified at first when he looked into the hatch to the conning tower with its inferno-like red lights glowing. But the crew got him below and began feeding him U.S. Navy chow. He soon became the ship's mascot.

O'Kane decided to patrol off Choppeki Point, the westernmost promontory of Korea jutting into the Yellow Sea, where coastal traffic had to swing west to keep clear. As the officers considered their tactical situation on the chart on the wardroom table, Dick O'Kane drew a circle several miles west of their current position.

"Is that where *Wahoo* sank one of her ships?" Fraz asked Dick.

"No, that's where Mush Morton dealt me a twenty-one cribbage hand."

"I can't think of a better criterion," Frazee said, drawing a course line to the circle.

Tang's radar picked up a pip moving away from Choppeki Point, at the very long distance of 34,000 yards. O'Kane decided on a night's end-around to get in position ahead of the target. He left the job to Fraz, Mort, and Frank, on the grounds that he did not need to supervise everything, and that his senior officers were perfectly competent to conduct the maneuver.

Meanwhile, Chief Ballinger had removed Firecracker from the after torpedo room to get him out of the way. He was still being loosely handcuffed to his bunk, but was attended by Chief Pharmacist's Mate Leroy Rowell and Ship's Cook Wixon. O'Kane stepped into the after torpedo room to chat with the torpedo gang about the upcoming attack. Chief Torpedoman Leland Weekley promised, "Captain, you put us in position, and we'll blow her out of the sea." It was a succinct way, O'Kane thought, to express the bond between captain and crew.

By the time that O'Kane returned to the bridge, *Tang* was ahead of the enemy and close to attack position. He ordered the two blasts of the klaxon which took the submarine under. It was 0227 on July 6.

O'Kane found the cold water and moist summer air tended to fog the periscope's exterior lens, making accurate sightings difficult, but he was afraid to keep the periscope up long enough for the lens to clear up. The sea was calm and the big freighter might have alert lookouts. He would have to take the chance—he didn't want to miss with only two torpedoes left. He might have fired by the so-called generated bearing method, figuring out where the final bearing should be, and firing without another periscope look. Other sub skippers used this frequently. But with only two fish, O'Kane preferred the "bow-and-arrow" method. He ordered *Tang* into a sharp turn to place her stern to the oncoming vessel.

Quartermaster Jones raised the periscope for his captain's last sighting for a constant bearing, which was cranked into the computer as the periscope went down.

Then: "Up periscope."

O'Kane saw the freighter's mainmast in his scope.

"Fire!"

Tang's last two torpedoes were on their way. O'Kane, his job done, turned the periscope over to Frazee. The first one hit.

"Her whole side's blown out!" Frazee exclaimed. Another explosion from the second torpedo. "She's capsizing!"

"Take the con, Frank," O'Kane said, "and take her up, and into any flotsam."

Three blasts and *Tang* broke the surface. There was a small amount of wreckage in the gray dawn that marked the grave of *Dori Maru*. There were no survivors sighted.

O'Kane's first chore was to plot a homeward journey from the Yellow Sea in a wide arc that would take *Tang* well clear of the areas where she had sunk an unprecedented number of ships in a handful of days. When daylight came, he took *Tang* under, running at 4 knots. He could have made 6 knots but that would have been harder on the batteries. You never knew, he mused, what emergency might arise and then you would need all the juice you had in the can.

As the crew took the day off, except for those on watch, O'Kane went over the menus with Murray Frazee. They both decided to instruct the cook to lay on all the steaks, roasts and fresh-frozen strawberries in the cold room. No use saving that good stuff simply to turn it in at base.

As darkness fell, *Tang* surfaced and raced eastward charging her batteries. Everyone was eager to clear the area and reach the deep, blue Pacific.

Steward Walker stuck his head in O'Kane's cabin. "I think we're in the news, Captain," he said.

O'Kane moved to the wardroom to listen to the ship's radio. Tokyo Rose predicted a dire fate for any submarine "foolishly" operating in the East China or Yellow Seas. She was obviously referring to *Tang*'s sinkings in the Yellow Sea, and *Tinosa*'s and *Sealion*'s in the East China Sea. Wait until she gets word of *Tang*'s last few days of action, O'Kane said, when more Japanese ships fail to reach port. Then she'll really be bothered.

O'Kane and Frazee plotted their departure through the Nansei Shoto chain into safe water beyond. The transit could be tricky because Japanese anti-sub forces had been alerted by the sinkings carried out by *Tang, Tinosa,* and *Sealion,* which would be exiting within days of each other. The Japanese forces could close off the passes through the island chain and the bright moon coming up these nights would help the enemy.

Tang spotted a group of escorts at night and saw the blinker signals between them. O'Kane surmised this could be a special killer group. He steered well clear of them and kept *Tang* heading somewhat southerly to transit the Nakano Strait, where he hoped to meet less opposition.

Running on the surface and racing for the Strait, *Tang*'s new APR1 radar detector picked up strong enemy signals near the Gaja Shim light on a small island. Then a searchlight began sweeping the area. O'Kane ordered full power. The enemy radar was searching. *Tang*'s own detector showed the Japanese were tracking *Tang*. That was a twist, O'Kane wryly observed.

Tang raced through the Strait into a rising moon. Japanese radar signals were at their strongest. Lookouts reported small, probably slow, surface vessels ahead on both sides of *Tang*'s course. Dick O'Kane chose to run the gauntlet and not be bluffed into diving. Murray Frazee climbed to the bridge and reported the crew at unofficial Battle Stations. Each command from the bridge was relayed quietly from man to man below. *Tang* was in a dicey position. O'Kane and Frazee worked out their plan. As an escort seemed to head *Tang*'s way, the submarine would veer slightly off, maintaining speed and distance. When this drew *Tang* toward another escort on the other side of the Strait, they would do the same with that ship. It was a form of zigzagging through the Strait while maintaining *Tang*'s speed. In a pinch, they would dive.

Tang got in front of the first escort and then swerved by the second without being spotted. The next maneuver to starboard seemed closer to O'Kane, but it took *Tang* past two more enemy ships. Finally, the last patrol ship was left behind. *Tang* outran her for the open sea. The tricky maneuver had lasted only 15 minutes but the whole crew had held their breaths. O'Kane thought *Tang*'s run was like a punt return: there were fewer tacklers—but they were playing for keeps. The boat rolled eastward. O'Kane decided to dispense with the recommended zigzag: it would save a day, and running at high speed, *Tang* would make a very difficult target. O'Kane estimated a straight, fast course would reduce the chance of being torpedoed—by foe or friend—by one-eighth.

He signaled ComSubPac on *Tang*'s departure from patrol and gave the location of the hunter-killer group for other American submarines to avoid. The return signal was highly congratulatory on *Tang*'s most successful patrol—ten ships down, a record for a single war outing. But the second half of the message was not too well received: *Tang*'s refit would be at Midway rather than Pearl.

While wandering through the ship, Captain O'Kane noticed that the midnight duty cook, James Roberts, was still busy over the galley range. The cook seemed to be taking special measures to get the mix of some dough just right. Curious, O'Kane queried the cook.

"Oh, I'm just trying to get the texture of Firecracker's rice the way he's used to, Captain. We've been cooking it too hard." O'Kane was amused. Cook Roberts was so sincere that O'Kane didn't have the heart to remind him that Firecracker was a prisoner of war rather than an honored guest. The captain quickly learned that Firecracker was indeed considered a guest by the crew, who would take him to the forward torpedo room to watch the evening movie. In turn, in pigeon English, Firecracker revealed his name, Mishuitunni Ka, his hometown, Kyoto, his ship's name, her cargo of iron ore, and her ports of call, Tientsin and Kobe. He also believed that the Hawaiian Islands had been captured by Japan as well as half of Australia. Firecracker would soon learn.

Torpedoman Don Sharp was proud of *Tang*'s performance. He thought O'Kane tops, while he disparaged another skipper, writing, "He must have been a shoe salesman." After the last sinking, Sharp scrawled: "All I can say is we done it. If this don't rate the Presidential Unit Citation, I don't know what will. Now we're heading for the barn and may God guide us there safely. Amen."

It was a curious turn of human nature that Sharp couldn't get along with another crewman in the torpedo gang, who annoyed him, as he noted in his secret diary. "Things haven't went so well for me in the torpedo room this run, since a new third class came aboard. I asked for a transfer today. If it hadn't been for this punk, I wouldn't have done so." The transfer request was approved. No questions were asked on *Tang*.

At the dock, Midway's Navy band was on hand. But before it could strike up, Boatswain's Mate Raymond Aquisti, *Tang*'s accordionist, stepped from behind the ship's bridge and, to the ragged accompaniment of *Tang*'s crew, ground away with the Midway Hymn:

Beautiful, beautiful Midway,
Land where the gooneybirds grow,
Beautiful, beautiful Midway,
The goddamnedest place that I know!

CHAPTER SEVENTEEN

Relaxing with Gooneybirds

Four husky Marines met *Tang* at the dock. They were prison guards, armed and with handcuffs and blindfolds, come to collect Firecracker. The crew watched from the deck, not knowing whether to laugh or cry at the handover of *Tang*'s mascot. Partly to assuage the crew's feelings, Chief Ballinger demanded a signed receipt for one Japanese prisoner of war in good health. O'Kane and his crew later learned that for days Firecracker's only response to questioning by intelligence officers was "ten thousand tons." That was what the crew instructed the prisoner to say if anyone asked him the size of his ship. The POW insisted for some time that his name was Firecracker—until he eventually identified himself as seaman Mishuitunni Ka. At the dock, O'Kane released *Tang*'s crew, each with his customary $10.

Fraz finished the patrol report, which Yeoman Walter Williams typed up. *Tang* had travelled 9,700 miles in thirty-six days, making ten attacks with ten sinkings. To top it all, *Tang* experienced only three depth charges—from the freighter. For her first three patrols, *Tang* under Dick O'Kane was awarded the coveted Presidential Unit Citation, a ribbon the submarine's crew would proudly wear.

Though submarines were not officially rated according to their results, because so many variables entered into performance, *Tang*'s officers knew their boat was moving sharply up in the unofficial tables. *Tang* had one of the best records in the Submarine Force: fifteen ships sunk, plus the extraordinary rescue of aviators at Truk. Only O'Kane's old *Wahoo, Silversides, Tautog,* and Slade Cutter's *Seahorse* were in the same league. No skipper came close to O'Kane's ten ships down on one patrol, except Mush Morton's nine on *Wahoo*'s fourth patrol with Dick as exec.

O'Kane and Frazee were invited to dinner with Captain Charles Edmunds, Midway's top submarine officer. *Tang*'s officers were anxious to depart early and get back to the Gooneyville to swap stories with other submariners. They were surprised not to find any senior officers at the bar which was usually frequented by all sub officers. O'Kane and Frazee were informed that the Gooneyville now boasted a "senior officers' bar."

The second bar had been built to give the junior officers more privacy in their own space—supposedly more relaxing than drinking and cutting up under the noses of their own senior officers. O'Kane disapproved. He believed that the separate bars undercut the finest war patrol school there was. At the old corner room, officers had cast aside ranks: skippers, PCOs, execs, and junior officers had all learned from one another in frank talks about tactics and operations. While O'Kane made token appearances at the senior officers' bar, he insisted his top echelon spend time at the corner room to keep it buzzing while *Tang* was in port.

Tang's wardroom learned of the progress of Allied forces in Normandy. Cherbourg had fallen. In the Central Pacific, the Marianas were taken with high casualties. Unlike their earlier support of major fleet operations, submarines performed well in the battle for the Marianas.

Dick was pleased to hear that Slade Cutter in *Seahorse* had sighted the Japanese fleet heading toward the Marianas, and though he couldn't pursue at full speed because of a motor bearing failure, he got off a vital contact report to ComSubPac. Cutter's report backed up a previous sighting by Robert Risser in *Flying Fish* (which had nearly been sunk by a circular run of her own torpedo in an earlier attack), promptly transmitted to SubPac and then to Admiral Spruance, Commander of the Fifth Fleet.

ComSubPac alerted O'Kane's Academy classmate, Herman Kossler commanding *Cavalla*, to Cutter's and Risser's contact reports. Kossler, his first time out as skipper after serving as exec to Burt Klakring in *Guardfish*, collided with a whale en route to his patrol station to screen for Task Force 58. The whale was severely wounded from *Cavalla*'s screws. Kossler was worried that the impact might have damaged the screws or shafts, but they appeared not to have been affected. *Cavalla* was poised across the Japanese fleet's route from the San Bernardino Strait in the Philippines to Saipan, where the U.S. forces were about to invade. Kossler spotted a convoy of naval tankers. He was ordered to trail them to a possible rendezvous with Japanese main fleet units.

Kossler followed the units but lost them. Then he ran into a Japanese task force. He submerged and approached. He raised his periscope and could hardly believe his luck. In the lens was the big Japanese carrier, *Shokaku,* which had led the attack on Pearl Harbor and the Battle of the Coral Sea. Kossler fired six torpedoes. Four hit the huge target. The carrier was wracked with internal explosions as aviation gas ignited. *Shokaku,* 30,000 tons, dropped out of the formation and slowly capsized, slipping beneath the sea. It was a Navy Cross performance for Herm Kossler on his first patrol as skipper.

Another skipper racked up a major kill on the same day, June 19. Commander J.W. Blanchard in *Albacore* found himself in the middle of a fast-moving Japanese carrier group. At periscope depth, Jim Blanchard zeroed in on the second carrier in the formation. As he was about to fire, he realized something had gone wrong with the torpedo data computer, so he fired six fish purely by calculated guesswork. Three destroyers closed in on *Albacore* and gave the submarine a rough going over. As the depth charges rained down, Blanchard heard a huge explosion farther off. Only one torpedo hit. The target was the carrier *Taiho,* at 31,000 tons the biggest and newest in the navy and the flagship of Admiral Jisaburo Ozawa, Japanese fleet commander. One of his carrier pilots had flown into an oncoming torpedo from *Albacore* 100 yards short of the flagship, exploding the fish as he destroyed himself. At first, Admiral Ozawa thought damage from the torpedo, which had exploded in an elevator bay, was minimal and containable. Two carrier raids were launched from the flight deck. But a young officer in damage control decided to open the ship's ventilation system to disperse the gasoline fumes. The fumes spread throughout the ship. *Taiho* was like a huge vapor-filled bomb awaiting a spark to ignite it. The spark came just after 3:30 p.m. An enormous explosion ripped the flight deck apart and blew out the sides of the carrier. The ship began to settle rapidly. Admiral Ozawa wanted to go down with his flagship but his staff insisted he transfer to the cruiser *Haguro,* with Emperor Hirohito's portrait. A second massive blast doomed the 31,000-ton *Taiho.* It sank with 1,650 Japanese sailors aboard.

Dick O'Kane learned, too, of Gene Fluckey's successful patrol with *Barb.* Commander Fluckey, an outgoing officer with an infectious smile, had a quiet early war. After five fruitless patrols as a junior officer on the elderly *Bonita* out of Panama, he took a postgraduate course in naval engineering. Finally he arrived in the Pacific, and made a PCO patrol aboard *Barb* (which had spent her first five patrols without luck in European waters) before assuming command during a refit at Midway. In his first patrol as skipper, and *Barb*'s eighth, Fluckey was given a personal send-off by Admiral Lockwood during a brief inspection trip. Fluckey was apprehensive about the meeting: he thought Lockwood might have had a change of heart about putting him in command. He decided to brazen it out.

"Good morning, skipper," Admiral Lockwood said. "How do you feel about taking the *Barb* out on patrol?"

"We're ready in every respect, sir. How many ships do you want us to sink?"

"How many ships do you think you can sink?"

"Will five be enough, Admiral?"

Lockwood smiled. "Yes, five will be enough."

True to his word, Fluckey with *Barb,* operating in the Sea of Okhotsk, sank five ships on his maiden patrol in a three-sub wolf pack. The other two submarines, *Herring* and *Golet,* were lost on the patrol. When Fluckey returned to Pearl Harbor, Lockwood offered him hearty congratulations.

"Gene," he said, "you're the first skipper to tell me what he would sink and do it! Five ships sunk are enough. My hat is off to you and your crew." His first patrol as skipper earned Gene Fluckey a Navy Cross.

The officers at the Midway bull sessions also learned that Jack Coye had another fine patrol in *Silversides,* Creed Burlingame's old boat, with six ships down—one of the best patrols of the war.

U.S. naval intelligence intercepts of Japanese communications confirmed the sinkings O'Kane heard about. But other confirmations were harder to come by, which sometimes angered skippers who believed in their claims to sinkings. The subject of confirmed sinkings was a troubling one during the war. Returning from patrol, a skipper would give a concise report listing the ships he thought he had sunk or damaged. He would note the circumstances of the sinking: whether he had seen the ship go down, photographic confirmation if pictures were taken, or the sound of explosions and breaking-up noises if the submarine went deep after an attack. In many cases, of course, there could be no on-the-spot verification. A captain's first duty after an attack was to make sure his ship survived.

The squadron commander would review the report, and, possibly with the aid of intercepted Japanese reports about the attack, revise the skipper's estimate downward, or occasionally upward. Headquarters insisted on "eyesight evidence" or other proof: periscope photographs, witnessed sinkings, testimony of survivors, recovered debris. The Submarine Force Commander made awards on the basis of the wartime credit. Many skippers thought their own estimates had been arbitrarily lowered. But as the war progressed, staff officers realized that many of the hits reported by the captains were actually from defective torpedoes: prematures, duds, or the airflask exploding, which could resemble a true torpedo hit. The flawed torpedoes often only damaged ships, which appeared to be sunk. Of course, in the middle of a night-time mêlée in an attack on a convoy, a captain could genuinely believe that he had done more damage than was actually inflicted. Still, post-war analysis showed most skippers had been fairly close in their estimates of sinkings and the type of ship hit. However, the Japanese salvaged some sunken vessels in shallow water and did not list them.

After the war, a Joint Army–Navy Assessment Committee (JANAC) carefully compiled a list of sinkings from a thor-

ough study of Japanese records, but these did not include
ships under 500 tons and many Japanese destroyer-type escorts, which appeared to be larger, might have fallen under
that limit. Further, the JANAC group realized that Japanese
records were not perfect by any means, and its accounting
undoubtedly missed many ships that were sunk—the Japanese
didn't know some of their ships were downed by subs—thus
denying U.S. submarine skippers credit for their loss. For
many years, the JANAC figures were accepted as final. In the
1980s and 1990s, however, historian John D. Alden, a retired
Navy Commander, studied Japanese records and learned they'd
been updated with more precise figures. He undertook a thor-
ough study to reflect those statistics, which were more accurate than the older JANAC study. Though Alden recognized
that his figures were not the final word, they are probably
more accurate than any other set of data on enemy ships sunk.

Over-optimistic estimates of enemy sinkings were not restricted to submariners. They were common to Navy (and
Army) aviators, as well as to the action reports submitted by
cruiser and destroyer commanders early in the war.

Skippers like Pete Galantin of *Halibut* believed more
wartime credit should have been apportioned for damaging
enemy ships. Wounding a ship with torpedoes, he argued,
meant that a lot of effort and money went into repairs. A
badly damaged ship would be out of service for a long time,
tied up at dry dock, and might cost the Japanese more than a
vessel that was sunk.

Tang's stay at Midway was short, marked by fish fries, baseball games, cold beer, and some sport fishing in the lagoon
organized by the island's new recreation department. Officers and men let off steam with a lot of drinking, often restricted to beer, but sometimes supplemented by torpedo
juice, guilly, and the rare bottle of bourbon.

Though Dick O'Kane liked his share of cold beer after a
patrol, he was not in the category of the hard-drinking, hell-
raising type of skipper, like his friend Slade Cutter. Cutter's
antics on shore were legion, as were those of his former skip-

per, Lew Parks, Chuck Triebel of *Snook,* Fritz Harlfinger, and Dusty Dornin of *Trigger* fame.

After an early patrol aboard *Pompano,* Cutter and his skipper Lew Parks were in the bar of the Sub Base. Parks bought a load of beer for everyone. Present were two young Army officers. Cutter and Parks were trying to get to the Royal Hawaiian but couldn't find a ride because the nightly curfew was on and the two young Army lieutenants needled the Navy officers. "That's the trouble with the Navy," one said. "You have no morale. Here we are, just second lieutenants, and we have a command car." They did. Cutter looked at Parks. The Army officers made two mistakes, as Cutter told it. One was to stay behind in the bar after sounding off. The other was to leave the keys in the car. "Parks was the skipper and got behind the wheel," Cutter recounted. "The exec was Willis Thomas, who was later skipper of *Pompano.* Parks got the thing going, and went through the hedge right in front of the officers' club. Finally we got out on Dillingham Boulevard. There was a rifle in the back with a bandolier of ammunition."

Cutter sprayed rifle fire at some sodium vapor streetlights and a water tower. After a merry chase, they were pulled over by Marine shore patrols and taken to the brig. Dusty Dornin, then exec of *Gudgeon,* heard about it and talked to the sergeant of the guard—offering to bring down bread and water to his submarine friends. But Lew Parks had connections: his brother was prosecuting attorney and they got out on bail, the charges finally dropped.

Cutter was proud that submariners stuck together. Captains stood by their men, as O'Kane stood by the crew of *Tang.* Cutter swore by Parks. "If anybody got in trouble with the shore patrol," Cutter said, "Parks would go to bat for them. He'd say: 'That's my problem, not yours.' We all knew he was behind us, and we had a very high *esprit de corps,* even though he was tough. A lot of tough skippers didn't have any *esprit de corps.* They didn't have the qualities of leadership that Parks had. He was very loyal, and he expected loyalty, too. It was up and down both ways with him."

Of his escapades, Cutter admitted, "It sounds childish, but

you know, we didn't give a damn. I didn't care what happened. These things would happen just when we came in from patrol. We would get unwound, and then we would settle down and be reasonable. I didn't expect to survive the war. I don't think anybody did, really. I know that when we dived every morning I would look at the morning stars and wonder if I would ever see them again."

Later, during a *Seahorse* refit at Midway, Commander Dick Harlow, football coach at Harvard before entering the Navy, complained to Slade that *Seahorse*'s men were overdoing it on the beach. He didn't understand how they could drink like they did.

"Slade," Harlow said, "you are all destroying yourselves. This is terrible—all this booze. What you should do is rest and exercise and get your health back rather than tearing it down."

Cutter's view was the opposite. The men were exuberant. Sure, they drank too much, but in Cutter's opinion there was such a thing as mental health—which was much more important than physical health. After all, they were all young. They were all healthy. As soon as the two weeks rest camp was over, they would go back to work. Cutter took Harlow on a day's training in *Seahorse* to show him the crew at work. Harlow didn't change his mind.

Cutter admitted that perhaps more injurious to his own health was taking aluminum hydroxide pills for his acid stomach while drinking twenty-five to thirty cups of coffee a day and smoking two or three packs of cigarettes—just to keep going while at sea. During one four-day period of very little sleep while tracking and sinking a convoy, Cutter lived on coffee and Benzedrine. He had to be calmed down later by the pharmacist's mate who administered sedatives, and when that failed to work, slugs of Old Crow bourbon.

Most captains, like Mush Morton, Dick O'Kane, and Slade Cutter, administered the small, two-ounce bottles to the crew after a severe depth charging, or in honor of a sinking. One skipper, Gene Fluckey, finding that his young crewmembers didn't much care for hard liquor, issued cans of cold beer instead.

*   *   *

As *Tang* readied for sea, Dick O'Kane's mind turned to the upcoming patrol. Freshly assigned to *Tang* were new officers, Lieutenant (j.g.) Charles O. Pucket, a small, slight officer from Chattanooga, Tennessee; and a husky football player, Ensign Basil Pearce, of Palatka in northeast Florida, who both volunteered from the relief crew at Midway.

The other addition to *Tang*—and a real find, O'Kane thought—was Lieutenant Lawrence Savadkin, who came aboard as engineer. Larry Savadkin, dark-haired and wiry, from a Jewish upbringing in Easton, Pennsylvania, was a reserve who took naval training at Lafayette College. It was his first assignment out of Submarine School, but Savadkin was an expert engineer and destroyer sailor having served aboard *Mayrant* in the Mediterranean invasions and fighting for two years. As engineering officer of *Mayrant,* he was wounded in action off Palermo in a German bombing attack during the invasion of Sicily. He was awarded the Silver Star medal for conspicuous gallantry in helping preserve the ship from sinking and saving his fellow crewmen's lives. Also receiving a Silver Star and Purple Heart in the same action to save the destroyer was Savadkin's shipmate and friend of many months' standing: Lieutenant Franklin D. Roosevelt Jr., the President's son.

Skipper O'Kane was keen to break in the new men during the training exercises at Midway. On his first dive, Larry Savadkin acquitted himself well. O'Kane would have no worries about Larry. He wished to give third officer Frank Springer conning experience so he could be designated "qualified for command" of a fleet submarine. O'Kane arranged for a patrol boat to drop depth charges 100 yards or so away from *Tang* to give new crewmen indoctrination for the coming experience at the hands of real enemies. The result was unexpectedly jarring because the shallow water and hard coral bottom seemed to magnify the shock waves from the charges, rattling sailors' teeth in *Tang*.

O'Kane was impressed by Frank Springer's performance. But he was faced with the dilemma that confronted other captains, from Lew Parks on down: if he named Springer

qualified for command, his valued officer would undoubtedly be snatched away for an executive officer's billet on another submarine. O'Kane knew that Murray Frazee was due
for rest and rotation after this next patrol. O'Kane did not
want *Tang* deprived of two valuable officers at the same
time. For admittedly selfish interests, but for the good of
Tang, O'Kane asked the division commander to hold up for-
warding the endorsement of Frank Springer until *Tang* was
heading back from her fourth patrol.

At Midway, the awards came through for the previous
Tang patrols for Murray Frazee, Chief Ballinger, "Boats"
Leibold, Quartermaster Sidney Jones, and Gunner's Mate
James White.

A message concerning the next secret operation arrived
from ComSubPac's Captain Joseph Grenfell. O'Kane sent
Exec Frazee and Quartermaster Sidney Jones to draw detailed charts from the Sub Base, but before *Tang* departed
there was one unusual, pending matter. O'Kane had checked
into the Midway dental office for some routine fillings. Returning to the ship, Chief Ballinger asked a strange question.

"Did they charge you for cleaning your teeth, Captain?"

O'Kane looked quizzical.

"Well, I just found out those bastards have been charging
our troops five bucks apiece, and no one could get a dental
appointment in the afternoon because the dentists were always out sport fishing!"

Dick O'Kane was furious. He barrelled over to the division commander's office and spelled out a complaint in no
uncertain terms. The division commander ordered an investigation. Shortly before sailing time, O'Kane was instructed
to leave behind witnesses who could testify to the dental office's misdemeanors.

O'Kane messaged the reply: "WITNESSES HAVE IMPORTANT
BATTLE STATIONS AND ARE NEEDED IN *TANG* ON THIS WAR PA-
TROL." As far as Dick O'Kane was concerned, that was that.

CHAPTER EIGHTEEN

Close to the Japanese Shore

On the afternoon of July 31, *Tang* barely managed to wait long enough for a late arrival, Steward's Mate Walker, who was delayed at the dice game. He hastily piled aboard. *Tang* sounded a blast on the horn, backed into Midway lagoon, executed a smart turn, and headed for the channel and open sea. Dick O'Kane put *Tang* on course for the Empire.

The *Tang* team meshed. There was an easy feeling of informality aboard. Clay Decker came to the boat as a torpedoman third class, but he didn't get along with the leading torpedoman, so Murray Frazee allowed him to shift to the engine room as a motor mac, and in successive patrols was promoted to MoMM 2nd Class. His Battle Station Submerged was at the bow planes in the control room: Fraz thought he was especially adept at this post. Decker was a good man at "catching the bubble," or keeping the dive steady. At Battle Surface, Decker would man the throttles in the engine room.

O'Kane ordered Chief Ballinger to post *Tang*'s operation order in the messroom. It read: "When in all respects ready for sea proceed to the Nampo Shoto and areas 4 and 5. Conduct offensive patrol against all shipping. There will be no friendly submarines in the adjacent area." Areas 4 and 5 covered much of the south and east coast of Japan's main island, Honshu. The areas held great possibilities but also dangers. O'Kane wrote his night orders which forbad the use of the aircraft radar without his permission, because it was easily detected, and warned: "Do not be lulled by the 2,500 miles between us and the enemy's front door. He can be here just as surely as we will be there. Do not hesitate to call me to the bridge, or to dive."

As *Tang* approached Empire waters, Dick O'Kane asked Murray Frazee into his tiny cabin. He showed him a handwritten note from Vice Admiral Charles Lockwood. It read:

Dear Dick,
   I want to tell you why I am sending you and your *Tang* right back to the Empire, with hardly a breather. We have had two poor and now a dry patrol in these areas, the boats reporting a dearth of shipping. Intelligence reports indicate that the merchant traffic must be there, and I am certain that *Tang* can rediscover it.

Sincerely, and Godspeed,
C.A. Lockwood.

Fraz read the note and commented, "It requires nothing that we wouldn't do anyway."

O'Kane nodded. "Well, we don't need intelligence to tell us that the ships are there and running. The war is still going on, so they have to be either loading or at sea. I don't expect that we'll find them off the 10-fathom curve. The admiral's note underlies my responsibilities."

Frazee agreed. It was a compliment to *Tang,* and a challenge to the crew, but it meant that *Tang* was expected to prowl dangerous shoal waters winkling out elusive Japanese coastal shipping.

O'Kane finally had a chance to experiment with the gadget he purchased with his daughter Marsha in the San Francisco music store: a metronome. He thought it out-of-date for a submarine's soundman to count a target ship's propeller beat with a stopwatch. It was important to determine any change quickly for it meant the ship was speeding up or slowing down, which could affect the data for torpedo firing. The stopwatch counting method was often too late for an accurate solution. "Why couldn't there be an instrument for instant readings of propeller sounds?" O'Kane asked. In San Francisco, an electric metronome had caught O'Kane's eye in a store just off Union Square. The metronome's scale was graduated in beats per minute. The instrument's range covered those of screw beats of Japanese merchantmen or heavy ships. The beats came through the water as pulsed swish-swish sounds at regular intervals. These could be matched to a metronome. Changes would be registered and spotted immediately. Experimenting with the metronome had had a low priority since O'Kane brought it aboard, but now the information it could provide would be imperative. O'Kane had technicians at Midway mount the metronome next to the sound receiver, where the soundman with his headset pushed off his ears could hear it directly.

O'Kane was pleased to see that *Tang*'s camouflage seemed to be effective: each night a few flying fish would land on deck. For fish-fanciers like him, there was fresh seafood for breakfast, done up by Steward Walker.

The first concrete indication that *Tang* was approaching the Japanese home islands came with Basil Pearce's booming order "Clear the bridge!" when the lookouts sighted a Japanese Betty bomber. *Tang* dove for 30 minutes, until the scouting plane disappeared over the horizon.

Just before midnight on August 8, *Tang* spotted the pinnacle of Inamba Jima, part of the Nampo Shoto island chain stretching due south from Tokyo Bay. Iwo Jima was the southernmost isle in the chain.

O'Kane decided to move near the Honshu coast where the 100 fathom curve closed in only 3 miles offshore. This would provide a deep-water escape route. As a *Tang* officer remarked, "The skipper always calculated a way out of any tactical set-up."

O'Kane found what he was looking for. Ed Beaumont, on the search periscope, spotted a tanker moving up the coast, near the shore, with search planes overhead. *Tang* went to Battle Stations Submerged. Larry Savadkin held the boat at periscope depth with not much water under the keel. The tanker was at an awkward angle. O'Kane knew he had to get into firing position quickly in order that the target did not get away. It would be like shooting from the hip. O'Kane called for the outer tube doors opened, and steadied on an approach course. He ordered three torpedoes fired. Frazee hit the plunger three times. The set-up seemed fine. O'Kane headed

Tang toward deep water, but there were no explosions. He took a quick look through the scope. The tanker was proceeding along the coast, now well out of range. *Tang* went deep to evade depth charging and bounced lightly off the soft bottom before stopping engines.

After cooling down for an hour, the disappointed officers proceeded to discuss what had gone wrong on the approach. Led by O'Kane, they dissected the data. The evidence indicated that *Tang* should have gotten at least two hits. O'Kane's guess was that the hard bottom in shallow water may have affected the torpedo run. Next time, *Tang* would try for an attack in deeper water.

As *Tang* waited and looked for a new target, the men went about their off-duty chores: two crewmen worked the washing machine, cleaning sacks of the crew's underwear and dungarees, hanging the wet clothes in the warm engine room to dry. The clothes were stenciled with the owners' names and each man picked his clean laundry off the line after it dried. Electrician's mates carefully monitored the battery charge. Others checked the batteries, making sure the specific gravity was correct. In the forward torpedo room, the nightly movie was underway. While the battery charge was finishing, the smoking lamp went out. This was to prevent an explosion before blowers carried away any hydrogen accumulated during the charge.

O'Kane followed the Honshu coastline, a mountainous mass with bays and headlands and a few beach areas. He was convinced the Japanese were running night shipping along the coast to escape attack in daylight, but *Tang* was up against increased surface and air patrols, guarding shipping and looking for American submarines. She moved near the Miki Saki promontory, which had to be rounded by Japanese ships.

"This is the spot, Captain," Frazee said, over a cup of coffee. O'Kane nodded. Dick Kroth and Larry Savadkin were at the table. As engineer, Larry would normally have been the diving officer. But, as in the case of Roger Paine aboard *Wahoo,* Savadkin found he had a flair for operating the torpedo data computer in the firing party, so he sometimes took over the equipment at Battle Stations.

Tang's skirting the coast was hampered by a strong current, running northerly, making it difficult for the sub to present a minimum angle to Japanese patrols. One escort forced her to seaward and shortly after, a small tanker appeared around the promontory leaving *Tang* out of position. The cold water rising to the surface, which created humid conditions fogging *Tang*'s periscope lens, didn't help the situation.

Two columns of smoke were sighted at the horizon to the north, and O'Kane rang up speed for an attack. The captain took a periscope look. The smoke resolved itself into two large freighters. Both ships were heavily loaded, but with escorts. O'Kane turned on the loudspeakers so the crew could follow the attack party's actions in the conning tower.

Soundman Floyd Caverly, using the newly installed Sherman Clay & Co. metronome, reported, "No change in speed, Captain, still seven-two turns."

O'Kane was ready. "Open all outer doors forward. Stand by for final bearing. Up scope." Caverly interrupted urgently. "Fast screws bearing three four zero, Captain!"

O'Kane swung the periscope left. It was an escort gunboat with a zero bow angle heading directly for *Tang*. O'Kane chose to continue the attack.

"Constant bearing—mark! Keep the sound bearings coming, Caverly."

"Set."

"Fire!"

O'Kane launched three torpedoes at the first freighter, and three more at the second ship in column. He ordered *Tang* toward the escorts. Expecting the worst, O'Kane was relieved to see the gunboat racing past *Tang*'s stern, badly misjudging the submarine's position. O'Kane turned the periscope to the leading freighter, just as it blew up from a torpedo hit.

The captain turned *Tang*'s stern toward the gunboat and ordered, "Flood negative. Take her deep. Rig for depth charge."

As *Tang* went under, Signalman Ogden timed the torpedo runs and noted two sharp detonations of *Tang*'s fourth and fifth torpedoes. Soundman Caverly reported scrunching, breaking-up noises very loud in the direction of the targets.

Tang's conning tower readied for depth charges. O'Kane

sensed that this time the boat might get a real going over. She had led a fairly charmed life, as far as her experience with depth charging went, but the law of averages was catching up with *Tang*. As usual, Captain O'Kane wedged himself between the radar well and Floyd Caverly's sonar equipment. The soundman had already moved his earphone outward so that he would not be deafened by the expected explosions. Watertight doors were closed and dogged down. Bulkhead clapper valves in the ventilation system were secured. All machinery not used for propulsion was shut down. The gunboat on the surface was already echo ranging for *Tang*. The noise of her screws and steady bearing meant the vessel was getting close. Moving right or left would bring part of *Tang* closer to the gunboat. There was only one way to go. "Keep her going down, Larry," O'Kane said. Savadkin was on the way to 180 feet, only 2 fathoms off the bottom. *Tang* was caught in shallow water.

Then came the sharp crack of explosions, which went off in quick succession all around *Tang*. The boat underwent a terrific beating as O'Kane ordered twists and turns, running silently, in a desperate effort to outwit the Japanese gunboat captain. The Japanese skipper made five separate passes over *Tang*. He dropped twenty-two ear-splitting depth charges that landed near the submarine, confined in 200 feet of water rather than operating in the ocean deep. O'Kane was concerned. This depth charging was getting serious. How to get away from this persistent Japanese captain?

"All ahead full," O'Kane ordered. "Left full rudder!" O'Kane maneuvered out of the Japanese path as the gunboat completed another run. His evasive measure succeeded. On the last pass, the depth charges were slightly to shoreward and *Tang* was heading in the other direction. O'Kane called for damage reports from all compartments. He was surprised to hear that there were few problems except for broken light bulbs.

O'Kane's crew was cheered by the sounds of breaking-up noises from the sinking ships behind, but Dick took his hat off to the Japanese skipper. It was the worst depth charging he experienced on *Tang*. He was impressed with the anti-sub tactics that seemed sharper and more dangerous than in the past. In 38 minutes, *Tang* returned to periscope depth and saw the gunboat 4,000 yards astern. Beyond the first was a second escort, apparently recovering survivors. *Tang* cleared the scene safely.

In the wardroom, Dick O'Kane was about to compliment Larry Savadkin on his excellent control of the ship underwater, when the diving officer said, "Captain, if I'd known depth charges would be like those, I might just have stayed in surface ships."

"Larry," O'Kane kidded, "they just seemed close because you're not used to them. When we get some that are really close, these won't seem too bad. Just wait and you'll see."

Fraz, sitting across, tried to keep a straight face. It was Fraz's worst depth charging in his eleven patrols.

Then Dick O'Kane admitted the truth to Larry: this was his tenth patrol and the gunboat had laid them down faster and closer than any he had experienced before. If *Tang* were not blessed with the new, strong hull, they'd probably be wrestling with repairs. The confession cheered up Savadkin, who reached for the cribbage board, while Murray Frazee took a turn through the boat to reassure the crew. As he left Frazee made a drinking motion with his hand, and O'Kane nodded approval of the tacit request to pour a round of depth charge medicine for the crew—though Dick O'Kane preferred to think of the drink as a celebration for the sinking.

O'Kane was relieved that *Tang* had broken the ice with a sinking on her fourth patrol, but he was unhappy that the boat had only downed one ship and damaged another with nine torpedoes used so far. He was upset because while *Tang*'s officers were convinced the second enemy ship was sunk, SubPac rules now called for visual evidence, otherwise the enemy ship was listed as damaged. Earlier in the war it had been easier to take periscope photos of sinking ships, but with the ratio of escorts vastly increased around the Japanese home islands, U.S. submarines hadn't the luxury of hanging around for photos. At least, O'Kane thought, *Tang* had had the chance to see the first maru break in two.

O'Kane was conscious that the crew was under another pressure: rarely had a submarine stayed near enemy aircraft and surface escort echo-ranging equipment for so long. But that was the price *Tang*'s crew paid for staying in close to find the enemy. O'Kane thought Admiral Lockwood's letter left the boat little choice: they were instructed to find shipping that had eluded earlier U.S. submarines off Honshu.

On August 14, *Tang* spotted a large yacht, armed with plenty of machine guns and extra antennas. O'Kane decided to surface and sink the vessel. Though he avoided gun con-tact with trawlers and fishing boats, this merited more atten-tion, and it would provide a break in routine for the crew, which responded to the "Battle Surface" order. The gunners unlimbered *Tang*'s 4-inch gun and at "Commence Firing," began shooting at the yacht at 7,000 yards. The yacht re-turned fire with what appeared to be 20-millimeter guns, and neatly dodged *Tang*'s attack. *Tang* was hampered because, with her gun forward of the bridge, her fire was masked whenever *Tang*'s stern was toward the yacht. O'Kane grimly thought it proved his contention that the gun should be astern of the superstructure. He observed eight hits, which demol-ished the ship's deckhouse and damaged its sides. After eighty-eight rounds, O'Kane ordered, "Cease firing." He wanted to keep the remaining forty rounds of 4-inch ammu-nition for a real emergency.

O'Kane prowled the area around offshore islands for a time but finding no targets, he decided to go back to Honshu. "Fraz," he said, "let's head in and get a ship!" Fraz's answer was a broad smile and an OK sign. O'Kane's concern was to place *Tang* where she could interdict coastwise shipping, but still be close to deep water for evasion and escape. He had to consider the Kuroshio, the offshore current which moved northerly along the coast at up to 3 knots. While changing position, O'Kane and Fraz made sure the senior petty offi-cers destined to move up after the patrol stood the watches and performed the jobs of the chiefs they were to replace— with the chiefs looking on.

Tang got into position 5,000 yards offshore where O'Kane could monitor Japanese shipping. As the sun set, he saw evenly spaced lights offshore, which could be lighted buoys marking a channel for Japanese shipping clinging to the coastline.

"Captain to the conning tower." The word came over the intercom. "Ship bearing zero-two-two."

"That puts her inshore," Fraz said to Dick as they climbed the ladder from the control room to the conning tower.

O'Kane conned *Tang* tracking the target, a modern engine-aft freighter running on the inside of the 10-fathom curve. Two patrol escorts, both to the seaward side, accompanied the freighter fore and aft. That didn't give *Tang* much maneuvering room for an attack. Larry Savadkin held *Tang* at a depth of 64 feet.

Chief Jones raised the periscope for O'Kane. The set-up was a good one. O'Kane ordered two torpedoes fired.

Frazee pressed the plunger. The first fish left the tube with the customary zing. But the second torpedo left with a loud clonk. It seemed to have sunk. The seconds went by. Disappointingly, the first torpedo exploded on the beach having missed the freighter. *Tang* quickly retreated into deep water as the two escorts began depth charging at random.

The officers gathered around the wardroom table trying to figure out why the first torpedo missed, and the second didn't even run. They were unable to do so. O'Kane was gaining an appreciation of the problems previous skippers had in the area—trying to position themselves near the ten-fathom curve, armed with some faulty torpedoes.

Tang's lookouts sighted another freighter with two escorts running along the coast. Taking advantage of the Kuroshio Current, O'Kane maneuvered in front of the target, and waited for it to come into his periscope sights. The freighter was close to the beach and the difference in speed estimates caused by the Kuroshio might upset the firing set-up. O'Kane decided to offset that possibility by firing a wider than usual spread of torpedoes. At his command, Frazee pressed the plunger for a three-fish spread of Mark 18 electrics.

O'Kane sweated out the long wait for the slower electric torpedoes to reach their targets. Signalman Ogden called out, ". . . two . . . one . . . zero . . ." Nothing happened. No explosions. They had missed. *Tang* had a minute more before the three fish exploded on the beach, and those 60 seconds were needed to streak for deep water and safety from a counterattack. *Tang* reached deep submergence.

What had gone wrong? O'Kane prided himself on his torpedo marksmanship, the best in the Sub Force. Frank Springer, Mel Enos, and Dick Kroth checked the log for firing bearings, gyro readings, depth setting, and torpedo data computer. O'Kane believed his spread had covered speed estimate errors. He was convinced that one or more of *Tang*'s torpedoes had run too deep.

He sensed the attack party's confidence had been shaken and his own pride was dented. It was a humbling experience, but the only thing to do when you fall off a horse, he thought, is to get back on it again. He decided there was one solution: to conduct some test firings, observing exactly what was happening to *Tang*'s torpedoes. He and Fraz decided to test them at night in a nearby bay called Owashi Wan, but they were troubled because the charts were not up-to-date enough to determine *Tang*'s exact position. As they moved into the bay, a patrol ship followed at some distance behind, unaware of *Tang*'s presence, and anchored for the night.

Dick O'Kane would rather test his fish against a Japanese warship than a cliff. He identified the vessel as similar to the gunboat that had given *Tang* such a hard time a few days before. Moving slowly on batteries for quiet, O'Kane turned *Tang*, bringing the after tubes with electric torpedoes to bear. The set-up was fine: the gunboat, *Nansatsu*, hadn't detected *Tang;* the wakeless torpedo would not alert her crew. The firing party was on the bridge and O'Kane ordered a single torpedo fired. It whined cleanly from the tube, but halfway to the target there was a muffled explosion. Tracking it, Floyd Caverly reported the torpedo had hit bottom, 250 feet under, according to *Tang*'s chart.

O'Kane calibrated *Tang* slightly for another deadeye shot from the after tube. There was no sign of activity on the gunboat. Two minutes later, he ordered another torpedo fired, and it went off properly, but there was no explosion from the target. The second torpedo apparently passed under the gunboat. It was now 4 minutes since the first shot. Fraz joined Dick on the bridge and shared his disappointment.

O'Kane maneuvered *Tang* to bring the bow tubes with steam torpedoes to bear. Everyone on *Tang*'s bridge spoke in whispers. It seemed incredible that they were not yet sighted.

"Fire!" O'Kane commanded.

The torpedo was set to run on the surface. *Tang* was steady. There was a zero gyro angle—a dream shot. But the fish took a 30-yard erratic jog before settling down toward the target. It missed astern.

By this time the gunboat's crew was showing signs of waking up; lights flashed on. O'Kane ordered another torpedo readied. His periscope wire was on the forward gun mount. "Fire!" The torpedo jigged slightly but settled down, running close to the surface. Everyone suddenly crowded up to *Tang*'s bridge. The fourth torpedo hit with a resounding explosion, one of the most spectacular O'Kane had seen. The impact shattered the gunboat. It quickly sank in the fiery darkness.

Dick O'Kane ordered *Tang* to full speed to clear the bay for deep water where he could take the boat under and turn her into a floating torpedo overhaul shop. He believed the malfunctions were due to faulty depth engines and sluggish steering devices. He was confident the fish could be repaired by torpedomen whose lives depended on the quality of their work.

Tang had six torpedoes left: three steam fish in the forward tubes and three electrics in the after room. The investigation led by Hank Flanagan revealed that three of the fish had flawed depth rudders, which caused them to run deep.

The torpedo room gangs pulled the fish, hoisted them in the chain falls, and checked the vertical and horizontal rudders by running the motors. All the mechanisms were freshly calibrated and reset—gyros, rudders, valves and engines. Hank Flanagan was satisfied. Torpedomen had painted fresh eyes on the fish to guide them to the enemy. They reloaded the tubes, a backbreaking job. The work was topped off with a big dinner. O'Kane surfaced *Tang* to give the boat a long blast of fresh air.

Two days later, *Tang* patrolled close to Honshu's coastline. Smoke was sighted, and O'Kane found a convoy hugging the shoreline so closely they looked to be aground. Quartermaster Jones rang the general alarm. Steward's Mate Walker appeared with piping hot coffee for O'Kane and Frazee. Dick viewed the situation with the periscope: two freighters with escorts. He prepared the set-up, but a last minute zig turned the convoy toward *Tang,* closing too near for O'Kane to get off a spread.

O'Kane then spotted a destroyer which seemed to be circling *Tang.* He maintained periscope depth to observe the warship, and as the enemy moved in a lazy arc, O'Kane kept *Tang's* nose pointed at him, partly to reduce his profile, partly to shoot if he had to. Captain O'Kane preferred to save his torpedoes for loaded merchantmen. The destroyer turned out to be a persistent customer. It was a long, tense stretch for *Tang.* O'Kane kept his bow pointed to the tin can; the conning tower party listened carefully to learn if the enemy increased its pinging, which would indicate *Tang* was in their echoes. It seemed like hours to O'Kane, but *Tang* outwaited the escort, which gradually moved away.

O'Kane soon learned the reason for the destroyer's lingering presence. A periscope glance picked up a big ship heading *Tang's* way. As it came closer, O'Kane could see the decks lined with sailors in white. It was a naval transport, with three escorts. This was a really choice target: the *Tsukushi Maru,* 8,155 tons. *Tang* readied for a shot.

O'Kane ordered the three forward torpedoes fired.

"All hot, straight, and normal," soundman Caverly reported.

At Signalman Ogden's count of "thirty seconds," first one, and then a second blast rocked the target and *Tang.* Two torpedoes hit, one just forward of the bridge, the other in the superstructure. The transport quickly settled under the surface with a 20 percent down angle, and disappeared into the waves. O'Kane had Fraz and Chief Ballinger view the fast-sinking ship for visual confirmation. O'Kane ordered *Tang* to clear the area. The escorts were slow to drop depth charges, which were well astern as *Tang* went deep.

*   *   *

By this time, *Tang*'s patrol track on the chart table was showing a confusion of criss-crossing lines, testifying to O'Kane's
policy of putting at least 100 miles behind the submarine
after each attack. This was a tactic, O'Kane thought, that
would provide additional safety for *Tang*. It also served to
confuse the enemy anti-sub warfare forces. O'Kane hoped
the enemy would believe there were other U.S. submarines in
the area and disperse their forces accordingly. Murray Frazee
suggested that *Tang* had certainly carried out ComSubPac's
orders, and their patrol endorsement should read: "Excellent
area coverage is indicated."

As the off-watch officers gathered in the wardroom, the
conversation turned to the behavior of the destroyer that had
kept them at periscope depth so long that morning, August 23.
While O'Kane was a stickler for learning what went wrong
on an attack, he found that doing the same for what went
right was more fun, and instructive. In the discussion, he encouraged junior officers to add their views.

"Maybe she never did train her sound gear far enough aft,"
Mel Enos suggested. "As I remember we were almost con-
tinuously on her quarter."

Dick O'Kane picked up on Enos' suggestion. "I figure she
had a fixed sonar and was searching by maneuvering in lazy
circles," the captain added. "We stayed on the inside keeping
our bow to her, and as Mel said, never did get off her quarter
for any appreciable length of time nor into a forward sector
where she could have obtained an echo."

Dick Kroth asked: "Could it have been just a fathometer
we heard?"

O'Kane hadn't considered that, but thought it plausible. A
fathometer was just a vertical echo ranger. Its pings would
sound the same and could drive a submarine out of position
just as effectively as horizontal echo ranging—and might
even make a contact. Whatever the case, O'Kane decided the
failure of the destroyer to make contact would remain a
pleasant mystery.

Underwater just after daylight, *Tang* sighted a convoy
moving close to the shore. Examination by periscope showed

two freighters with four escorts, one forward, one aft and
two abeam of each freighter. O'Kane guessed the escorts
guarded the convoys from point to point along the coast,
turning their charges over to other escorts as they left the
sector. *Tang* worked her way in to intercept the track of the
freighters and get inside the seaward escorts. On O'Kane's
next sighting, he saw *Tang* would have to move inshore another 1,000 yards for a proper shot, but there were five escorting vessels in view, poised in an arc between *Tang* and
deep water.

"Fraz," O'Kane said as Jones lowered the scope, "this situation stinks!"

Frazee replied by pointing his thumb in the direction of
the open sea.

O'Kane decided to break off the approach. He ordered
Tang seaward in a great, descending helix, under the patrol
craft and toward the safety of the deep. O'Kane analyzed his
unusual decision not to attack. His was always a calculated
risk. This risk, he decided, was not worth taking. He thought
the enemy suspected *Tang*'s presence, the water was far too
shallow for defensive measures, and he would have expended
his last three torpedoes. Japanese anti-sub vessels were already in place and waiting to take counter-measures. Dick
was going against his usual audacious style, but retreat had
its place in battle, even for an intrepid submarine like *Tang*.
They would fight another day.

As *Tang* cruised through the night, Dick O'Kane sat
drinking coffee and considering new tactics. He didn't think
they'd been used before by U.S. submarines so he hoped his
plan would come as a surprise to the Japanese.

O'Kane ordered *Tang* submerged and moved to within
1,500 yards of the rocky promontory around which shipping
traffic would have to sail. Hardly had she got into position
then patrol vessels showed up. A low-flying Japanese air patrol announced the arrival of shipping. Two freighters came
over the horizon, but they turned into a bay shielded by escorts. O'Kane decided to wait and see. The tension was getting to the crew. In his cabin, after turning over the conn to
Fraz, O'Kane switched on the speaker by his ear and heard a

voice from the control room grumble: "Jesus Christ, I wish the Old Man would get rid of these three goddamned torpedoes!"

The patrol boats, which were pinging with their sound gear, moved off. O'Kane returned to the conn and took a look through the scope, hoping to catch the merchantmen they had been screening. He spotted two masts and a long hull in a passing rain squall. The range was 8,000 yards. Using his new tactic, O'Kane moved *Tang* inshore of the oncoming target, which was identified as a heavily loaded tanker, *Nanko Maru,* with five escorts loosely scattered around. O'Kane turned *Tang*'s stern, with the three remaining torpedoes, toward the target. It was a delicate maneuver, and involved avoiding an offshore island.

Finally O'Kane heard Frazee's confident voice. "Any time, Captain." He was at the firing panel.

Quartermaster Jones raised the scope. O'Kane found the tanker in his scope wire. "Fire!" he said.

Fraz pushed the firing plunger. O'Kane fired two more torpedoes. Caverly reported them running smoothly. Ogden counted the seconds until impact. "Torpedo run 40 seconds," Frazee said. The crew listened intently to the conning tower dialogue over the intercom system.

The first two torpedoes hit the tanker, blasting out the entire stern. The third torpedo hit an escort, breaking her up. As the other Japanese escorts milled about, O'Kane ordered *Tang* to head for deep water and rig for depth charge.

As the boat ran for cover, depth charges plummeted down, but well astern. Larry Savadkin took *Tang* down in a long glide, all the way to 500 feet and safety.

The Japanese anti-sub forces were now alerted and kept echo ranging, seeking *Tang.* As night set in, she went to periscope depth. Then the moon rose and Larry Savadkin gingerly brought *Tang* up. O'Kane spotted a dark cloud about to cover the bright moon. As soon as it did, *Tang* surfaced fully and the whole crew cheered. *Tang*'s escape was assured, the enemy searchlights astern lost in the rain squalls.

In the lively discussion over a steak dinner in the wardroom, O'Kane said the inshore attack would not become

standard operating practice on *Tang,* but he thought it a prac-
ticable tactic off a deep-water promontory in Japan's front
yard. The attack set-up, O'Kane argued, was less dangerous
than trying to approach from seaward. An inshore-side attack would come as a surprise, and the boat was in position
to shoot torpedoes and head for deep water before the escorts could get organized for a counterattack. It wasn't a
comfortable feeling being underfoot of a convoy, backed up
against the beach, but it was more effective—and safer.

That night the torpedo gang selected the movie *Flying
Down to Rio* with Fred Astaire and Ginger Rogers. O'Kane
couldn't decide whether it was played because the crew
thought it one of his favorites—or because of the subliminal
message in the title. O'Kane got the message.

Tang's patrol was short; she still had plenty of diesel fuel.
Dick O'Kane pleased the crew by ordering a full-speed run
to Pearl Harbor with no refuelling stop at Midway. It was a
long way from peacetime steaming practice at the most eco-
nomical speeds, but the all-out dash for home was actually a
safer way to return. Dick thought it improved the war effort
by making *Tang* ready for another patrol that much sooner.
Since her first patrol, including refits, *Tang* had averaged one
enemy ship on the bottom every twelve days, at several million dollars a copy. *Tang* would save three days in running
for the barn. That would justify the added expenditure of
diesel.

Heading home, O'Kane didn't slow *Tang* down with the
daily trim dive, which would have given up the equivalent of
5 or 6 miles. Instead he devised a "dunk" dive. This began
with the usual two blasts of the diving klaxon, but as the ship
went under, and the OOD called "decks awash," O'Kane
sounded three blasts for surfacing. He was satisfied that *Tang*
was buttoned up and could go down. The dunk dive took
only 4 minutes instead of the usual 20. O'Kane thought the
dunk dive fun. The crew loved it.

On the bridge, Bill Leibold, who had made Chief Boatswain's Mate in July, reflected that his captain showed a mas-
tery of night surface attacks. O'Kane thought things out well
ahead. He always had an escape route in mind. The skip-

per was a marvellous tactician to watch in action. Captain O'Kane might sometimes be hard to understand, Leibold thought, but after four war patrols he was sure he would rather go to war with the skipper than with anyone else. Below in the engine room, the confidence in the skipper was seconded. Clay Decker thought O'Kane always had a smile when the crew needed one, and no bullshit. The captain left the ship's detail to Frazee and Ballinger and that's the way it should be. Floyd Caverly sensed O'Kane gave everyone the feeling he knew what he was doing, that he knew how to get out of tight spots. The crewmen had come to admire their skipper.

O'Kane posted the arrival date for Pearl—0900, September 3—in the messroom. The crew ate lavishly. Chief Ballinger ordered the extra steaks be cut up and taken off the ship in Pearl for a big fry-up at the Royal Hawaiian.

Tang was right on schedule, after only thirty-four days on patrol. Captain O'Kane noticed two other U.S. submarines on the surface behind *Tang* and off to the quarter, heading toward Pearl Harbor still some miles distant. The first boat began signalling with a flashing light: "FORM ONE EIGHT." This was a signal instructing *Tang* to fall in directly astern, 180 degrees, of the sending submarine. The signaller turned out to be Hank Munson, captain of *Rasher* finishing up a fine war patrol. He travelled from Midway with *Pompon*. Since Munson was senior officer of the three skippers, he was insisting on a sort of seagoing parade into Pearl's Submarine Base—with himself in the lead. Dick O'Kane was having none of this stuffy, peacetime protocol. He told signalman Ogden to play dumb. Ogden returned Munson's instruction with, variously, IMI (repeat), INT (interrogatory, I don't understand), and JIG (verify and repeat) as *Tang* poured on the coal to disappear over the horizon.

In O'Kane's view, *Tang* kowtowed to no one. Hank Munson was reported to be furious. Dick O'Kane couldn't have cared less.

CHAPTER NINETEEN

The Hottest Boat

The band at the Submarine Base turned out to welcome *Tang*—her crew in freshly washed dungarees and white hats—along with the assorted SubPac brass on the dock. *Tang*'s reception was warmly congratulatory. Dick O'Kane believed he had sunk five ships and damaged two. Admiral Lockwood credited *Tang* with five ships down, and awarded another Navy Cross to his favorite skipper. The post-war JANAC accounting reduced this to two ships, but the authoritative summary of historian John D. Alden raised *Tang*'s total to four ships confirmed sunk. *Tang* was a leading scorer in the Sub Force, but Dick O'Kane was equally proud that fifteen crew members, through their studies supervised by Murray Frazee, achieved a higher rating at the end of the patrol, while eighteen newcomers became "qualified for submarines."

As for the dicey tactics requested by Admiral Lockwood—but considered overly dangerous by some skippers—Captain Charles F. Erck, Commander, Submarine Squadron Four, in his endorsement of *Tang*'s patrol, praised O'Kane for his pioneering inshore patrol as targets grew scarce. He declared: "The evasion tactics employed by the Commanding Officer allowed penetration of shoal water for attacks on coast-wise and anchored shipping with excellent results. As the wide-open sea areas diminish by reason of further U.S. Naval conquest, it is incumbent upon all submariners to develop the tactics of attack and evasion in shoal water. The tactics used in this patrol point the way." Admiral Lockwood enthusiastically endorsed the report, declaring that Captain O'Kane "sought out enemy traffic with daring and skill."

Dick was happy to find on his return that he had been promoted to full commander—three stripes on his sleeve and scrambled eggs on his visor. O'Kane then called on Captain Erck for some bittersweet business. Murray Frazee was due for relief as his executive officer, after an overall total of eleven war patrols. O'Kane strongly recommended Fraz be given command of his own boat, preferably after a tour at the Prospective Commanding Officer's school at New London. This would give Frazee a well-earned, long break in the States with his wife and family. Further, O'Kane thought Fraz's hard-earned knowledge would rub off on others at PCO School. O'Kane pointed out to Erck that an officer to replace Frazee was already aboard *Tang*. As if to underline that fact, a blast from the waterfront caught Captain Erck's attention. It was *Tang* backing away from her pier to enter the nearby floating dry dock. Just then Frazee walked into the squadron commander's office.

"Who has the conn?" O'Kane asked in mock surprise.

"Oh, Mel Enos is backing her down," Frazee replied, "but Frank Springer will be putting her in dry dock, of course."

"You certainly have confidence in your executive officers," Captain Erck remarked, and with the use of the plural, implicitly approved O'Kane's request that Frank Springer relieve Murray Frazee as *Tang*'s exec.

Frazee informed O'Kane that there were plenty of volunteers to fill vacancies for crewmen transferred off: *Tang* had acquired a reputation as the hottest boat in the Pacific Fleet. While at the Submarine Base, O'Kane did some horse-trading. He promoted some crewmen. In cases where he wanted to promote a man but the complement did not call for a higher rating, he switched the men temporarily to the Sub Base to get their rate, and then quietly took them back aboard at the higher rate. O'Kane liked to move men up to get them higher pay and insure that their next-of-kin received a larger allowance. O'Kane's wheeling and dealing impressed Larry Savadkin: he viewed it as an example of how the Old Man looked after his people.

Dick and Fraz arrived at the Royal Hawaiian in good spirits. One topic of conversation was the second war patrol of

Parche, under Lawson "Red" Ramage. After his confrontation with Admiral Christie in Perth while skipper of *Trout,* "Red" Ramage returned to the U.S. and new construction as Commanding Officer of *Parche.* Following a first successful patrol when Ramage sank two good-sized marus in one day, Admiral Lockwood assigned *Parche* to a three-boat wolf pack with *Steelhead* and *Hammerhead* operating in the Luzon Strait. The commander of the wolf pack was Lew Parks, ex-skipper of *Pompano* who was now a division commander. The pack was dubbed "Parks' Pirates." He rode in *Parche* with Ramage. The two veteran combat submariners did not hit it off. Slade Cutter, who knew Parks well, thought the trouble was that two strong personalities were trying to run the same ship. Parks was giving Ramage a hard time with his backseat driving; the wolf pack commander simply couldn't keep his nose out of Ramage's business. The "Commodore" was on board in theory only to give overall tactical orders to the three boats. To skippers like Cutter and O'Kane the fractious relationship that could develop between a skipper and a wolf pack commodore was a good argument for giving command to the senior skipper, rather than packing along a supernumerary senior officer. For that matter, neither O'Kane nor Cutter developed any enthusiasm for the wolf pack concept itself.

The situation between Parks and Ramage was aggravated by lack of enemy contacts. The two officers had words. Ramage thought Parks was needling him. Possibly because of the prodding, Ramage took on a large Japanese convoy early on July 31, 1944. Steaming on the surface at night, he first tried to swing around the escorts to get at the big ships, but the convoy changed course heading at *Parche.* Ramage bored directly into the convoy and began firing torpedoes at tankers, a transport, and destroyer escorts, maneuvering wildly through the enemy ships. At one point, "Captain Red," steering *Parche* as if she were a PT boat, cut under the stern of a tanker, purposely staying in close so the enemy deck guns couldn't train down on the submarine.

"The whole place was alight with gunfire," Ramage noted.

"Everybody was shooting at everybody and anything. But nobody could see us going through at 20 knots." An escort tried to ram *Parche* but Ramage managed narrowly to avoid it. Bridge crews of both ships screamed at one another. There wasn't room for everyone topside, and Ramage ordered, "Clear the bridge," including Commodore Parks. Ramage remained topside to conn *Parch* with his quartermaster as lookout. Enemy escorts opened up with their guns. In forty-six minutes, Ramage fired ten torpedoes, a full load from bow and stern tubes, at various ships. Sweating torpedomen reloaded as *Parche* twisted and turned. Ramage fired the remaining nine fish. He believed he had sunk four ships and damaged at least one. After the action was over, Admiral Lockwood credited *Parche* with five vessels down. He also credited *Steelhead* with two ships sunk in the same action. Ramage believed *Parche* probably sank ships attributed to *Steelhead*. The post-war accounting gave *Parche* only two confirmed ships sunk that night. *Parche* shared one or two ships down with *Steelhead*. This was no record patrol, but the wild and woolly surface action convinced SubPac staff that Red Ramage deserved more than a Navy Cross for his heroics. With Lew Parks' favorable endorsement, Ramage was put in for a Medal of Honor, which was approved, the first to be awarded to a living submariner. Parks got a Navy Cross.

As was customary, SubPac Chief of Staff Merrill Comstock wrote Ramage a letter about the patrol, which reflected the tightrope skippers treaded between being too cautious and too rash. "This was foolhardy, very dangerous and an undue risk," Comstock said, adding, "I guess it's okay as long as it came out all right. You got away with it but don't do it again. That isn't exactly what we expected you to do."

In an ironic footnote, on his next patrol Red Ramage drew a blank. Ramage ruefully thought every skipper should go through that humbling experience.

During O'Kane's fourth patrol, *Flier,* which had grounded at Midway, departed Fremantle on August 2, aiming for the waters off Indochina. On the night of August 13, *Flier* was moving through Balabac Strait, between northern Borneo, and the Philippines island of Palawan, running on the surface. At 2200 the boat was wracked by a thunderous blast. Captain John Crowley on the bridge and several others were injured. Men grappled their way up the ladder behind him. Air rushed out behind them followed by the sound of flooding compartments. *Flier* had struck a mine. She sank within 60 seconds.

Thirteen survivors, including Captain Crowley, found themselves in the water. They began a desperate nighttime swim to the nearest land, which appeared to be the coral reefs to the northwest. At first they tried to remain together, but the swift tide tended to break up their group. Two badly injured officers, Lieutenant William L. Reynolds and Ensign Philip S. Mayer, drifted off. Lieutenant Paul Knapp separated from the group and disappeared in the night. The moon rose at 0300, which helped the remaining swimmers to see each other and orient themselves toward the north. The weaker swimmers, like Lieutenant John E. Casey, blinded by oil and salt water, drifted off in the night to their deaths. The next day, Commander Crowley, Lieutenant Jim Liddle, Ensign A.E. Jacobson, Chief Radio Technician G.A. Howell, and Motor Machinist's Mate E.R. Baumgart found a floating palm tree and managed to hang on, pushing it to Manatangule Island after fifteen hours in the water. There they found Quartermaster J.D. Russo, Fire Controlman D.P. Tremaine, and Motor Machinist's Mate W.B. Miller, who had made the island independently, swimming all the way.

The survivors lived like Robinson Crusoe castaways for five days. They constructed lean-tos of palm leaves and caught shellfish in the inlet. With driftwood they built a raft and worked their way from island to island, reaching the long, narrow island of Palawan at the western edge of the Sulu Sea. There they made contact with friendly natives who guided them to a U.S. Army coast watcher unit on Palawan. *Redfin,* commanded by Cy Austin, had landed the coast watchers some weeks previously. They learned that Manning Kimmel, skipper of *Robalo,* had been sunk by a mine, too, and was a POW of the Japanese. (He did not survive captivity.) The guerrillas contacted Australia and made arrangements for *Redfin* to return and rescue their submarine colleagues. Early on August 31, *Flier*'s eight survivors in small boats were picked up by *Redfin,* and after a sometimes harrowing passage landed safely in Australia.

The *Flier* episode had an awkward sequel. Because there were survivors, an official inquiry was held. Admiral King in Washington named Commander Submarines Atlantic Fleet, Rear Admiral Freeland Daubin, to head the investigation. Commander Crowley, whose ship had sunk, was technically a defendant. He named as his counsel veteran submariner Herb Andrews of *Gunard* fame, who was now on Admiral Christie's staff. Commander Andrews got the impression that Admiral Daubin was manipulating the inquiry to get Admiral Christie's job by showing he was negligent in assigning his subs to mined areas. Admiral King, too, was bothered with the way Daubin was conducting the inquiry and complained to his naval aide, submariner Dusty Dornin, "Goddamnit, I sent Daubin out there to get facts, not to get in a pissing contest with Christie. I ought to relieve them both."

Commander Crowley was exonerated. Christie ordered the Balabac Strait off-limits to his submarines.

The sad story making the rounds of the officers' bars was the loss of *Harder,* and its highly regarded skipper, Sam Dealey, a soft-spoken, mild, unassuming officer. A member of the Texas publishing family, Dealey had a quiet career until he took over command of the new boat *Harder.* In short order, he rang up a series of fine patrols, operating out of Australia under Rear Admiral Christie. He made a name for *Harder* with his daring attacks, specializing in hitting destroyers, a most dangerous occupation. His boat's motto was "Hit 'em *Harder,*" and Sam Dealey was known as the "destroyer killer."

On his fifth patrol in May 1944 from Fremantle, Dealey had a passenger: base operations officer Captain Murray Tichenor, who hadn't made a war patrol and decided to join the boat as an observer. Submarine captains didn't appreciate senior officers going along for the ride. Dealey was asked to pick up some guerrillas on the coast of Borneo, a task he did not relish, since he thought submarines were basically misused in special operations.

In a stunning patrol, *Harder* sunk three Japanese destroyers to add to the one Dealey torpedoed on his previous patrol. He fired at two more destroyers and thought he had sunk them, but was mistaken. Sam Dealey also picked up a half-dozen Allied intelligence officers in Borneo.

Dealey returned to Darwin. The crew was exhausted, and was looking forward to topping off the fuel tanks and running down to Fremantle for an eagerly awaited refit period of relaxation. At Darwin, however, they found Admiral Christie at the dock. He had planned to make his second war patrol on another submarine, but the boat was delayed for repairs, so Christie requested Dealey that *Harder* go out on a "supplementary" patrol, with the Admiral aboard, taking the place of operations chief Murray Tichenor. The crew was bitterly disappointed at having to turn around and go out again, according to Admiral Lockwood. "They felt they had done a tough job and that a speedy return to the rest camps was indicated," Lockwood said.

The supplementary patrol was a bust. The target was a large ore carrier, which picked up nickel in the Celebes about once a month. Alert escorts kept *Harder* underwater and the "nickel ship" got away. *Harder* returned empty-handed in this anti-climax addition to a great patrol.

Dealey was dead-tired. Christie planned to send him home after his five patrols; it was up to Sub Force leaders to determine when a skipper became affected with "burnout." Lockwood made sure Slade Cutter went back to the States for rest after four top-scoring patrols as skipper of *Seahorse.* Dealey was certainly ready for a rest. Frank "Tiny" Lynch, a huge man who was regimental commander at the Naval Academy, was *Harder*'s exec; he could easily fleet up to skipper. But Dealey vetoed the idea, arguing that Lynch should stay on the beach for a "blow" during *Harder*'s sixth patrol since he, too, had five patrols on *Harder.* Then he could take over as commanding officer. Dealey was staying at Christie's comfortable quarters in Perth, so the Admiral could keep an eye on him to judge whether he was fit for patrol number six (or six-and-a-half).

Sam Dealey then got innocently caught in a bureaucratic spat involving the top officers in the Southwest Pacific. Paying a courtesy call on General MacArthur, Admiral Christie mentioned he'd accompanied Dealey on *Harder*'s fifth patrol extension. MacArthur said he wanted to award them both Army medals. Christie pointed out that when MacArthur earlier mentioned presenting Army awards to submarine captains, Christie put forward Walt Griffith on *Bowfin*. MacArthur said he never received the recommendation; Christie suspected Admiral Kinkaid had intercepted it. MacArthur then declared he was presenting Dealey with the Distinguished Service Cross (the Army's equivalent of the Navy Cross), and Christie with the Silver Star. When word got back to Admiral Kinkaid, he fumed over Christie's maneuvering around him.

Christie decided that Sam Dealey was fit enough for a sixth patrol. *Harder* Exec Tiny Lynch was not so sure. "Sam was showing unmistakable signs of strain," he said. "He was becoming quite casual about Japanese anti-submarine measures. Once, on the previous patrol, I found Sam in a sort of state of mild shock, unable to make a decision."

Promised a job at the Submarine School on his return to the U.S., Sam Dealey set off on his sixth patrol, leader of a three-boat wolf pack with *Haddo* under Chester Nimitz Jr., and *Hake,* with Frank Haylor. *Harder* was credited with sinking two ships before encountering an escort fiercely dropping depth charges on June 24. Dealey was never heard from again. After searching for days, Chester Nimitz radioed: "I must have to think he is gone."

The loss of Sam Dealey, who had sunk seventeen ships, among them four destroyers and two frigates, was deeply felt throughout the Submarine Force, perhaps mourned second only to Mush Morton. It caused further friction between Ralph Christie, and Admirals Lockwood and Kinkaid. Some Lockwood staff officers believed Christie had needlessly extended *Harder*'s grueling fifth patrol, and should not have kept Dealey in command for a sixth.

When he learned *Harder* was overdue and presumed lost, Christie recommended Sam Dealey be awarded the Medal of Honor for his fifth patrol. Admiral Kinkaid replied that, since MacArthur was already awarding the Army Distinguished Service Cross to Dealey for that patrol, he couldn't be awarded a Navy decoration for the same action. Christie was livid. He asked MacArthur to rescind the Army award so that he could recommend Dealey for the Medal of Honor. MacArthur agreed.

Then Christie, in an action some thought close to hara-kiri, sent Kinkaid a low-priority code message, which most everyone could read: "YOUR ENDORSEMENT THAT NO NAVY AWARD BE GIVEN DEALEY IS A VERY SERIOUS BLOW TO THE SUB-MARINE SERVICE PARTICULARLY IN VIEW OF *HARDER*'S LOSS. EARNESTLY REQUEST RECONSIDERATION." Kinkaid, the senior admiral, replied coldly: "I CONSIDER YOUR [message] INAP-PROPRIATE AND UNNECESSARY."

To many in the southwest Pacific, it seemed Ralph Christie had become upset because he allowed Sam Dealey to go out on the final patrol. Christie was thrown, too, by the loss of *Robalo* and *Flier* from his command at the time. Kinkaid, in turn, may have blamed Christie for the loss of *Robalo,* whose skipper Manning Kimmel was the son of the Pearl Harbor commanding admiral, Husband Kimmel, and was Tom Kinkaid's son-in-law.

Eventually, Christie pressed his case in Washington and Sam Dealey was awarded a Medal of Honor, which was presented to his widow.

In a poignant encounter in September, a wolf pack with *Pampanito* (Commander Paul E. Summers commanding), *Growler* (Commander Ben Oakley), and *Sealion II* (Commander Eli Reich) attacked a convoy of ships loaded with valuable oil and raw rubber. The group included *Rakuyo Maru* and *Kachidoki Maru,* which were sunk. Unknown to the U.S. skippers, the ships also carried some 2,000 British and Australian prisoners-of-war, who were crammed in the holds and were being shifted to Japan. Many had been forced to build the infamous "Bridge on the River Kwai" in Thailand. Four days later, moving through the area, *Pampanito* spotted survivors and picked up seventy-three men. *Pampanito* called in three other boats to assist in the rescue. *Sealion* picked up fifty-four men, *Queenfish* (Commander Charles Elliott Loughlin) rescued eighteen, and *Barb* (Commander Eugene Fluckey) took aboard fourteen men. The Japanese picked up more than 1,000 Allied POWs. The rest were lost. The survivors were elated at being saved and finding themselves free men again. They even volunteered to enlist in the U.S. Navy and serve in submarines.

In Pearl Harbor, Dick O'Kane said farewell to his valued friend and exec Murray Frazee. They had become close personally and professionally, but Murray was due for a long rest. "We had been through much this past year," O'Kane reflected, "and with results that neither of us could have accomplished without the other. The skipper–exec was a unique relationship in submarines but I was blessed." Dick O'Kane sensed with Frank Springer as exec, the captain and *Tang* would be blessed again.

Tang had patrolled at a record rate; her turnaround-time was the shortest of any boat in the Submarine Force. Dick O'Kane seemed able to find targets, sink them, and return home for more torpedoes. Fraz thought Dick was single-minded about sinking ships and killing Japs. Not all the crewmen were thrilled by the shorter periods in port, and the additional periods of action, but O'Kane knew that after the next patrol *Tang* would be due for a long, stateside overhaul. That should mightily please his hard-working crew.

After this patrol, Dick himself was also due for a long break, either staff duty ashore or assigned to new construction. He had made ten war patrols. Admiral Lockwood worried about keeping top skippers in action too long. He saw what happened to Mush Morton and Sam Dealey, who may have burned out. He took Slade Cutter off *Seahorse* after four terrific patrols as skipper and sent him home for a long rest and new construction. O'Kane privately thought he might serve in a new role, directing sub-air lifeguarding and rescue on SubPac staff or with a carrier task force.

As O'Kane prepared *Tang* for her fifth patrol, he was among the most decorated officers in the Navy: three Navy Crosses, the Legion of Merit, three Silver Stars, the Commendation Ribbon, two Presidential Unit Citations, and battle stars for ten war patrols. Dick made sure that his crew received their share of medals, among them a third Silver Star for Murray Frazee; Silver Stars for Frank Springer and Quartermaster Sidney Jones; Bronze Stars to Chief Motor Machinist Robert MacDonald, Chief Torpedoman Leland Weekley, now Chief Signalmen Earl Ogden and Floyd Caverly; and commendation ribbons to Torpedoman James Montgomery, Motor Machinist George Robertson, Chief Electrician's Mate Joseph Kivlen, Radioman Charles Andriolo, Boatswain's Mate Raymond Aquisti, and Ship's Cook Frederick Wixon. With recommendations submitted as a result of *Tang*'s last patrol, O'Kane believed his ship led all others in personal and unit awards. No submarine captain was prouder of his ship or men.

At SubPac headquarters, O'Kane conferred with Admiral Lockwood. Uncle Charlie asked his favorite skipper whether he wished to join a wolf pack or go out alone. O'Kane opted for patrolling solo and was assigned the Formosa Strait. He hadn't changed his opinion that boats could do better on their own, rather than being tied down to a pack leader and his movements. He thought any spark in a wolf pack, which could encourage pack mates, had to come from within, rather than from a pack leader. He noted that only one wolf pack had sunk more ships than *Wahoo* and *Tang* did when they were alone in the Yellow Sea.

Lockwood asked how soon *Tang* would be ready for patrol.

"Four days, sir," O'Kane said. "But there is one thing I request."

"Yes, Dick."

"Admiral, *Tang* has been banging out patrols at nearly twice the customary rate. Most have been short, but so has every upkeep. My ship needs a new radarscope, and I need something to take back to my crew. I'd like our next upkeep scheduled for Mare Island."

"I appreciate what you say, and I'll take care of it," Lockwood said, extending his hand to seal the bargain.

Murray Frazee had mixed feelings about leaving *Tang*. He was tired and needed a rest—he had made eleven combat runs, way above par—but he loved *Tang*. As exec, he had with Dick welded the crew into a proud ship, famous within the Silent Service. He watched O'Kane take over *Tang* and, through rigorous training and expert tactics, create a fine-honed fighting machine, probably the best, ton-for-ton, in the United States Navy. He and Dick brought off the war's best war patrol.

Fraz remembered being slightly put off at first by Dick's single-minded manner, but he had come to admire, respect, and have a fondness for his captain. He remembered O'Kane losing his temper only once when Frazee as navigator was unable to get star sights on a dark night with no horizon. "Get some goddamn stars," O'Kane snapped, "or I'll get someone who will." The two officers never spoke of the incident again.

Dick O'Kane, Fraz had soon learned, was competitive and wanted *Tang* to do well—and be recognized for it. O'Kane worked his officers hard but stuck by them. Fraz believed that Dick was a hard-charger, but never crossed the line into recklessness. As far as Fraz was concerned, the more you got to know Dick the more you realized that under the sometimes abrasive exterior, he was a pleasant, patient, and generous man. They had become cribbage partners; Frazee was amused at how O'Kane hated to lose. Fraz shared the captain's suite at the Royal Hawaiian and O'Kane included him in all social events to which he himself was invited. Their wives were friendly; they went out to dinner together when they had the chance.

Leaving *Tang,* Murray Frazee was proud of his friendship with Dick O'Kane, whom he thought a striking-looking officer with a commanding presence. O'Kane was abrupt at times, and not a diplomat. He was a maverick, Fraz thought, and an American original. Fraz departed sensing he left a more mature Dick O'Kane, a brilliant tactician, and a complex mix of toughness, fairness and loyalty. He said goodbye, not knowing that *Tang* was embarking on a patrol that would make history.

CHAPTER TWENTY

"Let's Head for the Barn"

Captain O'Kane readied *Tang* to depart four days early. As he set out on patrol with eighty-seven men aboard on September 24, he received Vice Admiral Lockwood's fond farewell. O'Kane knew the expectations of the ship's company continued to increase. The constant flow of new hands in no way lessened this, for *Tang*'s reputation spread—indeed, it was the reason sailors sought billets aboard. O'Kane thought he must maintain *Tang*'s fine name; and if possible better her previous performances as a fighting ship. But the submarine war against the Japanese was at the high-water mark. So proficient were the fleet boats that Japanese targets were harder to come by. Subs' bags were dropping and even first-rank skippers came back empty-handed. By now, advance sub bases were established west of Midway at Majuro in the Marshall Islands, Guam and Saipan in the Marianas.

Tang topped off diesel tanks at Midway. The wardroom lost Charley Pucket there, but gained Lieutenant (j.g.) Paul Wines, a tall, athletic reservist from Ridgewood, New Jersey, and Lieutenant John Heubeck, from Baltimore, Maryland. Larry Savadkin moved up to third officer and senior watch officer; O'Kane trusted him completely. Bill Leibold, now Chief Boatswain's Mate, was working in as prospective Chief of the Boat. After trim dives heading westward, O'Kane was satisfied that he had a first-class team.

Then a personal mishap occurred. O'Kane was inspecting the boat to make sure it was secure for the heavy weather in prospect when his attention was momentarily distracted, and he fell through an open-deck plating into the lower engine room, about 5 feet, breaking his fall on the bottom rung of the ladder. The impact fractured his left foot. In great pain, he was helped up and taken to his stateroom. Chief Pharmacist's Mate Paul Larson took a look. With his hands, he straightened the foot—another sharp burst of agony for the skipper.

"You've got some small broken bones, Captain," Larson said. "I can feel them but they're pretty straight now—and one hell of a sprain. There's nothing they'd do ashore that I haven't done except to take some X-rays and I already know about what they'd look like."

O'Kane was relieved. There was no question of returning to port. Lying on his bunk, his ear next to his intercom, and his foot stretched out, he would command from that unusual post. Frank Springer took over in the conning tower and directed *Tang*'s passage through the Bonin and Volcano Islands, diving when Japanese planes appeared.

A few days later, the worsening weather developed into a violent storm, verging on typhoon strength. O'Kane ordered the ship buttoned up and conned slowly on the surface on batteries. Doc Larson gave his captain a pain-killing shot in the foot. O'Kane struggled to put on an oversized field boot, laced tightly to bind his broken bones. Chief Larson and Frank Springer helped O'Kane into the control room, and prepared to bring him up the ladder to the conning tower. O'Kane was worried about the mountainous seas. The storm caused *Tang* to roll sharply, almost 70 degrees. For a dreadful moment, O'Kane wondered if *Tang* would recover. "Jesus Christ," he said, "is she ever coming back?" Losing his balance, Frank Springer landed on the open switchboard. The 110-volt current shocked him as he tried to get clear. Springer responded cheerfully to O'Kane's question: "Sometimes they don't, Captain."

Tang recovered, but then rolled twice more to 60 degrees, before righting herself on the surface. Springer helped pull the captain up to the conning tower. Quartermaster Jones raised the periscope to full height. With the lens of the "high" periscope 55 feet above the sea, O'Kane stared at a single, monstrous wave blowing spume from wavelets on its crest. He was astonished at its size. Instinctively, O'Kane ducked and green water roared over the superstructure. The weight of it was like a solid force that buried the submarine. The captain was amazed that the periscope wasn't torn away—Jones quickly lowered it.

O'Kane soon realized the storm had escalated to typhoon strength, greater than the one that engulfed *Wahoo* a year previously. *Tang* was in the dangerous semicircle of the tempest. "It was a sight such as none of us had witnessed before," he noted.

The on-watch team managed to maneuver to a course that got *Tang*'s roll down from 45 to 20 degrees. Larry Savadkin reported that the crew had wedged themselves between bulkheads, equipment and bunks; they could only remain in their bunks by clutching the railings tightly.

Tang was in a perilous situation. It was too late to dive, and in any case, O'Kane hesitated to submerge in these seas because the ballast tanks might flood unevenly, contributing to the instability of the boat. O'Kane decided that *Tang* must turn in front of the mammoth seas and cut into them, instead of being pushed toward the Ryukyu Island chain. This meant risking foundering while broadside during the turn. O'Kane made up his mind.

"All ahead standard," he ordered.

Chief Marvin De Lapp, watching the inclinometer, called out: "Twenty-five degrees."

A wave hit *Tang* and the boat rolled badly, but O'Kane thought the list was acceptable.

"All ahead full," he ordered. "Right full rudder."

Tang responded and rolled through the trough. As she turned, another huge wave struck her on the starboard bow, knocking the ship around. But the wave action failed to stop the swing to a new reverse course. "All ahead two-thirds," O'Kane said. "Ease the rudder to fifteen. Meet her. Steer two-one-zero."

The typhoon was still dictating *Tang*'s course, but now it was not pushing her into the dangerous islands. She was pitching up and down wildly, but not rolling so dangerously. Doc Larson reported no injuries. O'Kane chalked that piece of news up to the fact that, for a submarine lying low, a steep roll was much slower than the whip of a surface ship. It was easier for crewmen to handle their balance. O'Kane privately thanked Frank Springer for continuing his inspection tour after the captain broke his foot. The ship's gear had all been tightly secured; nothing broke loose to cause injury to crewmen or damage to equipment.

For five grim hours, *Tang*'s best steersmen worked in pairs, with the engine order telegraph close at hand, using their muscles to keep *Tang* heading into the seas: they were coached by O'Kane and Springer with the OODs manning the scope. Then suddenly, *Tang* found herself in huge swells, with torrential rain, but the wind had moderated. Were they in the eye of the typhoon or at its edge? O'Kane ordered the conning tower hatch cracked to get a new outside barometer reading: 28.4. That meant, O'Kane saw with relief, that the typhoon was moving on, leaving *Tang* behind in relative safety. Dick O'Kane was impressed with his ship and crew: she was the toughest submarine in the world.

As operations normalized, O'Kane figured that the typhoon had carried *Tang* about 60 miles off course; he was thankful they had been no closer to the Ryukyus. Quartermaster Jones consulted his notebook. He had recorded periods when the periscope had been completely underwater, the longest being 14 seconds. By Jones' recordings and with the help of calculations by the OODs, they estimated that a minimum of 40 feet of sea had rolled above the lens of the extended periscope, which was 55 feet above the normal surface. O'Kane thought an accurate measure of the highest waves therefore was 95 feet, trough to crest. He estimated the winds reached 150 miles an hour. *Skate,* which also endured the typhoon, made the same estimate for wind strength and wave height.

Once back on track, *Tang* headed for its patrol area, carefully skirting known minefields, and lookouts sighted the towering mountains at the northern tip of Formosa. Two hours later, off the capital port of Taipei, *Tang* spotted a target. "Range seventeen thousand, and closing," came the word. O'Kane thought he had the choice of seeking a night surface action, or doing an end-around and submerging for a dawn torpedo attack. Chief Leibold helped the captain, who found he could walk on the heel of his boot with less pain, topside to the bridge. O'Kane followed *Tang*'s tracking of the target, which was developing into a good-sized, zigzagging merchantman. He thought that as morning twilight was coming up, a submerged attack would be preferable.

"Clear the bridge," was followed by two blasts of the klaxon and *Tang* went under. Larry Savadkin trimmed the boat. Floyd Caverly tuned in the target's screws with the Sherman Clay metronome. O'Kane brought the boat up to raise the surface radar reflector. Ed Bergman on the radar showed the target zigging toward shore.

O'Kane ordered: "Make ready tubes One, Two, and Three forward, and if there's a wide zig, tubes Seven, Eight, and Nine aft." He tracked the cargo ship in the periscope lens, waiting for the ultimate zig. It came. This was the firing leg. The target would never zig again, at least not horizontally.

"Stand by for constant bearings," O'Kane said. "Up scope."

"Constant bearing—mark!"

"Set," said Mel Enos.

"Fire," O'Kane ordered.

Exec Springer pushed the firing plunger. O'Kane launched two more fish. The run was 47 seconds. Two hits! The freighter *Joshu Go* exploded and quickly sank stern first. O'Kane took a second look. Only the tilted bow was above the surface and he could see no survivors, only flotsam with what appeared to be empty, half-swamped landing craft.

O'Kane ordered the crew to take a break. He was pleased with reservist Frank Springer's performance as exec and would recommend him qualified for submarine command when they returned to Pearl Harbor.

Before the day was out, *Tang*'s periscope lookout reported another Japanese ship sighted. "Head for him, Hank," O'Kane told Lieutenant Flanagan.

Steward Walker brought O'Kane a cup of coffee. "We going to get this one, too, Captain?" Walker had become like a shadow to his skipper. O'Kane nodded. *Tang* launched into a long chase. The target hugged the Formosa coastline heading south, but *Tang* followed underwater at some distance seaward. O'Kane worried that the boat's battery can would be depleted before a firing position would be reached. A possible shot before nightfall was thwarted by planes overhead. In the evening O'Kane surfaced and gave chase, but progress was slow, since two of *Tang*'s engines were needed to recharge the batteries. O'Kane worked abeam of the target, pulled ahead, and into position for a night surface attack. The set-up was textbook.

The target was alone. O'Kane fired only one torpedo at the freighter *Oita Maru,* but was prepared to back it up with a spread. The fish slammed into the vessel's side and exploded with an enormous roar, the torpex apparently blowing up the ship's boilers. Steam and fire rose skyward. The coastline was illuminated by the blaze. O'Kane invited the fire control party to the bridge for a look. They hadn't much time before the target hissed and went under.

In reply, anti-aircraft guns on the nearby coast opened up. O'Kane was content to allow the enemy to think their assailants were planes from China. In the middle of the night, a couple of Japanese patrols forced *Tang* to seek deeper water away from the coast. O'Kane ordered the crew to take a long rest; they were still worn down by the typhoon and battle stations for two successful attacks.

Then radar picked up a large target and O'Kane looked it over. He noted it had illuminating cargo lights, which showed a white hull, a green stripe and a huge red cross—the markings of a Japanese hospital ship, but Larry Savadkin said he couldn't see the difference between an enemy ship and an enemy hospital ship. O'Kane replied calmly, "We play by the rules, Larry." He did not chide Savadkin for suggesting otherwise. Chief Ballinger summed up the crews' reaction: "Aw, the bastard's probably transporting 10,000 troops, all with athlete's foot."

Tang moved south toward the port of Tsusho. There the crew watched a strike on the island by the planes of Admiral Halsey's Third Fleet. *Tang* had orders to stand by as a lifeguard for the attacks on Friday, October 13, but no downed aviators were spotted.

After a couple of days without sighting enemy ships, but with plenty of planes overhead showing up on radar, O'Kane felt more hunted than hunter. He planned to take *Tang* around the northern tip of Formosa to patrol off the port of Kiirun on the Pacific side of the island. Hardly had they arrived when a priority dispatch came in that evening: "TASK FORCE PROCEEDING NORTH ALONG CHINA COAST." *Tang* reversed course and headed at full speed back to China, to a destination called Turnabout Island, where shipping headed west for the big port of Foochow. There, *Tang* picked up a Katori-class cruiser and two escorting destroyers heading south. *Tang* pulled in behind the Force, which was zigzagging. This enabled *Tang* barely to keep up, but the enemy force presented a stern target: the slow electric torpedoes would have a very difficult time overtaking the cruiser, which at best did not present a good target position. O'Kane's best hope was to catch the cruiser during a sharp zig, when his electric fish had a chance of hitting.

As he tried to keep up with the Katori captain's clever zigs, Boats Leibold lightened the tension on the bridge with the crack: "I just never expected to be maneuvering with enemy warships!" O'Kane thought grimly that it was nice to have someone around who could see the lighter side of *Tang*'s predicament. She was running out of darkness. As the cruiser kept zigging, O'Kane planned a desperation "up-the-kilt" shot from behind. The captain readied for firing, but Frank Springer said, "They wouldn't reach him, Captain. I've held up the maneuvering order." O'Kane agreed with Frank. The slow electrics couldn't catch the speeding cruiser. Then a battery of searchlights snapped on aboard the enemy ships, and O'Kane thought *Tang* might have been spotted.

"Clear the bridge," he ordered, and *Tang* dived to evade. The cruiser group sped on into the lightening sky, leaving O'Kane frustrated beneath the sea. He was cheered, however, by the optimistic response of his young officers.

"I wonder what that cruiser's captain would do if he knew that five times in a row he'd missed getting six pickles in his side?" Dick Kroth asked. "And a half-dozen up the fanny," Paul Wines added. *Tang* had done her best in the long, strenuous, dangerous chase, O'Kane reflected, and she still had her torpedoes. That was enough. Next time he would not be without the faster steam torpedoes in the forward tubes. O'Kane took a quick turn through the boat to congratulate the crew for an exciting chase that almost paid big dividends.

O'Kane picked up a destroyer escort patrol in stormy weather, with the seas rolling over *Tang*'s bridge. The heavy seas and the escorts' zigs made a successful approach unlikely. When the range closed to 2,500 yards, as if by mutual consent, the DE reversed course and high-tailed it away. So did *Tang*. O'Kane thought he was as happy as the Japanese skipper at the outcome.

A little more than twenty-four hours later the word came from the conning tower, "We've got a convoy, Captain." Floyd Caverly picked up perhaps ten ships on his radar heading *Tang*'s way. O'Kane was excited. The night had time to run, and there appeared to be no nearby port to which the convoy was heading. The radar pips seemed to be separating into five larger ships with five escorts, a submariner's dream, thought O'Kane. There were three large tankers or freighters in column, a transport on the starboard hand, and a freighter on the port, flanked by destroyer escorts.

Steward Walker was ready with O'Kane's cup of steaming coffee. The captain was satisfied with his set-up: in front of the convoy with Boats Leibold and Chief Jones on the bridge as well as four lookouts, and the OOD, John Heubeck. The freighters were riding low in the water, filled with supplies, high-priority targets. The convoy was zigzagging, and Jones and Frank Springer in the conning tower were figuring out a base course. *Tang* was inside the escort screen, dropping back among the major ships. Springer reported all forward torpedo doors open. O'Kane picked out his targets.

"Any time now, Captain," Springer said.

Just after midnight, October 23, Dick O'Kane fired two torpedoes at the first enemy vessel. He shifted targets to get three more fish in the water at two other enemy ships before the first salvo hit. The maximum range was 800 yards. Explosions racked three Japanese ships.

Chief Quartermaster Jones reported: "They all hit as we aimed 'em, Captain. They're on fire and sinking."

Frank Springer asked for another target bearing for the last bow torpedo. O'Kane peered into the target bearing transmitter, but Bill Leibold, O'Kane's "extra eyes," grabbed the skipper and pointed. A transport in the fiery night had sighted *Tang* and was heading toward the submarine to ram it. It was too close for *Tang* to dive. *Tang* had to cross her bow. O'Kane rang up flank speed and hard left rudder. The maneuvering room laid on emergency power: never had so many amperes poured through *Tang*'s motors. Small arms fire from the transport crackled overhead. So close was *Tang* that a rifleman on the transport's deck would have had to lean over the rail and shoot straight down. *Tang* almost brushed the transport, the two vessels passing in opposite directions at the combined speed of 40 knots. The submarine was in the middle of a rousing free-for-all. O'Kane was about to dive when he noticed the transport had to turn to avoid running into a freighter. Suddenly O'Kane had two targets for the stern tubes as the two Japanese ships collided. He fired a quick salvo of all four stern tubes, and focused on two Japanese escorts steaming ahead on both sides of *Tang*'s bow. The sky lit up as the four stern torpedoes hit the transport and freighter. The last detonation set the escorts firing at one another. The confusion was understandable and complete. The escorts were milling about looking for survivors.

Tang's radar screen was clear and Dick O'Kane ordered full speed to sweep the area for more targets, and then clear Formosa Strait to the north. He had downed four ships, freighters *Toun Maru, Tatsuju Maru,* and *Kori Maru,* and the transport *Wakatake Maru,* and badly damaged another in the convoy.

Tang's wardroom and crew were ecstatic. It was one of the most dramatic and successful attacks on a convoy during the war. O'Kane and his officers figured out the night's sequence from the Quartermaster's Notebook: 1 hour and 20 minutes for the approach and positioning; only 20 minutes for penetrating, shooting and pulling out; a 40-minute sweep to clear; and an hour's run northward.

As *Tang*'s crew relaxed and the boat settled in on the prowl, O'Kane instructed that the understudies for all key positions on the boat were to take over so that they could continue the breaking-in process. He suggested the crew enjoy a rare afternoon movie.

Just before lunch the next morning, Larry Savadkin reported the masts of patrol vessels at the horizon and changed course to avoid them. O'Kane approved—no point taking on these pesky, dangerous patrol craft when there were much bigger fish in the pond. Larry Savadkin, O'Kane thought, would be a gold mine to any skipper in a new assignment. He thought Savadkin's presence on board was like having a second executive officer, somewhat like Commander Mort Lytle on his PCO patrol.

For his part, Larry Savadkin was impressed by O'Kane's style. He thought Dick was a shrewd Yankee, who never went anywhere with *Tang* if he didn't have two ways to get out. That's what made O'Kane such a great skipper.

Dick O'Kane limped through the boat, chatting with the men, and offering congratulations. Without question *Tang* was now the number one submarine in the Force. The captain posted a list of awards for the previous patrol which he had recommended in Pearl Harbor: Ed Beaumont, Mel Enos, and Chief Ballinger for Silver Stars; Murray Frazee, Chief Electrician's Mate James Culp, Chief Motor Machinist's Mates Albert Hudson and Marvin DeLapp for Bronze Stars; Commendation Ribbons for Fire Controlman Emil Brincken, Torpedoman John Foster, Electrician's Mate John Kanagy, Radiomen Fred Schroeder and Edwin Bergman, and Motor Machinist George Zofcin. Dick admired Fraz for requesting a lesser award so that someone else could get a Silver Star, since he already had three.

After lunch, Frank Springer dropped by Dick O'Kane's cabin to discuss the next action, and their conversation drifted to the nature of submarine command. They agreed that skippers of U.S. surface warships in those days simply carried out orders, including maneuvering and firing, from their task group commander. Few had the freedom and latitude that submarine commanders did. O'Kane observed that such freedom brought with it heavy responsibility. Men volunteered for a demanding and tough task when they entered the Submarine Service. War brought about the need to put aside normal humane considerations in commanding a combat submarine: you could not waver in your aim to put enemy ships on the bottom, whatever that meant in terms of human lives lost. That was what being a submarine commander in war was all about. O'Kane said, and Springer agreed, that superb commanders and friends—like Slade Cutter, Dusty Dornin, Eli Reich and many others—would not let doubts get in the way of their task. It was not just a task but a duty in war to use their daring to sink enemy ships, whatever the obstacles.

The captain and exec decided to head back to the vicinity of Turnabout Island to see what the pickings might be there. Nearing the China coast, O'Kane heard a report from radar. "We've got another convoy, Captain, range thirty-five thousand, and the navigator says there's no hurry."

O'Kane made sure his boot was firmly fixed on his broken foot. He ordered *Tang* to close the convoy, which was heading their way. The time was 2300, October 24. The attack party was in place: Captain O'Kane and OOD Lieutenant Heubeck on the bridge with Boats Leibold and Chief Jones on either side. Above them were four lookouts and a man in the crow's nest, including Radioman Andriolo, Gunner's Mate White, and Gunner's Mate Rector, who had had his appendix out on *Seadragon*. Below, Frank Springer and Larry Savadkin worked the conning tower. Floyd Caverly took over on radar and reported many ships in the convoy.

It was the largest concentration of ships O'Kane ever encountered, strung out in an elongated formation. Several ships carried planes or crates of supplies on their decks. The formation was heading south to reinforce Japanese troops on Leyte in the Philippines. O'Kane ordered the general alarm sounded for Battle Stations Surface. The convoy rounded the eastern side of Turnabout Island with escorts to the seaward side. The range was down to 9,000 yards as *Tang*'s fire control party was able to sort out the ships from the island's background.

O'Kane identified a leading ship as a large two-stack transport. He decided to get in quickly and fire before the enemy was alerted. O'Kane knew the Japanese had finally put a good radar on their ships, and the chance of discovery was high. As *Tang* neared, the lead ship signalled with a flashing light and 36-inch searchlights were turned on. This only served to help *Tang*'s attack party make out ships more clearly. *Tang* was in position to fire at the three-deck, two-stack transport, the second tanker and another one behind. Dick O'Kane thought *Tang*'s best chance was to dispatch as many torpedoes as possible, disrupting the escorts' view of the situation and any counterattack.

O'Kane peered through the binoculars on the target bearing transmitter. The crosshairs were between the ship's two stacks. He waited for the transport's mainmast to cross the reticule.

"Fire!" he commanded. The electric torpedo was on its way. O'Kane ordered a second fish launched at the transport. Then he shifted his sights to the next transport in column. "Fire!" A third torpedo sped toward the Japanese ship. He quickly ordered another fish dispatched. O'Kane then focused on the third target in the column and he fired two electrics at the tanker. They exploded and broke the vessel's back, setting the wreckage ablaze. The 7,000-ton *Matsumoto Maru* went under.

The escorts began firing wildly. A mad mêlée ensued with *Tang* running and weaving down the reverse course of the convoy, firing torpedoes and dodging return gunfire. For the second time in twenty-four hours, *Tang* was boxed in among the ships of the convoy and angry escort vessels, but O'Kane's expert handling saved her from destruction. Below Frank Springer was pleading with Chief Electrician Culp for more speed as O'Kane maneuvered sharply. "To hell with the overload," Springer ordered. "Pour on the coal."

Tang fired her stern tubes at the ships behind her at ranges of 600 and 700 yards. The escorts shot back. Explosions lit up the sky. Fires burned on the sea. *Tang* cleared the immediate turmoil amid the sinking 7,000-ton *Ebara Maru* and damaged ships. At 5,000 yards distance, *Tang*'s torpedomen carefully checked the last two torpedoes and reloaded them in the forward tubes. The submarine was still untouched, the enemy fire passing overhead. O'Kane could see the transport had been damaged but was still afloat. It was now past midnight, early morning on October 25. O'Kane ordered *Tang* to approach the damaged transport slowly and quietly at 6 knots. The submarine's bow was pointing directly at the transport, which was now much lower in the water, but was not sinking. The escorts had departed to guard the rest of the convoy. The torpedo set-up was textbook—range 1,000 yards.

"Stand by below," O'Kane commanded. The time was 0230 hours.

"Ready below, Captain," Springer reported.

"Fire!" The electric's phosphorescent wake sped straight ahead, 900 yards to the target.

Tang had one more torpedo left. Twenty-three fish had worked perfectly. Richard O'Kane was now determined to put the transport under, once and for all. He would fire the second fish before the first one hit. Then he would order *Tang* to head for the barn, for safety and glory, after one of the most dramatic submarine patrols of the war.

Larry Savadkin was on the torpedo data computer. There was no rush, no particular excitement in the conning tower. Larry matched the pointer on the computer with the data. Everything tracked fine. *Tang* was going to finish off this ship. He heard the first fish hit.

"Fire!" O'Kane commanded from the bridge.

From below someone yelled happily: "Let's head for the barn."

In the forward torpedo room, Pete Narowanski said, "Hot dog. Course zero-nine-zero, head her for the Golden Gate!"

The bridge party watched closely in the dark. They had seen and heard *Tang*'s first torpedo hit the transport but to their horror, the final torpedo broached above the sea. Phosphorescence in its wake showed it turning sharply left. It began porpoising above and below the surface, moving in a circle. *Tang* was threatened by her own torpedo! A dreaded circular run!

"All ahead emergency!" O'Kane shouted. "Right full rudder!" This was his desperate attempt to push *Tang* outside the erratic torpedo's turning circle. The jammed fish was 20 yards directly off *Tang*'s port beam and turning toward the 300-foot submarine. There were only seconds left to escape.

Boats Leibold, dumbfounded, still thought *Tang* would get past the torpedo's turning circle. He thought Captain O'Kane would make it. "Left full rudder!" O'Kane ordered, hoping to fishtail *Tang*'s stern clear of the oncoming missile. It would be close.

Abruptly, a devastating explosion ripped *Tang*'s stern. Twenty seconds after firing the errant torpedo hit the submarine on the port side aft between the torpedo room and the maneuvering room. O'Kane's sharp maneuver kept the torpedo from hitting amidships. The stern of the submarine went down instantly, the three after compartments flooding, before the bridge party could react.

O'Kane saw there was no time to clear the bridge. He ordered, "Close the hatch," to protect the conning tower below, but it was too late to carry out the order.

As the *Tang*'s stern went under, the bow flipped up, throwing the men on the bridge into the dark waters of the Formosa Strait. Captain O'Kane was tossed into the ocean. As he struggled to stay afloat, Dick was almost overcome by a deep feeling for those in the water facing the sea, and for those in the submarine below.

CHAPTER TWENTY-ONE

The Incredible Escape

Dick O'Kane, a strong swimmer, found himself floating away from the others in the water. He swam and tread water. He was alone, but later that night found a plank of wood, part of a ship's door, to hang on to. In the water, the bridge crew had quickly become separated in the darkness and swirling current, which seemed to change direction frequently. The powerfully built Bill Leibold was cool-headed and a good swimmer. He heard Sidney Jones and Darrel Rector calling to one another in the water. They seemed to be paddling, but Leibold decided against swimming off toward the China coast. It would mean struggling against the current. He merely floated alone, wondering what would come next. After a while, he saw Floyd Caverly, and they managed to stay together.

Caverly had been in the conning tower manning the radar when the torpedo hit. The blast knocked out the radar and sonar and the ship's power. Exec Frank Springer told him, "Get up there and tell the Captain what the situation is." Caverly clambered up the ladder to the bridge, through the hatch that hadn't been closed, to report to O'Kane. That move saved his life. Once on the bridge, Caverly, too, was washed overboard into the sea. Just before he was thrown into the water, Caverly saw a lookout, Radioman Charles Andriolo, hanging on to the guardrail. His binoculars were around his neck. He told Caverly he couldn't swim. Though every U.S. sailor was presumed to have passed a swimming test in boot camp, some slipped through without taking the exam. Andriolo remained inside his railing on the periscope shears, seemingly frozen there. He went down as the bridge

sank under water. In the sea, Caverly took it easy: he was not
a great swimmer but was in good physical shape, having
been a boxer.

Caverly passed closed to Gunner's Mate White. Attempting to swim, White asked Caverly the direction of the nearest land. Caverly told White he didn't know, and was struck
by a touch of black humor: the closest land was only 180 feet
away—but it was straight down. Caverly calmly took stock:
he remembered looking at the chart; *Tang*'s position was
10 to 15 miles from the China coast and offshore islands. He
floated on his back and checked the North Star. He now
knew which way was west. Then he suddenly saw Lieutenant
John Heubeck, the OOD.

"Who are you?" Heubeck gasped.

"Caverly, sir."

"Which way is land?"

Caverly told the officer he thought the China coast was
10 miles away. Heubeck had been a swimmer at the Naval
Academy and struck off, apparently heading for China. Caverly never saw him again. A bit later, Caverly found Leibold.
They agreed the current was too strong for swimming anywhere and decided to float with the tide. The two sailors
stuck together through the night—the only ones from the
bridge who managed to do so.

When the errant torpedo struck, Larry Savadkin was operating the torpedo data computer in the conning tower, standing near Radioman Edwin Bergman, who was manning the
sonar. Savadkin sensed *Tang* was in extremis. Suddenly, he
was thrown against a bulkhead as the ship tilted sharply
down by the stern. Water was pouring into the conning tower
and down into the control room before the hatch was closed
from below. The rushing water and steep deck angle knocked
people down and they were washed around in a tangled mess.
The lights in *Tang* were out. Savadkin grabbed the smooth
sides of the periscope. "What a hell of way to die!" he
thought. His head popped up into an air pocket. He could
breathe, but he wondered how long the air would last. Did
one really fall peacefully asleep and feel no pain before suffocating? Was drowning more painless than suffocating? But

his mind was alert. He had to do something—because staying put wasn't going to get him home.

Larry ducked under water and felt around to try to figure out where he was in the conning tower. At first, he sensed that *Tang* was upside down; she had turned turtle. He didn't want to go the wrong way, and wind up in the pump room. He wanted the bridge. Larry touched a knob which he recognized as the engine order telegraph. That meant he was in the forward part of the conning tower near the ladder and hatch to the bridge above. He reached upward, grabbed the ladder, and felt the edge of the hatch. He pulled himself up through the hatch to the bridge, planning to make his way to the surface holding his breath. Savadkin emerged into another air bubble, which he figured was under the cowl of the bridge. That gave him time for another long breath of air and the opportunity to think clearly.

The head of a sailor popped up in the dark.

"Who is it?" the sailor asked.

"Mr. Savadkin. Who are you?"

"Bergman."

Ed Bergman asked Larry Savadkin, "Do you know where we are?"

"I think we're under the bridge cowling," Savadkin replied.

"What are you going to do?" Bergman asked.

Savadkin told Bergman he planned to get out of *Tang*'s superstructure and fight his way to the surface.

"Can I come with you?" Bergman said.

"Sure," Savadkin replied.

"How?"

"Hold on to my legs."

Larry Savadkin had no idea how far the surface was, and Bergman seemed confused, uncertain where they were headed. He grabbed Savadkin's trousers and hung on. Savadkin pushed off from the air pocket and began swimming with his arms. Along the way, Savadkin felt Bergman letting go of his legs. Larry was now committed and kept going up to the surface, while expelling his breath on the way up. He guessed it was some 60 feet or more, and knew that if you went up too fast with your breath held you could burst a lung. Just as it

seemed that Savadkin had exhaled all his air and desperately
needed to breathe in, or burst, he broke the surface. In fact,
his was the first case of a free ascent without a Momsen
Lung from a submarine.

On the surface, Larry Savadkin was alone. There was no
sign of Ed Bergman, but he could see the bow of *Tang* and
watched it descend into the sea. Savadkin thought he was a
long way from home. Recalling his survival training at officer's school, he got his trousers off, tied off the legs and
waist and fashioned himself an impromptu life buoy, like
water wings. Then, some distance away, he saw the bow of
the sunken Japanese ship. He thought he would try to reach
it to hang on, but the current coming through the Strait was
too swift. Occasionally he yelled out, but there was no reply.
He thought he was the only person to get off *Tang* alive.

Swimming seemed futile so Savadkin floated on his back,
shivering in the water. He could see the stars. Then he noticed an island he believed he might reach and treaded water
toward it, but the strong current carried him in a different direction. He heard depth charges and felt the shock waves,
arching his back to lessen the force of the explosions. There
was plenty of oil, debris, and some Japanese survivors in the
sea. In training Larry had jumped off a diving board into an
oil-covered pool and at the time his attitude had been "None
of this applies to me." Now, he knew how wrong he had
been.

Below in *Tang,* the personnel in the control room succeeded
in closing the hatch above to the conning tower—but only
after tons of water had poured through, and boiled down into
the pump room and the bilges.

One of the heroes of this terrible night was Clayton
Decker, a motor machinist's mate who was on duty in the
control room. During Battle Stations Submerged, he manned
diving planes near the chart table in the center of the room.
Decker had been in the forward engine room, which was his
Battle Station Surface. When someone called out "Battle
Stations Submerged," he moved into the control room. All
hydraulic and electrical power went out when the maneuver-

ing room was destroyed. *Tang* went to battery power, which provided dim light. The ship sank at an angle of about 45 degrees, stern stuck in the mud bottom, bow still exposed on the surface. Men were flying down through the conning tower hatch, head first, followed by rushing water. One sailor damaged his neck, another his spine. In the rough and tumble, Signalman John Accardy fractured an arm, another man broke a leg. Men struggled to close the conning tower hatch to stop the flow of water. The hatch lanyard got caught in the gasket and it wouldn't seat fully. Water kept coming through from the flooding conning tower, but at a reduced rate.

In the chaos, Decker thought clearly. The rear compartments were flooded, everyone presumed dead, so the only usable escape trunk was in the forward torpedo room. But with a 45-degree angle on the boat, the crew couldn't climb forward through two open watertight doors. They weighed several hundred pounds each and would have to be raised against gravity in order to close them once the crew passed through. Having qualified for his dolphins, Decker was familiar with the hundreds of valves, lines, and tanks aboard. Most of the hydraulic systems, he knew, had a back-up that could be operated by hand.

He recalled there was a long lever above the chart table attached to the overhead, a back-up that operated the forward ballast tanks. He knew *Tang* must get level on the bottom if crewmen were to have a chance to escape, and he could feel the stern of the boat already resting on the floor of the sea. There remained an outside chance for some of those aboard, but he had to flood the forward ballast tanks to put the boat on an even keel. There were no officers around to give orders.

Clay Decker climbed up on the chart table and lay stretched out on his back with his legs around a stanchion to brace himself. He reached up and grabbed the ballast tank lever, which was a couple of feet long, and like a broom handle. It was held in place by a pin. Decker pulled the pin out and with all the weight of his body, pulled the lever down. His actions opened the vent valves, which flooded the ballast tanks. *Tang*'s bow sank to the bottom levelling off in 180 feet of water. When *Tang* hit seabed, she rocked a bit and settled fairly evenly.

The way was now clear for the crew to move to the forward torpedo room and the escape trunk. Clay Decker was among the first from the center compartments of *Tang* to struggle to the torpedo room.

As the torpedo headed for *Tang,* Jesse DaSilva, a motor machinist's mate who was on duty in the engine room, entered the crew's mess to get a cup of coffee. He was standing between the crew's quarters and the messroom when the torpedo hit. The submarine whipped around violently, "like a giant fish grabbed by the tail," he thought. Someone dogged down the watertight door between the forward and after engine rooms, thus sealing off the rear three compartments of *Tang,* and the fate of their occupants. The boat was still upended and DaSilva, a powerful man, clutched a ladder to keep from being pitched off his feet. Forward motion was almost impossible. Water was pouring into the crew's mess from the control room. Together with a couple of mates, DaSilva wrestled shut the door from the messroom to the control room and dogged it down with a great effort. This effectively sealed off the messroom.

Japanese patrol boats above were charging around and dropping depth charges as DaSilva and about twenty men clung on in the mess. They knew that when the seawater reached the batteries below it would generate deadly chlorine gas, and decided their only chance was to get into the control room and to the forward torpedo room. They weren't sure how much water they would find. Earlier it had reached above the eye port in the watertight door, but now with the boat in a level position, the control room seemed clear.

Jesse wrenched open the rear door to the control room, as the men stood on the mess tables. Water rushed in, rising around their legs, but then it gradually subsided. One by one, the men moved forward. In the control room crewmen were destroying secret publications and records. Unfortunately, an officer began burning them in a wastebasket, which created acrid smoke; the men convinced him to put out the fire. DaSilva noticed the depth gauge was registering 180 feet.

There was still compressed air in the tanks and an attempt was made to blow the boat to the surface, but the air simply passed through ruptured tanks.

DaSilva and the others clambered past officers' quarters above the forward battery room into the forward torpedo room, with its sleeping berths. They carried injured shipmates forward in blankets. The quick-thinking Clay Decker jammed some of the half-burned secret documents into the top openings of the batteries. The sulfuric acid in the batteries ate away at the papers, destroying them.

In the torpedo room, somewhere between thirty and forty men were gathering. Many were injured, some badly. The air was foul, and the lighting became even dimmer as the batteries began to short out. Battle lanterns were turned on.

By the time Clay Decker reached the torpedo room escape procedures were beginning. They had been held up because of the constant depth charging: no one had ever tried to leave a submarine in the middle of underwater explosions. Everyone was given a Momsen Lung packed in celluloid. Every submariner in Sub School learned to use the Momsen Lung in the 100-foot escape tower in New London and in Pearl Harbor, but most never practiced the procedure again. Submariners stoically believed they would never have a chance to use it, since escape had to be made from relatively shallow water.

The procedure of escape by Momsen Lung was for four men at a time to enter the escape trunk, or chamber, and close the lower hatch to the torpedo room. The trunk contained gauges showing depth, and inside and outside pressures, and an air manifold to fill the Momsen Lungs. Sea water was slowly allowed into the trunk until the air pressure inside was slightly higher than sea pressure outside. The seawater then stopped entering, and the escape hatch—actually, a rounded, rectangular door—could be opened outside the pressure hull of the submarine. The men charged their Momsen Lungs with air.

A line with a buoy attached was then released, and extended to the surface. The men climbed out of the submarine through the escape door and made their way slowly up the line. When the last one was out, the escape door was closed using a lever inside the torpedo room. The water inside the trunk was then released into the torpedo room and down into the bilges, and the exercise repeated. That was the plan, and it worked well in New London, but ostensibly simple escape procedures can be quite different when lives depend on them, and few submarines ever practiced escapes from torpedo room trunks.

Things in *Tang* did not go to plan. Lieutenant Hank Flanagan, torpedo officer, was directing the escape from the torpedo room. Much time was spent in discussing alternate ways to get out. Some torpedomen suggested firing the surviving crewmembers from *Tang* out of a torpedo tube, but Flanagan argued that the air pressure during the shot would be fatal to a human. Besides how many of the broad-shouldered crew could fit in a tube only 21 inches in diameter? Others wanted to go back to the control room and see if they could get out through the conning tower. That idea was shot down when a quick investigation showed fumes in the forward battery room: no compartment aft of the torpedo room was habitable.

When the depth charging finally stopped, Lieutenant Mel Enos and two other men led the first escape, but this attempt became confused. Enos left the hatch before the buoy was released and the line attached. He was not seen again. The others stayed inside the trunk. They disagreed on the proper escape procedure and on how to release the escape line buoy. Valuable time was lost because of the delay: the men were reluctant to take action for fear of endangering their shipmates below. The men in the torpedo room took a half-hour or more to determine whether anyone had left. Of those remaining behind in the trunk, some did not want to try again. The failure of the first escape left some crewmen rattled.

A second attempt led by Hank Flanagan was also botched. The escape party became disoriented because the extra pressure was too strong for them. The sea pressure was 90 pounds per square inch while normal air pressure is only 15 pounds per square inch. It made their voices sound high pitched and almost inaudible. They decided to return to the torpedo room. Hank Flanagan nearly passed out, and had to be taken below. Precious time was wasted while the crew in the torpedo room waited for those in the escape chamber to clear it. The re-emergence of Flanagan, a submarine veteran and a tough mustang, left others in the torpedo room unsettled: they were fearful of attempting what their officers had been unable to accomplish, and they were puzzled as to what was happening because there was no communication between the torpedo room and the sealed escape chamber.

Chief of the Boat Ballinger led the next attempt, sometime around 0600. Ballinger called for volunteers. Clay Decker considered Ballinger a salty sea-dog who knew what he was doing. He stepped quickly forward. "I'm with you, Bill," he said. Decker grabbed his buddy, Motor Machinist George Zofcin, and pulled him with him. Zofcin had a small house in San Francisco, and their wives shared the premises.

"No, no," Zofcin protested.

"Let's get our ass outta here, George," Decker insisted.

"No, Clay. I've got to confess. I can't swim."

Decker found this hard to believe. A sailor who couldn't swim? In the submarine navy?

"Look, George, the Momsen Lung—when you close the mouthpiece—acts like a Mae West. You can hang on the buoy that's at the end of the line."

"Clay, you go now. I'll go with the next wave."

They unpacked the lung from the celluloid wrapper. There was an air release valve at the bottom of it that expelled air, but the new lung came with the valve closed by a small wire. Zofcin unfastened Decker's wire, which may have saved his life. Decker was reluctant to leave his buddy behind, but had to move up the ladder to the escape trunk. He was followed by two sailors he didn't know. George Zofcin pulled himself into a bunk and appeared to go to sleep.

Decker and Ballinger and the two others ascended the ladder to the escape trunk. Decker did not know whether Ballinger had unfastened the wire around his release valve. If the wire wasn't undone before the lung was used, the air could not be expelled and would back up into a man's lungs.

They closed the hatch below and flooded the chamber up

to their armpits. The air pressure became intense. When it equalized with the outside sea pressure, Ballinger opened the escape door. There was a buoy, constructed of light wood, and a long line knotted at regular intervals. Ballinger handed the line to Decker who began paying it out, the buoy lifting it to the surface. When Decker felt the line jerking he knew the buoy was bobbing on the surface. He connected the lower end of the line to a steel rung on the ladder to the pressure hull, and tied it in a triple knot. There was another complication: to get out of the escape door a man had to bend his head and clamber over the sill. This was easy enough in broad daylight, but in the pitch darkness of deep water, it took some doing for sailors under such pressures. There were several steps in the companionway ladder leading up to the submarine's decking, but in the blackness one could get hung up in the space between the pressure hull and the decking. Disorientation in deep water made it difficult to tell which way was up.

Decker calmly followed the drill as he remembered it and had no problem. He climbed out of the escape door first, got up the few steps of the ladder to the deck, and hung on to the line, moving up as he had been instructed in Sub School, pausing at each knot. He made it to the surface. He wiped his hand across his face and noticed blood, but he didn't feel pain. In his logical way, Clay Decker decided that he had come up a little too fast. Not fast enough to get the bends or a burst lung, but fast enough to break the blood vessels in his face. On the surface, he saw Chief Ballinger bleeding badly and flailing around. He appeared to be drowning and disappeared. Decker figured he had come up too fast, letting go of the line, or failed to remove the new wire from the release valve. In either case, he must have suffered a burst lung. Decker thought that Ballinger had the "bends," an extremely painful and often fatal condition that occurs when nitrogen absorbed into the bloodstream under high pressure is forced into lung tissues when the air pressure is too suddenly reduced. Clay Decker never saw the other two sailors behind them in the escape attempt. He hung onto the buoy, which had a lanyard stitched around the edges for a handhold in the water.

Below, things were in a mess. Those trying to escape found the Momsen Lungs difficult to unwrap and put on. The valves and connections were stiff and hard to work properly. Further, the lungs had no internal air supply—they needed to be connected to the submarine's air manifold to load them— and *Tang*'s oxygen supply was dwindling.

Torpedoman Hayes Trukke, well built, and knowledge-able about the Momsen Lung and escape techniques, led the next escape attempt to leave *Tang*. He entered the chamber with another torpedoman, Pete Narowanski, and two other men. Narowanski was a colorful character who was wearing swimming trunks and a loud Hawaiian sport shirt. Pete had stuffed a can of soup into his trunks. Trukke, not knowing the status of the escape line or the buoy, carried with him a life ring, a souvenir picked up from *Yamaoka Maru,* which *Tang* sank previously. He tried to fill his lung with air from the manifold in the chamber but found that it was dry. It needed to be replenished by a valve inside the torpedo room. He began to get dizzy, but remembered a description of the "free ascent" technique of rising to the surface. The other men in the chamber with him didn't want to escape with-out the necessary oxygen in their Momsen Lungs—though Trukke explained how it could be done. The principle was simple: air inhaled in the submarine was already compressed. As a man ascended, the air in his lungs expanded in response to lowering outside sea pressure. The expanded air was ex-haled on the way up. There was still enough air for a man's lungs as the pressure decreased.

Hayes Trukke decided he would get out while he could, still hanging on to consciousness. Holding the *Maru*'s life ring, he stepped out of the hatch onto the pressure hull and made his way up through the deck opening. He wore his Momsen Lung at first, but after he cleared the submarine, the lung got loose and fell off. So Trukke made a free ascent the rest of the way up, allowing his lungs to expel air as he rose. He reached the surface still holding the life ring. He was ex-hausted, sick and vomited for a half-hour, but he was free.

He heard Clay Decker calling to him. They tied the life ring to the escape buoy for added support.

Trukke's companions remained behind. Two climbed back down from the escape chamber, but Pete Narowanski stayed and waited for the next group to come up. By this time, the situation was very bad in the torpedo room. The gaskets in the watertight door to the forward battery room were leaky and smoke seeped in. Depth charging had started an electrical fire in the forward battery room, causing fierce heat, and further fouling the air. Men were coughing and gagging. Some appeared unconscious, and were lying in bunks.

There was no longer much interest in escaping. Some men who entered the escape chamber decided they couldn't breathe and climbed down the ladder. Others feared an error on their part would jam up the works and endanger the chances of those waiting to escape. By now in the torpedo room lassitude had set in, partly as a result of the heat, the pressure, and the lack of breathable air. As minutes dragged on, many of the men indicated no desire to escape, though they knew what the alternative was. Their conversation turned to thoughts of family and loved ones. The badly injured could not make the escape attempt. Chief Pharmacist's Mate Doc Larson did his best to bind up the wounds of the injured men, and one chief petty officer gave a pep talk about remaining calm and conserving energy. Then he climbed into a rack and just seemed to go to sleep. Some men appeared to prefer to die quietly in *Tang* rather than face the dangers of an escape attempt: the possibility of drowning on the way up or on the surface, or, worse, at the hands of the Japs.

However, a fourth escape party was organized. A revived Hank Flanagan joined Torpedoman Narowanski in the chamber, and called for two more volunteers. Jesse DaSilva, who had been waiting, said, "Hell, I'm not afraid to try." He climbed into the chamber with a crewman behind him, but the second man hesitated and stepped down. Another sailor took his place. The hatch to the torpedo room was closed, the flood valve opened, and the sea water began filling the chamber. It was hard to breathe but Jesse DaSilva got his Momsen Lung strapped on. The incoming water compressed the air in the top part of the chamber and finally stopped. The pressure was equalized. They wrestled the outside door open. The escape line was secured. DaSilva was third to go out, and when his turn came, he ducked his head under water, clambered out of the door, grabbed the ascent line, wrapped his feet around it, and started up in the pitch darkness. He understood why some shipmates might become disoriented and get tangled in the decking near the escape hatch.

DaSilva worried: how fast or slow to go? Remember to stop every 10 or 15 feet to allow the nitrogen in the blood to adjust. Take your time. What would be waiting on the surface? He went up 10 feet at a time, stopped and counted to ten, then continued. Finally the water grew lighter and DaSilva broke through the surface. He was surprised to see that there was a faint light in the sky. He had been in the submarine several hours since the explosion.

Hank Flanagan was already on the surface. The last thing he saw before leaving *Tang* was the bulkhead of the torpedo room peeling because of the heat generated by the fire in the forward battery room. He believed that the chances were against any more crewmen getting out. Pete Narowanski made it to the surface, too.

Jesse DaSilva was heartened to spot Clay Decker and Hayes Trukke hanging onto the buoy, treading water. Soon DaSilva saw two more heads bob up. Paul "Doc" Larson, the Pharmacist's Mate, and a steward's mate DaSilva thought was possibly Howard Walker, Dick O'Kane's favorite. DaSilva didn't remember their being in his escape party. They may have come up in a last escape group. Possibly they had left in an earlier attempt. Doc Larson was obviously in poor shape, blood pouring from his nose and mouth. Jesse and Pete pulled him over to the group at the buoy. Clay Decker hung on to him, and Jesse attempted to get him to cling to the buoy, which was the shape of an oversized basketball. Larson was only semi-conscious, probably dying. He had difficulty keeping his head above water. DaSilva thought he had come up too cold.

The steward's mate had apparently lost his grip on the line, for he surfaced some 50 feet from the buoy. DaSilva and

Trukke swam to reach him, but the sailor began flailing his arms wildly. His head went under the water and he disappeared, carried away by the fast-running current. DaSilva and Trukke swam to the buoy, linking up with Hank Flanagan, Pete Narowanski, and Clayton Decker, who was holding Doc Larson. Narowanski and Trukke could see the coast of China and thought they could swim to it. They struck off, but after some 25 yards or so, the current ran strongly against them and they swam back to the group around the buoy. Hank Flanagan thought as many as thirteen men may have got out the escape chamber. Hayes Trukke guessed the figure was nine, but no one was sure. There was never an accurate accounting of the men who left the escape chamber for the outside sea, nor who they were. Whatever the case, five men plus the dying Larson were left alive on the surface at the buoy.

It was an incredible escape: never before had any U.S. sailor escaped in wartime from a sunken sub. The fact that more did not reach the surface and survive could be attributed to the fact that submarine sailors tended to scorn the Momsen escape practice: it was almost a given that everyone would go down with a ship in combat. The unfamiliarity of the crew with the unused Momsen Lungs fresh out of their wrappers added to their ineffectiveness. The devices were difficult to work, particularly for crewmen weakened by cold, dark, fear, and shock. In fact, it was surprising that anyone made it out of a submarine 180 feet below the surface of the sea at night. It was a tribute to the stamina, fortitude and nerve of *Tang*'s survivors, men who behaved bravely under great pressure.

The six Navy men from the torpedo room hung on to each other and the buoys. Larson never regained full consciousness. They had no idea of how the men on the bridge had fared after the explosion. The sunken Japanese freighter's bow was about 500 yards away. Hank Flanagan and his shipmates hoped to wait until the tide changed, swim to the bow, salvage a boat or raft from the ship and make for the China coast under cover of the still poor light.

For their part, Boats Leibold and Floyd Caverly in the sea

out of sight of anyone else estimated they were about 20,000 yards, or some 12 miles off a little island near Foochow, but their own plan to head for China was spoiled when they saw a Japanese patrol boat picking its way toward them in the brightening day.

CHAPTER TWENTY-TWO

"Good Morning, Captain. Do You Want a Ride?"

The Japanese patrol craft assigned to look for survivors from *Tang*'s successful attack on the convoy inched through the waters of the Formosa Strait where the bow of the maru still protruded above the water. There were several figures bobbing in the oil-darkened sea. Among them were Bill Leibold and Floyd Caverly who had been swimming, or floating, in the open ocean for more than seven hours. The Patrol Boat, *P-34,* lowered a whaleboat over the side, with two sailors at the oars. It had already picked up a couple of Japanese in the water when the coxswain spotted Leibold and Caverly and came alongside. The two *Tang* sailors were hauled into the boat by the Japanese crewmen and set down on a thwart in the bow. As they looked at *Tang*'s men, the Japanese said several times, "Deutsch, Deutsch."

Caverly said to Leibold, "God, they think we're German." German specialists had ridden aboard Japanese ships, and U.S. forces in the Western Pacific sank a couple of German submarines. But soon the Japanese began to suspect that Leibold and Caverly were Americans, probably even submariners. Their view was confirmed a while later when the whaleboat sighted Dick O'Kane in the water, hanging on to a piece of wood, which appeared to be part of a door. He had been floating for hours, kept going by his determination to survive for the sake of his family. As the boat came alongside O'Kane, Boats Leibold leaned over and said: "Good morning, Captain, do you want a ride?"

The whaleboat coxswain seemed to catch the word "Captain." When O'Kane was pulled aboard, his fractured foot still hurting, he was placed in the transom seat in the stern,

traditionally the place of honor in a small naval boat. Leibold mentally kicked himself for addressing O'Kane as
"Captain." Then the Japanese sailors spotted Larry Savadkin,
still using his pants as water wings. He was quickly picked
up and the four *Tang* survivors were taken to the *P-34*.

The patrol craft moved slowly, searching for more Japanese survivors. The ship spotted the six Americans hanging
on to the buoy, and circled them several times. The vessel
then stopped and trained guns on the *Tang* survivors. Jesse
DaSilva watched carefully. "Well," he said to himself, "this
is where they are going to shoot us." Instead, the ship lowered a small boat into the water; sailors rowed over and
picked up the six survivors, including Doc Larson. Without
apparently giving it thought, the boat's coxswain tugged on
the line connected to the buoy. *Tang*'s crew didn't tell him the
line was attached to an American submarine. The Japanese
sailor then cut the line from the buoy—losing physical
contact with the submarine and any possibility for salvage.
"That was a relief," Leibold thought.

The boat rowed back to the warship. Decker and others
tried to help Doc Larson, but he seemed to be unconscious
and didn't respond. Hayes Trukke saw the Japanese sailors
try to revive Larson by slapping him but still he didn't move.
The men from *Tang* struggled up a rope ladder to the deck of
the patrol boat. Clay Decker was the last man up and looked
behind to the boat. He saw the Japanese sailors lift up Doc
Larson and throw him over the side. Decker didn't know
whether Larson was alive or dead.

As Floyd Caverly climbed aboard he looked closely at a
Japanese petty officer's wristwatch. It read 10:30. The sailor
punched Caverly in the mouth for his impertinence. The oncoming *Tang* crewmen were amazed to find their captain and
three other survivors on the forward deck of the *P-34*. The
nine men were all that was left of the proud crew of eighty-
seven who had manned the finest submarine in the Pacific
fleet. Dick O'Kane hoped that more of the survivors picked
up would be from *Tang*, but they were all Japanese.

The Japanese sailors tied the Americans' hands behind
their backs and ordered them to sit on the forecastle deck of

the ship, in the sun, on hot plates. The Japanese were angry with *Tang*'s survivors. They didn't know who they were but suspected they were an American submarine crew, the one that had caused so much havoc to the Japanese merchant marine in the previous few days. On board the *P-34* were survivors of *Tang*'s lethal handiwork. Many had been scalded by live steam from exploding boilers on their ships.

The Japanese crewmen and survivors aboard were equally rough on *Tang*'s crew. They would grab the U.S. sailors' hair, pull their heads backwards, and then stub out cigarette butts in their face and nostrils or throat. An officer hit *Tang*'s Caverly on the head with the broad side of his sword. *Tang*'s crewmembers, except for the man the Japanese now knew was "Captain," were kept out on deck in the blistering sun. It was about 95 degrees. Everyone was badly sunburned. The Japanese gave the men on deck only teacups with hot water, soda crackers, and a bit of rice. Some *Tang* sailors tried to drink their urine but found it no solution to their thirst.

During the day, the Americans were questioned singly. When it was Jesse DaSilva's turn, the Japanese took him to a cabin, sat him down between interrogators and offered him a ball of sticky rice. He could not eat it. One Japanese had an electrical prod and jammed it in DaSilva's ribs, causing him to twitch and jump. The Japanese laughed. An English-speaking Japanese carried a club the size of a baseball bat. He asked DaSilva questions and when he didn't like the answers, whacked him on the head. Once they had decided Jesse wasn't going to reveal much, the Japanese brought him back to the others on deck. *Tang*'s crew thought the questioners were amateurs at interrogation.

In the evening, the *Tang* men were stuffed into a tiny deckhouse on the forecastle, so small that most of the nine had to stand. It turned cold and the salt water splashing into the deckhouse exacerbated their bruises. The sailors exchanged rough notes on their escape.

In their conversations, Captain O'Kane was philosophical about his and his crew's mistreatment at the hands of Japanese sailors and survivors. He thought that when his men realized their clubbings and kickings were at the hands of burned and mutilated survivors of *Tang*'s handiwork, they would take it with less prejudice.

The *P-34* speeded up and headed for Takao, a port on the southwest corner of Formosa. The men from *Tang* were blindfolded as they entered the harbor, and driven to a jail, separated, threatened with beheading, and beaten. Worse for Dick were the mosquitoes, biting the men whose wrists were chained to a ring in the wall of the cell. *Tang*'s survivors were paraded around and laughed at. Children threw rocks and screamed at them. The next morning, the U.S. sailors were issued tattered white uniforms and put on a train for a day-long ride up the coast, past peasants tilling fields with oxen and hand-ploughs. Their journey ended at the port of Kii-run, which was at the opposite end of Formosa from Takao.

There they were thrown into a medieval, stone, Portuguese prison complete with massive wooden bars, a scuttle for food, a slit near the ceiling for light, and a hole in the floor as a latrine. To their surprise, an evening meal was shoved through the scuttle: hot balls of rice and fish wrapped in cane husks. It was the same food the guards ate. The men dubbed the jail the Kiirun Clink. They were given blankets, and were allowed to sleep, the first real rest they had had since before *Tang* sank. Much to his amazement, Larry Savadkin was handed a Popsicle, of all things, by a guard.

Shortly before dawn, a guard brought Popsicles to the crew. He said, "I am a Christian." Dick O'Kane never figured out what he meant. In a matter of hours, O'Kane and eight *Tang* crew were transferred and split up between two destroyers and a cruiser for the voyage to Japan. The Japanese Navy observed strict protocol with Captain O'Kane. There were side-boys as O'Kane boarded one of the destroyers. The captain, a lieutenant commander about the same age as Dick, offered O'Kane his cabin. There was a guard outside the door but from a porthole O'Kane could observe the ship's company going about their duties. He was impressed by the efficiency of the gun crews he watched drilling. He was also provided clothes and shoes, and meals.

The destroyer's skipper returned to the cabin in the evening and began a discussion with his prisoner-guest. The conversation ranged from naval tactics to literature. The Japanese officer pulled down a copy of *Gone with the Wind,* which he called *Went with the Breeze.* He said that if officials of both nations had read this story of the Civil War, Japan and the U.S. might have avoided conflict. Dick did not disagree.

"How is it, Commander, that you speak no Japanese but seem to understand my English?" the destroyer skipper asked. O'Kane replied that when he was at the U.S. Naval Academy Japanese was not a course, though now the language was on offer because of the war. The captain asked with feeling, "How could we, Commander, expect to understand each other's problems when you made no attempt to learn even a word of our language?"

The skipper departed for the bridge. Dick O'Kane, his mind seeking practical solutions to problems, considered *Tang's* circular torpedo run. He recalled that the torpedoes used in his destroyer, *Pruitt,* and his first submarine, *Argonaut,* had equipment specifically designed to prevent circular runs. But early in the war for obscure reasons the Bureau of Ordnance had done away with these safety devices. O'Kane suspected that *Tang* was not the only victim of her own torpedo. Other skippers had reported near misses from erratic fish, but sunken submarines rarely tell tales about their deaths. He thought it idiotic that submarine torpedoes did not have anti-circular run devices.

As the destroyer approached Kobe naval base, O'Kane, assured by the skipper that fresh clothing would be awaiting him ashore, returned the borrowed gear. He thanked his host, and asked his counterpart why it was that his crew had suffered such rough treatment on *P-34,* while receiving courtesies on the destroyer. "That ship and the escort force," he replied scornfully, "are not part of the Imperial Japanese Navy."

Dick O'Kane limped down the gangway. He was in Japan. His ordeal as a prisoner of war was beginning. He had shown his character and courage, annealed by combat in submarines. Now he faced a different challenge.

CHAPTER TWENTY-THREE

"Nobody Could Say I Was a Coward"

The Submarine Force was stunned when word spread that *Tang* was overdue and presumed lost. As Ned Beach of *Trigger* pointed out, word of a missing submarine did not come in a package; rather it circulated with bits and pieces surfacing here and there. Rumors first emerged from operations that a submarine was overdue and hadn't made contact with headquarters. Officers at submarine bases hoped that trouble with the radio transmitter might be the reason for the submarine's silence. A "blind" rendezvous with another sub was arranged for the missing boat by a radio instruction. If that didn't produce any results, an escort vessel was sent out from a forward base to scout for an incoming, overdue submarine. Only then did the grim truth become accepted. Only then was *Tang* listed as lost, her name taken off ComSubPac operations chart. As in all cases of lost submarines—unlike surface ships—there was no last-minute transmission from *Tang*.

Like other brave ships before her, *Tang* became the topic of talk in wardrooms and officers' clubs. She had become a Pacific War legend and her gallant skipper was widely recognized as the leading captain in the Submarine Force. "We knew only that she was gone," Ned Beach said of *Tang*, "leaving to the rest of us a legacy of consistent aggressiveness, success, and daring."

Japanese radio intercepts coming into the Pacific combat intelligence center indicated that O'Kane may have sunk more than ten ships on his last patrol, the highest ever patrol total of the war. Later JANAC figures reduced this to seven ships, which was still the third best patrol of the war, after

Dick O'Kane's own third patrol with ten ships sunk, and the Morton–O'Kane fourth patrol in *Wahoo* with nine. But historian John Alden's revised totals credit *Tang* with eight ships down on her last patrol. *Tang* sank more ships, twenty-seven, in its short career than any other U.S. submarine. Dick O'Kane probably sank more tonnage than any other skipper, although the figures vary slightly according to the source. His record of lifeguarding, saving twenty-two aviators, was bested by only one submarine, *Tigrone,* which picked up B-29 crews. O'Kane and *Tang* accomplished all this in only ten months in action. It was a dazzling record. No wonder that Vice Admiral Lockwood declared, "Commander O'Kane has, without a doubt, established himself as the most outstanding officer of the Submarine Force."

A day before *Tang* went down, the U.S. Submarine Force lost two other boats: *Shark II,* skippered by O'Kane's Naval Academy classmate, Ed Blakely; and *Darter,* captained by David McClintock. The loss of *Darter* was one of the more dramatic submarine stories of the war and involved sister ship *Dace,* under Commander Bladen Claggett. The subs were operating together as a two-boat pack, shadowing the Japanese main fleet, which was preparing to contest the vital U.S amphibious landings on Leyte by Admiral Kinkaid's Seventh Fleet, covered by Halsey's massive strike force, the Third Fleet.

Darter and *Dace* intercepted the main body of the Japanese fleet which was steaming from Brunei Bay in Borneo to Leyte Gulf. They filed contact reports to alert the admirals. Then in separate nighttime actions, *Darter* and *Dace* each sank a Japanese heavy cruiser; in *Darter*'s case, it was the fleet flagship *Atago,* 12,000 tons, whose commander, Vice Admiral Kurita, had to move his flag to another vessel.

Blad Claggett in *Dace,* thinking he was shooting at a battleship, let loose all six forward torpedoes. He sank the heavy cruiser *Maya,* 12,000 tons. Dave McClintock's *Darter* also severely damaged the heavy cruiser *Takao.* He spent much of the day with *Darter* at periscope depth, hoping to get in finishing shots at *Takao,* but Japanese escorts and search planes kept him down. *Darter* and *Dace* rendezvoused after dark and mapped a plan to launch another attack on *Takao,* which was moving slowly for her base in Brunei Bay, Borneo. But *Darter*'s navigator hadn't been able to get any navigational fixes for two days. He was operating in an area known as "Dangerous Ground," full of low-lying reefs and shoal water. McClintock and Claggett maneuvered for an end-around to sink *Takao* in the Palawan Passage. Then *Darter,* making 17 knots on the surface, ran hard aground on Bombay Shoal with a loud crash that some thought was a torpedo hit. Though he tried valiantly, McClintock could not maneuver *Darter* off the grip of the reef. The crew jettisoned excess weight and anything removable was thrown overboard. McClintock even tried rocking the boat, with the crew racing from one end to the other. High tide came at 0140, but *Darter* was stuck fast. McClintock reluctantly radioed Bladen Claggett, who broke off *Dace*'s planned attack and came to the rescue of her sister ship. Claggett knew he could be criticized for not following up his successful attack, but he never gave it a second thought. *Darter* was in peril, and that was that. Had *Darter* been left alone, her crew would most probably have been taken prisoner and possibly executed. Certainly, the enemy would have obtained valuable documents and gear. McClintock ordered all confidential documents destroyed— as well as radar, sonar, and torpedo computer gear.

Dace maneuvered alongside during the night, and with a rubber boat making several trips, hauled off *Darter*'s crew in two and a half hours. McClintock left demolition charges on *Darter* but when they were detonated they only fizzled. *Dace* fired four torpedoes one at a time. They all hit the reef and exploded without sinking *Darter.* The next morning *Dace*'s crew pumped a score of shells from her deck gun into *Darter* but the submarine remained high and dry on the reef. A Japanese plane arrived and dropped its bombs on *Darter* rather than *Dace.* Finally, when Japanese escort vessels nosed about *Darter,* Bladen Claggett decided to call it quits and shoved off for the eleven-day trip to Fremantle with two crews, 165 men, aboard his submarine. Despite two later at-tempts to destroy *Darter*—torpedoes from *Rock* and gunfire from *Nautilus*—*Darter* remained on Bombay Shoal for years afterward. Both ships were awarded Navy Unit Commendations for their actions.

Captain McClintock requested that he and his crew be transferred as a unit to new construction. Instead, the Bureau of Personnel informed him to his chagrin that he was assigned to a mine depot. In Washington, McClintock was summoned to the Office of the Chief of Naval Operations to describe *Darter*'s role in the battle. Admiral King himself came in to the meeting.

"That was a great job at Leyte," he said.

"Thank you, sir."

"Did you get a new sub with the *Darter* crew?"

"Not yet, sir."

King turned to an aide, Submariner "Dusty" Dornin. "Take care of it," he ordered.

The next day McClintock and *Darter*'s crew were all assigned to the new submarine *Menhaden,* which was being built in Manitowoc.

The two skippers remained close friends. McClintock said he was forever grateful to Claggett. Claggett pointed out that he could have been hailed as a hero for saving *Darter* and her crew or condemned in a court martial for breaking off his attack on the Japanese fleet. McClintock maintained a tradition of toasting Claggett once a year on the night of October 24 for saving him and his crew.

That autumn, *Sterlet* was having *Caine Mutiny* problems in what seemed a replay of the earlier situation aboard *Crevalle* with Hank Munson and his second and third officers. The exec of *Sterlet,* Paul Schratz, was puzzled by the behavior of his skipper, Orme C. "Butch" Robbins, an Academy classmate of Dick O'Kane. On *Sterlet*'s first two patrols, the captain seemed in a high state of tension. Frequently he called Schratz into his tiny cabin. Then Robbins would lay in his bunk, mumbling unintelligibly, and Schratz would have to ask for a repeat five or six times. Even then the captain still didn't make sense. During one depth charging, Exec Schratz thought Robbins' actions erratic and not responsible. Schratz seriously considered the extreme choice of relieving the captain and taking command himself, but if he did so, how could he justify his actions? If he sent a report to Commander Submarines, he thought, what would Admiral Lockwood do? It seemed likely that *Sterlet* would be ordered to rendezvous with another ship to get Robbins off the ship lest something worse happen. The exec was vaguely aware of Robbins' relief from a submarine and hospitalization early in the war, which Schratz suspected was stress related. *Sterlet* was badly needed to cover a strategic area in the Philippine Sea. Schratz thought he couldn't discuss the problem with other officers until he himself made a decision, although the other officers were upset by Robbins' bizarre behavior in and out of the conning tower.

Was he too rash, Schratz wondered, even to think of relieving the captain? Robbins had three times Schratz' experience in submarines and Schratz was just twenty-nine. The exec resolved to tough it out, but to be prepared for anything. In one action, the captain pulled himself together and sank a big tanker of 10,000 tons. But then, tracking a naval task force, Commander Robbins ordered *Sterlet* on a course that took the boat away from contact. By the time Schratz managed to change course, the submarine lost the opportunity for an attack. On *Sterlet*'s return to Saipan, the captain informed Schratz that he planned to ask for his exec's detachment. The skipper told the squadron commander that Schratz was "hot for combat" and didn't want a rest period.

While Schratz remained in Saipan, *Sterlet* returned to Pearl for refit. On arrival at Pearl on November 30, 1944, most officers said they would not go to sea with Butch Robbins again. Robbins was recommended for a Navy Cross, but at the end of the refit the thought of going on patrol again dimmed. He asked to be relieved, went to staff duty and disappeared from the Submarine Force.

Seawolf had a long and distinguished career: after first going into action under Freddie Warder in 1942, she made fifteen runs and engaged in fifty-six torpedo battles. On September 29, *Seawolf* left Manus in the Admiralties under Commander A.L. Bontier on a special mission to the Philippines with seventeen U.S. Army personnel aboard. En route to Samar, *Seawolf* entered a new submarine safety lane, where U.S. boats were supposedly free from accidental attack by friendly forces. She remained in the lane though she had to buck heavy seas, which set her behind schedule. This salient fact was reported to Commander Seventh Fleet Submarines and Commander Seventh Fleet.

About that time, a Japanese submarine attacked a Seventh Fleet task force and sank the destroyer escort *Shelton*. The American task force searched for the enemy sub; a U.S. Navy plane spotted a submerged boat and dropped two bombs and a dye marker. He was unaware that a safety zone existed. Destroyer escort *Rowell* was nearby, but though the commanding officer knew he was in a sub safety zone, he believed there were no U.S. boats in the area. He had not received word that *Seawolf* was running behind schedule. The DE skipper launched an intense depth charging, and continued even though *Seawolf* tried to issue sonar signals—which the DE captain claimed were "not proper recognition signals."

There was little doubt at ComSubPac about the boat's identity. Friendly forces sank venerable *Seawolf.* Though there were several close shaves, this was the only friendly sinking of a U.S. boat in the Pacific. It was an example of the failure of communications in the Pacific theater: the pilots and DE commander never got the word.

On a brighter note, submariners were cheered by a couple of brilliantly conducted patrols.

In late November, Eli Reich, a New Yorker who had helped solve electric torpedo problems at Newport while on *Lapon,* was plagued by two torpedo accidents. He was commanding *Sealion II* in the East China Sea off the coast near Shanghai. First, a battery fire in an electric torpedo occurred in a bow tube. Reich and his torpedomen decided to back emergency, up to 12 knots, and fire the torpedo from the forward tube, hoping that the fish would clear *Sealion II* before exploding. It worked. Then during a later inspection, a torpedo was accidentally fired from a stern tube with the outer door closed. The departing torpedo ripped off the outer door. *Sealion II* was left with nine operating tubes; more importantly, only the inner door of a stern tube maintained watertight integrity.

Despite these setbacks, *Sealion II* moved south toward the entrance to the Formosa Strait and was running on the surface at night. Reich received a report around midnight that radar had picked up a contact at 44,000 yards, which was an almost unbelievable range. He hurried to the conning tower, thinking at first that the contact was the northern tip of Formosa, but it turned out to be a ship some 20 miles away. At 30,000 yards, the single pip split into more than one target: what appeared to be a major ship task force, moving at 16 knots. *Sealion II* was ahead of the targets and Reich moved into an attack set-up, intending to shoot the second ship in the column. It would be a night surface attack.

Reich thought his target looked like a battleship with a pagoda mast. He got a firing set-up at about 4,500 yards but that was an extreme range for the slower electric fish. Exec Jim Bryant worried about the escorts. "Don't worry," the skipper said. "We've got to close this guy. Right now, we'll not worry about the escorts." Reich decided that if *Sealion II* was going to do anything, she had to do it fast—and "get the hell of there pretty soon." "Commence firing when ready," Eli Reich told Jim Bryant. "As soon as you get your bow fish out, we'll swing around 180 degrees and get the stern ready."

Eli Reich fired six fish out of the forward tubes at fairly long range, 3,000 yards. He swung the boat around and fired three torpedoes from the after tubes at what he identified as a second battleship, while heading in a getaway direction. Reich saw three explosions. He thought he had three hits under *Sealion II*'s belt. The escorts began depth charging but the submarine was on the surface and hauling away at top speed. *Sealion II* then paralleled the task force and reloaded tubes. The targets began to move faster. The sea was building up, the beginning of a typhoon. Under these conditions, *Sealion II* could only make 18 knots.

As Reich watched from the bridge, the biggest target slowed to stop, some 6,000 yards away. He saw a tremendous

explosion, and reported, "big ball of fire and then darkness—
nothing. She ignited and blew up. It was a major magazine
explosion."

Sealion II began chasing the other ships north but a huge
wave crashed over the bridge and poured water into the conning tower; gallons dumped into the control room and even
the pump room underneath. "It was a hell of a slug of water,"
Reich said. The wave wetted down electrical machinery,
switch boxes and other sensitive gear. Reich sent off a contact report and decided to call it a night. *Sealion II* dove and
sat on the bottom for five hours while the crew cleaned up
the mess.

The Japanese target was the battleship *Kongo,* 31,000
tons, the first and only battlewagon sunk by an American
submarine in the war. *Sealion II*'s torpedoes started fires that
reached the magazines some time later, and causing the blast
witnessed by Reich. The second battleship was *Haruna,* but
Eli Reich's second salvo from his stern tubes sunk the destroyer *Urakaze.*

Fellow skippers were also delighted when word travelled
round the New London–Pearl–Brisbane–Fremantle circuit
of Joe Enright's belated success story. After an unsuccessful patrol aboard *Dace* in 1943, Commander Enright, Dick
O'Kane's Sub School classmate, asked to be relieved—
believing he was not up to submarine combat command. He
went to a backwater submarine staff job at Midway, but a
year later in 1944, feeling more confident, he requested and
was given a second chance as CO of *Archerfish.* In his first
patrol, Enright was at the outer reaches of Tokyo Bay and
spotted a huge aircraft carrier. He pursued on the surface
with moonlight guiding him, and observed the carrier had
four escort vessels.

It was *Shinano,* laid down as a sister ship to the world's
largest battleships, *Yamato* and *Musashi,* but converted to an
aircraft carrier. It had been launched and was fitting out in
Tokyo Bay when the high command decided to move her to
the Inland Sea, which would be safer from attacks by carrier
planes and B-29 bombers. *Shinano* was still carrying dozens

of shipyard workers busy with preparing the vessel for sea trials. The crew on this shakedown was mainly green.

Enright, still on the surface, noticed the carrier and escorts were pulling away from him, making at least a knot more speed. The skipper got off a contact report and tried to follow the enemy group. As he fell farther behind, he sent out another contact report in frustration. But then Joe Enright's luck changed.

The five-ship group altered course radically, steering back toward *Archerfish,* and closing the range. As the enemy group neared him, Enright ordered *Archerfish* submerged. The range narrowed to 3,500 yards. An escort passed over the submarine. One more zig by the carrier put her in firing position. At 0317 on November 29, *Archerfish* fired six torpedoes at the carrier. Four hit.

A huge, glowing fireball climbed the carrier's side, but *Shinano* kept going. Captain Toshio Abe believed his damage control officers would have no trouble keeping the brand-new ship afloat, but they were inexperienced. *Shinano* was still being worked on, and some of her watertight doors were not in place. *Shinano* was shipping water badly and it sloshed through many compartments, but Captain Abe was oblivious. The world's largest warship at 59,000 tons began slipping beneath the sea. She sank with Captain Abe and 500 men, having known the open sea less than twenty hours. It had taken four years to build *Shinano* and she had the shortest lifetime of any capital ship.

This was the biggest warship ever sunk by a submarine and it made *Archerfish*'s patrol the best of the war in tonnage terms. It earned Joe Enright the Navy Cross. Curiously, *Shinano* was the only ship he ever sunk: he drew blanks on *Archerfish*'s last two war patrols.

George Grider, a skipper troubled by the loss of *Wahoo* and Mush Morton and then *Tang* and Dick O'Kane, was, like Joe Enright, a reflective, self-examining man. Grider, O'Kane's shipmate on *Wahoo,* was a great admirer of Mush Morton, though he had his reservations about Mush's aggressiveness. But he also thought himself fortunate to follow the rocketing career of Dick O'Kane. George Grider considered O'Kane a genuine legend in the Pacific War. He thought Dick had been a perfect exec for Mush Morton on *Wahoo* and the perfect skipper for *Tang*. Commander Grider watched Dick O'Kane's progress from brash, hard-charging, sometimes abrasive young officer to almost a different self: sure, steady, confident, an officer who developed the quality of command. Grider was pleased to see that every man who served with him on *Wahoo* discussed Dick O'Kane's exploits with affectionate admiration, particularly now that O'Kane was gone.

After hitches as exec of *Pollack* and *Hawkbill*, George Grider was eager to get his first command, *Flasher,* which had rung up a splendid record under Reuben Whitaker, Dick O'Kane's Academy classmate. But Grider, in his worrying way, wondered whether he would make good. Would he live up to Reuben's record? It was strange to realize, Grider thought, that his *Flasher* crew was a little afraid of him as he and Roger Paine had been a little afraid of Mush Morton when he took over *Wahoo*. Grider was aware he was an unknown quantity, and the crew's safety as well as their effectiveness depended on him. He was experiencing the loneliness of command. It was disquieting. In every wartime situation, no matter how much reliance was placed on him, he had known there was someone nearby who assumed final responsibility. Now, there was no one to call on but himself.

When George Grider got into action with *Flasher* on his first patrol in the South China Sea in December 1944, the fears, the inhibitions, the uneasy feelings vanished. When he spotted a convoy and fired his first torpedo spread at an escort destroyer, it was like the first kickoff in a football game. When Grider saw the vessel sink, a feeling of exaltation swept over him. He had paid his way as a skipper now, no matter what else happened. If they never accomplished another thing, even if none of them ever saw another day, they had justified their training, the cost of their boat and the sacrifice of their lives. He sensed the change in the crew's attitude toward him. They had been through a successful attack together and there would never again be a wall of watchful waiting between them. They were all on the same team now.

Grider surfaced, caught the convoy, and sank three tankers. In this first patrol, the captain accounted for a total of four tankers and two destroyers, a stunning performance. He had acquitted himself, and had taken over Reuben Whitaker's mantle. This run by *Flasher* was among the top patrols of the war: it earned George Grider a Navy Cross and *Flasher* a Presidential Unit Citation.

Ever reflective (perhaps too reflective, some skippers might add), Captain Grider thought: "I was in the midst of a triumph more personal than any I had ever experienced in combat before. Whatever happened, nobody could say I was a coward. I had cleared myself of the burden of guilt that had ridden my shoulders all day, and at that moment I didn't give a damn whether *Flasher* was sunk or not."

The close of 1944 marked the end of the biggest year for the U.S. Submarine Force. Boats were sweeping Japanese shipping from much of the Western Pacific and also scored great success in sinking Japanese warships: the battleship *Kongo* and seven aircraft carriers; two heavy cruisers; seven light cruisers; some thirty destroyers, and seven submarines. But the victories came at a high cost. The Japanese improved their anti-submarine tactics and the Sub Force lost nineteen boats. Some were the best in the Force, others were on their first patrol: *Scorpion, Grayback, Trout, Tullibee, Gudgeon, Herring, Golet, S-28, Robalo, Flier, Harder, Seawolf, Darter, Shark II, Tang, Escolar, Albacore, Growler,* and *Scamp.*

By contrast, the performance of Japanese submarines remained disappointing to the Imperial Navy. During the war, the Japanese failed to use their submarines as an independent naval arm. The vessels were treated as lone wolves and deployed erratically. Japanese submarines were huge boats ranging from 2,000 to 3,500 tons with a cruising range of 16,000 miles. Some carried airplanes in watertight deck hangers. One, *I-17,* fired on the Richfield Oil refineries in Southern California with a 5-inch deck gun two months after Pearl Harbor. It was the first time since the War of 1812 that an enemy had struck American shores, but it did little damage. The other submarine attack on American soil was near

Fort Stevens, Oregon. A sub-based seaplane from *I-25* took off alongside and bombed the forests to cause fires, but a heavy rain wiped out the effort.

In 1942, acting alone, enemy submarines sank some choice targets, among them the carriers *Yorktown* (already dead in the water from carrier aircraft attack) and *Wasp,* the cruiser *Juneau,* and twice-wounded *Saratoga.* But after sinking the escort carrier *Liscombe Bay* during the Gilberts invasion in late 1943, the Imperial Navy's submarines failed to down another major American warship until the cruiser *Indianapolis* in the last days of the war.

The Japanese submarine force seemed to lack a coherent strategy, with navy and army commanders shifting vessels around seemingly at will. They were used more for logistical purposes than for combat patrolling. The subs occasionally shelled U.S. outposts on Pacific atolls, which served only to call attention to their position. Worse for the Japanese, their frequent radio messages home were intercepted by U.S. code-breakers who tracked their courses. ComSubPac, thus alerted, ordered *Gudgeon* under Joe Grenfell to ambush one talkative submarine returning from the U.S. West Coast. He sank *I-173,* the first enemy ship put under due to Ultra. Poor radio discipline led U.S. boats to sink twenty-six Japanese submarines during the war, and caused U.S. ships to avoid known positions for Japanese subs.

Strangely, the Japanese never tried to hit the Panama Canal, the crucial Atlantic–Pacific artery, or its vulnerable locks, though some large submarines carried float planes, which might have made a successful attack. Instead, the huge, 3,500-ton I-boats were used as communications ships, and as transports bringing troops and supplies to garrisons on beleaguered islands. They carried out a successful evacuation of the Japanese garrison on Kiska Island in the Aleutians— concealing it from the Americans who were about to invade.

The big subs were used as tankers for flying boats at forward Pacific island bases. They were sometimes employed to seek out U.S. warships in task forces, but they never launched a systematic attack on the hundreds of U.S. cargo and troop ships plying regularly between the West Coast, Pearl Harbor, the Pacific Islands, Australia, and New Zealand carrying vital troops, equipment and supplies.

In the Indian Ocean, Japanese submarines carried out a short, effective campaign against Allied shipping, but their achievements weren't followed up: the Japanese only assigned ten boats to the task and despite the successes, pulled them out of the area.

During the war, the Japanese expended much time, money, and steel in building hundreds of midget submarines, the Kaitens. These vessels were engineering marvels, but never proved particularly useful in the war. They carried two torpedoes with warheads in the bow, and were designed to be transported on the decks of larger submarines. During the conflict, the U.S. Navy Department occasionally came up with suggestions that America build similar midget subs, but Admiral Lockwood vigorously opposed the idea on the grounds that Japanese harbors—where the midgets were designed to operate—were heavily mined and netted. Deployment would amount to suicide missions.

During 1944, the U.S. South Pacific Force was disbanded, and assimilated into the Central Pacific Force under Admiral Nimitz and the Southwest Pacific Forces under General MacArthur. Admiral Halsey took over the Third Fleet which alternated with the Fifth Fleet under Admiral Spruance for the rest of the war: the ships remained the same, but the commander, the staffs and the designators changed. "MacArthur's Navy," the Seventh Fleet, remained under the command of Admiral Thomas Kinkaid.

In the Submarine Force, everyone sensed that pickings were going to be slimmer for the fleet boats in 1945 as the U.S. armed forces drove the Japanese back to the home islands. Expert skippers would be unable to locate targets in the rapidly dwindling Japanese merchant fleet.

Charles Lockwood and his SubPac staff, particularly Captain Dick Voge, continued to dominate U.S. submarine operations. Admiral Nimitz and Admiral Lockwood prepared to move headquarters from Pearl to Guam to be closer to the westward-moving combat operations. In one administrative surprise, Admiral Ralph Christie was shocked to be removed from command of submarines in Australia—at Admiral Kinkaid's specific request. Their bitter relationship had escalated, and as Commander Seventh Fleet, Kinkaid was in a position to get rid of Christie, who was sent to the West Coast to command the Bremerton Navy Yard. Jimmy Fife took over Christie's position, and in early 1945 planned to move the Australia boats to Subic Bay in the Philippines, an unpopular jungle base which the puritanical Fife insisted submariners use as a "rest camp."

While the number of U.S. submarine sinkings of enemy ships crested in 1944, the year 1945 would see its share of American submarine derring-do.

CHAPTER TWENTY-FOUR

"May God Bless You. Abandon Ship"

Dick O'Kane and *Tang*'s survivors arrived at the big Kobe naval base on a wet, cold, sleety day early in November, 1944. By the time they had left the ship and marched to a building at the naval training station, everyone was soaking wet and miserable. A tall Japanese rear admiral looked over the *Tang* crew. He stopped at Boats Leibold, who was so cold his teeth were chattering. The officer spoke English.

"How old are you?"

"Twenty-one," Leibold replied.

"You look thirty-five," the officer said. "Frightened?" he then asked.

"No, cold," Leibold answered.

"Of course, you're cold, stupid," he said. "You have no shoes on." The Admiral thought it funny. Leibold had had no shoes since leaving *Tang*.

That was the sum of the inspection. *Tang*'s men were bundled on a train at Kobe for a journey through central Honshu northeast to the great port of Yokohama. Dick O'Kane was depressed by what he saw in the countryside: despite the blockade and bombing, it seemed to be thriving. The passengers got off the train briefly at the port city of Nagoya. Though it was night, O'Kane could see the blue-white arcs of welders' torches at the shipyard. It reminded him of Kaiser shipyards in California, and he worried that this level of activity suggested that the war had a long way to go before the enemy were brought to their knees. He thought invasion of Japan would be the only, but very bloody, answer. In Yokohama, a bus took the prisoners on an hour's ride to the secret naval intelligence base at Ofuna, arriving just before dawn.

Ofuna was justly infamous. It was a secret prison camp run by naval intelligence and designed to elicit classified information from inmates, who were exclusively submariners and aviators. Ofuna came to be known as the "Torture Farm." It was built in 1942 and was 30 miles southwest of Yokohama. There were three, one-story barracks around a large field, like a football gridiron, the compound surrounded by a 12-foot wooden fence. In one building, there was a long central passageway with thirty cells on each side, some 4 feet by 8 feet. The rooms contained an electric light, a bunk with a bamboo mat, and a door with a small window through which the guards could peer. There were interrogation rooms at both ends of the building.

The camp was constructed to house 100 prisoners in individual cells with interrogation rooms to which they would be taken frequently. When the Japanese decided they had got all they could out of the prisoners, the inmates were sometimes then moved to work camps, and treated like ordinary POWs. Crewmen from the *S-44, Perch, Grenadier,* and *Sculpin* had been imprisoned at Ofuna. The chief interrogator, accompanied by two assistants, spelled out Ofuna policy in English to a *Sculpin* survivor: "You have survived the sinking of a submarine. No one survives the sinking of a submarine. No one knows you're alive. We are going to ask you questions. This man and this man are going to shoot you if you don't answer the questions, and no one will ever know you were alive."

Tang's crewmen were assigned cells with a grass floor mat and blanket. They were issued with a shirt, pants, and tennis shoes, which were too small for the tall men. They were then placed in solitary confinement and warned not to speak with one another. However, a private communication system was soon set up. The barracks were divided between the older prisoners and the new. A fellow American brought them bowls of lumpy, warm rice. At the next morning's assembly, *Tang's* crew learned that they were not ordinary POWs but "special prisoners."

Their special status meant that the Japanese didn't consider them under the protective cover of the International Red Cross. Submariners and aviators were presumed to have

committed crimes against civilians, either by bombing them
or sinking ships with foodstuffs for the Japanese populace.
Further, since they were not listed as prisoners-of-war, their
existence was not messaged to the Red Cross in Geneva or
the U.S. government. Because Ofuna was not a work camp,
the prisoners were informed their daily rations would be cut
by a third. However, they were told that they could study
Japanese; no one was eager to learn the enemy's language,
but it did take up much of the time on their hands.

The camp's operative head was a warrant officer named
Taicho, who was in charge of the guards. He made the
nightly rounds, but O'Kane soon learned that the real power
in the complex was the Kangocho, or chief pharmacist, a big,
hulking sadistic officer whom Dick considered a navy misfit.

The *Tang* nine spent the first couple of days isolated from
other camp inmates. After a few days, they were marched to
the other side of the compound, and in a row of prisoners
O'Kane was astonished to see Commander John Fitzgerald,
skipper of the *Grenadier,* which had been listed as missing in
April 1943. Fitzgerald and two others, looking like skele-
tons, were called forward. To O'Kane's horror, guards began
to beat the prisoners in turn, holding up the men who slipped
into unconsciousness. They continued hitting the Americans'
limp bodies with clubs the size of baseball bats. Floyd Caverly
retched at the sight. *Grenadier* survivors eventually exchanged
notes with *Tang*'s crew and told of the submarine's loss.

Grenadier had seemed to be unlucky. Her first four patrols
had not been productive. On her fifth run from Fremantle,
she was captained by John Fitzgerald who was transferred
off *Gar* for complaining about his skipper's lackluster tactics. Fitzgerald showed positive combat strengths on his first
patrol in *Grenadier.* On his second, patrolling off Malaya, he
was sighted by a Japanese bomber. He dove *Grenadier* but
an explosion rocked the ship as a bomb went off over her
stern. It set off electrical fires and twisted the hull badly,
causing serious leaks. The crew worked all day in fierce heat
to stem the flow of incoming water. That evening, *Grenadier*
got to the surface, but her propellers wouldn't turn. Fitzgerald's ship was totally immobilized and he had to prepare to

abandon her. The crew destroyed the radio, radar, sound, and torpedo-aiming instruments, and threw the decoding machines and codebooks over the side. A Japanese aircraft hovered in sight, as did an enemy surface ship. Fitzgerald gathered the crew on the deck and spoke to them from the bridge. He looked haggard and despair was in his eyes.

"Men," he said, "the options we had at dawn have been stripped from us by the plane that appeared at daylight. You are all aware of the ship off our port bow. I don't know what will be our fate in a couple of hours, but this ship must not fall into the hands of our enemy. On my command, you will all go over the side and swim rapidly away from the boat. The Chief of the Boat will open the vents for the last time. Whatever the outcome, may God bless you. Abandon ship!"

The captain gave the order to scuttle the boat. The Japanese rescued the crew, and seventy-six *Grenadier* crewmen were picked up and dispersed to prison camps. *Tang* crewmen learned that four *Grenadier* sailors died from brutal treatment and near starvation. Interrogators looking for technical information tortured Fitzgerald, but despite his torment he managed to keep up his own and his surviving crew's spirits. Of his conduct, a crewman said, "I think as much of Commander Fitzgerald, our skipper, as I do my father. He went through hell for us. They beat him, jumped on his stomach, and tortured him by burning splints under his nails. He never talked."

At Ofuna, the prisoners received a daily food ration—a bowl of barley in the morning and evening, with a soup at lunch and a few slices of potatoes or beans and soy sauce. Sometimes the soup would contain leftovers called "dumpo," and was served at supper. The men never saw fish, meat, fruit, or vegetables, except for the potato slicings and carrot greens. It was estimated the diet contained about 300 calories a day, and there was precious little protein.

During the day, the prisoners were often forced to assume the "Ofuna crouch"—heels together, toes pointed in opposite directions, knees half-bent, standing on the balls of the feet, back straight, with arms above heads. As the minutes dragged by and prisoners trembled and toppled over, the guards would club those who had fallen. On various evenings, gangs of guards—with nicknames like "Fatso" and "Smiling Jack"—roamed the compound, beating the prisoners with clubs at random and on whim. The American officers were singled out for brutal beatings with 4-foot clubs or the knuckled fists of guards. Dick O'Kane was beaten often, put on reduced rations, and threatened with death.

The intelligence interrogators—who did not live at the camp—were often young, English-speaking naval officers; one told O'Kane he had been to the University of Arkansas. The Japanese wanted information from the prisoners about submarine secrets and operations against their ships. Dick O'Kane was thankful he had no knowledge about overall broader strategic plans, as might a wolf pack commodore who was a staff officer at Pearl or Midway.

O'Kane told the interrogators *Tang* sank only five ships. When her loss was announced with the name of her captain and details of her exploits, the Japanese broke some of O'Kane's teeth. Later, a Japanese officer pulled out a news clipping that said *Tang* received the Presidential Unit Citation for sinking 110,000 tons of Japanese shipping. The guards knocked Dick off his stool and beat him.

The interrogators thought *Tang*'s last patrol had been as part of a wolf pack. O'Kane was content to let them believe that, because *Tang*'s crew would have suffered even worse beatings if it were known that all the ships sunk in the Formosa Strait had been torpedoed by his submarine. The intelligence officers assumed that *Tang* was caught by depth charges; O'Kane and *Tang*'s crew let them believe that was the cause of her loss. It was clear to the nine men that the Japanese were trying to break their spirit, but they kept to their story. They lived with the knowledge that since they were not officially registered as POWs, they could be executed at will. No one would know the difference.

Skipper O'Kane was grateful that even after their ordeal of escape and rescue the men from *Tang* were healthy and perhaps better able than most to withstand the rigors of confinement, beating, and meager diet. Because of their size and good shape, *Tang*'s crew were assigned to work details outside their barracks, even emptying privies, which privately pleased them because it kept them active and away from the sadistic guards.

The interrogators frequently questioned the prisoners. *Tang*'s crew called them the "Quiz Kids." The guards would put blankets over the prisoners' heads so they couldn't see their surroundings when they were taken to the interrogation rooms. They didn't seem to have any set rules for treatment, Boats Leibold thought. It all depended on the whims of the guards and interrogators.

Clayton Decker considered that Dick O'Kane's leadership through their ordeal was 4.0. He instructed his men not to undergo any unnecessary beatings. "I'm the guy they're after," he said to *Tang*'s crewmen. O'Kane told the interrogators he had had a desk job before being assigned to the submarine. The intelligence people were unable to check on the lie, but they beat him just the same. Poor old Dick, Clay Decker thought, he was taking a hell of a lot of beating.

When the interrogators asked Decker a question about the diesels—he was a motor machinist's mate—Clay gave them a routine answer about Fairbanks Morse, as O'Kane had advised. The skipper was right on. After Decker replied, the interrogator pulled out a factory catalogue with a complete description of an engine obtained from Fairbanks Morse, presumably just before the war started. Another intelligence officer kept asking how many ships were in Pearl Harbor. Decker thought this stupid. "How would I know? And what difference would it make, since the composition of ships changed daily?" He told them American submarines didn't have portholes.

In Jesse DaSilva's case, one Japanese questioning officer was polite, and spoke good English. He would offer DaSilva a cigarette and ask how everything was. Then he would put the same questions, over and over. DaSilva would give the same answers. He was happy that the interrogators seemed to assume he did not have much information of value.

Larry Savadkin was asked about the age and training of submariners. He would give vague answers. He was questioned about *Tang*'s speed and patrol areas. He lied. He was queried about the seniority and ranking of officers. He was a little more accommodating. He knew that for seven dollars, anyone could buy a copy of the Naval Register, a listing of every regular officer in the U.S. Navy with his signal number.

Occasionally, to show their better side, the interrogators would give the men a tangerine or a cigarette. A Japanese Navy captain in civilian clothes even gave them the score of the Army–Navy game in late 1944—O'Kane was disappointed that Navy lost, 23 to 7.

Through the prison grapevine, Dick O'Kane learned the details about the death of Captain John Cromwell from the survivors of *Sculpin,* and the fact that half the *Sculpin*'s survivors were lost aboard the carrier *Chuyo* when it was sunk by *Sculpin*'s sister ship *Sailfish.* Gradually, they pieced together the losses of *S-44, Perch,* and *Grenadier,* from survivors who had been sent to prison camps in Japan.

They heard the dramatic story of the loss of *Tullibee* under Commander Charles F. Brindupke from that submarine's only survivor, Gunner's Mate Clifford Kuykendall. On the night of March 26, 1944, *Tullibee* fired torpedoes at a Japanese convoy from a range of 3,000 yards. The last fish made a circular run and sank *Tullibee.* The submarine went down almost instantly, stern first, bow swung upward. It was strikingly similar to the sinking of *Tang.* Kuykendall, a nineteen-year-old from Texas, was a starboard lookout on the bridge when the explosion occurred. There were three other lookouts, the skipper and the OOD on the bridge too.

Kuykendall was thrown around the superstructure, and his upper teeth were broken when his head hit part of the fairwater. He was almost unconscious when he hit the water, but the cold sea revived him. It was quite dark, but Kuykendall heard voices in the water for about ten minutes. He watched *Tullibee*'s bow go under as he swam away to avoid getting caught by the suction of his sinking ship. He had no life jacket and so he began to dogpaddle. The salt water helped keep him afloat and he was surrounded by diesel oil. He could feel the implosions of the submarine as it sank in miles-deep water. He noticed a Sunkist orange crate floating in the water with three oranges in it; he held onto the crate, an action he believed saved his life. The sinking occurred about 0300 with daylight expected at 0600. Then all was silent.

Kuykendall floated up one swell and down another, trying to keep from panicking. He succeeded. About 1000, a Japanese frigate headed Kuykendall's way and opened up with a burst of machine gun fire. The crew saw he was helpless, stopped, and picked up the American sailor. After being kicked and beaten on the frigate, he was taken to Palau and tied to a tree for two days during American carrier strikes. He was then flown by seaplane to Saipan, by air to Yokohama, and finally to the Ofuna interrogation center. There he met Commander Fitzgerald of *Grenadier* and Lieutenant George Brown, the surviving senior officer of *Sculpin.* After he was questioned, the Japanese sent Clifford Kuykendall to the Ashio camp to work in the copper mines for the rest of the war. If Kuykendall hadn't survived, no one would have learned the fate of *Tullibee.* Dick O'Kane suspected that other U.S. submarines had also been sunk by their own torpedoes.

It was a terribly sad holiday season for Ernestine O'Kane and other *Tang* wives and relatives. In early December 1944, she received a yellow Western Union telegram at her apartment in Ignacio across the bay from Mare Island. For three years she had feared that such a message might arrive. It read:

WASHINGTON, D.C.
THE NAVY DEPARTMENT DEEPLY REGRETS TO INFORM YOU THAT YOUR HUSBAND COMMANDER RICHARD HETHERINGTON O'KANE USN IS MISSING FOLLOWING ACTION WHILE IN THE SERVICE OF HIS COUNTRY. THE DEPARTMENT APPRECIATES YOUR GREAT ANXIETY BUT DETAILS NOT AVAILABLE NOW AND DELAY IN RECEIPT THEREOF MUST NECESSARILY BE EXPECTED. TO PREVENT POSSIBLE AID TO OUR ENEMIES AND TO SAFEGUARD THE LIVES OF OTHER PERSONNEL PLEASE DO NOT DIVULGE THE NAME OF HIS SHIP OR STATION OR DISCUSS PUBLICLY THE FACT THAT HE IS MISSING.

VICE ADMIRAL RANDALL JACOBS
THE CHIEF OF NAVAL PERSONNEL

It was the worst day of Ernestine O'Kane's life. She hoped that somehow the message was a mistake, that it was not the last word. She telephoned and wrote other *Tang* wives and tried to buck up their morale. She sent out a newsletter. She tried to give them hope. There was always a chance, she said. Later Ernestine worried that she might have been too positive to wives and mothers, but she wanted to give them comfort, just as she gave herself hope. She was solicitous and remained in touch with the relatives of the men on *Tang* for many long months, but no word on the fate of the boat, its captain or its crew ever came. Ernestine's hopes gradually dwindled.

A few weeks later she received a personal letter from Admiral Lockwood which said that Dick had been "the heart and soul of the ship. His leadership, his coolness under counterattack, his daring, his determination to destroy any and all enemy ships encountered, all combined to make him the idol of his fellow skippers and of his seniors." Mrs O'Kane replied that "if disaster had to be met by these officers and men, Dick would have wanted to be with them."

In Ofuna, Dick O'Kane relied on his classical education at Andover to get him through some bad patches. He practiced reciting passages of literature in Latin. He went over the French he once learned. He repeated poems by Robert Frost and Ralph Waldo Emerson. And he thought for long periods about his family.

He dreamed up mechanical inventions. He built a sundial in the camp. A guard asked: "What do you do when it's cloudy?" O'Kane decided to needle him, even at the risk of another beating. "Give me a match." The guard complied. O'Kane lit it and the light cast a faint shadow on the sundial. "See!" O'Kane told the perplexed guard.

At Christmas time, the *Tang* group were surprised to be given three packages from the International Red Cross containing food rations—cans of corned beef, jars of jelly, chocolate, coffee, cigarettes, soap, powdered milk, small blocks of cheese, and a tiny can opener. It was a cornucopia. This set the stage for trading among the men as they exchanged the various items for their favorite goodies.

At the first of the year, they saw more B-29s in formation in the blue winter skies. With snow on the ground, the *Tang* survivors were no longer given work to do. It was just as well. By this time Dick had developed skin ulcers from scurvy that would not heal. Worse, he contracted beriberi, a disease of the peripheral nerves caused by a vitamin deficiency, and marked by pain and paralysis in the arms and legs and severe emaciation of the body. It was common to the undernourished in East Asia.

Tang's crewmembers' uniforms were now in tatters. They used rags for shoes. They were allowed a blanket to wrap around their shoulders in Japan's harsh winter, but the men walked often outside on the snow-covered ground, stamping their feet to keep their circulation flowing and to ward off the creeping paralysis of beriberi and pellagra. *Tang*'s crew talked the guards into letting them share the same cell so that their body heat could provide additional warmth in the unheated barracks.

There the men of *Tang* were allowed to converse. Dick O'Kane found that imprisonment and shared hardship brought down the normal barriers between officers and enlisted men. They talked among themselves on subjects ranging from boyhood days to the operation of *Tang*. But conversation centered, Jesse DaSilva thought, on food, food, and food— especially when the rations were reduced.

For his part, Dick O'Kane was surprised to learn that on the first patrol, when they were badly depth charged near Saipan, *Tang* went deeper than he had realized. Down in the pump room, the sea-pressure gauge registered 350 pounds per square inch, which equated to about 700 feet in depth. The few enginemen who were aware of how deep *Tang* actually descended decided to keep the information to themselves.

The crew also griped that the captain held too many inspections, which O'Kane thought was a normal and legitimate complaint common in many well-run ships. But then came a surprise: despite the inspections, the skipper had never uncovered the secret still Radio Technician Caverly had stashed away in the radio spare parts locker. Caverly told his captain that he had engaged in this illicit activity so that the troops could have something more powerful than beer at the Royal Hawaiian. O'Kane remembered seeing some of the dismantled elements of the still—Silex coffee-maker, condenser, the transmitter's output coil, rubber stoppers—during an inspection, but hadn't put it together in his mind. "Skipper," Caverly said with a grin, "if you knew how many times we burned our fingers getting that damned coil from the Silex to the wastebasket, always expecting you to smell the stuff!"

O'Kane realized that Caverly and the torpedomen had ready access to the gallons of torpedo juice if needed and hardly had to construct a still, but he admired his men's ingenuity. O'Kane thought wryly: if sipping the produce of the home-made still helped get the crew of *Tang* back into fighting trim, then maybe Josephus Daniels, Secretary of the Navy in World War I, erred when he decreed ships should be dry.

The crew was proud of Dick O'Kane as their skipper and leader. Larry Savadkin thought that despite his wounds and illness, O'Kane was good company. They designed a set of makeshift cards and played cribbage, the submariner's popular card game. Larry saw that Dick tried to keep up discipline, not in the sense of giving orders, but in protecting his crew from their captors. O'Kane explained how to obey the Japanese rules to keep out of trouble and avoid beatings, but made it clear to his men never to cooperate with them. Hank Flanagan gave interrogators an inaccurate description of U.S. torpedoes. Savadkin and the crew tried to anticipate questions and arrive at common answers. "We all took Captain O'Kane's advice," Savadkin said. "I liked him and respected him immensely."

During his captivity, Dick O'Kane found another side to his character. In combat, he was all business—an officer geared to battle. Now, he developed more compassion for his crew and his fellow prisoners. He behaved like a benign father figure to them all.

In February, the prisoners were treated to the sight of a carrier air strike, which signified to O'Kane that the Philippines must now be secure, because only then would such strikes be launched on Honshu. The guards beat the men for watching the skies, but to Dick O'Kane the sight of Avenger carrier bombers was well worth it. The camp received more airmen who were forced down, and were placed in solitary confinement. One of them had two broken arms. Dick O'Kane was on a mess-cooking detail at the time. He delivered the airman's food and asked a guard if he could feed the new prisoner. The request was met with a "knuckle sandwich," a favorite response of some guards. The new arrivals in the camp brought the prisoners up to date on the state of the Pacific War.

In spring, beriberi began to affect Dick seriously. Word spread that two prisoners who could no longer walk died quickly. The Japanese interrogators, he thought, expected the weakness and sickness from beatings and poor diet to force the prisoners to tell everything they knew. Then they would be transferred to regular POW camps with a better diet. That hadn't happened, and the fact that prisoners were dying seemed to generate alarm among the captors. So the Japanese gave the prisoners vitamin shots to combat dysentery and beriberi. They introduced bread for the morning and evening meals instead of barley. Scraps from the officers' mess were put in the "dumpo" soup. But the remedies did not work and the men got weaker.

O'Kane knew that U.S. Marine Major Gregory "Pappy" Boyington was in another building in the Ofuna camp. Pappy Boyington was a hell-raising Marine Corps pilot who had shot down twenty-eight Japanese planes in the South Pacific before being brought down himself over Rabaul. He had kept his brilliant record secret from the Japanese—and also his previous service in China with the Flying Tigers. Boyington told interrogators that he was assigned to operations in his Marine Corsair squadron in the Solomons: he had just gone along for a ride. One day a new interrogator, a navy captain who had attended Princeton, opened up his briefcase. He withdrew some clippings. "I thought this might be of interest to you, Major," he said, handing over the papers. They were radio news reports from the U.S. announcing that

Boyington had been awarded the Congressional Medal of Honor for shooting down twenty-eight planes and that he had been killed in action. The stories mentioned his Flying Tigers fame. Pappy thought this might mean his execution.

"You don't have to lie to us," the Japanese captain said. "There are a lot of us around who know what the score is. I've spent many years in the U.S. personally. I was in the Japanese Embassy in Washington." The interrogator paused. "But do you know something else? We appreciate a hero here in Japan even though he's from another country." The captain offered Pappy a cigarette. Boyington was allowed to work in the camp kitchen from 4:30 a.m. to 9 p.m. and given an extra ration of soup and barley.

Larry Savadkin saw Pappy Boyington in the camp galley and stole some catsup from a bottle there to take back to his mates. Then he or another POW urinated in the bottle to make it look full. Savadkin alerted Boyington which bottle was defective so he would keep it on the shelf and eventually throw it away. Boyington sneaked the prisoners extra food when the guards weren't looking.

As the Japanese war effort continued to run down, the officers in charge at Ofuna became worried. They may have been concerned about the collapse of Germany and the announcement that those responsible for war crimes would be held accountable. In April 1945 the Japanese at Ofuna ordered Pappy Boyington to lead a group of enlisted men, including *Tang*'s six sailors, to Omori, a regular Army-run prison camp on an island in Tokyo Bay connected by causeway to Yokohama.

They took off with guards aboard a streetcar. O'Kane, Savadkin, and Flanagan remained behind at Ofuna, with O'Kane getting steadily weaker as beriberi dug in. The Omori prisoners were given a new set of clothes, and though this was a standard POW camp, the submariners and aviators were kept in a separate area. They were still considered "special prisoners." No word of their presence was made known to the Red Cross.

There were 500 other prisoners at Omori and life was better than it had been at Ofuna. They were fed rice and nourishing soup, and the food was palatable—if they didn't look at it too closely. There were other POWs to talk to, and the guards didn't single anyone out for special punishment. After some time, the Japanese said that if the new prisoners joined work details they would be given two-thirds rations. That's when Boats Leibold realized they had only been getting half rations. They worked digging caves on the mainland that were used for storage areas and for air-raid shelters. The prisoners were given shoes to wear to work.

Jesse DaSilva and others talked the guards into letting them plant a vegetable garden just outside the camp. Those that were well enough could work in it. They took along a 5-gallon can of water for making tea during breaks. DaSilva volunteered to be the tea maker. He would scrounge for bits of garbage like fish-heads and pieces of vegetables and toss them in the water to take back to camp for soup for his mates. At one time during a tea break, the sailors saw an old stray dog shuffle by. They immediately argued about the feasibility of eating dog meat if only someone had the stomach to kill it. Nobody had.

In Pearl Harbor, Murray Frazee was now skipper of *Gar*. He was deeply grieved when he heard the news about *Tang*. As exec, he was the mail censor for four patrols and he had got to know something about the crew's personal lives. He had also met some of their wives while putting *Tang* into commission. Frazee later wrote to every family involved, telling them what he knew about the men. Fraz thought of himself as the chaplain aboard *Tang*. *Gar* was such an old boat, with fifteen war patrols behind her, that she was assigned only to training duties.

Fraz was told highly confidentially by a senior submarine officer with connections to Jasper Holmes' intelligence staff at Admiral Nimitz' headquarters that Ultra intercepts indicated there were survivors of *Tang,* including Dick O'Kane! He was a POW, though not officially so. Fraz was sworn to silence. Any hint the Navy knew there were *Tang* survivors alive could compromise the priceless Ultra secret.

Murray Frazee desperately wished to inform Ernestine that her husband was alive, but he could not. He had to bite his tongue. In writing to her, he could not even hint at what he knew. It was a great pain for him. But in order to insure the Ultra secret, and possibly to protect *Tang* survivors, Ernestine O'Kane and the other wives and families had to suffer in the dark.

Two months later as summer began, the three *Tang* officers were transferred to Omori. Dick O'Kane could hardly walk but he was assigned a work detail, digging caves near Yokohama. Japanese civilians, seeing the wretched shape the prisoners were in, would sometimes leave roasted soybeans where the men could find them. O'Kane's guard caught one civilian doing this and whipped him in the face with a large pair of pliers. O'Kane thought the actions showed the strength of civilian kindness and their hatred for the military.

By now, even with the improved diet, most *Tang* crewmen were afflicted with one or more diseases. Others in the camp were terribly ill. They suffered from beriberi, malaria, malnutrition and skin diseases. They were emaciated and sometimes confused. Some had "rice brain"—memory loss from the wretched prison diet. The average sailor who arrived weighing 170 pounds was down to 120 or even 100 pounds. Soap was always short and men felt they could never get clean. Big, strapping Boats Leibold had hepatitis. O'Kane had hepatitis, beriberi, and jaundice. Jesse DaSilva's large frame was dwindling; he wasn't sure he could hold out.

The prisoners recognized that the frequency of the frightening air bombing raids around Yokohama and Tokyo, often close to the Omori camp, indicated the war was drawing to a close. All sorts of information filtered through the camp. The prisoners heard about the dropping of the atomic bomb in the southern cities of Hiroshima and Nagasaki.

Dick O'Kane was in bad shape and getting worse, crippled by his beriberi and jaundice. Boats Leibold thought his captain had only a few weeks to live.

CHAPTER TWENTY-FIVE

Walking on the Tops of Periscopes

The submarine year 1945 began with an illustrious patrol by Captain Gene Fluckey, red-haired, wide-grinned skipper of *Barb,* who had sunk five ships in his first patrol (*Barb*'s eighth). In his fourth *Barb* patrol as skipper, Fluckey was part of a wolf pack with *Queenfish* under Elliott Loughlin, and *Picuda* with Commander Evan T. Shephard, assigned to the southern area of the East China Sea. It was close to where Dick O'Kane and *Tang* went down. On January 8, the wolf pack picked up a large convoy heading south near the China coast. *Barb* bored in first and with good sharp shooting by Fluckey sank the *Shinyo Maru* in an enormous explosion.

Fluckey idly remarked after the torpedoes exploded with an enormous roar, "Now that's what I'd call a good solid hit." He heard a crewman remark, "I'd hate to be around when he hears a loud explosion!" The victim appeared to be an ammunition ship. Fluckey then fired his stern torpedoes and sank the tanker *Sanyo Maru.* "Can feel aggressiveness surging through my veins," Fluckey noted in his report, "since the escorts are more scared than we are. Commenced reload forward. Destroyer suddenly turned towards us! Nice spot for a down-the-throat shot, but no torpedoes forward. Aggressiveness evaporated. Assumed deep submergence at 140 feet. Mud below that."

Queenfish and *Picuda* attacked the convoy. *Barb* found another target and, attacking on the surface, scored three hits. Fluckey recorded a "stupendous earthshaking explosion. This far surpassed Hollywood." Personnel were almost sucked out of the hatches by the high vacuum created by the pressure wave from the blast. "The horizon was lighted as bright as day," Fluckey reported. "The volcanic spectacle was awe inspiring. Shrapnel flew all around us, splashing in the water in a splattering pattern as far as 4,000 yards ahead of us." *Barb*'s target was the 9,256-ton, passenger-cargo *Anyo Maru*. Fluckey turned away to reload and let his pack mates get in their shots. It was difficult to determine which of the wolf pack sank which ships, but Fluckey was credited with downing three and sharing another one down.

For the next eleven days *Barb* dodged Japanese patrol planes while he looked for vanishing targets. He, like Dick O'Kane before him, had to move close inshore since Japanese marus hugged the coast and tended to anchor at harbors at night, sailing only during the day when U.S. submarines could be held down by escorts and planes.

Barb found a group of anchored ships in lower Namkwan Harbor, on the China coast in Fukien Province northwest of Taiwan, and headed in to get them with a night surface attack.

Fear is natural to all creatures, Fluckey thought, necessary for self-preservation. To win, however, fear must be controlled, enabling expertise to determine when to fight and when to retreat to fight another day. The subconscious weighs the odds almost automatically. Fluckey and his attack party looked at the chart: the position for firing was a few thousand yards from the anchored ships. This was 6 miles inside the 10-fathom curve. There were 19 more miles to the 20-fathom curve where safe diving lay. Fluckey planned to attack with bow tubes, swing right for the stern tubes, and then gallop out of Namkwan Harbor.

The skipper announced to the crew that he thought the odds for a successful attack were ten to one in *Barb*'s favor. The control room was dead quiet except for the occasional sounding. Ahead Fluckey saw targets—some thirty ships—anchored in three columns. He thought this must be the most beautiful target of the war and moved quickly in to 5,000 yards. He fired four bow tubes, then spun *Barb* around and with 5 fathoms under the keel fired his four stern tubes. Then he ordered: "All ahead flank!"

Barb highballed it out of the anchorage, running for the open sea, leaving marine carnage behind. An hour and nineteen minutes after the first fish was fired, Gene Fluckey reached the 20-fathom curve and since he figured the Japanese would expect him to dive at dawn, he decided to stay on the surface at 21 knots to clear the Namkwan area. *Barb* got away unscathed.

As was Fluckey's custom, he had beer put in the cooler and ordered all hands to celebrate. He believed he had sunk at least three ships and probably four, with three more damaged. Post-war records credited him with only one, *Taikyo Maru,* 5,244 tons, but others may have sunk in the shallow water of the anchorage, then been salvaged and not listed in Japanese records. As for the daring raid into port, Fluckey pointed out that the first skipper could get away with a surprise raid, but not the second. He wouldn't have done it twice. Gene Fluckey was awarded the Medal of Honor for this most successful patrol and *Barb* the Presidential Unit Citation.

"Lucky" Fluckey followed this up with his last patrol on *Barb.* An inventive captain, Fluckey rigged rockets from his own special-made launcher to fire 5-inch missiles for the first time from a submarine at the port of Shari on the Japanese half of Sakhalin Island. *Barb* followed the missiles with a deck gun attack on an observation post on Kaihyo Island, just offshore. Next, she took a breather from the artillery attacks to sink two ships. Then moving inshore, Fluckey observed a railroad with regular traffic running along the coast. At night when clouds darkened the moon, he landed a group of eight *Barb* crewmen in two boats under Lieutenant William Walker, USNR. The commando party set demolition charges under the tracks and blew up a train—engine, a dozen freight cars, and two passengers cars, all piled up off the tracks. "Wham!" Fluckey exclaimed. "What a thrill! The charge made a much greater explosion than we expected. The engine's boilers blew, wreckage flew 200 feet in the air in a flash of flame and smoke, cars piled up and rolled off the track in a writhing, twisting mass of wreckage. Cheers!"

Gene Fluckey reported this was the first time in the war

that U.S. forces had set foot on Japanese home islands. He
launched a couple more rocket attacks on the factory towns
of Shiritori, Kashiho, and Chiri, shooting up everything in
sight. Afterward, he ordered beers broken out for his young
crew.

Barb returned to Midway and Pearl to Lockwood's fervent
congratulations. Fluckey stepped down from command of
the submarine with four Navy Crosses and the Medal of
Honor for five patrols; he was among the submarine elite and
Gene Fluckey's war was over.

In January 1945, *Extractor,* a fleet salvage vessel commanded
by H.M. Babcock, was sailing from Apra Harbor, Guam, to
the Philippine Sea to pick up a damaged warship in a joint
safety zone, where positive identification was needed for a
sub or air attack. A radio message from Guam ordered *Extractor* to return to Apra, but the message was garbled and
Extractor continued, not wishing to break radio silence, and
expecting a repeat transmission.

The proud submarine *Guardfish*—the only warship at the
time to have won two Presidential Unit Citations, under skippers Burt Klakring and Bub Ward—entered the same area
while returning from patrol. *Guardfish* picked up a night
radar contact. The skipper, Commander Douglas T. Hammond, sent a message to submarine authorities in Guam requesting guidance. He was told that there were no friendly
ships in the area, but was reminded that he was in a safety
zone, and that if the contact was a surface ship it was probably friendly. The Guam operations officer apparently believed
Extractor had received the earlier message and was returning
to Apra.

Guardfish did not attempt to use the IFF (Identification,
Friend or Foe) communication with the unknown surface
ship. The U.S. boat submerged and in the morning twilight
of January 23, Hammond and his exec identified *Extractor*
as a Japanese I-365 class submarine running on the surface.
Hammond fired four torpedoes at a range of 1,200 yards.
Two hit. *Extractor* exploded and sank by the bow. One
glance at the stern coming out of the water showed that the

target was no submarine. *Guardfish* picked up seventy-three survivors. Six crewmembers were lost.

To Admiral Lockwood, three officers were at fault: *Extractor*'s captain for not taking action on a dispatch addressed to him which he could not read; Guam's operations officer for not contemplating that the ship picked up by *Guardfish* might be the vessel he directed into the area; and *Guardfish*'s skipper for not using additional means to identify his target. A court martial found both captains guilty of negligence. Admiral Lockwood was depressed by the incident: though U.S. submarines had often been attacked by friendlies, this was the first and only attack on a U.S. ship by a U.S. submarine during the whole war.

Admiral Lockwood suffered another severe embarrassment through a second major casualty inflicted by a U.S. submarine. One of the more successful skippers in 1944, Charles Elliott Loughlin, was CO of *Queenfish*. He chalked up two Navy Crosses and a Silver Star in three patrols, winning a Presidential Unit Citation for his boat. From Wilmington, North Carolina, Elliott Loughlin was a popular officer who had been an all-American basketball and tennis player at the Naval Academy, graduating in the Class of 1933. He was in the same bright Sub School class as Dick O'Kane, Dusty Dornin, Slade Cutter, and Bub Ward. It was Loughlin's misfortune to commit, in Admiral Lockwood's words, "the biggest error in the history of American submarine operations," one that might have resulted in serious reprisals by Japan.

In early 1945, through neutral Switzerland the U.S. State Department requested Japan to take Red Cross packages to Allied prisoners held in Southeast Asia. Japan finally agreed. Tokyo used the gesture as a device to bring vital war supplies with the Red Cross packages to their beleaguered forces in Indonesia, Singapore and Hong Kong. The ship chosen was *Awa Maru,* 11,600 tons. She bore 11-pound Red Cross gift packages as well as 500 tons of ammo, some 2,000 bombs, and 20 crated planes, which were unloaded at Saigon, Vietnam.

The ship was to be painted with a white cross on each side

of her funnel, illuminated at night, and two white crosses on both of her sides. There was no procedure for identification in the case of heavy fog. However, in the second week of February (when *Queenfish* had been on a previous patrol), a plain-language dispatch giving the markings, description, route, and schedule of *Awa Maru* was broadcast to all U.S. submarines. It was repeated three times a day over three days. Loughlin was not briefed on *Awa Maru* when he returned to Saipan between his third and fourth patrols. Early in March, the Japanese altered the route of the vessel, and a second message conveying this change was broadcast from SubPac in plain language. On March 28, two days before *Awa Maru* was to pass through the waters patrolled by Sub-Pac submarines, ComSubPac sent a general reminder to all vessels, this time in code. "Let pass safely *Awa Maru* carrying prisoner of war supplies. She will be passing through your areas between March 30 and April 4. She is lighted at night and plastered with white crosses." But the message did not signal out *Queenfish* as an addressee, nor did it give details of speed, course, or routing.

At 2200 on April 1, *Queenfish* picked up a pip on its radar at 17,000 yards, or about 10 miles. The sea at the time—in the northern end of the Formosa Strait—was covered with a thick fog. Skipper Loughlin and his attack party decided, from the size of the radar pip, that the fast-moving ship must be a destroyer, which Loughlin believed was rushing to forestall an attack on a convoy by Loughlin's wolf pack mate, *Sea Fox*. Since visibility had descended to 200 yards, the crew of *Queenfish* could hardly see past their own bow and were unable to make a visual sighting of the enemy vessel. Using radar bearings, Loughlin fired four torpedoes from the stern tubes. All hit and the radar target disappeared. Loughlin reversed course and searched for survivors. One was found. He said he was from *Awa Maru*. The ship was not sounding a foghorn, as she should have been under the rules for safe passage. Had *Queenfish*'s officers heard the fog warning, they would not have attacked. *Awa Maru* carried about 1,700 passengers, mainly sailors from sunken Japanese vessels. Loughlin immediately radioed the dreadful news to Admiral Lockwood in Guam.

The sinking placed the U.S. government in an awkward position. Washington had given Japan a safe-passage guarantee. The State Department was angry. Admiral King, Chief of Naval Operations, was furious. He commanded Admiral Nimitz in Guam: "Order *Queenfish* into port. Detach Loughlin from command and have him tried by general court martial."

Loughlin was shattered. So was Charlie Lockwood—that such a fine officer made such a serious and fatal mistake. There was also the fear that the Japanese would wreak barbarous reprisals upon U.S. submarine prisoners. *Queenfish* was ordered to Guam. Along the way, Loughlin got word that some airmen were down, and he managed to pick up thirteen men, the crew of a four-engined Navy patrol plane, who had been drifting in rubber rafts for four days.

Lockwood personally intervened to persuade Admiral King that there were mitigating circumstances in the case. Lockwood admitted his messages might have been confusing. He wanted to share any blame. Lockwood was loyal and fair, as usual. King's own chief-of-staff, submariner Admiral Richard Edwards, pleaded with his boss to calm down and reconsider, but Ernie King was adamant. Loughlin was tried by the general court convened in Guam and top-heavy with gold braid: two vice admirals, three rear admirals, and two captains, including submariner Lew Parks. The defense, to show lack of intent, introduced evidence that Loughlin believed he was shooting at a destroyer, since the torpedoes were fired at a depth setting of 3 feet, rather than much deeper as they would have been for an 11,000-ton liner.

The reason for the mistake was that *Queenfish*'s wayward communication officer, who deemed them not important enough, had not brought the earlier messages in plain language concerning *Awa Maru*'s route and schedule to Loughlin's personal attention. The officer filed the dispatch without telling anyone. In fact, many officers ignored plain-language dispatches on the grounds that anything important would be coded. Elliott Loughlin saw only the coded dispatch of

March 28, which could not make much sense to him—since it contained no details—unless he had seen the previous messages. The coded message mentioning a submarine's area, Loughlin thought, could have referred to any boat from Australia to the Aleutians. Every submarine in the Western Pacific was given the same dispatch. However, Loughlin readily accepted he was responsible for his officer's actions. He was not a man to pass the buck: he believed in loyalty down.

Loughlin was acquitted of the first two charges against him: culpable inefficiency in the performance of duty, and disobeying the lawful order of his superior officer. He was found guilty of the third count: negligence in obeying orders. The popular skipper was punished with a Letter of Admonition.

Admiral King was outraged by the mild verdict and light sentence. He and Secretary of the Navy James Forrestal put the heat on Admiral Nimitz, who was forced to issue Letters of Reprimand to the entire court martial board—an even heavier penalty than a Letter of Admonition. The incident seemed to show naval justice and Admiral King at their worst.

King vowed that Elliott Loughlin would never again get a Navy command; his career appeared to be in ruins. But Charlie Lockwood believed that his own staff might have been responsible for not spelling out the details concerning *Awa Maru*. Lockwood ordered Loughlin to the sub training command. He was then shifted to the staff of Commander Submarines Atlantic, a choice assignment, after Admiral Edwards called the submarine detail officer and ordered: "See that the young man gets a good job."

Once Admiral King retired, Loughlin continued a successful career in the Navy, reaching the rank of rear admiral, perhaps because much sympathy had developed toward him over what many considered Admiral King's high-handed tactics—which amounted to railroading a brave, young captain. Loughlin had no reason to change his opinion that "based on the information I had I felt that I was justified in making the attack."

*   *   *

Queenfish's blunder was more than balanced by the remarkable first patrol of George L. Street III in a new boat, *Tirante.* Street was a Virginia gentleman who made nine patrols on old *Gar*—four of them under the hapless Don McGregor as skipper. George Street's model as a skipper was Dick O'Kane at whose dining table he sat as a plebe at the Naval Academy. Street was fortunate to have as his exec the redoubtable Ned Beach, the most experienced and impressive officer of his age (Class of 1939) in the Submarine Force. Beach had served under skippers Roy Benson, Dusty Dornin, and Fritz Harlfinger in *Trigger* before moving to *Tirante.* He was overdue for his own command, which was to come soon. George and Ned made a great team—mutually admiring like Morton–O'Kane and O'Kane–Frazee. Among his officers was a reserve lieutenant, Endicott "Chub" Peabody II, future Governor of Massachusetts.

Ned Beach had a special concern: one of the *Tirante's* torpedoes made by the Westinghouse Corp. at Sharon, Pennsylvania, was donated to the Navy by the factory's workforce. It was elaborately decorated and George Street promised—amid many flashbulbs and toasts—to send the torpedo into a Japanese ship.

The new boat made the passage from Portsmouth to New London to Panama to Pearl for final training exercises. *Tirante* passed all tests with flags flying. Ned Beach reflected, however, that it often happened in life that the most expert, aggressive, far-seeing officer in training exercises somehow never quite found the same opportunities open to him in battle. Conversely, an individual who hadn't made an impression could rise to astonishing heights of effectiveness under the stimulus of extreme danger. So it was in submarines.

Once on station, in the Tsushima Strait between Japan and Korea, George Street, like Dick O'Kane earlier, found that targets in the open sea were scarce. So he searched for them, nosing through shallow coastal waters that were supposedly off-limits to submarines. Street and Beach wanted to blood *Tirante* as soon as possible because successful patrols usually began with successful first attacks. They needed to get their "Sharon Special" fish into action.

Like the Morton–O'Kane set-up, Ned Beach with his fine eye manned the periscope in a submerged attack, and he sighted the TBT binoculars on the bridge during surface fights. In their first attack, Street used the stern tubes as *Tirante* sank a freighter off Nagasaki. Three days later a larger freighter came into range, which Street tracked with the help of Chub Peabody on the torpedo data computer. Street fired a spread including the "Sharon Special," serial number 58009. The torpedoes hit the freighter, which jack-knifed as it sank. Street called for a camera, which Beach handed him. Here was proof on March 28 for the people back in Sharon that their torpedo worked well indeed.

Three nights later Ned Beach received a shock that seemed almost physical. *Tirante* was supposed to make contact with *Trigger*, his old boat, to explore working together. But *Tirante* was unable to raise *Trigger:* "*Trigger* from *Tirante . . . Trigger* from *Tirante . . . SS 237* from *SS 420 . . .* Come in please . . ." The calls went out all night long.

For three nights, *Tirante* tried to raise *Trigger.* By then Ned Beach knew the chances were that *Trigger* was gone. He could visualize the end: a bomb, a depth charge, a mine, a torpedo. The angry water taking possession. Most crewmen struggling in indescribable confusion. Eyes turned to the depth gauges as the needles began their crazy spin. The deep-sea gauges reaching the limit on the dial. The rush of water. The groaning and creaking of *Trigger*'s dying body. The trapped and pounding pulses of the men. Down, down, down, to who knew what depth, until the ribs gave way, the sheet steel collapsed. Beach thought of *Trigger*'s gallant spirit ascending to the Valhalla of ships, bearing with her the souls of eighty-nine loyal sailors. His heart felt like lead.

The next morning, *Tirante* sent men aboard a fishing vessel to capture a prisoner for interrogation later at the home base. *Tirante* picked up three prisoners in the commando-type boarding party led by Chub Peabody, All-American, Harvard 1942, carrying a dagger, and wearing a beat-up, black sweater with a huge, red "H." Chub thought his team looked like a bunch of pirates. He had developed a real gung-ho attitude after his first depth charging. "Hey," he realized, "these people are trying to kill us. We have to sink them before they sink us. We have to kill them before they kill us."

On April 9, *Tirante* sank a large transport and on April 14, *Tirante* closed on Quelpart Island, which Mush Morton in *Wahoo* and Dick O'Kane in *Tang* had explored in their journeys to the Yellow Sea. Street and Beach worked out a plan. They would nose into the Quelpart harbor anchorage when the enemy would least expect, and attack. *Tirante* had to move between the shore and a minefield, which fortunately they had plotted on their chart. Ned Beach looked at the chart and said: "Let's do it."

Admiral Lockwood's citation told the rest of the story: "In order to reach this anchorage, he would have to take his submarine through many miles of shallow water in which his ship would not be able to dive. The harbor was inevitably mined, numerous reefs and shoals were known to exist, and shore-based radar, numerous patrol vessels, and extensive air coverage closely guarded the whole area. Fully realizing the mountainous dangers involved, the commanding officer made his decision—'Battle Stations, torpedo'—a decision to attempt an act far above and beyond the call of duty. Disregarding the possibility of minefields and the five shore-based radars in the immediate vicinity, *Tirante* closed the shore land and progressed into the harbor through numerous anti-submarine vessels. The gun crews were at their stations, as *Tirante* would have to fight her way out on the suface if attacked. Once in the inner harbor, the current was checked and a rapid set-up was made on a nearby 10,000-ton tanker. Torpedoes were skillfully fired at this target and a great mushroom of white blinding flame shot 2,000 feet into the air and a thunderous roar nearly flattened the crew of *Tirante*. In the light of the burning tanker, two new Mikura-class frigates spotted *Tirante* and started in for the kill. Quickly bringing his submarine to bear on the leading frigate, the commanding officer tenaciously fired two 'do or die' torpedoes at this vessel, which was endeavoring to block his escape and then swung his ship and fired his last torpedo at the other frigate. With all his torpedoes expended, the commanding officer headed his ship out of the confined harbor at full speed just as the torpedoes hit the first frigate and blew it sky-high. Seconds later, the sister ship was hit and it, too, followed a like fate and disintegrated. The commanding officer slipped right out of the enemy's hands and passed undetected along the shoreline before retiring to deeper water. In addition to this history-making offensive against the enemy, a 100-ton lugger was sunk by gunfire, three prisoners were captured from a schooner and two aviators were picked up from a downed Jap aircraft."

On *Tirante*'s return to Midway, with six enemy ships sunk, George Street, Ned Beach and company received a triumphant welcome. Lieutenant Ralph Pleatman, who served on Lew Parks' *Pompano* and Slade Cutter's *Seahorse,* was now on *Devilfish* between patrols. He greeted Ned Beach with his hand held out. "Congratulations on your patrol," Ralph said. "You and George have called out the biggest celebration I've seen yet on this damned island." Pleatman's demeanor turned serious. "Have you heard about your old ship?"

Hope flooded through Ned Beach. Maybe *Trigger* had somehow turned up.

"No. What is it?"

"Awfully sorry, Ned. She's three weeks overdue. She's been turned in as overdue and presumed lost."

Beach knew Ralph Pleatman's sorrow was genuine. Dave Connole, *Trigger*'s skipper, had served with Pleatman aboard *Pompano,* which had gone down in August 1943.

George Street was awarded a Medal of Honor for *Tirante*'s first patrol; Ned Beach received a Navy Cross, rare for an exec; Chub Peabody got a Silver Star; and the submarine's crew won the Presidential Unit Citation. A magnanimous man, George Street gave Ned Beach half the credit for his Medal of Honor, and his *Tirante* crew the other half.

Admiral Lockwood was amused when he finally learned the story of H.H. "Hank" Quanstrom, a Motor Machinist's Mate with a refit crew at Midway Submarine Base. Quanstrom had served aboard the old *S-31* on a patrol out of Dutch Harbor in the Aleutians. The submarine was bombed by a friendly plane and in the resulting getaway, Quanstrom's arm was chewed up in an engine room accident.

After hospitalization he was eventually assigned to the refit crew; he kept trying to get back on a fleet boat going on patrol without success. After seven months at Midway, Quanstrom was desperate to make a run and win a combat pin. After a farewell beer bust for *Snapper,* Quanstrom persuaded a member of the engine room gang to smuggle him aboard. The next morning *Snapper* left on patrol with Quanstrom hiding in the bilges. He waited until nightfall to reveal himself to the ship's officers, figuring it would be too late to turn back to Midway. Skipper William Walker, who was in Dick O'Kane's Sub School class, was furious. He had to break radio silence to report the stowaway's presence on board. Walker put Hank Quanstrom to work washing the crew's dungarees, and peeling potatoes. Eventually, he was assigned to the engine room, where he turned out to be a valuable asset on the patrol, which was a success and qualified the crew for the combat insignia. Returning to Midway, Walker considered preferring charges of "jumping ship" against Quanstrom. He gave Quanstrom a deck court martial at Midway and sentenced him to ten days restriction, a mild form of punishment. Walker admired Quanstrom's desire to get into the fight against the Japanese, so the ten days restriction was served aboard *Snapper* traveling to Mare Island for overhaul. Stowaway Hank Quanstrom wound up with his coveted sub combat pin—and home leave in the States!

By early 1945, U.S. submarines blanketed constricted areas like the South China Sea, leading one Japanese officer— victim of a sinking—to complain that it was possible to walk from Singapore to Hong Kong on the tops of U.S. periscopes.

Flounder under Commander James E. Stevens was cruising submerged off the coast of Indochina. *Hoe* skippered by Commander Miles Refo, former exec of *Jack,* was running submerged in the area just to the north of *Flounder,* but was pulled south by a 4-knot current. At 1700 hours, February 23, 1945, while creeping at 60 feet depth, speed 1.8 knots, Refo felt his sub crash. He first thought it had hit an undersea rock. The shock seemed to be forward on the starboard side. The boat turned up with a 4-degree angle and broached the surface. The CO ordered Battle Stations and blew all main ballast tanks. Topside, Refo found the sea all clear. *Hoe* seemed to have suffered no serious damage. Refo was puzzled.

Flounder, meanwhile, felt a violent crash with a stem-to-stern shudder. Water poured through a shear valve. An alert crewmember closed the valve and the leak stopped. A soundman reported a tremendous rush of air and the swish-swish of high-speed screws starting and stopping on the starboard bow.

Skipper James E. Stevens sensed that his boat had been run over by another submersible. The screw noises faded out. Eleven minutes later *Flounder* reached periscope depth. The surface was clear. That night an exchange of signals with Pearl Harbor established that the two subs had collided underwater. The damage to *Flounder* was fairly extensive, since *Hoe* had run over *Flounder* from left to right, just forward of the periscope shears. Stanchions and the forward gun platform were damaged. The radar mast was bent and the antenna broken. *Flounder* had to return to port. The incident was the only submerged collision on record during the war.

In April, *Besugo,* commanded by Herman E. Miller, sank a surfaced submarine flying a Japanese flag in the Java Sea. A survivor was picked up and identified himself as the officer-of-the-deck on the German *U-183.* A few months earlier, the *Flounder* under skipper Stevens had sunk the *U-537* in the Java Sea. Two other American boats sank German vessels in the Pacific: Thomas Wogan's *Tarpon* torpedoed the German commerce raider *Michel* which was bringing high-priority cargo to Japan; and Herb Andrews commanding *Gurnard* sank a freighter.

In the spring of 1945 Rear Admiral Jimmy Fife moved his

headquarters from Australia to Subic Bay in the Philippines. He travelled aboard *Hardhead* on a war patrol in the South China Sea. *Hardhead* sank a ship, qualifying Fife for the submarine combat insignia.

Guam and Saipan were now major forward bases. Boats from the Mariana bases expanded their lifeguard duties along the flight path to Tokyo, scooping up carrier aviators and B-29 bomber crews. *Pomfret* picked up a downed carrier aviator in Sagami Nada, sometimes called Lower Tokyo Bay, and the incident was widely reported. *Stingray* submerged and used its tall periscope to tow a pilot in his life raft away from an enemy-held island for a full hour, until he was safely out of reach of the Japanese guns.

Lifeguard subs found they were picking up large crews of B-29 bombers, which could not make it home from Japan. The Army Air Force supplied B-29 "superdumbos" (named after smaller rescue Catalina flying boats called "dumbos"), which orbited along the standard B-29 flight paths. They radioed U.S. submarines when their big bombers got into trouble and had to ditch. *Pintado* picked up the entire eleven-man crew of a bomber, with the bomb group commander aboard. In thanks, the B-29 command named one of their planes "Pintado." Submariners were welcomed by the pilots in General Curtis Lemay's bomber command on Guam and Saipan. Some even went along on superdumbo missions, among them Murray Frazee, *Tang*'s fine exec, who now had his own boat, *Gar,* which was used for training at Guam. He volunteered for a superdumbo mission over southern Japan and acted as a submarine contact with the boats in case of an emergency. He was to radio a submarine and vector it to a downed B-29 crew. Fraz's mission was exciting but his talents on the long flight weren't needed. No bombers were down. However, he did get a look at Japan and took the controls on the way back to Guam. So Fraz qualified for eleven submarine war patrols and one B-29 mission.

Another submarine officer temporarily based on Guam, Paul Schratz, who had served on the troubled *Sterlet* and was now a prospective commanding officer in temporary command of boats in refit, made a B-29 mission over Japan on the massive night fire raids. He was put on a "Pathfinder" plane, one of three lead aircraft over the target, Nagasaki. It was a sixteen-hour, 3,200-mile flight and Schratz was both exhausted and elated on his return. Later, General LeMay recommended Schratz for an Air Medal. When the recommendation came to the attention of the Sub Base staff, they were not pleased. Schratz was informed that he had committed a serious offense: jeopardizing himself and his knowledge of Ultra on a mission over Japan. So for the same mission Schratz was being considered for a medal by the Air Force and a court martial by the Navy. Both recommendations were quietly forgotten. Lockwood issued an edict that no submariners were to take B-29 bombing rides: submarines on lifeguard duty were there to pick up downed aviators—not sub sailors.

While Guam could be dangerous for submariners taking B-29 rides, it proved fatal to a group of submariner souvenir hunters from Camp Dealey, the rest area at the new Sub Base. In early 1945, seven crewmen from *Sea Fox* went sightseeing with a Guamanian constabulary officer through the scrub jungle. Only a mile from Camp Dealey, they were ambushed by a couple of dozen Japanese soldiers who had not surrendered and were living in the bush. Six men were killed. Two wounded sailors managed to escape back to camp to tell the story. Submarine sailors were angry but were dissuaded by officers from roaring off into the jungle to look for Japanese soldiers still at large. From then on, anyone leaving the vicinity of Camp Dealey carried side arms. Admiral Lockwood did not appreciate the irony of his men surviving war patrols only to be killed near a submarine base.

With submarines now running out of targets, the boats were spending more time in constricted waters, many of which were mined. Lockwood expended much effort trying to figure out how to cope with the minefields hampering his vessels. U.S. submarine skippers were justly skittish about Japanese mines, and knew most straits and other passages that they had to negotiate were mined in parts. Several sinkings were attributed to mines, among them *Escolar, Robalo, Scorpion, Runner, Pickerel, Albacore, Swordfish, Scamp,* and *Pompano.*

Lockwood had ruled the enclosed, traffic-rich Sea of Japan off limits to U.S. submarines after *Wahoo* was lost in the autumn of 1943. Minefields at the only three entrances heavily guarded it: Tsushima to the south, Tsugaru between Honshu and Hokkaido, and the northerly La Perouse Strait.

Operating close to minefields was especially hard on the nerves of submariners, inching around shallow waters where the explosives were suspected. It was bad enough spotting them floating—Eli Reich reporting seeing a hundred in the East China Sea. Even more unnerving was the thought of the ones that weren't visible.

Submarines sometimes took any anti-mine precautions they could. In *Bluefish,* the Chief of the Boat ordered the forward torpedo room door dogged shut because of the danger of mines. He figured, not incorrectly, that if the forward part of boat hit one, the ship might still be saved. However, the torpedomen were decidedly unhappy about the order; it made them feel expendable. Officers used the head in the forward torpedo room, and on his next visit, the captain asked the torpedomen why the door was dogged. "The Chief of the Boat wants it that way, Captain," a torpedoman replied. Skipper George Forbes promptly ordered the door opened except during Battle Stations, the normal procedure. "We'll all go back to base together," Forbes said, "or we don't go back at all." The tenants of *Bluefish*'s forward torpedo room received the countermanded order with some relief.

To counter the growing mine threat to submarines, U.S. scientists at the War Research Laboratory of the University of California in San Diego were developing a device to detect mines underwater—allowing subs to operate in mined waters. This invention used the echo-ranging principle with FM sonar sending out electronic pulses that allowed a submarine to "see" a mine in the sea ahead, and avoid it. It also meant that submarines could search a defended area for mines before a big Allied amphibious operation.

The FM gear was installed in *Tinosa* during an overhaul in Mare Island in late 1944. The captain was Commander

Richard Latham and his exec was Roger Paine, who was briefly exec of *Wahoo* before he was left in Pearl Harbor, hospitalized for appendicitis. *Tinosa* began an extended series of tests with the FM sonar using simulated minefields in San Diego Bay. Skipper Latham and Exec Paine were up to the painstaking task. Roger Paine had become skipper of a training boat, *S-34*, after leaving *Wahoo* and it was eventually installed with the FM sonar. He, therefore, was used to the equipment, in practice at least. Latham found his crew unhappy with their task: searching out minefields hardly appealed to submariners. Some had expected a longer period stateside before going out on patrol again. A few asked to get off in San Diego but Latham, like Dick O'Kane in *Tang,* insisted that transfers wait until Pearl Harbor. Roger Paine knew the crew had qualms about the FM gear, fearing they were being used as guinea pigs on a mission completely different from a war patrol. While Paine thought the FM gear was a fine piece of equipment, he knew it was not perfect. Some crewmembers thought that experimenting with the FM gear involved more risk than they were willing to take.

In Pearl, those crewmen who wanted to get off were allowed to do so, and replacement volunteers quickly filled *Tinosa*'s complement. The boat patrolled in the Okinawa area, and Latham and Paine began testing the FM sonar and mapping minefields—information that would be useful in the invasion by the Pacific Fleet amphibious forces. At one point, Paine said, a mine cable brushed along *Tinosa*'s steel hull. A cool officer, Paine conceded that this was a scary experience. Then the FM went on the blink; *Tinosa* had to stop and anchor underwater until repairs were made. When they fixed the FM and tried to pull up the anchor, the chain broke, and *Tinosa* finished its patrol without an anchor.

Admiral Lockwood, who was fascinated with technical devices, was delighted with *Tinosa*'s first FM mission and declared it had earned the combat insignia, even though no ships were sunk. He awarded Dick Latham the Navy Cross and Roger Paine a Bronze Star for his deft navigation during the dangerous patrol.

Not everyone was as happy as Lockwood with the FM device. Captain Jasper Holmes, the former submariner whose Pacific Fleet intelligence officers plotted Japanese mine-fields from U.S. submarine reports and captured Japanese documents, confessed that the project did not appeal to him. The thought of conning a submerged submarine probing blindly for mines that could blow the boat to smithereens gave him nightmares.

By the spring of 1945, the new FM gear had been installed and tested on other U.S. submarines in American waters and then near the Japanese coastline. In charge of the submarine project was Commander W.B. "Barney" Sieglaff, the successful captain of *Tautog* who was now on Lockwood's staff. When he was satisfied that the FM gear was working well, and that the Sea of Japan could be penetrated, Admiral Lockwood assembled nine submarines at Guam to conduct joint training. Lockwood asked Admiral Nimitz for permission to lead the operation personally. Nimitz refused.

When Barney Sieglaff thought the skippers could handle the mine-detecting gear, he sent the boats off to the Sea of Japan. An older and relatively inexperienced officer, Commander E.T. Hydeman, captain of *Sea Dog,* led the submarines, all equipped with the new FM equipment.

The boats, called "Hydeman's Hellcats," were: *Crevalle,* Commander Everett H. Steinmetz; *Spadefish,* Commander William J. Germershausen; *Tunny,* Commander George E. Pierce; *Skate,* Commander Richard Lynch; *Bonefish,* Commander Lawrence L. Edge; *Flying Fish,* Commander R.D. Risser; *Bowfin,* Commander Alexander K. Tyree; and *Tinosa,* Commander Dick Latham. By this time, Roger Paine had been transferred off *Tinosa* to new construction—commanding officer of USS *Cubera* which was being built at the Electric Boat Company in Groton.

In early June, the submerged Hellcats crept through Tsushima Strait, the southern entrance to the Sea of Japan. Shooting was timed to begin at sunset, June 9, after all the submarines were in position in their assigned individual operating areas. Believing the Sea of Japan a privileged sanctuary for their shipping, the enemy was caught off-guard when the Hellcats stole into the forbidden sea.

The Hellcats sank twenty-seven enemy merchant ships and a submarine in twelve days—for some 57,000 tons. The top scorers were pack leader Earl Hydeman's *Sea Dog* with six ships, followed by Bill Germershausen in *Spadefish* with five sinkings. Dick Latham's *Tinosa* sank four ships. *Skate* with Tiny Lynch, got the submarine.

Then according to plan, they rendezvoused at the western approach to the northern La Perouse Strait. On the night of June 24 they ran on the surface at 18 knots in two columns through a wool-thick fog. The operation was a great success. But it cost the Submarine Force *Bonefish,* which did not make the rendezvous and was never heard from again. She was the last submarine under Admiral Lockwood's command to be sunk in the war.

During 1945, before the loss of *Bonefish,* six U.S. submarines had gone down: *Swordfish, Barbel, Kete, Trigger, Snook,* and *Lagarto.* On August 6, a few days before the ceasefire with Japan, USS *Bullhead,* departed from Fremantle, reported she was passing through the Lombok Strait to operate in the Java Sea. A Japanese pilot later said he dropped two bombs, hitting a submarine in the area. *Bullhead* went down with all hands, the last U.S. submarine to be lost in World War II.

Other submarines had by now entered the Sea of Japan. On August 14, a few hours before the cessation of hostilities, *Torsk,* a new boat on her second patrol under Commander Bafford Lewellen, made two attacks on frigates. He sank one and then fired his last torpedo shot at the other, Coast Defense Vessel 47, about 800 tons. It went down—the last Japanese vessel sunk by a U.S submarine in the Pacific War.

At the end, some 288 U.S. boats had been commissioned. Of those, 185 sank at least one enemy ship. Of the 465 skippers who went on war patrols, 76 sank 5 or more ships. The Submarine Force in the Pacific launched 1,682 patrols, of which 1,050 were rated successful, or just over 62 percent. U.S. boats accounted for more than 5 million tons of merchant shipping, in effect blockading Japan, and another 600,000 tons of warships. Twenty major warships were sunk, including 1 battleship, 8 aircraft carriers and 11 cruisers. But these tremendous deeds went largely unnoticed by the general public because of the secrecy surrounding the Silent Service. During the war, 52 American boats were lost. At its peak, the close-knit Submarine Force had no more than 4,000 officers and 46,000 enlisted men—with only 16,000 sailors actually manning the combat submarines. The Submarine Force lost men at a rate six times higher than the surface Navy: 3,505 submariners are, as they say, still on patrol.

CHAPTER TWENTY-SIX

The Sub Force Ace of Aces

Tang's crew was physically burnt out at Omori camp, but spirits brightened when word circulated of the blast of a new kind of bomb at Hiroshima and Nagasaki. They were buoyed, too, by the almost daily sight of aircraft carrier planes on bombing and strafing runs over Tokyo Bay. Overhead the B-29s bombed frequently. The POWs sensed the war was nearly over. On August 15, the camp's loudspeaker system carried the voice of Emperor Hirohito giving a speech. With their rudimentary Japanese, they could make out the phrase: "The war is over."

When the news came, the Japanese guards slaughtered an old horse and carried it with them as they fled the Omori camp, presumably for their homes. But the canny prisoner cooks had scraped out the intestines of the animal. They chopped them up and mixed them with "gyp-corn," a rough meal fed to pigs. The POWs celebrated the Pacific victory with their horse-gut "dumpo" stew, the first meat any of them had had since arriving in Japan.

There were no immediate plans for the prisoners. They stayed put in the camp, since most were not capable of walking very far. Dick O'Kane's physical condition had deteriorated further because of beriberi and jaundice. He was exhausted, frail, going downhill fast. Dick had provided leadership to his men in a difficult situation, vastly different to the one he had trained and worked in. He neither cracked under torture and the many beatings nor gave the Japanese vital information: *Tang*'s depth capability, a description of the night surface tactics he developed, or the existence of Ultra.

B-29 bombers began dropping parcels of clothing, canned

goods and other foodstuffs from the sky—so much, in fact, that prisoners took cover for fear of getting hit. Dick O'Kane thought the camp looked like a giant salad bowl. Pappy Boyington headed for an air-raid shelter, declaring, "After living through all I have, I'm damned if I'm going to be killed by being hit on the head by a crate of peaches."

On August 28, 1945, Captain Harold Stassen, the Governor of Minnesota who was on military leave with Admiral Halsey's Third Fleet staff, arrived to make arrangements for the removal of the 604 prisoners from Omori. Appalled by what he found, Stassen ordered an immediate evacuation of the POWs to ships of the Third Fleet that were gathering in Tokyo Bay for the formal surrender on September 2. Without a precise plan for repatriation and with everything in flux, *Tang* prisoners became separated during the evacuation, as U.S. landing craft pushed up on Omori Island in the Bay.

Jesse DaSilva, who had gone from 170 pounds to 100 pounds, was taken to the hospital ship *Benevolence* where he was put to bed and given blood transfusions and food. He was in no condition to fly home so he was transferred to another hospital ship, *Rescue,* for a 21-day voyage to the U.S.

Larry Savadkin, who also had a bad case of beriberi, made a do-it-yourself trip home. Over the camp loudspeaker, he heard that C-54 transport pilots bringing in relief supplies would informally take prisoners back to Guam. On the spur of the moment, he took a boat to Yokohama, hitched a ride to the airport, and hopped aboard a C-54 for Guam. There he was taken to a hospital. Savadkin was one of the first POWs to arrive from Japan. This was the first news hospital officials heard of submariner prisoners, and immediately notified SubPac headquarters. They sent a car for Larry to take him for a chat with Admiral Lockwood; then to the Officers Club for a Saturday night dance. He was to dine with a nurse, but his hepatitis and jaundice meant he found it hard to digest fatty foods. The nurse persuaded him that he'd be better off in the hospital than at the dance. Larry was flown to Pearl Harbor and the Aiea Naval Hospital there. Intelligence officers and the Red Cross debriefed him and he bought a new uniform. He was soon flown to San Francisco, and Oak

Knoll Naval Hospital in Oakland. On September 10, he arrived by plane in New York City. "It was all *ad hoc,*" he said.

Clayton Decker fared better than most because of a hearty constitution. In the Omori camp, his roommate was Major Pappy Boyington. They boarded a landing craft together for the hospital ship *Benevolence.* After a couple of days aboard *Benevolence,* Decker stuck with Boyington. They went ashore to the airport at the Yokosuka Naval Base and boarded a C-54, the military version of a DC-4 airliner. Decker was the only enlisted man aboard the flight and attributed his presence to his friend Pappy. Eventually, Clay Decker arrived at the Alameda, California, Naval Air Station. There, he was met by his wife and four-year-old son.

His wife informed him that she thought he was dead and had remarried. "It was a great shock," Clay recalled, "to both of us. She was shocked to find out that I was alive. I was shocked to find that I was no longer Papa-san." Decker obtained a divorce, remarried, and remained happily with his second wife for more than fifty years.

Boats Leibold's weight had also dropped from 170 to about 100 pounds, and he had a badly infected foot. He stuck with his skipper. Like the other POWs, Dick O'Kane had suffered a huge weight loss: he was less than 100 pounds. In addition, he was running a high fever that could easily have killed him in his weakened state. Leibold accompanied Dick to the hospital ship *Relief* in Tokyo Bay. After emergency treatment they were moved to an LST, which was fitted out as a hospital ship. Leibold and O'Kane were then put in an isolated ward aboard. One morning, the doctors informed Leibold that he was being flown out immediately to the United States. He went to O'Kane's room to tell him the news, but Dick was in a deep sleep, apparently heavily sedated by the medics. Leibold was taken to the airport and flown via Guam, Johnson Island, Kwajalein, and Honolulu to Pearl Harbor and Aiea Naval Hospital. At every stop, a representative of the Submarine Force was on hand to see that the men were looked after, and if there was anything they needed.

After a few days' rest in Pearl, Boats Leibold was driven to

meet Admiral Lockwood. He offered the men a room in the
Royal Hawaiian, but Leibold and a few other Navy POWs
were anxious to get home. In San Francisco, another Sub
Force representative suggested a room at the St. Francis
Hotel, but a Navy nurse insisted Leibold be taken directly to
Oak Knoll Naval Hospital for treatment. A submarine officer
managed to sneak Leibold out of the hospital to get him a
new set of blues, the chief's uniform he had never worn, with
all his attendant ribbons.

Each man was sent to a naval hospital closest to his home:
in Leibold's case, this was the Long Beach Naval Hospital
where he was a patient with Jesse DaSilva.

Ernestine O'Kane had no word about the fate of her husband in the months after *Tang*'s loss was announced. She
moved to a rented house in Dick's family's home town of
Durham, New Hampshire, so that the children could be near
their grandparents. There was no immediate word about
Dick when the war ended. Her hopes sank. Then twenty-four
hours after Harold Stassen's visit to Omori, Washington informed Ernestine that her husband was alive.

Dick O'Kane reached Guam in slightly better shape than
when he left Ofuna. Larry Savadkin, preceding him, informed Admiral Lockwood his skipper was treated with special barbarity, but had not cracked under it. Dick O'Kane,
Savadkin reported, did the Navy proud. O'Kane consulted
with Lockwood and said he didn't want to go directly home.
It was Lockwood's opinion that Dick thought his physical
condition was too pitiful and shocking for his family to see.
He was just skin and bones. His arms and legs looked no bigger than an average man's wrists. His eyes were bright yellow from jaundice. Lockwood was convinced that O'Kane's
dysentery and jaundice would have killed him had he been
kept prisoner a few more weeks. Dick's case was the worst
Lockwood saw among the returned submariner POWs. It infuriated Charlie Lockwood to see this human wreckage from
the Japanese camps: he compared them to the well-fed, even
contented, German, Italian and some Japanese POWs in the
United States and Canada, but he remarked that "nothing
ever has, and nothing ever will, daunt Dick O'Kane."

After six weeks of overseas recuperation, Dick O'Kane returned home in early October and was sent to the Naval Hospital at Portsmouth, New Hampshire, as an outpatient. Early in 1946, he was considered fit for duty again.

When the submarine records were added up, revised by JANAC after the war, and re-revised by Commander Alden more recently, Dick O'Kane and *Tang* led all the rest. O'Kane's updated total of sinkings came to twenty-seven, making him the leading skipper by far. He probably sank more tonnage than any other captain. *Tang* was the leading submarine in terms of the number of ships sunk: *Tautog* was second with twenty-three, under three different skippers. Dick O'Kane's third patrol with ten ships sunk was the single most success-ful of the war. According to Alden, the eight ships sunk on *Tang*'s last patrol was the second highest patrol total of the conflict, exceeding by one the sinkings during *Wahoo*'s fourth patrol with Mush Morton as skipper and Dick O'Kane as executive officer. Alden suggests that two of the ships listed as sunk by *Wahoo* in JANAC's figures were only damaged. *Tang* received a rare second Presidential Unit Citation for the fourth and fifth patrols, one of only three ships in the U.S. Navy to win two of the prized awards.

Yet Dick O'Kane was no bloodthirsty warrior interested only in setting records. He had respect for the courage and ability of Japanese ships and sailors. As he reflected, "The total destruction and loss of life on both sides may seem ap-palling, but this was total war waged against a stalwart and equally dedicated enemy. I know of no submariner, however, who would not have gladly settled for half his sinkings or less if that number could only have sufficed in terminating the war. We are, after all, mariners first and submariners sec-ond, with a continuing love for all ships and the sea."

On March 27, 1946, for his exploits on *Tang*'s fifth patrol, President Harry S. Truman presented Commander Richard O'Kane with the Medal of Honor at the White House. The President cited Dick's last two attacks on the convoys in the Formosa Strait "for conspicuous gallantry and intrepidity at the risk of his life above and beyond the call of duty . . . This is a saga of one of the greatest submarine cruises of all time, led by her illustrious, gallant and courageous commanding officer, and his crew of daring officers and men."

Dick O'Kane thus became arguably the most highly decorated U.S. naval officer of World War II. He was awarded the Medal of Honor, three Navy Crosses, a Legion of Merit, three Silver Stars, a Commendation Ribbon, and three Presidential Unit Citations—as well as winning battle stars for eleven war patrols.

O'Kane's Medal of Honor award allowed him to nominate Larry Savadkin and Frank Springer for Navy Crosses, and request Silver Stars for Ed Beaumont, Floyd Caverly, James Culp, Jesse DaSilva, Clayton Decker, Mel Enos, Lawrence Ericksen, Hank Flanagan, John Heubeck, Dick Kroth, Paul Larson, Bill Leibold, Pete Narowanski, John Parker, Basil Pearce, Hayes Trukke, Leland Weekley, James White, Paul Wines, and George Zofcin. A Bronze Star went to Marvin De Lapp, and a Letter of Commendation to Charles Andriolo. The decorations were quickly approved for the gallant crew.

So ended the wartime exploits of Richard O'Kane, the Submarine Force's Ace of Aces. In summing up, Ned Beach, himself a heroic submariner, said simply, "*Tang* was the best," and Dick O'Kane "the most daring skipper."

CHAPTER TWENTY-SEVEN

"When Heroism Truly Meant Something"

Dick O'Kane initially adjusted to post-war life in the U.S. Navy. After his recuperation period, and his reception at the White House, he joined the staff of Commander Mare Island Group, Pacific Reserve Fleet, with additional duty as Commanding Officer of the submarine tender *Pelias*. During that assignment, which extended to July 1948, he attended and testified at the War Crimes Trials in Tokyo in September–October, 1947.

He then served as Executive Officer of *Nereus,* a sub tender based at San Diego. In August 1949 he became Commander Submarine Division 32, also based in San Diego. He was selected as a student at the Armed Forces Staff College, Norfolk, Virginia, from August 1950 until January 1951. He then moved to New London where he became Assistant Officer in Charge of the Submarine School, and in July 1952 became Officer in Charge of the Sub School. He won his fourth stripe to full captain. When possible, he looked after former *Tang* crewmen, helping them get assignments they wanted.

In 1953, O'Kane became skipper of submarine tender *Sperry,* and the following year moved up to command Submarine Squadron Seven, with *Sperry,* a submarine rescue ship, and twelve boats in his charge. He was then chosen to attend the Naval War College at Newport, Rhode Island, thought to be a choice assignment for future promotion.

Dick O'Kane seemed headed for flag rank. In his career, he had avoided duty in Washington or, for that matter, much in the way of any staff duty ashore. He was a man of action and not keen to serve in bureaucratic jobs, but most officers climbing the ladder to flag rank needed to serve their time

behind a desk and to learn their way around the naval bu-
reaucracy. Dick couldn't evade desk duty forever. Captain
O'Kane was assigned to the Ship Characteristics Board, Office of the Chief of Naval Operations in the Navy Department in the Pentagon.

In this job, Dick was bored and unhappy, his restless mind
not put to good use. Pete Galantin, wartime skipper of *Halibut* whom O'Kane succeeded as ComSubRon 7 and who
eventually made four-star admiral, explained, "Dick was a
pragmatic innovator, impatient with routine and scornful of
any rigidity in planning or procedure. In a Pentagon assignment that was little more than clerical, updating an interior
communications manual, he was completely miscast." O'Kane
himself observed of that job, "What I have accomplished in
one year could be done in one month." He believed that the
many short-term postings, characteristic of the peacetime
Navy, left him with "a feeling of uselessness and futility."

Old shipmates thought Dick's lack of tact and outspoken
nature might not set too well with senior brass in Washington. "He was always progressive, always looking ahead," Bill
Leibold said. "In the peacetime Navy, he might not be happy
as a flag officer."

In 1957, Dick O'Kane, now forty-six, and his friend and
fellow wartime submarine skipper, Chester W. Nimitz Jr.,
fretted over the lack of challenge in their careers, and the difficulties of supporting their families as children approached
college age. Both requested early retirement, as of July 1,
1957. Under the rules then in effect, they could retire one
rank higher because of their combat decorations. They both,
therefore, retired as rear admirals. It was an action widely
noted in the Navy and it prompted Hanson W. Baldwin, the
military affairs expert of the *New York Times* (and an Annapolis graduate) to write a column that received much attention.
Baldwin decried the loss of such respected, combat-proven
officers to the U.S. Navy.

Admiral Arleigh Burke, the Chief of Naval Operations,
asked Pete Galantin to look into the underlying reasons why
two such eminent submarine officers quit so early. "I was
certain," Galantin said, "that their decisions were prompted

by disenchantment with peacetime Navy duty, whereby many experienced officers, accustomed to high responsibility and command at sea were relegated to dull administrative chores ashore. Men with the energy, initiative, and daring of Dick O'Kane and Chester Nimitz, qualities that had made them good submarine officers, could not be happy and productive in such an environment."

Larry Savadkin followed his *Tang* skipper's later career, expecting O'Kane to make flag rank. "I had great confidence in Dick's abilities," he said. "Dick did not care for things that didn't count. So much stuff in peacetime consists of things that don't count."

Savadkin remained in the Navy. He commanded submarines then shifted into the amphibious forces, served in Korea and commanded an amphibious squadron in Vietnam, before retiring as a captain.

Murray Frazee stayed in submarines and then took a law degree courtesy of the U.S. Navy. He commanded a submarine squadron and served in the Judge Advocate General's office. He retired as a four-stripe captain. He practiced law in his hometown of Gettysburg, Pennsylvania, becoming mayor.

Boats Leibold was offered a commission, became an officer in the Submarine Force as a specialist in diving operations, and captain of the sub rescue vessel *Florikan*. He retired as a full commander.

Wahoo's Roger Paine stayed in the Navy, first in submarines then moving into destroyers and other commands and, as an expert in nuclear power, he reached the rank of rear admiral before retiring.

George Grider commanded a peacetime submarine—he relieved Roger Paine as CO of *Cubera*—then developed heart problems and received a medical discharge. He became a lawyer and was elected from Memphis to the U.S. House of Representatives.

Forest Sterling, too, remained in the Navy as a Chief Petty Officer, and eventually retired to the Naval Home in Gulfport, Mississippi.

They all agreed that Dick O'Kane was a brilliant maverick

who adored serving on ships, and detested bureaucratic assignments—and showed it.

So Dick O'Kane—like his famous wartime submarine colleagues Creed Burlingame, Slade Cutter, Dusty Dornin, George Street, Tommy Dykers, Burt Klakring, Roy Gross, Gordon Underwood, and especially Ned Beach (who many combat veterans thought was destined for four stars)—left the Navy without serving as a rear admiral. Slade Cutter summed up: "The bottom line is that all of my post-war assignments paled in comparison to command of a fighting submarine in wartime."

The Great Lakes Carbon Corp. in New York City employed Dick O'Kane for five years until he went into final retirement on a horse ranch in California's Sonoma County. He lived simply, comfortably, and productively with Ernestine. He wrote about his wartime experiences and liked to putter around the ranch fixing the mechanical equipment. Ernestine believed her husband might have later regretted his early retirement from service: his heart was always with the Navy. But he didn't complain about his decision. He delighted in seeing old shipmates, showing visitors around the modest ranch, and pointing out the natural geysers spurting up in the distance.

O'Kane's one bane in retirement was the depiction by some historians of what he considered an incorrect version of the incident on *Wahoo*'s third patrol—a picture that had Mush Morton relentlessly gunning down thousands of Japanese troops in the water after the sinking of the transport. O'Kane maintained that the Japanese shot first before Morton gave the command to open fire and *Wahoo*'s gunners aimed for the boats rather than for the troops.

O'Kane believed the inaccurate version was picked up by writers who hadn't studied the track charts of the incident. He thought that Mush Morton's gift for casual hyperbole and Forest Sterling's ambiguous remarks might have created a false impression of an atrocity. "The time spent in destroying the boats was less than twenty minutes," O'Kane insisted. "Some troops were in the sea, but no individual was deliberately shot in the boats or in the sea." Further, he pointed out that the sunken transport could carry less than 500 soldiers, not the thousands portrayed in some hyped accounts. Roger Paine, a member of the attack party of *Wahoo,* solidly backed Dick O'Kane's post-war version.

"I was on the bridge," Paine said. "We had surfaced and were trying to pick up a prisoner. The Japanese opened fire on us. We returned fire and it lasted only about fifteen minutes, not an hour or more. Mush Morton overstated the amount of time we were there. He never bothered to correct himself." *Wahoo* crewman William Young, a machine gunner that day, remembered returning fire from the boats, sinking everything they could. "They shot at us from their boats. We shot at them. We fired at the lifeboats. The hatred for the Japs in those days was very high. We killed everyone we could."

Mush Morton gave a couple of debriefings in Pearl Harbor in which he said *Wahoo* fired for about an hour. O'Kane and Paine thought that figure a typical Mush Morton exaggeration. Mush was casual about such data, particularly at a time in the war when such talk was admired. In later years, Forest Sterling said he couldn't recall how long *Wahoo* remained on the surface near the Japanese survivors before heading off to chase the convoy. "Time was moving very fast," Sterling said. "I never had any regrets," he added. "You have to remember how badly we hated the Japs, and how far behind we were in the war then."

In his recent book, *Unrestricted Warfare,* James F. DeRose says *Buyo Maru* carried 1,126 men, but 491 were Indian soldier POWs. A total of 87 Japanese and 269 Indians were lost in the sinking. This would seem to substantiate O'Kane's view that there were never "thousands" of Japanese killed— or even in the water. Differences of opinion about shooting Japanese soldiers on sinking ships continued among *Wahoo*'s crew long past the wartime days. Torpedoman Chester Myers believed: "The idea was to kill as many Japs as you could before they killed you. How you did it was up to you. That tended to be the consensus of opinion." But fellow *Wahoo* torpedoman David Veder, a seventeen-year-old from Cincinnati, Ohio, when he joined the boat, believed: "My view was that you sank ships, not people. These were humans in life-boats. We were shooting them. That was the only time I thought we were taking advantage of the Japs. My war wasn't against persons but ships, though there were people on those ships." (Four war patrols with combat stars and a Presidential Unit Citation must have been a wartime record for a seventeen-year-old sailor.)

The *Wahoo* incident, as it circulated through the Submarine Force during the war and among historians after the conflict, remained a controversial one with no agreed resolution. Certainly, no real opprobrium attached to *Wahoo* or her crew, then or now. *Wahoo* and Morton remain great names in the annals of submarine warfare.

On February 16, 1994, two weeks after his eighty-third birthday, Rear Admiral Richard H. O'Kane died of pneumonia, complicated by Alzheimer's disease, in a hospital in Petaluma, California. He was buried in a simple grave next to comrades-in-arms in Arlington National Cemetery. The U.S. Navy named a training facility at the San Diego Submarine Base for him (and an enlisted men's barracks for *Tang*'s Chief Quartermaster Sidney Jones), as well as a Bachelor Officers' Quarters at New London. In March 1998, a new destroyer, USS *O'Kane*, was launched at the Bath Iron Works in Maine. Ernestine O'Kane, Murray Frazee, Bill Leibold, and Floyd Caverly were guests. U.S. Representative Tom Allen spoke.

"Today," the Congressman declared, "we have devalued terms like 'hero' and 'courage,' applying them loosely to athletes with multi-million dollar contracts and movie stars whose feats are no more than celluloid fantasies. The destroyer we launch today," he said, celebrated Richard O'Kane, "a genuine hero from an age when heroism truly meant something."

It was an age when heroism was in fashion—a time of threat, risk, danger, challenge, and sacrifice. Dick O'Kane did not think of himself as heroic, simply as a naval officer carrying out his duty. "He had a deep sense of contributing to the war," Larry Savadkin said. "He believed he could be effective. He was not foolhardy. He did not worry about being a hero. But he was."

Dick O'Kane stayed in touch with *Tang* survivors. He remained heartbroken over those he did not bring back, those shipmates left "still on patrol." Long after Richard O'Kane's death, his widow Ernestine reflected, "Dick always thought about those men on *Tang* he left behind. I don't think a day went by in his life when Dick didn't think about *Tang* and his crew."

Afterword

We were the corsairs in the Pacific conflict, and I believe we were the last of the corsairs. We were granted what may have been the last taste of individuality in modern warfare.

War has been hell through the centuries, but until the single unit was lost in the masses of groups, squadrons, fleets, and army corps there was still something bearable about it, an opportunity to see the conflict in personal terms, a chance to hang on to some shred of romance in a sea of hatred. When you think of yourself as a lone wolf stalking the seas, searching down the enemy and engaging him in personal combat, it is a thing you can grasp. It is man-sized rather than incredibly colossal; an element of sanity remains. The cavalry had it in the Civil War, this feeling that the individual still amounted to something. The war birds, my father among them, had it in World War I. And we in the Submarine Service had it during those grim years in the Pacific.

But the submarine of the future will be too big, too important, too thoroughly integrated into overall strategy, for corsairs. In a world of nuclear physics, it is unlikely that any new element of romance, whether by land or sea or air, will temper the wars of the future. We were the last of the corsairs.

George Grider, Submarine Captain,
from War Fish

Acknowledgments

I became interested in submarine lore while assigned as a signalman to the submarine rescue ship USS *Florikan* in 1946 at the Submarine Base in Subic Bay, the Philippines. We were part of Submarine Squadron Seven, and operated with the boats *Plaice, Pomfret, Sterlet* and *Queenfish*. Later, I avidly read Theodore Roscoe's *U.S. Submarine Operations in World War II,* then Clay Blair's seminal *Silent Victory,* which depicted the submarine war in the round, positives and negatives.

As a correspondent for *Newsweek,* I interviewed Samuel Eliot Morison in Boston and Admiral Raymond A. Spruance in Pebble Beach. I was fortunate to meet Richard O'Kane in retirement at his ranch in Sonoma County, California, in 1990 and we had a long conversation about his role in the submarine war. My thanks are due to his widow, Ernestine G. O'Kane, who shared her reminiscences with me, as did their son, James O'Kane, and daughter, Marsha O'Kane Allen. I'd also like to thank Harriet Morton Bradford, Mush Morton's widow, for her memories of that great submarine captain, and their son, Douglas Morton.

My special thanks to Murray B. Frazee who received me at his home in Gettysburg, Pennsylvania, and who read the manuscript, suggesting several improvements. Also, to members of *Tang*'s crew—Lawrence Savadkin, William R. Leibold, Jesse B. DaSilva, Clayton O. Decker, and Floyd M. Caverly—for the insights they provided me. Among *Wahoo*'s crew before the last, seventh patrol, I'd like to thank Roger W. Paine Jr., a retired rear admiral I interviewed at his home in El Cajon, California; and Forest J.

Sterling, a retired chief petty officer I met at the Sailor's Home in Gulfport, Mississippi. Thanks, too, go to other members of *Wahoo*'s crew: William F. Young, Chester M. Myers, David Veder, James E. Lavine, Richard H. Lemert, and Walter Heiden, who provided me with their memories of that great submarine.

Those submariners who were very helpful in interviews include: Captain Edward L. Beach, USN, Captain Slade Cutter, USN, Rear Admiral Eugene B. Fluckey, Admiral I.J. "Pete" Galantin, USN, Captain George L. Street III, Captain Bladen D. Claggett, Captain David H. McClintock, Endicott "Chub" Peabody (and his wife "Toni"), Joseph L. McGrievy, and Clifford W. Kuykendall. I'd like to thank George Hogue for his observations and research material about USS *Wahoo,* aboard which his brother, Robert, was lost. Dick O'Kane's classmate Roy C. Smith, a retired captain, provided an insight into the life of a middie at the Naval Academy in the 1930s, as did Captain James C. Hay, Editor of *The Submarine Review.* Ruth Quattlebaum spoke about life at Phillips Academy at Andover while Richard O'Kane was there.

My thanks, also, to Steve Finnigan, curator of the U.S. Submarine Museum in New London; Ariana Jacob and Jack Green of the Naval Historical Center in Washington; John Urlock of the U.S. Naval Institute; and Daniel Finney of the Naval Historical Foundation; and historian John D. Alder, for clarifying in conversation his study of Japanese ships hit by U.S. submarines. I'd like to thank author A.J. Langguth in Los Angeles, who made suggestions; editor and writer Bruce Lee in New York, who made recommendations on the outline; and military publisher Leo Cooper in London, who read the manuscript, for their encouragement. Thanks are also due to publishers Little, Brown & Co. for permission to reproduce the extract from George Grider's *War Fish* (1958) on page 403.

I'm particularly grateful to my New York agent, Tom Wallace, for his enthusiastic support of the book, and to his associate in London, Bill Hamilton of A.M. Heath. Special thanks go to the editorial team at Sutton Publishing who did such a splendid job with the text and photographs: Jonathan Falconer, Sarah Moore, and Georgina Pates.

Finally, I'm indebted to my wife, Rose Marie, for her patience and for proofreading the manuscript.

Sources and Bibliography

SOURCES

The primary source materials used in the compilation of this book are the war patrol reports of various submarines, which each captain prepared after a run, as well as the books, articles, interviews, and papers written by various submariners after the war. I consulted the war patrol reports of *Wahoo* and *Tang*. I interviewed many of the surviving officers and men involved in the war patrols written about here.

The early chapters are drawn also from *Wahoo* by Dick O'Kane, *Wake of the Wahoo* by Forest Sterling, and *War Fish* by George Grider and Lydel Sims. *Tang* chapters rely heavily on O'Kane's *Clear the Bridge,* Murray Frazee's recollections and printed stories in *Naval History,* and interviews with those who survived *Tang*'s sinking.

Other research material comes from the U.S. Submarine Force Museum in New London, the Naval Historical Center (NHC) in the Washington Navy Yard, and the Nimitz Museum in Annapolis, Maryland. Ariana Jacob of the NHC provided many biographies of the officers who appear in the book. The U.S. Naval Alumni Association in Annapolis was helpful in supplying biographical information. They also had copies of *The Lucky Bag,* the U.S. Naval Academy Yearbook, with its thumbnail sketches of graduates. The Lockwood papers at the Library of Congress were a most useful source for ComSubPac's view of the submarine war in the Pacific. From the U.S. Naval Institute, I consulted the oral history submariner interviews with Rear Admiral John S. Coye Jr. (Retd), Captain Slade D. Cutter, USN (Retd), Captain Robert E. Dornin, USN (Retd) Rear Admiral Charles E. Loughlin, USN (Retd), Vice Admiral Lawson P. Ramage, USN (Retd), and Vice Admiral Eli T. Reich, USN (Retd).

I also found useful information in copies of the *United States Naval Administration in World War II, Submarine Commands,* Volume 1 and 2. Similarly, copies of *Submarine Warfare Conferences,* which were regularly held with submarine brass during World War II, were helpful: submarine staff officers went into every detail of design and combat operations. Ships' histories were provided by the *Dictionary of American Naval Fighting Ships.* I also consulted some ships' deck logs, which provided the rough draft for the patrol reports. The internal workings of a combat submarine are described in many places, the more technical in *The Fleet Type Submarine,* a training manual published by the Bureau of Naval Personnel.

I consulted, too, back copies of *Naval History* and *Proceedings* of the U.S. Naval Institute; *Polaris,* the magazine of the U.S. Submarine Veterans of World War II; *The Submarine Review,* published by the Naval Submarine League; the *Analysis of Air Operations,* published by the Commander Air Force Pacific Fleet for descriptions of B-29 rescues after ditching; *Japanese Naval Operations,* by the U.S. Strategic Bombing Survey, Naval Analysis Division; and Japanese monographs on their submarine operations, prepared by the Military History Section, headquarters, Army Forces Far East. I also found a wealth of detail in the four-volume history of submarine veterans published by the Taylor Publishing Company of Dallas, Texas.

Lastly, I recommend that anyone interested in submarines visit World War II boats on display at several sites in the United States. My thanks to the officials I met on visits to *Drum* in Mobile, Alabama, *Ling* in Hackensack, New Jersey, and *Lionfish* in Fall River, Massachusetts, and *Pampanito* in San Francisco.

BIBLIOGRAPHY

Alcanay, Jim, *Hero of the Upholder,* Shrewsbury, England, Airlife, 1991

Alden, Cdr John D., USN (Retd), *U.S. Submarine Attacks in World War II,* Annapolis, United States Naval Institute Press, 1989; updated and revised, 1999, 2000.

——, *The Fleet Submarine in the U.S. Navy,* USNIP, 1979

Anderson, William R., with Blair, Clay, Jr., *Nautilus 90 North,* New York, Harper & Row, 1959

Barrows, Nat A., *Blow All Ballast!* , London, Harrap & Co., 1940

Bastura, Bernard A., *History of U.S. Submarine Veterans World War II,* Middletown, CT, Submarine Library and Museum, 1981

Beach, Edward L., *Submarine!,* New York, Henry Holt & Co., 1952

——, *The U.S. Navy: 200 Years,* New York, Henry Holt & Co., 1986

——, *Salt and Steel,* Annapolis, USNI Press, 1999

——, *Around the World Submerged,* New York, Holt Rinehart & Winston, 1962

——, "Charles Andrew Lockwood Jr.," in *Men of War,* edited by Stephen Howarth, London, Weidenfeld & Nicholson, 1992

Bischof, Guenter, and Dupont, Robert L., eds, *The Pacific War Revisited,* Baton Rouge, Louisiana State University Press, 1997

Blair, Clay, Jr., *Silent Victory: The U.S. Submarine War Against Japan,* Philadelphia, J.P. Lippincott Company, 1975

——, *Return from the River Kwai,* New York, Simon & Schuster, 1979

Bouslog, Dave., *Maru Killer: The War Patrols of the USS Seahorse,* Sarasota, Seahorse Books, 1996

Boyd, Carl, *American Command of the Sea: Through Carriers, Codes, and the Silent Service,* Newport News, Virginia, 1955

——, and Yoshida, Akihiko, *The Japanese Submarine Force and World War II,* Annapolis, USNI Press, 1995

Boyington, Gregory, *Baa Baa Black Sheep,* New York, G.P. Putnam's Sons, 1958

Breuer, William B., *The Sea Wolf: Biography of John D. Bulkeley, USN,* Novato, Ca, Presidio Press, 1989

Buell, Thomas B., *Master of Seapower: A Biography of Fleet Admiral Ernest J. King,* Boston, Little Brown, 1980

——. *The Quiet Warrior: A Biography of Admiral Raymond A. Spruance,* Boston, Little Brown, 1974

Calhoun, C. Raymond, *Typhoon: The Other Enemy,* Annapolis, USNI Press, 1983

Calvert, James F., *Silent Running: My Years on a World War II Attack Submarine,* New York, John Wiley & Sons, 1995

Casey, Robert J., *Battle Below,* New York, Bobbs-Merrill, 1945

Clausen, Henry, and Lee, Bruce, *Pearl Harbor: Final Judgment,* New York, Crown, 1992

Cline, Rick, *Submarine Grayback,* Placentia, Ca, R.A. Cline Publishing, 1999

Compton-Hall, Richard, *The Underwater War 1939–1945,* Poole, England, Blandford Press, 1982

Conner, Claude C., *Nothing Friendly in the Vicinity: My Patrols on USS Guardfish,* Mason City, Iowa, Savas Publishing, 1999

Cope, Harley, and Karig, Walter, *Battle Submerged: Submarine Fighters of World War II,* New York, W.W. Norton, 1951

Crenshaw, R.S., Jr., *Naval Shiphandling,* Annapolis, USNI Press, 1955

DeRose, James F., *Unrestricted Warfare: How a New Breed of Officers Led the Submarine Force to Victory in World War II,* New York, John Wiley & Sons, 2000

Dull, Paul S., *A Battle History of the Imperial Japanese Navy,* Annapolis, USNI Press, 1978

Enright, Joseph F., with James W. Ryan, *Shinano! The Sinking of Japan's Secret Supership,* New York, St Martin's Press, 1987

Fahey, James C., *The Ships and Aircraft of the U.S. Fleet,* Annapolis, USNI Press, 1945

Fluckey, Eugene B., *Thunder Below!,* Chicago, University of Illinois Press, 1992

Foster, Col Frank, and Borts, Lawrence, *U.S. Military Medals, 1939 to Present,* Fountain Inn, South Carolina, Medals of America Press, 1994

Friedman, Norman, *U.S. Submarines Through 1945,* Annapolis, USNI Press, 1995

Galantin, I.J., *Take Her Deep! A Submarine Against Japan in World War II,* Chapel Hill, Algonquin Books, 1987

——, *Submarine Admiral,* Chicago, University of Illinois Press, 1995

Gray, Edwyn, *Submarine Warriors,* Novato, Ca, Presidio Press, 1988

——, *Few Survived: A History of Submarine Disasters,* London, Leo Cooper, 1996

Grider, George, with Lydel Sims, *War Fish,* Boston, Little Brown, 1958

Gugliotta, Bobette, *Pigboat 39: An American Sub Goes to War,* Lexington, University Press of Kentucky, 1984

Holmes, Harry, *The Last Patrol,* Shrewsbury, England, Airlife Publishing, 1994

Holmes, W.J., *Undersea Victory: The Influence of Submarine Operations in the Pacific in World War II,* New York, Doubleday & Co., 1966

——, *Double-Edged Secrets: U.S. Naval Intelligence Operations in the Pacific During World War II,* Annapolis, USNI Press, 1979

Horton, Edward, *The Illustrated History of the Submarine,* London, Sidgwick & Jackson, 1974

Hoyt, Edwin P., *Submarines at War: The History of the American Silent Service,* New York, Stein & Day, 1983

——, *Bowfin: The Story of One of America's Fabled Fleet Submarines in World War II,* New York, Van Nostrand Reinhold, 1983

——, *MacArthur's Navy,* New York, Orion Books, 1989

Howarth, Stephen, ed., *Men of War: Great Naval Leaders of World War II,* London, Weidenfeld & Nicholson, 1992

Icenhower, Joseph, *Submarines in Combat,* New York, Franklin Watts, Inc., 1964

Kaufman, Yogi, and Stillwell, Paul, *Sharks of Steel,* Annapolis, USNI Press, 1993

Keegan, John, *The Price of Admiralty,* London, Viking Penguin, 1989

Kimmet, Larry, and Regis, Margaret, *U.S. Submarines in World War II: An Illustrated History,* Seattle, Navigator Publishing, 1996

——, *The Attack on Pearl Harbor,* Seattle, Navigator Publishing, 1991.

Lanigan, Richard J., *Kangaroo Express: The Epic Story of the Submarine Growler,* Laurel, Fla, RJL Publications, 1998

LaVO, Carl, *Back from the Deep: The Strange Story of the Sister Subs Squalus and Sculpin,* Annapolis, USNI Press, 1994

Layton, Edwin T., with Pineau, Roger, and Costello, John, *And I Was There, Pearl Harbor and Midway—Breaking the Secrets,* New York, William Morrow, 1985

Lockwood, Charles A., *Through Hell and Deep Water,* Philadelphia, Childon, 1956

——, *Down to the Sea in Subs,* New York, W.W. Norton, 1967

——, *Sink 'Em All,* New York, Bantam Books, 1984

——, and Adamson, Hans C., *Hellcats of the Sea*, New York, Greenberg, 1955

——, *Tragedy at Honda*, New York, Chilton, 2000

Longstaff, Reginald, *Submarine Command*, London, Robert Hale, 1984

Lowder, Hughston E., with Scott, Jack, *Batfish: The Champion Submarine-Killer Submarine of World War II*, Englewood Cliffs, NJ, Prentice-Hall, 1980

Lucky Bag, The (U.S. Naval Academy Yearbook, 1930, 1931, 1932, 1933, 1934, 1935, 1936, 1939)

Maas, Peter, *The Rescuer*, New York, Harper & Row, 1967

Mack, William P., and Konetzni, Albert H., Jr., *Command at Sea*, Annapolis, USNI Press, 1982

Mansfield, John G., *Cruisers for Breakfast: War Patrols of USS Darter and USS Dace*, Tacoma, Washington, Media Center Publishing, 1997

Mars, Alastair, *British Submarines at War. 1939–1945*, London, Purnell Book Services, 1971.

Mason, John T., Jr., *The Pacific War Remembered*, Annapolis, USNI Press. 1986.

McCants, William R., *War Patrols of the USS Flasher*, Chapel Hill, NC, Professional Press, 1994

Mendenhall, Corwin, *Submarine Diary: The Silent Stalking of Japan*, Annapolis, USNI Press, 1991

Morison, Samuel Eliot, *The Two-Ocean War. A Short History of the United States Navy in the Second World War*, Boston, Little Brown, 1963

——, *History of U.S. Naval Operations in World War II*, Boston, Little Brown, various editions

Navy Times Editors, *They Fought Under the Sea*, Stackpole, Harrisburg, 1962

O'Kane, Richard H., *Clear the Bridge! The War Patrols of the USS Tang*, Chicago, Rand McNally, 1977

——, *Wahoo: The Patrols of America's Most Famous World War II Submarine*, Novato, Ca, Presidio Press, 1987

Padfield, Peter, *War Beneath the Sea: Submarine Conflict 1939–1945*, London, John Murray, 1995

Polmar, Norman, *The Naval Institute Guide to the Ships and Aircraft of the U.S. Fleet*, Annapolis, USNI Press, 1965

Potter, E.B., *Nimitz*, Annapolis, USNI Press, 1976

——, *Bull Halsey*, Annapolis, USNI Press, 1985

Reynolds, Clark G., *The Fast Carriers: The Forging of an Air Navy*, Annapolis, USNI Press, 1992

Roscoe, Theodore, *U.S. Submarine Operations in World War II*, Annapolis, USNI Press, 1949

——, *U.S. Destroyer Operations in World War II*, Annapolis, USNI Press, 1953

Ruhe, William J., *War in the Boats: My World War II Submarine Battles*, McLean, Va, Brassey's Inc., 1994

Sasgen, Peter T., *Red Scorpion. The War Patrols of the USS Rasher*, Annapolis, USNI, 1995

Schratz, Paul R., *Submarine Commander: The Story of World War II and Korea*, Lexington, University Press of Kentucky, 1988

Shelford, W.O., *Subsunk. The Story of Submarine Escape*, New York, Popular Library, 1960

Smith, Ron, *Torpedoman*, Ron Smith, 2000

Spector, Ronald H., *Eagle Against the Sun*, New York, The Free Press, 1985

Sterling, Forest J., *Wake of the Wahoo*, Chapel Hill, NC, Professional Press, 1997

Stern, Robert C., *U.S. Subs in Action*, Carrollton, Tex, Squadron/Signal Publications, 1983

Sweetman, Jack, *The U.S. Naval Academy: An Illustrated History,* Annapolis, USNI Press, 1995

Trumbull, Robert, *Silversides,* New York, Henry Holt & Co., 1945

U.S. Naval Historical Division, *U.S. Submarine Losses in World War II,* Washington, D.C., 1963

——, *The Submarine in the United States Navy,* Washington, D.C., 1969

Van der Vat, Dan, *Stealth at Sea: The History of the Submarine,* London, Orion, 1994

——, *The Pacific Campaign,* New York, Simon & Schuster, 1991

Walkowiak, Thomas F., *Fleet Submarines of World War II,* Missoula, Mont, Pictorial Histories Publishing Company, 1988

Werner, Herbert A., *Iron Coffins,* New York, Holt, 1969

Winton, John, *Ultra in the Pacific: How Breaking Japanese Codes and Ciphers Affected Naval Operations Against Japan,* London, Leo Cooper, 1993

Wheeler, Gerald, *Kinkaid of the Seventh Fleet,* Annapolis, USNI Press, 1996

Whitehouse, Arch, *Subs and Submariners,* London, Frederick Muller, 1963

Index

Headings are in alphabetical order; subheadings are arranged in chronological order of initial page numbers. A ship's name following a person's name indicates he was the Commanding Officer at that time. Personnel are generally listed with the rank identified first in the text, although most were later promoted to higher rank.